"Tussawehee, Bigfoot, Red Wolf. It is gratifying to
see in print the names of people, stories and events
that have been part of our oral history. Mr. Ontko's first
two volumes of *Thunder Over the Ochoco* have been
informative and exciting reading. The Western
Shoshone look forward to Volume III, *Lightning
Strikes!*"

Western Shoshone National Council

"The most factual writing by any author on the
Shoshone Nation."

Raymond D. Yowell
Western Shoshone Citizen

"I wholeheartedly support the truth as written in
Mr. Gale Ontko's series, *Thunder Over the Ochoco*.
This writing is most exciting, factual and represents
the Shoshone oral history as close as could be
expected. He represents our heroes as no other
could—dog soldiers such as Red Wolf, Wolf Dog and
Has No Horse, men who played such important roles
in our history and culture.

Jack C. Orr (Dogowa)
Citizen of the Western Shoshone Nation

THUNDER OVER THE OCHOCO

THE GATHERING STORM

Volume I

GALE ONTKO

— A Maverick Publication —

Copyright © 1993 by Andrew Gale Ontko
Volume I

Second Printing 1993
Third Printing January 1996
Fourth Printing   August 1997

ISBN 0-89288-245-X

Library of Congress Cataloging-in-Publication Data

Ontko, Andrew Gale, 1927-
    Thunder over the Ochoco / Andrew Gale Ontko.
       p.   cm.
    Includes index.
    ISBN 0-89288-245-X (v. 1) : $16.95
    1. Oregon—History.   I. Title
F876.057   1993
979.5—dc20   93-18698
                                CIP

Cover oil painting by Larry B. Milligan

Maverick Publications, Inc. • *P.O. Box 5007* • *Bend, Oregon 97708*

TABLE OF CONTENTS

FOREWORD

"Why waste time in the middle of nowhere?" was the initial reaction of gubernatorial candidate Neil Goldschmidt in 1986 for a proposed debate with his opponent at a site east of Oregon's Cascade barrier. Politically and economically his point was well taken. But this barren, sparsely-settled inland empire has an early history as explosive as the volcanic action and land upheavals which shaped it. In *Thunder Over the Ochoco*, Gale Ontko relates that story with a sensitivity, sense of perspective and attention to detail not previously seen.

Early on, the reader is introduced to the Nokoni—the Homeless People—a prehistoric band of Indian agriculturalists driven out of the southern Blue Mountains area and set adrift in the Great Basin. He is able to watch them become the first Horse Indians of the west as they round up, tame and master the stray animals left in the wake of the Spanish explorers of the Southwest. And he is witness to their evolution into the Shoshoni nation and their return to the ancestral home as *Saydocarah*—the Conquerors. Their war tribes become the scourge of all their red neighbors and at a later date the most implacable foes ever faced by any of the white colonizers. Strictly speaking, their domain was the Ochoco, the land between the Deschutes and Snake Rivers, and the Eldahow which extended on eastward to the Tetons. In a broader sense it was anywhere the magnificent war horses they learned to breed could carry them.

So it is no surprise to see them as the decisive force in expelling the Spanish from Santa Fe in 1680.

The events which at various times led groups to break away from the Shoshoni nation and pursue separate identities as Aztecs, Comanches and Utes are carefully described.

Part I, however, is primarily the story of the conquistadors, sea dogs and adventurers who, starting in the 16th century, discovered the land called Oregon and sought ways for their home country to possess it and of the contacts that ensued between the white strangers and the

Saydocarah. Readers may be surprised to learn of Spanish and probably Russian penetration into mid-Oregon. On the other hand the stories of the coming of Robert Gray, George Vancouver, Meriwether Lewis and William Clark are not new but the wealth of detail gives them a very special freshness.

It is no accident that as the new nation moved into the 19th century Oregon became the tail that wagged the dog in American foreign policy, culminating in the clamor of "54° 40' or Fight" during James Polk's run for the presidency. The colonial appetites of England, Spain and Russia were still very strong and the lands on the Pacific tempting morsels.

Part II is the story of the multinational contest for the furs of the Northwest, but it is also the story of a half century of political intrigue as the major powers tried to use fur trade as a stepping-stone to political control. This theme has reality because the reader is kept constantly aware of how decisions being made in Montreal, Quebec, Fort William, London, St. Petersburg, Madrid or Washington, D.C. affect the lands south of the Columbia. But the charm of this second section is in its delineation of character. All of the principal persons of the fur trade era appear in the narrative as unique and interesting personalities, but there is no hero worship. The trappers are portrayed just as with few exceptions they were—coarse, cruel, volatile and self-serving but with an incredible ability to withstand suffering. Although representatives of a civilized way of life, they ate bugs, ants, crickets, mice or snakes as readily as the most despised savage if survival demanded it.

This is not a book "written from the Indian point of view" but it does at least recognize that Indians had occupied the land in question long before any white man ever saw it and that they had an important part in making the subsequent history of the region. It allows the Indians to explain their beliefs about the sanctity of the land. And it gives sufficient insight into their patterns of daily living for a clear understanding that their way was not without desirable features. But it is also a portrayal of the total unpredictability of behavior when almost none of the restraints of civilized life are in place. Repeatedly, the Indians behave with as much brutality or insensitivity to other Indians or even their own tribesmen as any of them are receiving from or dealing out to the worst of the white invaders.

Given this clash of cultures and objectives, conflict was an inevitability and the victory of the white man a foregone conclusion. But there is a sense of frustration that it could not have occurred on the field of battle in a fair fight. No sadder story has been written since the time of the Black Death than the extermination of most of the native populations of North and South America and Hawaii when the natives picked up the germs of white man's diseases for which their bodies had no immune systems. Before the first wagonload of emigrants crossed the borders into Oregon Territory the once great Shoshoni nation was reduced to a few scattered groups, the survivors of malaria, cholera, typhoid and other similar sicknesses beyond the power of their medicine men.

Individual reactions to the contents of this book will, of course, vary, but no one who reads this book will ever see the area once known as Shoshoni land through the same eyes as before, for this book traces the contacts of the Snake war tribes with white men down to 1840 in a way that has not been done before.

Robert Harris
Prineville, Oregon
Fall, 1992

ABOUT THE AUTHOR

Mix together equal portions of the intellectual curiosity and organizational abilities of Benjamin Franklin and the steely determination of Ulysses S. Grant, let simmer in the Ochocos of Central Oregon for nearly seven decades and the product is Gale Ontko, the writer of *Thunder Over the Ochoco*.

In most respects this is a man who became an author because of circumstances rather than desire. He grew up in the Ochoco Valley area east of Prineville and unlike most Oregonians has spent his life on the land. His employment as a BLM fire management supervisor took him into back country for long stretches of time and the Indians of the area got to know him so well they finally gave him an Indian name of his own.

It all began innocently enough when he realized that native Americans—except for brief reports of an encounter on the Little Big Horn—had been ignored in the writing of American history as totally as our other non-European minorities. He began to talk with Indians, take notes and enter the world of historical research until one day he felt he was able to add something to what had been written about early days in the Northwest. His other motivation was an increasing belief that the rather desolate land mass of the Ochoco had itself profoundly influenced the history of the region and had an interesting story of its own to be told, if someone was willing to do the work of putting it in proper order.

To a greater extent than is usually the case his writing is a mirror reflection of the man himself. It is said that only the very rich and/or those who live alone can afford the luxury of very strong attitudes and convictions. Gale has lived by himself for many years and the two special gifts of that experience which he brings to his writing are an iron-willed determination to be sure that he has the facts right and an incredible degree of patience. The first has led him to an extraordinary depth of research. There was no solid backlog of Indian data, because the Shoshoni had no written language. So he listened carefully to the oral histories of all the principal tribes and then sought verification by crosschecking contemporary written materials. He has known that his writing breaks new ground and has been determined that regardless of the amount of research required that it stand solid against all inquiry. His remarkable patience has let him continue for years the assembling of his facts before doing the writing.

His book has the refreshing directness and, when necessary, the bluntness that back country people still retain and which their urban cousins have largely abandoned. He has made every effort possible to learn the truth about the people who made the history about which he writes and then to state it. Hudson's Bay Company is not likely to send him a thank-you note, genteel readers may feel they could get along with fewer details of the way the trapper brigades lived and any descendants of Protestant missionaries to Oregon might well consider putting out a contract on this man. The good news is that when most readers finish this book they are very likely to say, "I had no idea non-fiction could be so interesting."

Robert Harris
Prineville, Oregon
Fall, 1992

THE SEARCH BEGINS

"At a generous assessment, approximately half of this book is nonsense. Unfortunately, I don't know which half; and neither, despite all claims to the contrary, does anyone else."

Arthur C. Clarke

Thus commented Arthur Clarke—author and scholar—after a struggle for journalistic accuracy. In fifty years of extensive research I can sympathize with that reflection. The Indian history was especially challenging. Not that there wasn't ample source material once one discovered the clues and traced them through the maze of hundreds of documents but from the confusing and often contradictory way in which the information was presented.

Because of the current concept that the Indians of eastern Oregon were northern Paiutes, it became a major task to unravel their correct identity. The true natives of eastern Oregon were the Shoshoni who called themselves "Saydocarah," the Conquerors. Beginning in the early 1600's the Europeans would call the Shoshoni "Snakes," a name most frequently used in all 18th and 19th century journals. According to the Bureau of Indian Affairs, by 1960 the only Indians officially recognized as Snakes were confined on the Klamath Reservation in southern Oregon.

The majority of the survivors of the Shoshonean wars are of so-called Paiute ancestry and there is reason for that. The Indians we call Paiute knew themselves as "Numa,"—the People—but were identified by very different names by the Shoshoni. There were at least sixty clan names within the Paiute (Numa) grouping, but the principal bands were by tribal affiliation: Snake—Tekap'wi "Those Who Have No Meat" or more commonly, Hohan-dika "the Earth Eaters"; Comanche—Waa' ih-rika "The Maggot Eaters"; and Ute—Vain-units "The Diggers," sometimes called Goshutes.

Frederick Hodge of the Bureau of American Ethnology states that "Paiute is a term involved in great confusion. In common usage it has been applied at one time or another to most of the Shoshonean tribes." The name Paiute (in the Shoshoni language Pai means true, which would indicate that these people were Utes) did not come into official usage until 1890. From then, through 1930, the name was applied to all Shoshonean tribes. This made for difficult research as Paiute then defined all Shoshoni; Shoshoni included Bannock, Comanche and Ute; and Snake was synonymous with Shoshoni.

Major John Wesley Powell, the foremost authority on Shoshonean tribes, has this to say: "the name Paiute properly belongs exclusively to a tribe in southwest Utah." However, to save confusion the term "Paiute" will be used throughout this narrative but applied as the Snakes used it to denote their poor relation, the Earth Eaters.

Also, there was no such tribe as Bannock. These people, through attrition, were the Banattee (Robber) Snakes. Dr. Sven Liljeblad in his research of the *Idaho Indians in Transition 1805-1960*, discovered that "some Paiutes were fortunate in obtaining horses and did not delay in seizing the opportunity to join the mounted Shoshoni (Snakes) in their buffalo hunting expeditions to the plains." These Paiutes called their Shoshoni compatriots "Wihin-nakwate, the Ones on the Iron Side," thereby acknowledging the cultural superiority of the Snakes. The Snakes for obvious reasons called these Paiutes "Robbers" and as an in group in the Shoshoni ranks, the Robbers called themselves "Pan-nakwate, Hair Tossed Over the Head People" from their habit of wearing their hair in a pompadour over their forehead. The fur traders soon rendered this into a variety of forms which ultimately became "Bannock."

As Liljeblad would caution, "it is only to be remembered that nowhere was there a Bannock society separated culturally and politically from the Shoshoni society." Most often, I will use the term "Banattee Snake" in this writing. Ironically, a Snake warrior could have an Earth Eater brother or sister. In a way it could be likened to the yuppie and hippie lifestyles of the later 20th century. In short some believed in fighting for a living, while others took the path of least resistance no matter how degrading it might become.

Prior to the Shoshonean wars most of the white man's peaceful contacts with the Shoshoni were through the Paiutes, who were treated with contempt and considered incapable of hostilities other than petty theft and an occasional murder for personal gain. The 19th century historians would describe them as "beasts who lived in vermin infested holes from which they crawl forth to eat grass on all fours and bask in the noonday sun." How these men could have made such a costly mistake concerning the tribes of eastern Oregon—Indians whose record from 1812 on was one of hostilities—can be traced to many causes. Probably the most significant is the testimony of Peter Skene Ogden, who claimed credit for leading the first white party through Central Oregon in 1825. Actually, Ogden's party was the third to enter Central Oregon, being preceded by David Thompson's North West survey party in 1807 and Ramsay Crooks' lost members of the Hunt Overland Expedition in 1812.

Some of the earliest written records on the Shoshoni of eastern Oregon are contained in Ogden's journals, proving that there were two distinct lifestyles diametrically opposed within the Shoshoni nation.

However, Ogden—usually in a starved condition himself—was never alert enough to deduce this from his own observations, preferring to accept the popular, although erroneous, beliefs of that period. (See comments made by Ogden in Chapter 34). Ogden made a tremendous error. The Shoshoni was a man to be feared, for he was neither cowardly nor skulking. It takes a bold savage to rob a stage coach, but on March 25, 1867, as the Boise-Owyhee stage was coming down a ravine toward the Snake River that is what happened.

Eight Shoshoni, led by the daring war-chief Paulina, lay in ambush and mortally wounded the driver, William Younger. A passenger in attempting to escape was quickly overtaken and riddled with slugs from a .36 Navy Model Colt. . . a choice weapon for a degenerate race. The mail and contents of the coach were destroyed or taken. This accomplished, Paulina and his men rode into Silver City and killed a townsman who was slow in taking cover. Swooping north into Reynolds Creek, they burned a ranch house and drove off twenty-three head of cattle. Westward bound, Paulina and his warriors raided the Clarno stage station and stole twenty-five cattle and two horses belonging to Howard Maupin. On every road in any direction the Shoshoni struck with vengeance, firing on civilians and soldiers alike, stealing their stock, burning their settlements and making life on the Ochoco frontier as miserable as they possibly could.

Few indeed were the warriors whose years carried them back beyond the arrival of the Spanish explorers, the English fur traders and the American colonizers. Such men as Twisted Hand, The Horse, One Moccasin and Old Deer Running could remember what it was like to live in peace. To the others their first memory was that of a struggle to protect their hunting grounds from the ever present threat of white invasion.

In an effort to track the Shoshoni leaders through the gloomy corridors of time it became necessary to break down their names into the various forms in which they appear, as each journalist, interpreter, news reporter and Indian agent had his own idea as to the spelling of the Indian name. Each was known by many titles, some quite similar, others totally unlike. Any great feat performed by a Shoshoni warrior which added to his reputation and renown—such as scalping an enemy, successfully stealing a number of horses and the like—was celebrated by a change of name.

Because of this and the preference of the writer, many have lost their identity in the confusion of trying to solve who was where at any given time. For example, Cho-cho-co—the Man Who Has No Horse— is identified in the various accounts as Ochoco, Shoshoko, Ocheo, Ocheho, Ochiho, Otsehoe and Ochoho. Paulina—the War Spirit—appears as Paulina, Paluna, Pahnina, Pahninee, Pushican, Pandina, Poloni, Pauline, Poliki and Paunina.

This is the story of red men and white men locked in a death struggle for possession of an inland empire. There were brave and honest men on both sides of the conflict and all would petition their chosen deity, "God, where art Thou?" Call it the conquest of Shoshoni Land, the settlement of Central Oregon, the history of old Crook County—give it whatever name you choose, but in the end it all falls under one heading—*Thunder Over the Ochoco.*

ACKNOWLEDGMENTS

My heartfelt thanks to the many who helped make this account possible. Where to start? Perhaps with the search of historical records where the documented evidence of the past was eventually tracked down. To gain access to the records my appreciation to the staff of the National Archives, Washington D.C.; the Bancroft Library, Berkeley, California; the Oregon State Archives, Salem; The Oregon Records Division of the Bureau of Land Management, Portland; The State of Idaho Department of Commerce and Development, Boise; the Oregon, Idaho and Montana Historical Societies; the Crook, Deschutes and Lane County Historical Societies; The Oregon State, Crook, Deschutes and Wasco County Libraries; the Bowman Museum, Prineville, Oregon; and the Grant County Museum, Canyon City, Oregon.

Very special help was given for background material on the Shoshoni by John Crow, Deputy Commissioner, Bureau of Indian Affairs, Washington, D.C.; Frell Owl, Supt. of Indian Affairs, Fort Hall Agency, Idaho; Doyce Waldrip, Supt. of Indian Affairs, Warm Spring Agency, Oregon; Burton Ladd, Supt. of Indian Affairs, Nevada Indian Agency, Stewart, Nevada; Steven Bly, Director of the Idaho Department of Parks, Boise; and Dr. Sven Liljeblad, Idaho State University, Pocatello, for sharing his in-depth research of the Shoshoni language.

My thanks to the historians who granted me the privilege to share in their research and thus gain insight into my own endeavors. To these author friends I am deeply grateful: Francis Juris Rush, *Rails to the Ochoco Country;* Lawrence Nielson, *Pioneer Roads of Central Oregon;* Phil Brogan, *East of the Cascades;* May Miller, *Golden Memories of the Paulina Area;* Rube Long, *The Oregon Desert;* Vera Koch Ontko, *Through the Golden Gates of Yesteryear; Life on the Upper Ochoco 1907 through 1918;* Dorothy Lawson McCall, *Ranch Under the Rimrocks;* Norman Weis, *Ghost Towns of the Northwest;* Herman Oliver, *Gold and Cattle Country;* Irene Helms, *School Days of Old*

Crook County; Burr Henley, *Gold From the Grass Roots Down;* Donna Wojcik, *The Brazen Overlanders of 1845;* Elsie Stover Mitchke, *The Pioneer Story;* and Mary Montana, western artist.

Then, the native Americans without whose knowledge the Indian history of Eastern Oregon would have forever remained a blank. Thank you, Tom Ochiho and Agnes Banning Philips, grandchildren of Chief Ochoco; Wilson We wa, great grandson of Paulina; Dave Chocktote, son of the war chief Black Buffalo; Rueben Mariscall, who roamed central Oregon and found signs of his Aztec ancestors; Ray Johnson, Sr., Chief of the Warm Springs Paiutes; George Winishett, Paiute lecturer; Victor Scisson, Klamath; Rudy Paul, Warm Springs; LeRoy Saunders, Fred Rickard and Bill Hoptowit, Yakima; John Limberhand, Ute; Terry Courtney, Walla Walla; John Waseese, Umatilla; and Walt Sixkiller, who inspired the Warm Springs Indians to name me "The Man Who Sits On the Hill and Talks to Himself," an observation born of many years as fire management officer for BLM, sitting on a mountain top and talking by two-way radio to the district office.

Words can never express the heartfelt appreciation which I owe to Robert Harris and Martin Morisette. Through their patience, advice and above all, the countless hours of work each put into this effort, *Thunder Over the Ochoco* would never have gotten off my desk.

Finally, I am deeply indebted to those—many of whom are now a part of history themselves—who shared first hand accounts. I wish all to know they are recognized as having helped to make this writing possible.

Gale Ontko

THE DECEPTION

In the order of their occurrence, the Indian wars of the Pacific Northwest were: the Cayuse 1847-1850; the Rogue River 1850-1856; the Yakima 1855-1859; the Modoc 1872; the Nez Perce 1877 and the Bannock 1878.

Lancaster Pollard
Oregon historian

The obvious conclusion to be drawn from this statement is that prior to 1847, Oregon experienced no problem with its Indian population, and between 1859 and 1872, a thirteen year truce had been negotiated. However, it was during this period that the tragic finale to a medicine man's glorious vision of a Shoshoni-American brotherhood played its closing scene.

The extermination of the Ochoco Shoshoni was one of the United State's more time consuming and vindictive conquests. The cost in loss of life and destruction of property is unsurpassed in Indian warfare. Yet, this conflict knifed through western history without fanfare. . . unpublicized by those involved and therefore ignored by historians.

Clashes with other Amerindian tribes are given full coverage—even one day skirmishes. Why then does history by-pass the Shoshoni rebellion, giving the impression that it never occurred? Is it because no one took the time to consider the evidence or was there a deliberate concealment of the facts? Both conclusions are correct.

Extensive research of the records covering 1590 to 1890 indicates that there was a widespread cover-up of the details surrounding the Shoshoni campaign. The cloak of secrecy was cast at the outset of Oregon exploration and continued through the reconstruction period after the Civil War. Spanish naval logs, French exploration records, Russian historical notes, Hudson's Bay Company documents, North West Company journals, United States Army records, U.S. Indian

Affairs reports, U.S. Senate and House documents, personal diaries and obscure newspaper accounts confirm this theory.

Further search reveals that there was a definite purpose behind such massive censorship. The circumstances leading to and perpetuating this restriction of information were:

1. International tension among the major world powers over the ownership of Oregon territory.

2. The European attitude toward an Indian people who refused to conform to the standards set forth for native Americans.

3. The inability of the white men to recognize that all Shoshoni were not the same, ranging in cultural development from peaceful and often poverty stricken family groups to powerful and dangerously aggressive war tribes.

4. National political concern over westward expansion of the United States.

5. Oregon's obligation to its citizens to be accepted into the union of American states.

6. And, finally, the unfortunate timing of the Civil War.

When these issues are considered in their proper sequence, it becomes obvious that a strict security blackout was inevitable and had to be maintained by the nations involved for military, political, economic and social reasons.

By 1810, Spain, Russia and Great Britain were saturating the United States with propaganda about the undesirability of the area west of the Rocky Mountains, with special emphasis on the hostility of the Shoshoni war tribes. The United States, with dreams of westward expansion, had to discredit such rumors. To accomplish this the United States flooded Oregon territory with Protestant missionaries, who were to convert the heathen population to Christianity. As a counter-measure, Canada, Belgium, Spain and France were just as eagerly claiming the savages in the name of Catholicism. The apparent reasoning behind this reverent courtship was that a devout savage was a peaceful savage. . . and to a degree this was true.

For reasons known only to Parliament and Congress, the seemingly endless public domain lying between the Mississippi and Snake rivers was not a serious point of contention. It was eventually claimed fifty to sixty years after the Oregon dispute by a multitude of gamblers, prostitutes, murderers and thieves, lured into the wilderness by rich deposits of gold and silver. Their contribution to western history was a writer's dream. . . violent, raw and uncensored.

This interesting element also belonged to Oregon but they, like the Shoshoni, were not something a genteel person would advertise. Oregon was a treasure to be claimed by staunch servants of the Lord and honest tillers of the soil, men and women who were sober, dignified and sinless. Their mission was to secure Oregon for the United States and bolster the growing coffers of an ambitious nation as befits a dutiful and well-reared child. It would not be wise to tarnish the respected name of the parent. And so the deception initiated by Spain, Russia and Great Britain was to continue.

Unfortunately, the Shoshoni—officially called Utes, Comanches and Snakes, but more commonly referred to as renegades, animals and sons of bitches—wanted no traffic with the Americans, even going so far as to reject their God. Shoshoni contact with European culture had made a bitter and lasting impression. Singly and in groups, the Spaniards, the French, the Russians and the British had convinced them that whatever the white man desired—whether it be pelts, horses or women—they got. All the Shoshoni received in return was depletion of his hunting grounds, degradation of his women and death! The embrace of the white man was not to their liking and they were prepared to repulse any and all advances.

Because the backward Shoshoni were the only real threat to Oregon settlement, it was decided to play down any adverse publicity on their hostile acts. After all, they could be removed in a moment of small consequence. This "moment of small consequence" stretched into the unbelievable span of seventy-eight years. Had the Americans taken the time to question the Spanish on this subject, they would have discovered that these swarthy soldiers had been trying, unsuccessfully, to uproot the Shoshoni for 150 years.

It took a battle-hardened army—baptized in the carnage of Shiloh, Gettysburg and Appomattox—three years to beat the Shoshoni into reluctant submission and ten more years to completely destroy them.

The simple fact was that the Shoshoni occupied land that the westward-moving Americans wished to exploit for its economic value. In the inevitable clash which followed, the two opposing forces responded in a perfectly human manner. They went at each other's throats with all the moral fervor of rabid wolves.

This is the story of the European traders who packed the red hatchet onto Shoshoni soil. It tells of a conflict which began at the turn of the 18th century in a heat-drenched valley leading into the Crooked River basin and of its final death throes 200 years later on a frozen meadow less than forty miles from its place of birth. It is the record of hundreds of thousands of dollars—in prime furs, gold shipments, civilian property, arms and ammunition—stolen or destroyed. It is the obituary of thousands of casualties. It is the admission of millions of dollars in war expenditures at a time when the first Indian war west of the Mississippi River was launched with forty-seven dollars in the Oregon Provisional Treasury.

It is the history of a people whose lives were governed by the sun. . . the wind. . . the mountains, a people for whom time was dateless, without beginning, without end. It simply faded over the Cascade range, marked by seasons, by famine, by birth and by death. These were a people who developed a complex culture, suited to their own wants and needs, a civilization in much the same position as the Europeans had been 3,000 years earlier. In them, as one historian so aptly phrased it, "burned a small flame which could in time become a great light. Then the white men landed, wave on wave, with the savage strength that comes from steel, gunpowder and horses and the flame was put out for ever."

These were a people who in defeat were denied the privilege of being classed as natural-born citizens of their own country. This would not be granted until after World War I, during which many of their descendants gallantly fought and died on foreign soil to preserve the American way of life. When citizenship was granted in 1922, it was a flimsy affair, refusing the Indians practically every legal right and status which normally went with the act. Yet, 30,000 served in World War II, the highest per capita contribution to military forces made by any racial group in the United States. A full-blooded Shoshoni was the first U.S. soldier to enter Berlin and another was with the first contingent to make contact with the Russians on the Elbe.

This is a tribute to those first settlers of the Ochoco—men, women and children—who were left to wander and starve in a land they thought belonged to them through eternity, a people who in their final agony cried out ". . . Nimma ne-umpu—We too are human!" And it came to pass. The Ochoco—cradle of an ancient Shoshonean civilization—was to become its everlasting grave.

Many of the issues leading to the downfall of the Shoshoni nation and the ultimate settlement of Central Oregon are not discussed in this volume of *Thunder Over the Ochoco*, for it covers only that period beginning with the early Spanish discovery of Oregon territory and ending with the collapse of the North American fur trade. Future volumes will cover the tide of United States emigration; the political upheaval it caused, the Eastern Oregon gold strikes; the bitter Shoshoni wars; the growth of industry; the vigilante's brutal reign of terror in Central Oregon; and last, the devastating range wars that pitted neighbor against neighbor in a final struggle to survive.

THUNDER OVER THE OCHOCO

THE GATHERING STORM

Volume I

Part I

BEYOND THE SETTING SUN

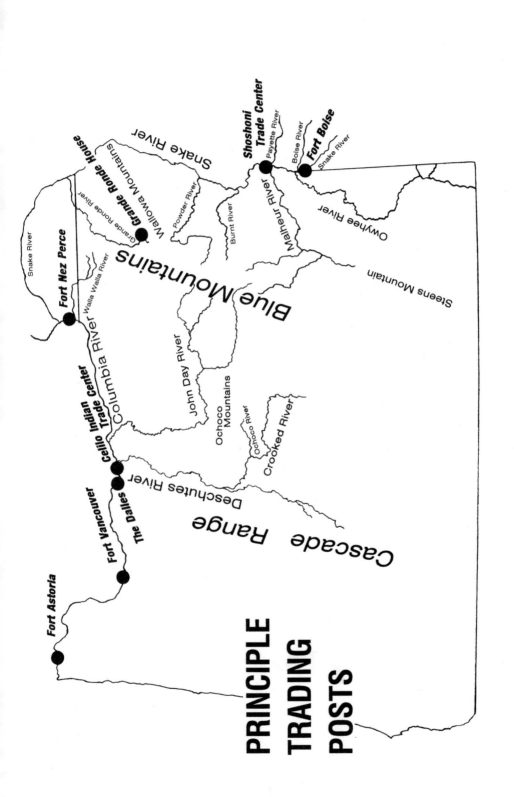

PRINCIPLE
TRADING
POSTS

Fort Astoria

Fort Vancouver

Celilo Indian Trade Center

The Dalles

Fort Nez Perce

Grande Rounde House

Shoshoni Trade Center

Fort Boise

Snake River

Snake River

Columbia River

Walla Walla River

Grande Ronde River

Wallowa Mountains

Blue Mountains

Payette River

Boise River

Snake River

Malheur River

Owyhee River

Powder River

Burnt River

Steens Mountain

John Day River

Ochoco Mountains

Ochoco River

Crooked River

Deschutes River

Cascade Range

BEYOND THE SETTING SUN
(THE PERIOD OF EARLY DISCOVERY AND EXPLORATION)

*Who were these bronze-colored people called the American
Indian who had numbered a million in their vast nearly
untouched wilderness when first the white men rimmed in
iron and clothed in velvet came in contact with them?
Were they Mongoloids. . .*

Stephen Longstreet
War Cries on Horseback

Beyond the setting sun lay the cloud-capped Blue Mountains and
the rolling sage plateaus designated on 19th century maps as Shoshoni
land. . . a distorted territory conceived in flame and born of fury, a
land which for countless centuries had been the home of Shoshonean
tribes. This land was their heritage. . . a birthright they would defend
against all odds. Judge them and their way of life if you must. . . but
do it by their standards.

*From whence they came we know no more than they.
Some would have us believe they were displaced Orientals but,
perhaps, the yellow men descended from the North American
Indian for one theory is just as feasible as the other.*

Al Look
In My Back Yard

3

CHAPTER 1

INCIDENT AT HELL'S GATE

The pit has come from underground,
Satan himself is out of breath;
He links the marksman to his mark,
With the hyphen-flash of death.

Owen Wister

Like a great vulture hovering in the dismal sky, a gray pall of dust announced the arrival of the emigration of 1851. Oregon's growing white population, which now exceeded 13,000, would again, like a loaf of leavened bread, engulf more Indian lands.[1] This was the Iowa-Illinois migration and like others before it, the numerous wagon companies were strung out for hundreds of miles across the Snake River Plateau. Each group traveled at its own pace, some eager to be the first to arrive in the lush, green valley of the Willamette, others dallying along the way, but all determined to crest the foreboding Blue Mountains before autumn snowfall.

In comparison to earlier emigration, the Iowa-Illinois crossing of western America had been uneventful almost to the point of boredom. Now, the advance party made up of Iowa families was within shouting distance of the promised land. Joyful hymns and thankful prayers would be offered this evening to a kind and generous God. High on the timbered shoulder of the northern Blues, cold, unrelenting eyes traced the column of dust marking the Oregon Trail from the Powder River as far eastward as the eye could see. The lead company had been

---

[1] By census of 1850 Oregon's population stood at 13,234. Pollard, *Oregon and the Pacific Northwest*, p. 300.

discovered by a Shoshoni war party.[2]

Near the headwaters of the Umatilla River two days before the arrival of the '51 emigration, the Tussawehee dog soldier, Cho-cho-co—The Man Who Has No Horse—sacked the village of Lawyer, Prince and Rotten Belly while they sat in council with the white chiefs from the Willamette Valley. His warriors had taken little of value on this raid other than the honor of demoralizing the Nez Perce tribes. Because of this, Has No Horse was in a surly mood. His pack-saddles were empty. His nerves were keyed for combat. . . a very explosive mixture. Now, a more lucrative target was lumbering into sight.

Well supplied with military information, Has No Horse knew he could strike at his own leisure. Early in the year, the Oregon Territorial Mounted Rifles had been called out of the mountains. For the remainder of the summer they sat idle at Fort Vancouver, awaiting orders to embark for Texas. At the same time the U.S. Dragoons, having scored a crushing blow on the Rogue tribes of southwestern Oregon, galloped across the country to Jefferson Barracks on the Missouri, placing them a thousand miles away from battle position. Secure in the knowledge that he would not be hampered by American troops, Has No Horse calmly watched his prey.

Has No Horse—a veteran brave not yet twenty—was well versed in guerilla warfare. He had earned his eagle feather at age fifteen in slashing raids against the Walla Walla, Sioux and Arapahoe. His full headdress, worn with dignity and honor, had been awarded two summers previously following the Shoshoni's first attack on United States Army personnel.

As he waited for the Iowa train to swing into assault position, it is likely the young war chief thought of past exploits with a twinge of remorse. Those had been the good days when warrior met warrior hand-to-hand and may the best man win. Umatilla, Blackfoot, Yakima, Klamath. . . he had faced them all in combat, but the most worthy opponents of all in the eyes of the Shoshoni were the daring Cayuse— more dangerous than the Bloods, more crafty than the Modocs, more

---

[2] Details in this chapter based on information by Claude Vandervert, great nephew of Thomas Clark; Alvin Grimes, grandson of James Miller, Jr. and Tom Ochiho, grandson of Has No Horse.

honorable than the Americans. To Has No Horse it would seem only yesterday that he and his troops had met the Waiilatpu in a cavalry charge.[3] In reality, three winters had tracked across the land since their last encounter. Ravaged by disease, hounded by the "Ghost Men," their final skirmish with the Shoshoni had been a mockery to the once powerful Cayuse nation.

Never again would the Shoshoni cross lances with Waiilatpu braves, for the Cayuse tribes were as dead as last year's campfire. This reality was confirmed in the official government census taken by Indian High Commissioner Anson Dart. In July of 1851 Dart combed the mid-Columbia basin and made the startling discovery that a mere thirty-six Cayuse survived in a world they once thought belonged exclusively to the Indians. It is not difficult to understand why Has No Horse watched dispassionately as the Iowans moved into his ambush. If necessary, the Tussawehee dog soldier would kill every man in the wagon train to achieve his goal.

Tawa—the sun god—was still high in the afternoon sky when a strange thing happened. The Iowa train was making preparations to camp. As the wagons creaked into the customary evening circle, the Shoshoni were convinced that the white chief was a fool, for the wagonmaster chose to spend the night in the Powder River Valley, disputed hunting grounds claimed both by the Nez Perce and the Shoshoni and the reason for Has No Horse's recent wolfish attack on old Joseph's tribesmen. In the Shoshoni mind any leader worth the title, even an Earth Eater, would not commit such a foolish blunder.

The war party watched this activity with scorn. Finally, the confusion of encampment subsided and again it was quiet. During the process of settling in for the night the unsuspecting Iowans dangled the lure which was to alter the course of history. . . blooded horses and modern firearms. Arrows were nocked, rifles loaded and lances raised to charge position in anticipation of the war chief's command.

Slowly, he raised his arm to which was strapped a sacred war shield. The shield was made from the entire fresh hide of a three-year-old bull

---

[3] Waiilatpu was the Shoshoni name for the Cayuse Indians. It meant Horse Men. Coming from the original horse men, this name bestowed upon the Cayuse by the Shoshoni was indeed a great honor.

elk which had been stretched by hand, shrunk by steam and pounded by bare feet until it was two and a half feet in diameter. Blessed in ceremony, the shield was considered a very important part of a warrior's equipment, not so much from the protection standpoint as from the virtues bestowed by the holy man which was supposed to render the bearer invulnerable. But caution was also used.

Now, like the murmur of the death wind, crying and body-wracking coughs of children drifted upward on the evening breeze. This was an unexpected turn of events and it had a sobering effect on the waiting warriors. Whether the cause of the children's sickness be smallpox, measles or the common cold, it made little difference. All were equally deadly to the Shoshoni and Has No Horse could ill afford the gamble of contamination. Already, many of his tribesmen were dying, including his infant son. Every dog soldier in his command recognized the folly of making contact with this group.

Has No Horse was faced with a difficult decision. Neither he nor his men could risk further exposure to disease or they most certainly would follow the trail of the Cayuse. However, if he and his tribesmen were to maintain life at all, they desperately needed supplies, especially good horses, guns and ammunition. Everyone in the war party realized how extremely important these provisions were to the survival of their people. Less than a month ago, Go'tia—the Red Wolf—speaking for the Shoshoni tribes had taken a vital stand. . . one from which there was no return. Because of Red Wolf's decree the young war-chief's course of action was crystal clear. He must attack.

Extreme caution would be exercised no matter what the plan and the raiders would wait until the war chief developed a new tactic. Four hours after sunset in an unprecedented night attack, Has No Horse struck. Silent war arrows took care of dozing guards. They also produced rifles, hand-guns and ammunition. Next, the marauders liberated the horse herd and methodically slit the throats of the draft oxen to discourage any thoughts of pursuit. During the operation they were careful not to come into physical contact with any member of this plague-ridden wagon train. By the time the Iowans realized what was happening, the Shoshoni had disappeared like shadows in the pine and by daylight the captured weapons and horses were miles on their way into the Ochoco.

At daybreak, August 24, 1851, as the advance column frantically searched for livestock and went about the heart-breaking task of burying their dead, Has No Horse—dangerously short on manpower —continued eastward along the Oregon Trail, intent on further destruction. North of the Snake River crossing, he took a bearing on the Sawtooth range, by-passing dozens of wagon companies. He was gambling on the chance that he could intercept some of his people who would be moving out of the Rockies toward the Blues on their return from the summer's buffalo hunt.

Miles to the east, Deer Fly—uncle to Has No Horse—was also in a mean frame of mind. In the lodges of the Blackfeet, he had learned that Gourd Rattler (known to the Americans as Washa'kie) had joined forces with the Crows and was heading toward a peace council with the Long Knives at Fort Laramie. Deer Fly was convinced that Red Wolf would become rabid on word of this sellout though it was camp gossip that Gourd Rattler—one of the important head chiefs of the Shoshoni nation—had been uncommonly friendly with the Americans since the late 1830's.

In the shank-end of August, Has No Horse and Deer Fly made contact. Borrowing as many men as his uncle could spare, Has No Horse returned to the emigrant road where—280 miles southeast of the Ochoco—a choking cloud of dust betrayed the Clark wagon company bearing an unerring course towards Hell's Gate. This bleak landmark on the great western thoroughfare was the entrance to Red Wolf's vast domain.

This group, organized by influential Charles Clark of Scott County, Illinois, and piloted by his brother, Thomas Clark, was made up entirely of Illinois families.[4] It was not due to misfortune that the Clark company

---

[4] Among the members of this train were the Powell, Hodges, Williams, Miller, Knox, Cartwright and Newsom families, all of whom retraced their grim trail into Central Oregon and settled in the Ochoco in the 1870s. Monroe Hodges platted the townsite of Prineville in 1871. Sam Newsom became the first assessor of Crook County by appointment of Governor Moody in 1882. Charles Cartwright became Crook County's first state senator in 1884. James Miller founded the Keystone Ranch in 1872, while his brother Cincinnatus (Joaquin) Miller was toasted by the crowned heads of Europe as the Poet of the Sierras.

was travelling late, for wagonmaster Tom Clark intended to leave the main stream of traffic and by-pass the most difficult leg of the journey, the crossing of the Blue Mountains, described by Narcissa Whitman, first white woman to cross the Blues in 1836, as the worst trail she had ever seen. "The long days of travel with only a few miles covered between daylight and dark were seemingly endless," she wrote. "And the heat of the mountains was unbearable. It was like a winding stair in its descent and in some places almost perpendicular."[5] Tom Clark was confident that he would eliminate this troublesome route.

Tom had drifted west with the emigration of 1848, looking for land and presently considered himself an expert on western affairs. By 1849 he had joined his brother, James, in the California gold fields, where they struck it rich. He used the money to buy livestock in Illinois to bring to Oregon. It was in the California gold fields that Tom formulated a daring plan. Although unqualified for such an undertaking, he was going to lead successfully a wagon train across the center of Oregon territory from the second crossing of the Snake River to the middle Willamette Valley, a feat never before accomplished even by such experienced wagon scouts as Jesse Applegate or Stephen Meek.

This inspiration was born when Clark made a chance acquaintance with Steve Meek in Sacramento. Meek, still smarting from his last adventure as a wagon scout, told Clark to visit his brother, Joe, up in Oregon, if he wanted information on wagon trails. And so in mid-September 1850, Tom was again in the Willamette Valley, seeking Joe Meek and advice.

Joe was full of information for a young greenhorn. Among other bits of local history he told Clark how the Willamette received its name. According to Meek, when the Corps of Discovery arrived at this tributary of the Columbia, Lewis asked Clark, "Will, am it a river?" Clark thought for a moment and decided that it probably was.

When asked if it was possible to bring wagons across the center of Oregon to the Willamette Valley, Joe's quick reply was, "Hell, yes!" For a man who had crossed the snow covered North American continent

---

[5] Diary of Narcissa Whitman, edited by T.C. Elliott, Oregon Historical Society, under the title *Coming of the White Women.*

Stephen Meek

on foot from the Pacific to the Atlantic in eighty-eight days anything
was possible. Besides, his brother had already blazed a trail across the
Ochoco. Joe failed to inform Tom that this route was known as Meek's
Terrible Trail.

With this information Tom headed east via the Isthmus of Panama
and in the spring of 1851 became a wagonmaster with all its inherent
responsibilities.[6] His own contribution to the sizeable caravan included
twenty-two brood mares and two stallions.

Pushing vast herds of pureblood sheep, cattle and horses through
the interior wilderness, the Clark company inched forward. Out on the
Dakota plains, normally the bottle-neck to westward progress, all had
been serene. Slowly, the train moved overland across the Continental
Divide, down the peaceful Bear River and into the dusty campsite at
Fort Hall. Contrary to the warnings offered at this outpost by Indian
Agent Narcisse Raymond, Clark knew the worst was behind them.
There would be no obstacles between Fort Hall and the Willamette
Valley.

Others in the company were not so certain. Raymond's ominous
report that thirty-one emigrants had been shot by the Snakes in the past
two weeks caused many to strengthen their guard on wagons and
livestock.[7] Then, when Clark decided to linger at the fort for half a day,
the big train split with five groups hurrying on. David Newsom would
record in his journal that "We perceived a great hustle among the Indians
at the fort and from their maneuvers we apprehended that they were
preparing for a war excursion. On inquiry, they stated that they were
fitting out to kill some Crow Indians up Snake River."[8] The uncertainty
was whether they were telling the truth.

Because they had moved so slowly, grazing their livestock enroute,
the Clark company now held the distinction of being the tail of the '51
emigration. . . not an envied position. There was already a hint of autumn
in the air and an early snowstorm in the treacherous Blues could spell

[6] *Oregon Historical Quarterly*, Vol. LXXVIII, No. 3, p. 214.
[7] *The Oregon Statesman*, December 9, 1851. Also the San Francisco *Alta* carried
news of this hostility.
[8] David Newsom: *The Western Observer*, 1805-1882, pp. 31-32.

disaster. As the wagons approached Hell's Gate on the Snake River, there were more distinct signs of impending danger.

On the evening of August 29, William Owens, trail scout, rode in from the west and joined the Clark train at American Falls.[9] He had just completed a reconnaissance to the Raft River, where the California Trail merged with the Oregon Trail. During the patrol Owens had observed some very disturbing signs—talking smoke billowing up from the crest of the Sawtooths, answering smoke from the distant Blues, no trace of Digger Indians waiting for a handout along the rutted track, a Shoshoni war lance imbedded in the center of the Oregon Trail.

The only information of interest to Tom Clark was that the scout had seen flocks of wild ducks on the Raft River. The following morning, shortly before daybreak, Clark told Owens he was going duck hunting and would meet the wagons at the Raft River crossing. He was also taking his pack of trained hunting hounds in the hope of flushing larger game. In view of the scout's warning this amounted to desertion in the face of danger. However, no one but Owens questioned Clark's decision to abandon the wagons in hostile country.

Within hours these people would learn firsthand why the Oregon Trail was gaining notoriety as the longest graveyard on the North American continent. Over the years in a span of 1800 miles thirty thousand people would be buried along the trail.

As the Clark wagons journeyed from Fort Hall, Has No Horse moved into the sullen rims below Hell's Gate and was silently closing on his quarry. Hell's Gate—1,251 miles west of the Oregon Trail's beginning at Independence, Missouri—was two massive basalt rocks, blocking the Oregon Trail with just enough gap between them to allow

---

[9] A famous landmark and camping place for emigrants, American Falls was a cataract where the waters of the Snake River dropped some 50 feet in six to ten foot steps among basalt fragments of a ridge of rock which compressed the stream to a width of 75 feet. On July 5, 1849, James Pritchard would make this entry in his diary: "We passed the great American Falls. The roaring of the water can be heard for many miles." The site of the falls is now submerged beneath the back-waters of an eighty-seven foot high dam constructed by the Idaho Power Company.

passage of a single wagon. Before this day was over it would receive the name of Massacre Rocks.[10]

Downstream and some twelve miles east of the Raft's confluence with the Snake, Has No Horse and his war party forded the river at Register Rock. This half-buried boulder 25 feet in diameter and 20 feet high was the autograph book for travelers of the Oregon Trail. Some of the names carved into the rock and even some of those painted with axle grease as early as 1849 are still visible. From Register Rock the Shoshoni closed in on the leaderless Clark train. They couldn't believe their good fortune. To the Shoshoni raiders the seemingly unlimited herd of Morgan, Spanish Barb and Arabian horses was like a glimpse of heaven. Armed with rifles taken a week earlier from the Iowa vanguard, they would take on the devil himself for a prize such as this. Keeping discreetly out of sight, Has No Horse planned the attack.

---

[10] Some sources such, as Haines in *Historic Sites Along the Oregon Trail*, state that ". . . the rocks were not even an important landmark for the emigration and their sinister name did not appear (in print) until well after the turn of the century." This does not appear to be true. For example, the diary of Hamilton Scott, covering his *Trip Across the Plains in 1862*, makes these entries. August 9, 1862 ". . . the Smart train had fought its way on to the vicinity of Massacre Rocks with the loss of two men killed." August 11, 1862 ". . .the five dead recovered. . .were buried at the south end of Massacre Rocks. . ." Jane Gould in her *Journal 1862* entry for August 10, 1862 ". . .asked to help recover the two dead men and brought them on to the camp near Massacre Rocks. . . ." Numerous other accounts refer to Hell's Gate as Massacre Rocks. Locations for the various Shoshoni attacks at Hell's Gate are:

> Attack on the Clark train, Township 9 South,
> Range 30 East, Section 6 NE 1/4, NE1/4;
> Attack on the Adams train, Township 8 South,
> Range 30 East, Section 22 NE 1/4, SW 1/4;
> Attack on the Smart train, Township 8 South,
> Range 30 East, Section 28 NE 1/4, NE 1/4;
> Start of Cold Creek fight, Township 8 South,
> Range 31 East, Section 20 SW 1/4, SW 1/4.

The opening between Hell's Gate as the emigrants knew it was destroyed by blasting in 1958 in preparation for the building of Interstate Highway 15 West.

The sun was approaching high noon. The white men were certain to stop and rest, for they had already traveled ten miles in the past six hours. When the weary travelers relaxed for lunch, Bear Hunter and Three Coyotes would hit the main body at full gallop, creating as much confusion as only a Shoshoni charge could. Has No Horse and his brother-in-law, Broken Knife, would be in position to cut out the entire horse herd and also be prepared to eliminate any opposition which might occur. From that point the sole objective was to wrangle the horses back to Red Wolf's hideout in the Ochoco.

Down on the flat Owens glanced nervously at the sun. It was mid-day and he had been pushing the wagons unmercifully from the American Falls camp. Time to halt for a badly needed rest. He felt uneasy. The thought kept crossing his mind about what Raymond had said: "Be careful, Owens. Prince, the pierced-nose chief, tells me the Snake tribes have joined forces and are striking at anything that moves. Don't make no difference whether it's a white man or an Indian. Keep double guards posted at all times. Those renegades ain't playin' games."[11]

Owens believed the Indian agent and he wasn't alone in his concern for the emigrant's safety. Jack Harpool, leader of twenty wagons from northern Illinois, had met with Owens that morning and asked bluntly if Clark knew what the hell he was doing. Owens seriously doubted that he did. Later, he talked to Jim Miller, who was in charge of the horse herd. According to Miller, the animals were unusually nervous, which was a bad sign. Little Sammy Newsom, who had been stuck on the cow column along with Miller's sons, Cincinnatus and James Jr., claimed, "Those darn critters have gone completely loco. You can't herd 'em at all."

Joe Jackson, brother-in-law to Miller, rode up and Owens gave him the order to halt the wagons. Jack Harpool saw the Clark train stop and he did likewise. It was now twelve hours before the Sabbath.

Fifteen minutes later the Snake River Plateau exploded. The shrill "whooo whooo yaaaaah"—dreaded war cry of the Shoshoni—froze the

---

[11] In an interview with Alvin Grimes, May 18, 1978, this is the message given to Owens at Fort Hall by Indian Agent Raymond as remembered by his grandfather, James Miller, Jr.

Illinoians in their tracks. Riding through a hail of bullets, Has No Horse's sacred war shield stood him in good stead. Within seconds six horse guards took their last look at the Oregon frontier. Twenty-eight others who got in the line of attack followed the horse guards up the Sundown Trail, and the Clark wagon company was paralyzed with wounded. The instantaneous destruction was beyond their comprehension.

It is recorded that Hulings James Miller, a Quaker schoolmaster, was the first one shot. Seconds later, Samantha Miller, rushing towards her father's crumpled body, was crushed under the slashing hooves of a Shoshoni war horse. Joe Jackson in an attempt to drag his niece's broken body to the cover of the family wagon, took a buffalo lance above the left kidney. It came out at his belt buckle. Jack Harpool screamed a warning filled with terror as hundreds of cattle stampeded blindly into his wagon column.

Five minutes after the initial attack, helpless confusion held sway. Bill Owens cursed in futile rage as he watched 300 head of the finest horses west of the Mississippi River fade into the ruptured land beyond Hell's Gate. Has No Horse—the fatherless boy who never owned a pony—was ecstatic. Ahead of him thundered a horse herd worthy of the greatest chieftain. . . to him more valuable than all the accumulated white man's wealth in the Pacific Northwest. This would be the grandest coup of his life, never to be equalled throughout his turbulent career.

Later accounts would say: "The Snakes went berserk, making life miserable for emigrants, killing 34 of them, wounding and outraging many and stealing $18,000 worth of emigrant's property."[12] This figure did not include the horses, which were valued at $45,000.

Back on the blood-drenched Oregon Trail, Margaret Witt Miller—her husband seriously wounded, her brother-in-law dying, her trampled daughter clasped in her arms, her infant son, George, screaming in terror—kept moaning over and over ". . . Why, oh God, why? We never harmed these damnable savages in any way. Oh, Lord, why did it happen? How much heartache must we suffer before the government

---

[12] *The Oregon Statesman,* December 9, 1851; Glassly, *Pacific Northwest Indian Wars,* pp. 50-51.

blasts these miserable heathen from the face of this wretched land? How much. . . . ?"[13]

Three months later on December 12, 1851, this same question would appear in print in the *Oregon Statesman*. "The residents of this country are at a loss to account for these outrages, so bold on the part of the savages and so injurious to the white people."

The Shoshoni knew the answer, for the circumstances leading to the incident at Hell's Gate had their roots buried deep in the tear-stained soil of the Oyer'ungun.

---

[13] Samantha (Ella S.) Miller would live and marry John L. Luckey July 21, 1864, in Eugene, Oregon. Luckey was Deputy Sheriff in Prineville in the early 1880s. [Luckey family records; 1860 census records of Lane County and obituary articles.] Hulings Miller also survived and settled in the Eugene area in 1852.

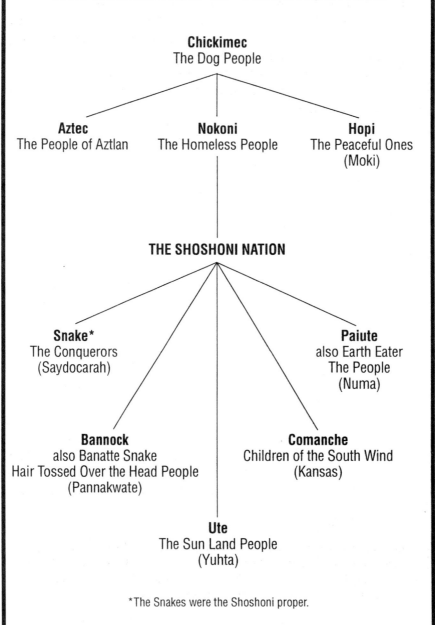

THE EVOLUTION OF THE SHOSHONI

Chickimec
The Dog People

Aztec
The People of Aztlan

Nokoni
The Homeless People

Hopi
The Peaceful Ones
(Moki)

THE SHOSHONI NATION

Snake*
The Conquerors
(Saydocarah)

Paiute
also Earth Eater
The People
(Numa)

Bannock
also Banatte Snake
Hair Tossed Over the Head People
(Pannakwate)

Comanche
Children of the South Wind
(Kansas)

Ute
The Sun Land People
(Yuhta)

*The Snakes were the Shoshoni proper.

CHAPTER 2

SAYDOCARAH—THE CONQUERORS

A horse nation all over the universe
Neighing, they come!
Prancing, they come!
May you behold them.

Black Elk
Sioux Holy Man

Three hundred years before the incident at Hell's Gate, Spanish galleons knifed through the northern waters of the sundown sea. Prowling the Pacific Coast, these ships carried the first white men to sight the towering cliffs of the Oregon mainland. That sighting was enough to satisfy their curiosity, for the reckless sailors harbored no desire to discover what lay beyond the pounding surf.

Aware that his sea-dogs had an aversion to land exploration, Antonio de Mendoza, governor of Mexico, initiated an overland thrust to coincide with the sea jab.[14] The ground armada clanked into the unknown wilderness west of the Rio Grande and took a bearing on the Oregon Country some 800 miles to the north. These iron-clad warriors—spurred on by rumors of cities whose streets were paved with gold—pushed through a desolate region, finding nothing but poverty-stricken natives and treeless prairies, swarming with "large black cattle." Garcia Lopez de Cardenas, scout for the expedition, gasped as he wandered onto the lip of the Colorado River's Grand Canyon. And there, some 350 miles

---

[14] For full details on the sea and land expeditions spearheaded by the Spanish, see *The North American Review*, January 1839; and Adam's *The Epic of America*, pp. 12-13.

short of its goal, Francisco de Coronado's army ground to a halt, defeated by the land itself.

At the same time Coronado marched toward the Colorado River, Hernando de Soto came up the Mississippi Valley and traveled as far west as the present state of Oklahoma before turning back. At one point, unknown to either party, the two expeditions were within nine day's march of each other.

Deep within the scorched interior an ancient Shoshoni civilization was fighting desperately for survival. Skilled agriculturists, their lifestyle had been destroyed by a 700-year drought, an endless dry spell which was still in progress at the arrival of the Spanish conquistadores.[15] Disease and famine had weakened them to the point where the barbarous Chinook and Sahaptin tribes were in complete command of their destiny. Hunted like animals for sport, traded for profit in the flourishing Columbia and Missouri slave markets, these people were on the brink of extinction.

Two hundred years before the Spanish made their appearance, the Shoshoni—who lived along the lakes and streams of Oregon's southern Blue Mountains—were driven out of their homeland by the Columbia Basin tribes and set adrift in the bleak Great Basin of western America. It was a bitter and traumatic experience for the Shoshoni, who had ruled the interior for perhaps 1,100 years and had resided there for a much longer period of time.

The forerunner of an ancient Shoshonean tribe may have settled in Central Oregon at a very early date. In April 1956, portions of pelvic bones which had not yet turned to stone were unearthed twenty-six feet beneath the surface of Combs Flat, southeast of Prineville, Oregon. Although they contained many features not found in modern man, local physicians who viewed the remains claim there exists considerable similarity to those of present day humans. Noted geologist, Phil Brogan,

---

[15] This awesome dry spell which began in 840 A.D. was accurately determined by tree borings taken by J.A. Jeanson and O.G. Ricketson of the National Geographic Society's first expedition into the Great Basin in the summer of 1923. The years of unbearable heat—with a slight reprieve between 900 A.D. and 1000 A.D., continued from 1067 to 1632. *The National Geographic Magazine*, Vo. LVI, No. 6, December, 1929.

of Bend, Oregon, also inspected the find and estimated it to be "at least 80,000 years old."

A greater puzzle which shed more light on their early existence is the Nampa Image. . . the figurine of a maiden flawlessly endowed with every feature of modern woman. This work of art, 1½ inches tall, with both hands and feet missing, was brought up from a depth of 320 feet by an artesian sand-pump at Nampa, Idaho, in 1889. Discovered in the heart of Shoshoni land, it lay in formations of late Tertiary or early Quaternary age. It is interesting to note that the age of the object corresponds with that of the Java Man. So, it follows that an ancient Indian sculptor had produced the Shoshoni Venus at a period when the Master of the Universe had succeeded only in blocking out the first rude suggestions of the human form in the Old World.

In their frantic search for food, the Shoshoni outcasts became intimately acquainted with every rock and gully from the Columbia Plateau to the Kansas Plains. They called themselves Nokoni—the Homeless People.

Long before the Chinook-Sahaptin invasion when the Shoshoni called themselves Chickimecs—the Dog People—some of the more adventurous members of the family drifted out of the Blue Mountains of their own accord. Over a span of centuries, during which they became hunters, this group worked their way south and between 700 and 850 A.D. established residence along the Colorado River. Here, some returned to farming, while others continued as hunters. The former changed their name to Moki—the Peaceful Ones. The Europeans would call them Hopi.

The hunting segment of the Chickimecs continued to move southward. Tough, brutal, hungry, they crowded into the valley of Mexico, where they seized, sacked and destroyed everything in sight. By 1300, this group of Dog People emerged as the rulers of Mexico. They took the name of Aztecs—the People of Aztlan—to honor a mythical city in their ancient homeland to the distant north.

During this same period one of the unsolved mysteries of ancient times took place. A group of invaders moved into the Mississippi Valley and near the geographic center of North America founded one of the greatest nations of the pre-Columbian world. All that is known for certain about its complex social system and capital city—called Cahokia for a local tribe of Indians who had no connection with the city but inhabited its ruins when the French arrived in the 1600's—is that it appeared suddenly, dated to the approximate time of the Aztec's invasion of Mexico and the Hopi's founding of the Pueblo dynasty. Bear in mind, the Hopi's were unsurpassed in agriculture and the Aztecs were scientists, astronomers and engineers.

Cahokia, whose city center covered six square miles, was the largest urban development to exist in North America until the mid-1800's, for it took that long for New York City to eclipse Cahokia, which had ceased to exist more than 400 years earlier.[16] This metropolis—built according to complex geometric and astronomical formulas worked out by scientists and engineers—was dominated by perhaps 140 huge earthen conical and pyramidal mounds. One of these, now called Monk's Mound, is the largest prehistoric structure in North America with a base area larger than Egypt's Great Pyramid of Giza.[17] Archeologists say Monk's Mound was "probably ceremonial in nature," which means they are completely baffled as to its true function.

A quarter of a million people lived in Cahokia, which was built on a plain sixty miles long and one to eight miles wide, containing some of the most fertile soil in the world and where four major rivers flowed into the Mississippi. An agricultural economy developed first with a scope never before seen in the New World. Everyday an estimated 30,000 pounds of corn flowed into the city and its suburbs just to feed the populace. From this base a surplus of food contributed to the growth of a substantial industrial and artistic community and traders ranged for a thousand miles in every direction.

From all across the continent flowed copper, lead, salt, buffalo hides, obsidian and hundreds of other articles. The rivers—Missouri, Illinois, Meramec, Kaskaskia and Mississippi—bore heavy traffic. Fleets of large canoes transported materials which highly skilled artisans trans-

---

[16] For a complete description of Cahokia see *Explorations into Cahokia, Illinois Archeological Survey*, Bulletin No. 7.

[17] Monk's Mound was named for a group of Trappist monks from Kentucky, who established a monastery here in 1809 on land donated to them by Nicholas Jarrot whose claim to 400 acres at Cahokia, including Monk's Mound, was affirmed on December 1, 1808. Jim Miles, *Cahokia: First American Metropolis*, Fate, Vol. 35, No. 10, October, 1982.

formed into beautiful, exotic goods. Shipments of these finished products in turn left the city by way of the rivers. Because of this there were many shipyards, acres of docks and warehouses, intricate canal systems, which meant there was probably a traffic control system on the waterways and perhaps even toll booths. The most important manufactured items were flint hoes and jewelry. Exotic artifacts that survive today are arrowheads, ceremonial spear points and pendants delicately chipped from obsidian. Cahokia was a highly structured society with classes of priests, civic leaders, warriors, farmers, merchants, artisans and slaves, the latter reflected in the mass sacrifices and the great amount of physical labor required in construction activities.

Early explorers knew of the existence of this city. J.M. Breckenridge—whose brother, Henry, was entering eastern Oregon with the Astorians at the same time he wandered into Cahokia in 1811—would comment, "Around me I counted 45 mounds or pyramids. . . a mile in extent. . . two were seen on the bluff at a distance of three miles. . . I conclude that a populous city had once existed here, similar to those of Mexico described by the first conqueror."[18] Yet modern archeologists were unaware of it until the 1960's when they discovered that "one of the greatest nations of the prehistoric world existed in the Mississippi Valley between A.D. 900-1400." By then it was a little late as the ancient townsite had been obliterated by East St. Louis, Granite City and Columbia, Illinois.

The Hopi and the Aztecs became separated from the Northern Chickimecs by a thousand miles of harsh desert and mountainous country, but always they maintained contact. A trail, etched deep through centuries of use, linked the Blue Mountains of Oregon with the east coast of Mexico, a prehistoric trade route which in time became overlain by the roads of the late-coming Europeans. It extended from Vera Cruz northward to the Rio Grande River. From there it continued north to Santa Fe, angled across western Colorado into Utah, where it crossed the White River; then on to the Green River crossing near where Fort Thornbury was located in later centuries. From this point the trail followed over the Uinta Mountains to the Snake River and thence west,

---

[18] J.M. Breckenridge, early American traveler, 1811.

where it followed the Malheur River into Harney Basin. Again it turned north to the headwaters of Crooked River and crossed Big Summit Prairie into the John Day Valley.[19] At Picture Gorge on the John Day River the Shoshoni Trail from Mexico joined the trade routes of the Columbia.

Trade goods passed back and forth along the Shoshoni Trail from family to family in a long series of exchanges. The Aztec and Hopi obtained gold, obsidian, silver, pine nuts and otter skins from the north. The Chickimecs received turquoise, corn, tobacco and parrot feathers from the south. More importantly, ideas were passed along with the merchandise and all sides of the family advanced in knowledge and wealth.

Then came the devastating drought. While the Aztecs fulfilled their destiny with the invasion of Mexico and the Hopi were building the pueblo dynasty, the Chickimecs became the victims of slavery and mass starvation. They were now Nokoni.

Unknown to Antonio de Mendoza, his land expeditions would provide the dying Nokoni with the means not only to survive but to emerge as the leading power in western North America. It is ironic that Mendoza's predecessor, Hernando Cortez, supplied the power to destroy the Aztecs, the most advanced civilization on the North American continent, one which by 1519 had an estimated population of more than eleven million people highly educated in engineering, brain surgery, architecture and astronomy.

In 1541, the Nokoni watched and marvelled as Coronado fought his way up the Colorado River, retreated to the Red River and then plunged north towards the Cimarron. However, it was not the Spaniards who inspired them with awe. They were men, no better and no worse than the ruthless Columbia tribes. But the conquistadores possessed something which held the starving Nokoni spellbound. Coronado and his soldiers were gliding across the sage, riding on the backs of large animals.

---

[19] Segments of the Chickimec or Shoshoni Trail eventually became parts of the Spanish Trail, the Mormon Trail, the California Trail and the Oregon Trail. Miles Cannon, "Snake River in History," *Oregon Historical Quarterly*, Vol. XX, No. 1, March, 1919.

Grass fires, which Coronado interpreted as evil omens, flashed the word ahead that strange men were prowling the southern wastelands. Up on the Arkansas River another group of Nokoni gathered their emaciated families to get out of harm's way only to run head-on into the horse-borne de Soto, plodding majestically but wearily across the sweltering prairies of the Kansas country. Like those who had given the initial warning, these people's imaginations were set aflame. Before them was the means for greatness. If they could capture some of these animals and master them, they had the potential for ruling the world.

After months of observation, the Nokoni were convinced that if the clumsy aliens could ride such a creature without fatality, then so could they. It was relatively easy to catch one for tired old Coronado and the dying de Soto left horses strung out for 900 miles in their epic crossing of the southwest plains. And thus the day of emancipation arrived when the Homeless People caught that fabulous creature they solemnly named Shirri won'gua. . . the Dog God.[20]

Within a very short span of time, small, mobile units of Nokoni, mounted on fast ponies, began to explore the land in which they lived. To them, a people who had walked every inch of ground between the Cascade Range and the Dakota Plains, a journey on horseback of 800 miles was nothing more than a pleasant outing. When their first small patrols encountered the Columbia Basin tribes and the equally cruel Plains Indians, they were rather intimidated, for these people had dealt them much misery. Nonetheless, they didn't let this dampen their spirits for a fight.

Being the product of a sterner environment, the Nokoni had been taught from childhood to bring down the wariest small game while outmaneuvering unseen foes. They soon discovered that they could handle a bow faster and see better than the Columbia and Missouri slavers. With the added speed and strength of a horse not only did they become dangerous predators, but they also held a decisive military advantage.

---

[20] Such authorities as Colonel Richard Dodge and George Catlin claim the Comanches were the first American horse Indians. Frank Roe and J. Frank Dobie give credit to the Utes. This is an academic discussion as none of the northern Shoshoni tribes had been formed prior to the acquisition of the horse.

As the 1500's submerged into the muck of time, the vanishing civilization grew strong and prosperous. Its citizens became fierce and warlike. No more did they scavenge the land for survival. Their livelihood was derived from the pursuit of large game, for they were now Horse Indians. . . feared and respected by all other tribes. They changed their name to Saydocarah, the Conquerors. Bordering nations called them Sho'sho-nee, the Enemy.

It is interesting to note that the Shoshoni called themselves "the Conquerors." Without exception other American Indians referred to themselves in their own language as "people." For example, the Arapahoe in their tongue are Inunaina, the people; the Navaho are Dine, the people; the Mandan are Numakiki, the people; even the poor relations, the Paiutes, called themselves Numa, the people. Not so with the Shoshoni. Had the white race taken the effort to discover this, it would have given them a much better insight into the character of the people called Shoshoni, the same people whom the Europeans referred to as "Snakes."[21] Through necessity the Saydocarah were forced to adopt the word "Shoshoni" into their language, where it came to mean "inland or plenty of grass."

Soon after the Shoshoni mastered the horse, long dormant agricultural instincts stirred memories of lush mountain meadows containing grasses of a high protein content. They reasoned, and correctly so, that their mounts required this quality of forage to maintain proper strength, so they abandoned their desert hideouts and headed for the high country of their ancestors. During this migration to the north the third segment

---

[21] Through a misinterpretation of the Indian sign language the Shoshoni received the name Snake. Over the years the explorers and early mountain men slowly came to the conclusion that all other Indian nations referred to these people as "Sho'sho-nees," a name believed to have been derived from the Cheyenne—shiski' noats-hitane—which as originally applied to the Comanche branch of the family meant "snake people." In the Shoshoni language, Comanche defined the enemy. The Shoshoni called the Comanche members of the family "Kansas," meaning the Children of the South Wind. Most historians, in keeping with the suppression of Shoshonean culture, will insist that the word "Kansas" is of Sioux origin.

of the family broke off and gained identity, which probably made the remainder of the clan quite happy.

In their eyes this group was pitifully shiftless. Worse yet, inasmuch as the rest of the Shoshoni family was concerned, these stocky characters were weak and lacking in enough good sense to come in out of the sun. They developed no political structure, lived in small family groups not unlike they had before the advent of the horse. By 1680 they were scattered over a vast expanse of Colorado mountains, Utah desert and Nevada salt flats which nobody else would be caught dead upon. The family referred to them as Yuhta—Sun Land People. The Europeans called them Utes.

In triumph the Horsemen entered their ancient homeland, the Ochoco (oooo'she-ho). . . the strange and haunting Shoshoni name for the Blue Mountains of eastern Oregon.[22] They returned as bold travelers, brutal fighters and daring raiders as savage as the animals they fought. To the terror-stricken Columbia Basin tribes the mounted warriors were nearly as god-like as the awesome beasts upon which they rode. By 1610 the Shoshoni claimed an immense territory—larger than most European countries—as their private hunting ground, a country they named Oyer'ungun. . . the Land of Peace and Plenty.

It is reasonable to believe that the name "Oregon" is derived from this Shoshoni word, for its similarity to Oyer'ungun cannot be denied. More of the original Oregon Territory was composed of this geographic area than by any other feature. As defined by the Shoshoni, the Oyer'ungun was bounded on the west by the Deschutes River and on the east by the Big Horn Mountains. It sprawled from the Blue Mountains on the north

---

[22] That the Shoshoni had been missing from eastern Oregon for centuries is confirmed by archeological evidence. In August, 1975, the University of Oregon conducted an archeological survey of the Glass Butte area within the southern boundary of the Shoshoni Ochoco. An analysis of the collected artifacts indicated that human use of the area was continuous from approximately 11,000 B.C. to at least 1100 A.D. Then there is a 500 year gap in usage. The absence of artifacts suggests that the area saw limited or no use from 1100 A.D. to 1600 (considered to be modern times). Joanne Mack, *Cultural Resources Inventory of the Potential Glass Buttes Geothermal Lease Areas, Lake, Harney and Deschutes Counties*, University of Oregon, Department of Anthropology, December 1, 1975.

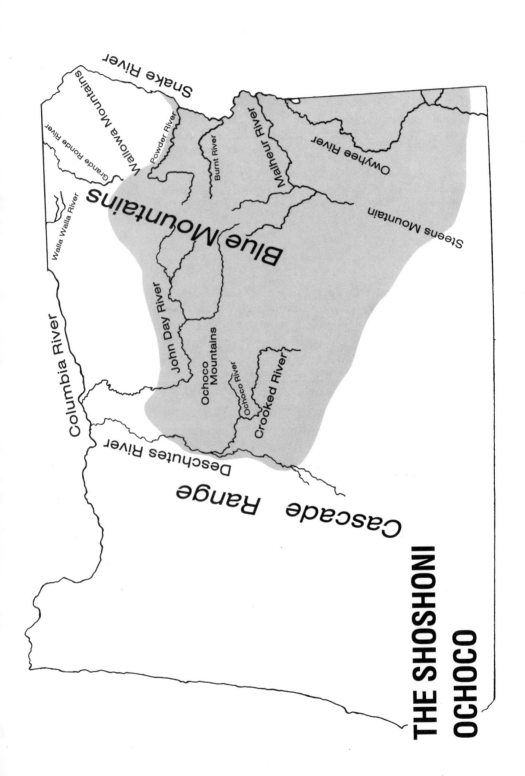

THE SHOSHONI
OCHOCO

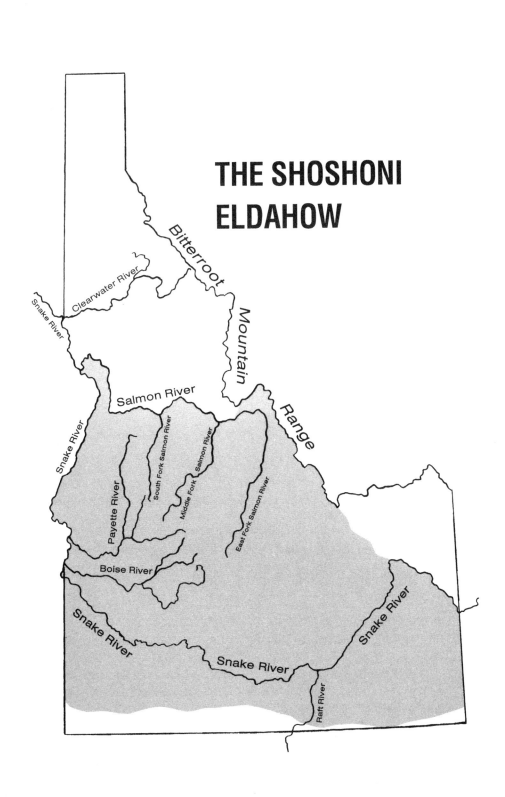

THE SHOSHONI
ELDAHOW

to the Spanish settlements on the south, covering an area of some 240,000 square miles. By Shoshoni description the Oyer'ungun was divided into two distinct land masses, which were comparable to the provinces of the European countries. They were the Ochoco—Land of the Red Willow—extending from the Deschutes River east to the Snake River and the Eldahow—Land of the Sun Marching Down the Mountains—running from the Snake to the crest of the Big Horn Mountains.[23] By 1700 the Shoshoni would expand hunting rights into three times the area of Oyer'ungun.

Another Shoshoni expression, originating from two Shoshoni words "ogwa" (river) and "pe-on" (water) may be the basis for the name "Oregon." Ogwa'pe-on was their name for the Columbia River. It meant "the trade river of the north" and was pronounced in the Shoshoni language the same way as Oregon is pronounced in the English language.[24]

Within a sixty year period, the Homeless People became a happy, musical, curious, poetic group full of dancing and mischief. Families combined into clans and clans into bands of a hundred people or more. It was then that the art of politics was perfected. Heads of families assembled and chose clan chiefs, spiritual chiefs and war chiefs. Promising youngsters were made sub-chiefs to carry out policies formulated

---

[23] Some claim the name "Idaho" (Eldahow) came from the Apache's name for the Comanche which was Idahi (Longstreet, *War Cries on Horseback*, p. 164). Not so. El-dah-how! was a Shoshoni exclamation announcing the sun coming down the mountains, heralding a new day. This became "Idaho."

[24] The name Oregon (or Oregan as he spelled it) was first used by Jonathan Carver who traveled west from Connecticut to the upper Mississippi Valley in 1763. In his book Carver speaks of the "Oregon or River of the West that falls into the Pacific Ocean at the Straits of Anion." This suggests the usage of the word Ogwapeon. Most likely Carver derived his idea of the existence of the Columbia River and the name from the Indians whom he lived with and who had either crossed the Rocky Mountains (which is unlikely) or more probably had received visits from the far-ranging Shoshoni traders. Whatever the circumstances, this appears to be the English origin of the name Oregon. *House of Representatives Document*, No. 101, 25th Congress, 3rd session. Also, see John Rees, *Oregon—Its Meaning, Origin and Application*, Oregon Historical Quarterly, Vol. XXI, No. 4, December, 1920, pp. 318-322.

by the elders. It soon followed that ambitious clan chiefs plotted to set themselves up as rulers of several large bands. And then came the tribes. Because of their vast horse herds it was impractical to stay together as a group, so it soon evolved that the various bands lived apart, joining together only for trade, festive occasions and war.[25]

By 1620, the Moki, Saydocarah, Yuhta and Kansas bands had formed into the four tribes of the Shoshoni nation. Or as ethnologists would classify them, the Hopi, Snakes, Utes and Comanches were the survivors of the Uto-Aztecan linguistic group. For by now the people of Aztlan, decimated by slaughter, disease and intermarriage with the Spanish colonizers, were little more than a memory to be noted in the passage of time.

Many small Shoshonean family groups, related by blood to the powerful war tribes, never mastered the horse. They continued to live as they had since being driven out of the Ochoco around 1340. These poor relations were known within the family circle by such descriptive names as Earth Eaters, Walking People, Diggers and Have No Meat. They grubbed a meager living from the hostile environment of the Great Basin. . . a land so poorly suited to survival that the best use they could put a horse to was to eat him. Here, they existed in relative peace, watched over and protected by the parent tribes. These timid souls called themselves Numa—the People. The Europeans called them Paiutes.

Few white men realized that they were associated with Saydocarah warrior clans. One who did would describe these stone-age, bug-eating relatives of the "powerful and prosperous tribe of the Snakes, who possessed a glorious hunting country" in this manner: "But there is another class called Diggers or Root Eaters. These are a shy, secret, solitary race, who keep in the most retired parts of the mountains,

---

[25] For a detailed description of Shoshonean customs and how they evolved, the following are recommended reading: Burton, *City of Saints*, London, 1861; Dunn, *History of the Oregon Territory*, London, 1844; Farley, *San Francisco Medical Journal*, Vol. III, p. 154; Farnham, *Life, Adventures and Travels in California*, New York, 1846; Taylor, *California Farmer*, April 27, 1860; Prince, *California Farmer*, Oct. 18, 1861; Ross, *Fur Hunters of the Far West*, 2 vols., London, 1855; James, *My Experience With the Indians*, New York, 1925; Simpson, *The Oregon Territory*, London, 1846.

lurking like gnomes in caverns and clefts of the rocks and subsisting in a great measure on the roots of the earth. Sometimes in passing through a solitary mountain valley, the traveler comes perchance upon the bleeding carcass of a deer or buffalo that has just been slain. He looks round in vain for the hunter; the whole landscape is lifeless and deserted. At length he perceives a thread of smoke, curling up from among the crags and cliffs, and scrambling to the place finds some forlorn and skulking brood of Diggers, terrified at being discovered.[26] Life was not easy for the Numa.

The Shoshoni were the wealthiest in horses of the American Indians with some warriors owning hundreds. They became the leading exponents of horse culture, which was to spread from them to all western tribes. As their own horse needs became filled, the Shoshoni started a real trade in horses.

To expedite transactions the forerunners of the Comanche tribe (and the reason for the name "Children of the South Wind") left the Oregon country and by 1680 the whole tribe had gradually migrated into the Kansas Plains so they could more easily raid Spanish settlements for more horses.

The Comanches became the principal procurers of horses, while the Utes were the middlemen in this lucrative business.[27] Immediately after a big raid the Comanches would turn the horses over to the Utes who would wrangle them over the southern Rockies and deliver them for a nominal fee to the Snakes. These traders would pass them along for a fat profit to the Nez Perce, Umatilla, Arapahoe or anyone else who could make the price.

The Shoshoni had now completed the pleasant transition from passive, starving, dirty proletarians to plump, clean, aggressive capitalists with time to explore or go fishing just for the fun of it. Their hunting parties probed the Great Plains in pursuit of buffalo and the Pacific Coast

---

[26] Washington Irving, *Astoria*, pp. 225-226.

[27] Even casual observers of the Shoshoni have recognized that the trade relations of the Comanches were especially complex due to the widely separated range of the various bands. Some of the important tribes were so far apart—800 miles or more—that they may have hardly been aware of each other's existence. For more on trade relations see *The American Heritage Book of Indians*, p. 378.

in quest of trade articles with no fear of retaliation. To stave off boredom they fought among themselves. Occasionally, they stopped these family squabbles long enough to stage a few wild raids on the Wascos, the Klamaths or the Crows. But, mainly, they occupied their time with hunting. This was a serious business, whereas fighting was pretty much a sporting proposition, carried on by individual initiative. Earlier war parties had eliminated any need for further conquests.

As early as 1706 the Comanches had cleared the Kansas country of Apaches and by 1739 they were the masters of the southern plains. During this same period the Snakes seized possession of the northern plains and by 1730 had driven the Blackfeet into the Saskatchewan prairies of interior Canada. The Utes swept through the southern Rockies and by 1690 claimed the present states of Colorado and Utah. Driving to the west the Snakes—shoving the Modocs, Washoes and Shastas ahead of them—expanded hunting rights into Nevada and northern California. In slashing raids to the north the Banatte Snakes cleared the northern Blues, the Idaho panhandle and the western Rockies of Nez Perce, Spokane and Flatheads.[28]

---

[28] In recent years two archeologists working on separate projects have found archeological evidence of the Shoshoni invasion of Eastern Oregon. (See James Teit, *The Middle Columbia Salish*, University of Washington publications in Anthropology 2 (4) 83-128, 1928, and Joel Berreman, *Tribal Distribution in Oregon*, American Anthropological Association Memoir 47, 1937.) This evidence confirms testimony by the defeated Chinook-Sahaptin tribes that they were driven to the Columbia River by the Shoshoni and supports the accounts of early explorers as to the war-like nature of these people. Further evidence of the Shoshoni intrusion to the Columbia was discovered in 1930 in the lower John Day River canyon. A cremation pit was located on a talus slope above Hoover Creek along with a crescent-shaped copper pendant and two pieces of hand-carved stone. The heat from the cremation fires had been so intense that it fused together pieces of basalt in the vicinity of the pit. (Strong, Schenck, Steward, *Archeology of The Dalles-Deschutes Regions*, University of California Publications in American Archeology and Ethnology 29 (1), Berkely, 1930.) The Aztecs practiced cremation. At this same site other searchers found basketry in which... "while the specimens were typically of a Northern Basin-Plateau culture, they also showed some affinities to the Pueblo culture of the Southwest." (Cressman, *Archeological Research of the John Day Region of North Central*

On the east the Cheyenne, Arapahoe and Sioux all fought the Shoshoni at various times or simultaneously. On the west the same situation prevailed with the Cayuse, Yakimas and Klickitats. In the strange manner of Indian wars this situation did not prevent the separate hostile bands from negotiating occasional peace treaties, which sometimes lasted for years. By means of gifts and conciliation the Wascos, Klamaths and Walla Wallas managed to co-exist fairly well with the Shoshoni until the arrival of the white men. The fish Indians seemed to consider it a small price to pay for even a shaky peace with the fierce raiders and appeasement became the order of the times as the Shoshoni plundered at will.

This is the way things were in western America at the dawn of the European invasion. Along with other fashionable contributions the white brothers would introduce the Shoshoni to loathsome disease and the latest innovation in modern warfare. . . that unholy weapon known to the civilized world as the smooth-bore musket.

Oregon, American Philosophical Society Proceedings 94:381, Philadelphia, 1950.) Yet, modern scholars refuse to accept these findings, still dwelling on the misconception that the Paiutes were the true representatives of the Shoshoni culture as attested by this statement: "The idea presented in the Teit-Berreman hypothesis that the Oregon Paiute forced the Plateau groups northward to the Columbia River during the early 1800s has been found to be wholly lacking in support." (Toepel and Beckham, *Cultural Resource Overview of the Brothers EIS Area, Prineville District*, Oregon, Department of Anthropology, University of Oregon, June, 1978.) Of course the Paiutes did not drive the Plateau groups to the Columbia. The Paiutes were incapable of such hostility, but not the Snakes.

CHAPTER 3

STRANGERS FROM THE NORTH

*The stage was first set in the forthcoming struggle
for empire by a long list of bold,
cold-blooded conquistadors. In the temper of
the times all were cruel, all skilled in the
technique of murder, rapine, assassination,
torture and pillage. . . .*

Ernest Swift
The Glory Trail

After the destruction of the Aztecs, the Hopi were the next members of the Shoshonean family to feel the bitter sting of European dominance. In 1512 the enlightened Pope Julius II—Giuliano della Rovere—at the 15th Lateran Council issued an official declaration, certifying that American Indians "are true descendants of Adam and Eve and hence human beings." The Hopi would now pay their dues for that membership. At the peak of the Shoshoni invasion of Oregon word filtered from Hopi pueblo to Ute tipi to Paiute hideout to the war camps of the Ochoco that the Peaceful Ones were being enslaved by a people whom the Hopi called Tiwa—Metal Men.

It was common knowledge that the Hopi were pacifists. Never had they practiced the fine art of warfare as a means to survival. For 900 years the Hopi had farmed the mesas along the Colorado River. Throughout the centuries they had not found it necessary to break the peace. Pedro de Castaneda, a soldier in Coronado's army, gave this description of the Hopi in 1542: "There is no drunkenness among them nor sodomy nor sacrifice; neither do they eat human flesh nor steal, but they are usually at work, tending their fields. . . ."

At the beginning of the Shoshoni expansion to the north, Spanish soldiers followed the Shoshoni Trail up the Rio Grande and in 1598 founded the first Spanish colony in what is now the southwestern United

States. They named the outpost Santa Fe. From this fortress the soldiers began colonization of all Indians from the Colorado River to the Kansas Plains. They encountered little or no resistance except for one pueblo.

Some 90 miles southwest of Santa Fe sat the ancient Anasazi pueblo of Acoma—Place of the White Rock. Perched near the crest of the Continental Divide on a rock-walled mesa 357 feet high, Acoma was—and still is—the oldest inhabited settlement in what is now the United States. At the time of the Spanish invasion, Acoma was inhabited by Indians of the Acoma tribe, belonging to the Pueblo nation. Because of its strategic location the pueblo people believed Acoma to be impregnable.

Impregnable or not, the Spaniards stormed the town. In less than four hours of brutal fighting, Acoma became a Spanish possession. The few men who survived the battle along with five hundred women and children were taken in chains to Santa Fe, where they stood trial for crimes committed against the Spanish crown. All—with the exception of children under 12 years of age—were sentenced to 20 years at hard labor. In addition the men suffered the loss of one foot severed at the ankle, making escape more difficult. Two Hopi farmers, who were visiting Acoma at the time of attack, had their right hands chopped off at the wrist. They were sent back to the Hopi pueblos as messengers that the Spanish were coming.[29]

Come they did. No longer would the Hopi tend their fields. Herded like cattle back to the Spanish settlements, the Hopi were sentenced to a life of. . ."personal services." They labored for the white men, who took their homes, their food, their blankets and their women. If Hopi complained, they took his life by sword, by fire, by rope. As the years of tyranny wore on the Hopi died in massive numbers from measles, smallpox, cholera and tuberculosis. Women, rotting with syphilis, could not give birth. The mark of progress was upon them. The Hopi died

---

[29] The governor of Santa Fe, Don Juan de Onate—son of one of the richest mine owners in Mexico and married to a great granddaughter of Montezuma—was fined and stripped of his honors by a Spanish court for this mass enslavement and amputation of limbs. However, this didn't occur until 1613, fifteen years after the crime had been committed. (William Brandon, The American Heritage *Book of Indians*, p. 119.)

drunk. They died insane. They died by their own hand. They died. . . and the priests cleansed their heathen souls for entry into the white man's heaven. There was no escape.

A visionary—the product of a Zuni farmer and a Hopi stable maid—dared to question Spanish authority. Even more astonishing, he refused to accept the Catholic faith. For this heresy he was thrown into a Spanish prison for three years of solitary repentance. His jailers called him Pope. In 1675 Pope was released from purgatory. He begged the Zuni, the Pueblo, the Hopi to unite in revolt against Spanish rule. Weak, tired, sick, frightened, they lacked the will to respond. It would take more years of misery and degradation before the pueblo people would react.

Finally, it was the long-suffering Hopi who were ready to fight. In the spring of 1680 their plea for help winged northward with the migratory geese, seeking aid from their Ute brothers. That was not forthcoming. The Utes—now dabbling in the slave trade—refused to join the pueblo revolt. Five years earlier in 1675 the Ute head chiefs at a meeting in Santa Fe with Antonio Otermin, Governor of New Mexico, pledged peace with the Spanish. However, they passed the message on and a heavily armed force of Snake dog soldiers rode for the land of the Hopi. In their wake came wives and children, parents and grandparents, horses and dogs. They packed with them all their earthly possessions in anticipation of an extended siege.

They raided, they plundered, they fought to the death, but the Snakes never lowered themselves to the base position of slavers. Five hundred years of enslavement by the Columbia and Missouri tribes had instilled within their minds an intensive hatred for human bondage. Unlike the Aztecs, who dealt in wholesale slavery, the Snakes would not condone such traffic. This practice, common to all other North American Indians, was the prime motivator in the devastating Snake attacks on the western tribes.

Seldom did the Snakes take a male prisoner. If forced into it, this luckless person was quickly disposed of unless he was truly a brave fighter. Then the captive's fate lay entirely in his own hands. He could become adopted into the tribe with full recognition as a Snake warrior, or he could choose to fight for his freedom and if victorious would be immediately set free.

If women and children had to be taken, which the Snakes tried to avoid, their lives became an improvement over that which they had left. The children were adopted into families and treated as equals to their newly acquired brothers and sisters and by maturity could rise to a very high position in the tribe, if they proved themselves capable. The women, if lucky, attracted some warrior's attention and gained a husband; if not, they were taken care of by some family and lived their lives in peace.[30]

The Shoshoni held a belief handed down from the time they wandered across the Great Basin on foot ". . .be merciful to those who are in your power. It is the part of a coward to torture a prisoner or ill-treat those that are helpless before you. It is the part of a warrior to take care of the weak, the sick, the old and the helpless."[31]

With this creed as the driving force the huge war party disappeared into the land-locked arroyos of the Great Basin. At the Ute camps they picked up fresh mounts. Twenty-nine days and 850 miles south of the Ochoco, the advance party galloped their lathered war horses around the eastern base of Tucayan Mesa into the nearly deserted Hopi pueblo of Kisa'kobi. When their families arrived in late July, 1680, they increased the town's population by almost 500.

The Hopi as the Shoshoni remembered them—a kindly people who fed them, clothed them, sheltered them when the Shoshoni were fair game for every slaver from the Pacific Coast to the Mississippi Valley—

---

[30] In 1836, Cynthia Ann Parker—a Texas farm girl—was taken captive and adopted by the Comanches. In her teens she became the wife of Peta Nocona, a rising young chief. To this union were born three children. In the 1850s some white hunters met Cynthia on the plains and offered to pay ransom for her freedom. She refused, saying she loved her husband. In 1860 a force of Texas Rangers and U.S. Cavalrymen took Cynthia Ann captive. She was never allowed to return to her husband and family. (Benjamin Capps, *The Great Chiefs, the Two Lives of Quanah Parker*, pp. 105-109.

[31] The Shoshoni when killing an animal offered this prayer to the animal's spirit: "I am sorry I had to kill you my brother. But, I had need of your meat. My children were hungry and crying for food. Forgive me, my brother." (Ernest Thompson Seton, *The Gospel of the Red Man*.)

no longer existed. Chronically ill, emaciated and scarred by the whip, the Hopi were now as vicious as their predatory brothers.

Fleet runners packed the word to Pope that the horsemen from the north. . . the dreaded Saydocarah. . . had arrived. This joyful message gave Pope's pitiful following of Zuni and Pueblo slaves the courage needed for revolt. On August 10, 1680, the united Pueblo Indians lay siege to Santa Fe.

The Spanish landlords would reap a bumper crop from the fertile seeds they had sown. Vengeance was swift, efficient and cruel. Clumsy iron-clad conquistadores were lanced in the fields they had stolen. Men, women and collaborators were slashed to ribbons beneath the stabbing hooves of frenzied war horses as they plunged recklessly through the streets and courtyards of Santa Fe. Priests were axed in their missions. . . their broken bodies draped in sacrifice across gory Christian altars. One fifth of the Spanish population of 2,500 was wiped out. The remainder, leaving their possessions and homes of nearly a century, fled south on the Shoshoni Trail, now called Deadman's Road. They did not stop until they reached the safety of El Paso del Norte on the border of Mexico. Spanish rule in New Mexico had been broken at least temporarily.

CHAPTER 4

VAMOS AMIGO

We came to serve God. . .
and also get rich.

Bernal Diaz del Castillo
Spanish soldier

The Spaniards retreated to El Paso; the Pueblos took possession of Santa Fe; the Hopi moved all their worldly belongings to the inaccessible mesas of northeastern Arizona; the Shoshoni—their appetite now whetted for blood—rode east to join forces with the Kansas horse rustlers located somewhere in the Texas panhandle.

From camps along the Canadian and Red Rivers the Shoshoni raided Spanish settlements for whatever they had to offer. War parties sometimes thrust hundreds of miles into Mexico and returned with as many as 1,000 stolen horses. The Spanish and Mexicans were regarded as a feeble enemy.[32] Most of the contraband was funnelled into the Oyer'ungun to aid in the war effort and bolster the economy. They found horses so plentiful in Mexico that this detached war party decided to take up permanent residence to serve as a supply depot for the northern campaign. These Shoshoni became the fourth segment to break away from the mother nation. They called themselves Kansas, Children of the South Wind. The Europeans called them Comanches.

Short-legged, ungraceful people when on the ground, the Comanches were some of the showiest horsemen the world has ever known. Mystically certain of their superiority in the way of born riders, they regarded other people, white or red, as inferior beings. This helped to make them tremendously successful in trade and war. With an

---

[32] For more on these predatory raids see Capp's, *The Great Chiefs*, p. 105.

estimated 17th century population of 7,000 they posed a real threat to Spanish expansion into eastern New Mexico, northern Texas and the Kansas Plains.

During this hectic period, England, Russia and France were smug in the belief that all North American natives could be subdued with a willow switch. Spain, having crossed swords with the best—Mayan, Aztec and Shoshoni—had considerable doubts on the validity of white supremacy. The displaced governor of Santa Fe upon his arrival in El Paso—only by the grace of God and a damn fast horse—reported to Mexico City that. . . "the Indians attacked with shamelessness and daring."

He did not exaggerate, and the Spanish government believed him. Spain's sweep through South America could be likened to a stroll through the streets of Madrid on a Sunday afternoon. . . challenging but pleasant and rewarding. Their conquest of western North America could be compared to a dash through a briar patch in the nude. . . not only was it embarrassing, but it also drew blood, specifically, Castillian blood.

Spain's army made four attempts in eight years to retake Santa Fe but weakened on the east by constant Comanche raids which in turn fired the Pueblo Indians with fanatic zeal to withstand further European aggression, they were unsuccessful. To further complicate repossession, Spain was bankrupt, a fact they were desperately trying to conceal from the rest of the world.

As early as 1596 Philip of Spain had managed to squander the millions in treasure his tough conquistadores had looted from the Incas, Mayans and Aztecs. In a last ditch effort to keep the rape of North America going Philip borrowed fourteen and one half million ducats from European money lenders only to default on repayment, thereby ruining Spain's credit on the world market.[33] By the late 1600's, if Spain was to survive as a major world power, it was imperative that it recoup its losses in the American southwest and, more importantly, it had to locate new deposits of gold and silver immediately.

---

[33] A ducat was a European coin valued from 83 cents to $2.32. It was first struck by Roger II of Sicily.

Twelve years after the destruction of Santa Fe, the Spaniards returned in sufficient force to recapture the colony in 1692. It took another four years of brutal fighting to bring their wayward children back under parental control. This struggle stirred memories of a time ninety-four years in the past when Don Juan de Onate shouted to the natives ". . . I take possession once, twice and thrice and all the times I can and must of the kingdom and province of New Mexico." Once more, the Pueblos were subjects of the Spanish crown and protected from evil by the Holy Catholic Church.

Fully aware of who had instilled their impressionable servants with the strength of Satan, the Spaniards chose not to reinvade Hopi country. From a military viewpoint this was a smart move, for Spain could ill-afford trouble from that quarter, especially with the Comanches applying pressure from the east. The conquistadores real target was that mysterious region somewhere beyond the gaunt desert to the north. . . a territory called Oregon.

From the meager evidence available it is apparent that a well-armed expedition complete with soldiers, engineers, priests, surveyors, Zuni mistresses, livestock, pack-mules and freight wagons was quietly outfitted in Santa Fe for a push into the interior. By early spring 1698 the conquistadores were again on the glory trail. Circling east of the Hopi and avoiding the Comanches, they slipped unobtrusively across Ute territory, for the Spanish believed the Utes to have been the Hopi allies in the Pueblo Revolt of 1690. Once clear of Ute patrols they plunged into the Great Basin and discovered that some of the Hopi had migrated hundreds of miles to the north, settling in the present Pueblo Mountains of Southeast Oregon.[34] Again bypassing trouble, they jammed north-

---

[34] The architect-engineer who constructed the Pueblo exhibition at the Louisiana Purchase Exposition in St. Louis in 1904 was surveying in eastern Oregon in the early 1900s. One day his horse wandered off and in searching for him he discovered the ancient ruins of a Hopi pueblo in what is now the Pueblo Mountains in the southeast corner of Harney County, Oregon. As early as 1863 a news item in the *Humboldt Register*, Unionville, Nevada, dated December 5, mentions the Pueblo Mountains by that name and they appear on Lt. Col. R.S. Williamson's map published in 1866. They were supposedly so named by Nevada prospectors.

ward and laid claim to Snake hunting grounds east of the Sierra del Nortes. . . the Cascade range.

Like their followers for generations to come, the Spanish invaders were unaware that the Aztec, Hopi, Ute, Comanche and Snakes were of a common origin. . . Chickimec, the barbarians. Imbued with a spirit of dash, the Snake members of the family were very intelligent—tall, big-boned, muscular, fine-featured—with every man being a born fighter. By contrast the women were slender, hard-working and peace-loving. A highly emotional people, the Snakes could one moment be frank and communicative, the next proud, sullen and intensely insolent. Known as a treacherous and dangerous group, the Snakes were the most resentful of the European's "I'm better than you" attitude. The conquistadores were now on a collision course with the ghosts of the Aztecs.

Following two centuries of frustration Spain's dream of expansion into the Pacific Northwest had become reality, but it wasn't advertising the fact. Spain, now operating with as much secrecy as possible, limited access to its exploration documents and for very good reason.[35] By 1700 Great Britain and France were shoving their way into North America in ever-increasing numbers and weakening Spain was unable to hold them back. The natives should have been worried also, for the English-French population—in excess of 290,000 by the census of 1700—was nearly equal to one-fourth of the total Indian population of North America.

By mid-summer of 1698 the Spaniards, according to their land instruments, had penetrated the interior to 43 degrees 12 minutes latitude. On a brooding basalt rim overlooking a warm desert stream now called Silver Creek, they set up camp three hundred and forty feet above the valley floor. Operating from this easily defended base, they

---

[35] For the next 200 years (1700 to 1900) researchers discovered that records dealing with Spain's early exploration not previously made public were inaccessible to outsiders. William Ray Manning, who did extensive research on Spain's exploration of the Oregon country and specifically the Nootka Sound controversy between England, the United States and Spain in 1787, made this observation in 1904: "I have not been able to obtain original diaries of the Spanish expeditions (to Oregon) nor has any previous writer in English seen them." (Herbert Priestly, *The Log of the Princessa* by Estevon Martinez, *Oregon Historical Quarterly*, March 1920, Vol. XXI, No. 1).

began colonization of the Paiutes. The timid Paiutes were even more docile than the Hopi. Short, heavy-set, fair-skinned, long-faced, they were the least warlike of the Shoshonean tribes. Apparently not as bright as their kinsmen, the Paiutes were quite eager to learn the white man's way of life.

The Spaniards found an ample labor force along the desert lakes and peaceful valleys south of the Blue Mountains. Once they got over their initial fear of the swarthy strangers, the Paiutes were anxious to work. The Spanish soon discovered that the Paiutes, although extremely poor, were scrupulously clean in their person and chaste in their habits. Although whole families of all ages and both sexes lived together in the same wickiup, immorality and crime were of rare occurrence. The Spaniards also learned that the Paiutes were a proud people and the only Shoshoni who considered it an insult to bear the name of an animal. Therefore, they took names for some identifying feature such as "Man with a Bad Face" or for some natural preference like "Prairie Flower."

Priests were kept busy baptizing Paiutes by droves as the soldiers herded them in from their desert retreats. By autumn the Rush Arrow People were constructing fortified rock shelters, harvesting grass, gathering firewood and tending flocks for their newly acquired friends.[36] Other Spanish patrols combed the interior from Crooked River to the John Day Valley in search of gold.[37] This expedition, coupled with

---

[36] On July 5, 1859, Captain Henry D. Wallen, Cmdg. 4th Infantry, made the following entry in his official diary. He had just come down Silver Creek in present Harney County, Oregon, and was in the vicinity of Silver Lake in Warm Springs Valley. . . "On the terrace of the adjoining bluff were several circular foundations carefully laid out in stone, evidently the work and habitation of man in his by-gone years." Wallen's report to Captain A. Pleasanton, 2nd Dragoons, Headquarters Department of Oregon, Fort Vancouver, Washington Territory., House of Representatives Executive Document No. 65, 36th Congress, 1st session.

[37] Evidence that the Spaniards made it as far north as Crooked River and as far west as longitude 120 degrees 50' was discovered in July, 1961. During the construction of Bowman Dam on Crooked River, 16 miles southwest of Prineville, Oregon, a Spanish bayonet dating in the 1600s was unearthed deep in a crevasse in a basalt bluff. For years this artifact was on display in what is now an auto body shop on East Fifth Street in Prineville. Articles of Spanish origin were found along

Heceta's coastal exploration in 1774-75 would be the basis for Spain's claim on Oregon in its quarrel of ownership with Great Britain, Russia and the United States in 1789.

Still in the process of clearing their territory of alien tribes, the Snakes were ranging in the farthest reaches of the Oyer'ungun. The Tebechya and Lohim tribes, dislodging Wascos, Umatillas and Walla Wallas, were securing a corridor from the Ochoco to the Columbia River to serve as a trade route to the great Chinook village at Celilo; the Hoonebooey, Watakin and Tussawehee tribes, slashing at Crows, Blackfeet and Minnetrees, were extending hunting rights into the northern Great Plains; the Banattee and Tuziyammo tribes were sweeping the southern trade route clean of Cheyenne and Arapaho horse thieves; the Tukarika, Walpapi and Waradika tribes were riding roughshod through

---

Crooked River by Hudson's Bay trappers as early as 1826. (Ogden's *Journals of the Second Expedition to the Snake Country 1825-26.*) Early Spanish maps show the northern boundary of Mexico at latitude 43° 59' which would place the boundary at the base of the southern Blues or Maury Mountains. It is also evident that the Spaniards had a trail from their holdings in the southwest through Big Summit Prairie to the John Day River. This old trail followed approximately the same route as the ancient Shoshoni Trail and is called the Spanish Trail. In the summer of 1910, Earl Hereford talked to a party of Mexicans on the headwaters of Marks Creek who were retracing this trail looking for long forgotten landmarks on a hand-drawn map which would lead them to early Spanish gold mines in the Ochoco mountains. They were from Nogales, Mexico. (Interview, Earl Hereford, Prineville, Oregon, 1968). About this same period (1912) Cecil Moore, his father and Shorty Low found "visible gold on a drainage of Stevenson Creek" south of Stevenson Mountain. The location was marked "by an ancient blaze on a mountain mahogany tree." They were acting on information that two gold nuggets traded for food in Sacramento, California, in the 1840s "were identical to a piece of sponge gold from the mines on Ochoco Creek." (Letters from Cecil C. Moore, Bend, Oregon, dated September 21 and October 13, 1986 and Mesa, Arizona, dated January 5 and 26, 1989.) In the 1890s Julius Cornez—born near Sacramento in 1850 only three years after California became a United States possession—slipped into the Marks Creek area and built a cabin on what is now known as Cornez Creek. Although no gold strikes have ever been recorded in that area, it was evident he had discovered gold in large quantities. (Cornez was well known by the author.) He passed away in a Prineville rooming house in 1944 without ever revealing his secret.

the northern Blues, laying siege to Nez Perce, Spokane and Flathead villages, thus giving the Spaniards free rein of the Ochoco.

On a sullen, sage-covered mountain some sixty miles northwest of the main Spanish garrison, the Spaniards discovered rich deposits of silver and gold. Two miles north of this strike in a barren valley resembling the Sonora Desert they found numerous strange holes filled with quicksand, vents which in later decades would become known as the notorious "soap holes" of Camp Creek—thought to be rich in silver held in liquid form. They also discovered a heavy flow of water gushing from one of these holes, enough to set up smelters and crushing machinery for the processing of gold and silver. Today, one of the holes has a rusted iron pipe in it from which flows the first artesian well found in Crook County.

In the mountains to the north, less than three miles from the soapholes known as Silver Wells, was an unlimited supply of wood to fire the smelters. Large iron crucibles, transported by freight wagons from Mexico, were installed and tunnelling began on Gerry Mountain. Ironically, the first recorded gold discovery west of the Mississippi River was made in this area in 1845. . . three years before the famous Sutter's Mill strike in California in 1848.[38]

---

[38] The mystery surrounding the Spanish mine (and including the Blue Bucket strike of 1845) has never been solved. All that is known is that there was an extensive mining operation in Camp Creek in the distant past. An investigation of the site known as Silver Wells made by the Bureau of Land Management in 1973 turned up evidence of ancient ore refining machinery. The first settlers in the Camp Creek area arrived in 1869. A post office was established at this site August 6, 1878. According to James J. Brown, first postmaster, the old building foundations appeared to be at least 150-200 years old. This is confirmed by Henry Barnes who built the first cabin on Camp Creek some 300 yards east of the Silver Wells site in 1869. (Interview, Ole Weaver, Camp Creek rancher, 1972). Military maps of the 1860s show Silver Wells by name and the military road from Fort Maury to Fort Harney passed by Silver Wells. (See map of the Military Department of the Columbia, Lt. Symons, 1881). Early settlers claim there was a 3,000' long tunnel dug into the west face of Gerry Mountain approximately 2-1/2 miles due south of Silver Wells. The entrance portal has now sluffed in and is covered with sage, making it virtually impossible to locate. (Interview, Gary Gumpert, Prineville, Oregon, 1970). Large disc-shaped iron

Not only were the Spaniards searching for gold but also for quick-silver, used extensively in the recovery of gold from the base ore. Although the Americans would not stumble onto the fact until the turn of the 20th century, the Ochoco was underlain with cinnabar, the parent ore of quicksilver.

Much of the rusted equipment found at Silver Wells was used in the production of quicksilver, leading skeptics to believe that the abandoned machinery dated much later than the Spanish invasion of Central Oregon. There is no doubt that the Spanish mining engineers in 1698 possessed the knowledge and technology to support such a massive mining operation.

The first furnace invented for exclusive quicksilver reduction was built in Peru in 1633. Owned by the Spanish, the Huancavelica mine was in operation for over 300 years. Thirteen years after its invention in Peru, the reduction furnace was introduced at Almaden, Spain, Ten furnaces built at the Almaden mine between 1646-1654 are still being used at the present time.[39]

During the search for gold and quicksilver the colonization of Harney Valley came to a standstill. The wedding of the two races had lost most of it charm insofar as the Paiutes were concerned. Their earlier enthusiasm for cooperation was dead. Old customs were destroyed. New ones, such as the worship of an alien God whom they could not understand, were forced upon them. Hard efficient workers, eager to learn, the Paiutes were being pushed to the limits of their mental and physical capabilities. Unfortunately, the poverty-stricken natives had nothing more than their bodies with which to appease the masters, and

---

crucibles used for smelting gold and silver found at Silver Wells were moved into the Maury Mountains by Frank McCullough in 1921 to serve as stock water-troughs. (Interview, Frank McCullough, Post, Oregon, 1972). Mr. McCullough was pledged to secrecy concerning details on Silver Wells by an unrevealed Portland, Oregon, couple who were doing extensive research on the area. Possibly, this involved Ruby El Hult, author of *Lost Mines and Treasures of the Pacific Northwest.*

[39] For a detailed account of quicksilver's role in history see C.N. Schuette, *Quicksilver in Oregon*, State Department of Geology and Mineral Industries, Bulletin No. 4, 1938, pp. 10-25.

they were to learn that back-breaking labor was only the beginning of their misfortunes.

Customarily, the Paiute women wore very short rabbit skin skirts.[40] Much to the consternation of the priests, when the ladies bent over to plant seeds, gather wood or hunker down to rest, they were "uncovered." According to Father Francisco Garces—who travelled 2,000 miles in his wanderings through Paiute camps of Nevada and who, with Juan Bautista de Anza, pioneered the Spanish Trail from Santa Fe to northern California in 1776—the Paiute women ". . . expose themselves most shamefully." This caused a certain amount of unrest among the hot-blooded Latins. The priests attempted to make the ladies wear under garments, but the Paiutes could not understand the reasoning for this strange attire.

Consequently, Castillian troops interpreted this rejection of "decency" as an open invitation of desire. If the object of attention did not submit willingly, it was rape. If Paiute men attempted to defend wives, sisters or daughters, they were publicly flogged. Some of these beatings were so severe that the men died from injuries received. Relations between Spaniards and Paiutes were at the breaking point when the Paiutes were herded out to the mine fields.

At this time Spain produced the best mining engineers in the world. They located heavy deposits of gold in the vicinity of Spanish Peak, and it is apparent they discovered the geomorphic province of lode and placer deposits that is now described as the gold belt of the Blue Mountains. As determined by geologist W. Lundgren in 1901, this gold belt is 150 miles long and 50 miles wide, extending from the head-waters of the Ochoco on the west to the Snake River on the east.[41]

---

[40] For a detailed description of Paiute clothing for both men and women see Whiting, Paiute Sorcery, Anthropology publication No. 15, pp. 95-96.

[41] This area is still the most untapped in the United States for gold and silver discoveries. The Armstrong nugget, weighing 80.4 ounces or 6-1/2 pounds and one of the largest high-grade gold nuggets in the nation, was found in this area in 1913. The Smithsonian Institution in Washington, D.C. has made a standing offer for this nugget of $18,000 to the U.S. National Bank in Baker City, where it is displayed. At the present world gold standard it would be $49,848. (See Jim Evans, "Klamath, Blues Hold Most Oregon Gold," *The Bulletin*, Bend, Oregon,

Because the pack-trains were needed to carry supplies between Silver Wells, Silver Creek and Santa Fe, ore was transported by Paiute power over the mountains and worked in the crucibles at Silver Wells. From there, it was taken by pack mule to Vera Cruz for shipment to Spain. Evidence found in records at the old Spanish Mission of Santa Fe indicate that some of the gold and silver was taken down the Columbia to Spanish galleons waiting off the Oregon coast and shipped to Mexico City.[42] How much gold and silver was taken by the Spanish from the Blues may never be known. It is known that millions of dollars in gold were taken between 1862-64 to finance the Civil War and by 1978 the Blues had produced 75% of Oregon's total gold and silver output. It is estimated that the total production from 1862 to 1978 ranges upwards to 5.8 million ounces of gold worth approximately 4.1 billion dollars at the 1978 gold standard. A significant portion of the gold taken was before 1880. This serves to illustrate how much gold the Spanish may have mined from the Ochoco. Based upon the length of the tunnel driven into Gerry Mountain, the diggings in Spanish Gulch and the smelter operation at Silver Wells, Spanish occupation lasted approximately three to five years.[43]

It is fairly certain that Great Britain and France were aware of this renewed activity in Oregon by the Spanish. In 1702 the British, moving in on the Kickapoos and Winnebagos, founded three outposts in Illinois country in an unsuccessful attempt to link the Great Lakes with French colonies in Louisiana territory to block off Spanish expansion into the

---

Jan. 31, 1979.)

[42] According to these records the Spanish also made it into northern Idaho. (Ruby El Holt, *Lost Mines and Treasures of the Pacific Northwest*, pp. 171-7).

[43] Noted linguist, Dr. Berry Fell, during research of his *America B.C.*, made a startling discovery which would indicate that centuries ago, some Shoshoni were either taken back to Spain or that the Spaniards spent considerable time teaching the Paiutes a Spanish dialect. He states that "it is quite in the cards that somewhere in the United States there are still spoken derivatives of the ancient Basque tongue. A fascinating letter I received from a Shoshoni Indian who had been traveling in the Basque country of Spain tells of his recognition of Shoshoni words over there, including his own name whose Shoshoni meaning proved to match the meaning attached to a similar word by the modern Basques." [Fell, *America B.C., Ancient Settlers of the New World*, p. 173.]

Mississippi Valley. Unknown to them, they had no worry for the Comanches had already stopped any Spanish activity in that direction.

It is believed that word travelled from the Mississippi Valley along the trade routes through the Comanches to the Snakes that Spain was encroaching upon their hunting grounds. Whatever the circumstances, they did find out. In late summer of 1702 Snake dog soldiers returned to the Ochoco.[44] Espana, a nation on the move, met Saydocarah, a nation on the rampage.

The sight of Paiutes serving as beasts of burden goaded the Snake warriors into a state of frenzy. There was widespread slaughter of Spaniards from Spanish Gulch to Silver Wells with the final destruction taking place 60 miles to the southeast at the main colony on Silver Creek.[45] The deathblow was complete. It is inconceivable that any survivors made it back across the thousand miles of hostile Shoshoni territory to Santa Fe. The Snakes had squelched forever Spain's claim on Oregon country.

---

[44] The year can be determined from British records on Spanish activity in western America. Henry Kelsey, a Hudson's Bay Trader, had been inland since 1691 and was the first non-Spanish white man to reach the Great Plains and see and shoot buffalo and grizzly bear. His journey was for many years in doubt but for over half a century he was the only known Englishman to have reached as far west as the eastern boundary of Snake hunting grounds. (The Henry Kelsey papers, Ottawa, Archives of Canada, 1929.) The time of year has been determined from an interview with Dave Choktote, son of the Snake war chief Black Buffalo, who stated that the Old People handed down a legend of a time when Toyah Tiva—Mountain White Men and the Shoshoni name for Spaniards—were driven out of the Ochoco during the Hot Moon (on the Shoshoni calendar this would be mid-August to mid-September) and were killed near Tonowama (Shoshoni name for Harney Lake in southeastern Oregon.)

[45] A continuation of the July 5, 1859, report of Captain Wallen, 4th Infantry to Captain Pleasanton, 2nd Dragoons, states: "We also traced the foundation of a kind of bastioned fortification (on the bluff above Silver Creek), this impressed us with the idea that a small party had been driven to this commanding eminence, entrenching themselves against a superior force on the plain below." (*House of Representatives, Executive Document No. 65, 36th Congress, 1st session*). Also see Captain Andrew Smith's Report of 1860.

CHAPTER 5

SPAWN OF THE COYOTE

From the hair and blood of a
gigantic beaver whom he had
killed in hand-to-hand combat,
Coyote created the most fierce
Indian tribe in all the world. . .
the Shoshoni!

Chinook legend

By 1720 the Shoshoni had been tested by every major power in their known world. They had emerged victorious. With the exception of the Spanish, this came as no great surprise to anyone, least of all the Shoshoni, for it was predestined. The Shoshoni were the direct descendants of the powerful deity, Coyote. . . supreme ruler of all earth creatures. It was a truth drummed into them from childhood.

The Shoshoni believed that human beings originally came from subterranean caverns at the bottom of Hell's Canyon. The Hopi later changed this to the Grand Canyon. Other tribes, including the Mandans, Crows and Gros Ventres, believed this also.

At night when campfires crackled and shadows danced, the Old People told how back in the distant past when time was still, an infant, the Great Spirit—whom they called Tobats—became very angry with humans. He commanded Tawa, the Sun God, to sear earth with a burning brand, causing all the lakes and streams to disappear. He ordered Okuwa, the Cloud God, to stop all lifegiving rain and from that moment the Great Spirit refused ever again to answer the Human Being's prayers.

One day in their agonized wanderings the desperate Human Beings came upon a stone column so high it seemed as though it must touch the sun. The Human Beings were certain that if they could scale this rock, they surely would be able to converse with the Sun God and persuade him that never again would they offend the Great Spirit. The strongest, bravest men attempted to reach the top of the Sun God's altar. Day after day they tried. Day after day Masauu, the Death God, hurled the intruders onto the jagged rocks below.

Finally, a slender girl went before the People's Council and begged permission to attempt to climb the Sun God's altar. The thought of a woman presuming she could succeed where the mightiest of warriors had failed was ridiculous. Her request was denied. Certain in her heart that she could triumph, the girl slipped away and began the treacherous ascent. The Sun God was unmerciful in his fury, but the girl would not give up. Many times her aching arms faltered and she was tempted to let the Death God take her to his realm. But, bruised and bleeding, she inched ever upward.

During her climb, the Great Spirit and Coyote visited the Sun God. Perched on the rim of the blazing sun, the Great Spirit observed the girl's progress with mounting interest, a fascination not shared by Coyote. The earth ruler watched with dread, torn between admiration and agony for he recognized the maiden as the woman whom he secretly loved—a love which must forever be denied, for she was an earth creature and he was a god.

Incredibly, the haggard girl reached the awesome dome of the sun altar, where she sank to her knees in prayer. The Great Spirit was deeply touched. Such courage he had never before witnessed in earth creatures. Because of her he would relent and give the Human Beings one more chance to mend their errant ways. As for the woman, he would bestow upon her favors beyond all earthly dreams.

The Great Spirit commanded Coyote to go to her and protect her throughout eternity. He promised that Coyote and the earth maiden would become the parents of a superior race of people. And for their children he would create a unique animal never before seen by Human Beings. True to his word, from the union of the great god, Coyote, and the earth woman came the Shoshoni. . . born enemies of all other people. And for them the Great Spirit created the horse.[46]

---

[46] This is the Shoshoni legend of Stein's Pillar, located in Mill Creek Valley, sixteen miles east of Prineville, Oregon. To them the rock pillar was sacred and religious ceremonies were held at its base. As late as 1890 they still returned to Mill Creek

Above: Stein's Pillar on the left, Goat Rock in the center, and Cathedral Rock barely visible on the right.

Below: Stein's Pillar on the left, Goat Rock on the right.

Because their mother was on an elevation with the gods by virtue of her marriage to Coyote, the Shoshoni honored their women as no other North American tribe did. Meriwether Lewis in his journals for 1805 made this observation. . . "the Shoshoni women appear to be held more sacred than in any nation we have seen." Women were treated as equals by the men and could hold high positions in the tribal council. Some even became powerful medicine chiefs. The practice of men and women dancing together originated with the Shoshoni and eventually spread to the southwest and the Great Plains.

Considering themselves superior, the Shoshoni were extremely rigid in moral conduct, and especially did this code hold true for women. With them perfect chastity was the rule, not the exception. Unfaithfulness was an unpardonable sin. A man could kill his wife if she committed adultery and public sentiment approved his act.[47] A maiden was not permitted to marry until 18 or 20 years of age and then it was a capital offense to wed any of another tribe without special sanction from the Council and tribal chief. This same restriction applied to men, and a man was allowed but one wife. If a man married outside of his tribe, he was required to become a member of his wife's tribe; she, however, was not required to become a member of her husband's tribe. This would all change with the arrival of the Europeans.

The Shoshoni had no reason to disbelieve their origin. Their creation and superiority was confirmed in the legends of other Indian nations. In 1789, when Alexander Mackenzie was exploring British Columbia, he asked everywhere for information concerning the Indians of Oregon country. He was told repeatedly that the natives living south of the great

---

Valley, believed to be holy ground, to worship at the sun altar. Coyote is a Shoshoni word adopted into the English language to define the wild dog of the western prairies. In Shoshoni it is pronounced Ky'o-tee and refers to the Indian god. The wild dog we call coyote is known to them as isha'ui—the desert wolf. According to Shoshoni legend, Coyote became earth-bound when he lost his grip on the edge of a star while on a visit to the Sky People. He fell continuously for 10 moons before he hit the earth, causing the deep split we call the Grand Canyon, homeland of the Hopi. Coyote never again returned to the sky, but lives in a huge cave deep in the heart of the Blue Mountains with his earth-woman wife.

[47] John James, *My Experiences With Indians*, pp. 64-65.

river "which falls into the Bel'haul-lay teo (White Man's Lake)" were of gigantic stature, very wicked and adorned with wings; that they fed on gigantic birds. And they possessed the extraordinary power of killing common men with a look of their eyes.[48] In 1883 *Harper's Magazine* would report that. . . "they have discovered footprints three feet long in the woods of Oregon, supposed to belong to a lost race." Even the unsophisticated Chinook swore by their sea gods that the Shoshoni were the most fierce people in the world.[49]

The belief that they were invincible was causing the ranking chieftains of the Shoshoni nation many problems. Since the mid 1700's there had been no serious challenge to their supremacy. Because of this the rank and file were getting more difficult to control. The tendency was becoming more and more to drift away from tribal guidance in the pursuit of individual achievement. Small family groups were strung the length and breadth of Oyer'ungun, either refusing or ignoring tribal authority. In their minds there was little or no need for tribal rule. It was an old-fashioned concept, clung to by the elders without meaning or purpose. They were certain that the land upon which they worked and played, loved and warred, would by decree of their Sky Father and Earth Mother remain unchallenged forever.

The clan chiefs knew this could not be. Almost daily their traders reported sightings of light-skinned men in ever increasing numbers. And the storm clouds of inevitable invasion were brewing on the distant horizon, nurtured by a group of rebellious English colonists, who were convinced that they, too, were children of God.

In passing the 18th century would witness a young and vigorous civilization take root on the fertile Atlantic seaboard. A restless offspring of European parentage, it yearned to hold an important position among the leading world powers. Striving for recognition, hungering for power,

---

[48] MacKenzie's, *Voyage From Montreal Through the Continent of North America,* Vol. I, Ch. VI.

[49] It was also the Chinooks belief that from the head of a giant beaver called Wishpoosh, Coyote created the Nez Perce, wise in council; from the arms, he made the Cayuse, strong with bow and war club; from the legs came the swiftrunning Klickitats; and from the belly he made the greedy Wascos—the easternmost tribe of the Chinook nation.

it expanded ever westward, probing deeper and deeper into the uncharted frontiers and spurring the parent nations into violent reaction.

CHAPTER 6

THE ADVANCING COLUMN

*While the Spanish were launching their
imposing expeditions, men of other nations
began to try the new continent for an easy
passage to the Orient. They all travelled
weary miles, suffered countless hardships
and what they saw was so fabulous their
tales were thrown back in their teeth as lies;
yet, the scoffers hastened on their back trail
to capture wealth, fame and more than likely
an unmarked grave.*

Ernest Swift
The Glory Trail

Two hundred years after the first faltering search for its actual existence, the Oregon country still remained a mystery. Was it really out there beyond the setting sun. . . or was it only the figment of some wanderer's imagination? No one but a ghostly Spanish battalion really knew.

The British, the French, the Russians. . . all were eager to find out. But underlying this enthusiasm to discover the answer were the ominous tales circulated by local Indians of a vicious inland tribe who would annihilate anyone foolish enough to enter their homeland. Because of this exploration during the 1700's was carried out cautiously with only a few hardy adventurers making feeble attempts on the unknown interior.

What little information these travelers did glean about the Shoshoni the east coast policy makers tended to forget, disbelieve or ignore. These gentlemen—secure from any harm—had a plan based on sound European logic on how to deal with the barbarians. The semi-civilized Atlantic Indians, who were also a hindrance to progress, would be used as pawns in a deadly game to force the Inland People into subjection. The Europeans would overwhelm the hostiles with sheer numbers.

With this in mind French voyageurs embarked up the Mississippi River, poking inquisitive fingers westward from the river's mouth to its source, subtly herding Osage, Wichita and Pawnee into the threatening war lances of the waiting Comanches. Advancing westward from the Atlantic, British merchants moved into the Great Lakes region, forcing Iowa, Sioux and Mandan ever closer to Snake hunting grounds. Russian traders, gaining a foothold on the north Pacific Coast, barred retreat for Salish, Kootenai and Spokane, trying to move ahead of the Snakes in the northwest. Spanish colonizers, entrenched along the southern border of Shoshoni territory from the California seashore to the Texas plains, were the only Europeans not looking for armed conflict with the Snakes, Utes and Comanches at the dawn of the 18th century.

The sons of Spain, trying to rebuild damaged muscle for another jab to the north, were having enough trouble just holding their possessions from seizure by the Shoshoni. To make matters worse, the Shoshoni had driven the Yosemites, Apaches, Shastas and Yumas deep into Spanish territory where they were becoming an unbearable nuisance in their own right. Spanish officials listened with apprehensive ears to rumors that guns were being supplied to the eastern Indians by the French and British to combat the undisciplined inland nation. They found it extremely difficult to believe that their fellow Europeans could be so naive. In two centuries of dealing with native Americans the Spanish had steadfastly refused to trade firearms for any reason.

Spanish intelligence also learned that French agents were scouting west of the Mississippi River. They couldn't allow this to continue. In June, 1720, a tough Castillian warrior, Don Pedro de Villasuer, with 110 battle-hardened troopers galloped out of Santa Fe to intercept the French intruders. Threading his way through Comanche patrols, Villasuer traced an erratic course across the Kansas plains, a reconnaissance which carried him as far north as the Platte River. In early August, as he moved warily up the Platte, Villasuer's army ran afoul of a united Snake-Comanche war party. The encounter was as swift as it was ruthless. The Spaniards were butchered like buffalo. When the dust of battle drifted away, Villasuer and forty-four of his veteran cavalrymen lay dead on the Nebraska prairie. During the next 146 years of warfare in the American west nothing would equal this Shoshoni victory. As one historian sadly put it. . . "no disaster of comparable proportions occurred to white arms in the West until the Fetterman defeat by the Sioux in 1866."

Strangely, perhaps because of a suspected French influence, an unlikely alliance of Otos and Pawnees were given credit for the Spanish defeat.[50] The Otos, a Sioux tribe living by Lake Superior, never came west of the Mississippi until around 1750. The Pawnees, a Caddo tribe living in the Louisiana bayous and usually held in slavery by other southeastern tribes never once made war on white men. Neither tribe had been to the Platte country until forced there by white advancement some 40 to 60 years after Villasuer's defeat.[51]

Four years after the Spaniards fatal push into Shoshoni hunting grounds the French explorer Bourgmont, veteran of the bloody Fox wars, traveled deep into the valley of the Arkansas River. French traders navigated America's major rivers a full century before pioneers of the English colonies which would become the United States. Most of this exploration went unrecorded, for those who accomplished it were often illiterate and their trade frequently illegal. A few were young men of good families who had gotten into trouble in France and were sent to the colonies in lieu of prison. Such a man was Etienne de Veniard, sieur de Bourgmont, who came to the lower Mississippi River around 1712 as a military deserter.

Alone and on foot Bourgmont entered a "vast camp of plains Comanche" in the fall of 1724. He observed that the Comanches were "amply equipped with horses, which they obtained from the Spanish." The Children of the South Wind neglected to say whether by trade or theft and Bourgmont was smart enough not to ask.

Superbly skilled at Indian diplomacy, the young Frenchman feasted with the chiefs on buffalo meat and dried plums, joined in the spacious oratory and proudly rode back to the French settlements with a present

---

[50] The official record reads: "at some point on the Platte, Villasuer's little army was cut to pieces by Pawnees aided by the Otos. The return of the frightened survivors occasioned the wildest alarm in New Mexico, for it was supposed that the French had been involved in the onslaught." (*The Book of the American West*, Monaghan, ed., p. 26).

[51] For more detail see Stoutenburgh, *The American Indian*, pp. 44, 303, 316.

of seven horses. Bourgmont, noted for being "a swash-buckler of the old breed with an appreciative eye for women—white or red—and having an uncanny flair for wilderness life" was the first white man to meet with a Shoshonean tribe on a friendly basis. Elated over this encounter, Bourgmont returned from the Comanche village with a firm conviction that he had opened a trade route from French Louisiana to Spanish New Mexico. But the years would pass with no trade article exchanging hands.[52]

In 1739 Spain's worst fear came true. The Comanches seized control of the French gun trade based on the Missouri and Red Rivers. Not that they were choice weapons, for the guns made a better bludgeon than a firearm, but this acquisition changed the balance of power. The Shoshoni were now on an equal footing with the Europeans. With .69 calibre French military muskets in their arsenal the Comanches and Utes kept the Spanish settlements bleeding well into the 1800's.

This same year, 1739, Pierre de la Verendrye, patriarch of French explorers, took to the field. He was no newcomer to western exploration. Unlike most pathfinders of those early days who came from France and England seeking adventure in the New World, Verendrye was a native of North America, a Canadian officer who had entered the French army at age 12. From 1726 to 1731 Verendrye was in charge of a post at Lake Nipigan north of Lake Superior. Many Indians from the west came to this post to trade. Their accounts of the vast country beyond, the river flowing westward into a great lake of bad tasting water (the Pacific or Great Salt Lake) fired him with zeal to undertake the much talked of discovery of an overland route to the western ocean. In the spring of 1731 Verendrye, three of his sons, his nephew, a Canadian army officer who had been stationed among the Sioux, and some fifty Canadian voyageurs set out by canoe from Montreal to discover it. They were unsuccessful.[53]

Now, in 1739, eight years later, the Verendryes were again on the prowl. They learned from the Mandans that Snake merchants were

---

[52] For more on Bourgmont see Novall, *Bourgmont; Explorer of the Mississippi, 1698-1725*.

[53] Grace Flandreau, *The Verendrye Expedition in Quest of the Pacific, Oregon Historical Quarterly*, Vol. XXVI, June 1925, No. 2, pp. 69-70.

herding horses from the Spanish colonies to trade with the upper Mississippi tribes, thus proving it was only a summer's march from the Great Lakes to New Mexico. This information turned out to be of little value, for the Verendryes also discovered that it was impossible to penetrate the Shoshoni's line of defense. Bourgmont's trade route existed only in his mind.

Convinced that civilized logic could induce the Shoshoni to lift their embargo, Verendrye's sons, Louis, Joseph and Francois, attempted to meet with the "Horse People" and negotiate a trade agreement. This meeting was to be arranged through the Mandans. In May, 1742, the Verendryes moved into the Mandan villages along the Heart River and waited until late July for the Snake traders to arrive. They never came. Failing in this venture, the Verendryes, accompanied by only two Canadians and two Mandans who volunteered to lead them westward, journeyed into the northern plains as far as the Black Hills of South Dakota.[54] From these highlands, they had hoped to sight the Pacific Ocean, but their Mandan guides, fearful of the Horse People, refused to take them to the crest.

Shortly thereafter the Verendrye brothers joined "a vast horde of Bow Indians who were marching westward to make war upon the Snakes." It is believed they eventually reached a point near Custer's battlefield. In any event on January 1, 1743, the brothers saw the snow-clad peaks of the Rockies. They wanted to press on, but the Bow Indians (probably Arikaras) suddenly got faint-hearted. The Snakes were a dangerous foe and the Bows, finding themselves this close to the enemy camps lost all desire for battle. In spite of protests from their war chief they retreated in disorder. The disappointed explorers had no choice but to return to the French settlements.[55]

The following summer another son, Chevalier de la Verendrye, headed a French expedition toward the Rocky Mountains. In late August

---

[54] In February 1743 the Verendryes returned to this area and at present-day Pierre, South Dakota, buried a lead plate which a 14-year-old schoolgirl kicked out of the ground in 1913, confirming this exploration. (*The American West*, Monaghan, ed., p. 27).

[55] Flandreau, *The Verendrye Expedition in Quest of the Pacific, Oregon Historical Quarterly*, Vol. XXVI, June 1925, No. 2, pp. 69-70.

of 1744 he blundered into a Shoshoni hunting camp on the Powder River. It was a detachment of the Tuziyammo (Big Lodge) clan. The camp was deserted except for a few women preparing the winter's meat supply. Committing what could have been a costly mistake, young Verendrye stalked into the Shoshoni camp and inquired through the western plains sign language about the women's identity.

No doubt the Shoshoni ladies checked their braids, their garments, their horse-markings and finding everything to be in order were amazed at Verendrye's wanton display of ignorance. Surely the anemic looking warrior was joking, for it was universal knowledge that the Shoshoni were the mightiest nation on earth. Certain that this uninformed traveler was making an attempt to determine their tribal affiliation, the Tuziyammo maids went into action. In sign language the Big Lodge women, whose furniture and huge willow woven homes were the envy of the Shoshoni nation, assured the stranger that they were the most skilled weavers of mats, baskets and lodges in the entire world. Not nearly so well-versed in Indian sign language as he tried to pretend, Verendrye misunderstood the graceful movements of brown arms and fingers weaving imaginary furniture, but he nodded knowingly and decided the natives must be "Gens de Serpents. . . the Snakes." Shaking his head over this odd name, the French explorer disappeared into the Big Horn Mountains never realizing he had brushed against the dangerous Inland People. From that day on the Europeans referred to the Shoshoni as "Snakes."

The Shoshoni men were not as favorably impressed with Verendrye's visitation as their wives and daughters. But since both parties, Shoshoni and French, were poaching on Crow territory, they decided to let the Tavibo (Sun Men) go their way in peace.[56] Because of that

---

[56] The reference to the French as Tavibo, meaning Sun Men, was applied because when the Shoshoni women first saw the Verendrye expedition, they were coming from the east out of the rising sun. In the years to come when the Shoshoni came to know the French intimately, their smooth manners and gentlemanly ways captivated the stern and somber Shoshoni and they renamed them Yoon Tivo, Polite Whitemen. When they met the American traders, the Shoshoni called them Soo Yawpi, Ghost People, because the Yankees always wanted to "swap," which word in Shoshoni means ghost. The Spaniards, the first white men they

fortunate decision Chevalier de la Verendrye went down in the pages of history not as the first white man to make peaceful contact with the Snakes but as the man who upon witnessing a sunset in the Big Horn range of the northern Rockies fervently shouted. . ."This is the land of the shining mountains."[57]

While Verendrye was making his push on Shoshoni country a second French expedition slipped into Comanche hunting grounds and established Fort Cavagnolle on the Missouri River. Although as a military trading post it would be short-lived, Fort Cavagnolle was the second white encroachment upon lands controlled by the Shoshoni nation.

By 1740 the estimated white population of the European colonies was 889,000, nearly equal to the total Indian population on the North American continent. The white men were now approaching sufficient numbers to realize their eventual goal of occupation.

The Great Plains saw trouble first. Shoved westward into the Mississippi valley by advancing American hunters with their Kentucky rifles, the Chippewa forced the Sioux into the northern plains. The Sioux found themselves in trespass on Snake hunting grounds. It meant war and war it was. The frantic Sioux with nowhere else to go forced the Shoshoni back by sheer weight of numbers—but only to the border of the Oyer'ungun. If a Sioux war party was so foolish as to cross the border, the Snakes would lure them into their mountain retreats west of the Rockies and annihilate them.

At the same time other tribes were being pushed into the danger zone. Notable among these were the Blackfeet or, as the Shoshoni called them, the Pah'kees, a belligerent group of natives whom the Shoshoni hated with a passion. It was Shoshoni practice to separate the best horses from their herds and keep them for their own use. Only the culls were traded to foreign tribes, thus insuring Shoshoni supremacy in horses. In

---

contacted in the Blue mountains, they called Toyah Tivo, Mountain White Men. (Original Journals of Lewis and Clark Expedition, Thwaites (ed) pp. 365-81; *History of the Expedition Under the Command of Lewis and Clark*, Cones, ed., p. 454; Bancroft, *History of the Northwest Coast* 1800-1842, p. 416.)

[57] For a full account of Verendrye's push into Shoshoni country see *The Montana Historical Quarterly*, Vol. VI, No. 2, p. 65.

the early days of the horse industry the Blackfeet became the Shoshoni's best customers. The Blackfeet would accept the mangiest broomtails without question and for very good reason. As soon as they bought enough horses to get off the ground, they began sneaking out of the northern Rockies into the Blues to steal Shoshoni mounts. This was an unforgivable sin. Before this practice could gain momentum and spread to other Indian nations, the Snakes tangled with the mountain horse thieves and swept their land clean, a purge which had kept Shoshoni territory free of Blackfeet since the late 1600's.

Now the Blackfeet (a displaced Algonquin tribe) were being shoved southward by pressure from the advancing British and by 1753 Shoshoni lands were infested with Blackfoot horse rustlers. All trade relations were broken off between the two nations and in a wild frenzy of vengeance the Snakes and Utes joined forces and drove the Piegons and Bloods deep into the Canadian Rockies.

This action did not please the British. Their fur supplies were rapidly diminishing, while demand for pelts on the world market was increasing. It was imperative that they trap the interior without interference from a group of backward natives. The Hudson's Bay Company began toying with the idea that perhaps the Blackfeet were the answer to a quick defeat of the Shoshoni.

With this in mind Hudson's Bay shipped Anthony Henday, an outlawed smuggler from the Isle of Wight, into Blackfoot country in 1754. Capable of matching wits and stamina with Shoshoni and French alike, Henday was charged with a twofold mission. First, he was to corner the intermountain fur market by working through the Blackfeet, thus keeping it out of French hands and second, he was to enlist the aid of Blackfeet in the overthrow of the Shoshoni nation. Although Henday never penetrated the interior any deeper than the present site of Calgary, Canada, he was the first Englishman to lay eyes on the spine of the continent. Of more importance to the Bay Company, Henday reported Indians using horses for transportation instead of canoes. This startling news would herald a change in the fur business, for it was obvious that horse-borne Indians would not float their furs to the Hudson's Bay outposts.

With mounting rumors of white encroachments Snake dog soldiers took to their mounts and scoured the country, finding nothing more than a few displaced Modocs, Nez Perce and Crows. Causing further unrest, the Chinooks, looked upon as one of the more backward nations with whom the Shoshoni held commerce, were spreading tales of impending danger. Now, or so the Chinooks claimed, huge war canoes were again plying the sundown sea. Sometimes the vessels ventured too close to shore, enraging the sea gods, who hurled the intruding craft onto the wave-battered cliffs of the Chinook homeland. The Chinook interpreted these encounters between ships and sea gods as a good omen, for the wrecks were laden with unbelievable trade items. This the Shoshoni could not discount, for some of their people were the owners of fantastic objects reportedly taken from the shipwrecks. Therefore, the dog soldiers were on the alert for any interference from this direction also.

Joining forces with the Comanches and Utes, they formed an impenetrable barrier to European commerce between the Mississippi settlements, Santa Fe and the California coast. While the Shoshoni were reinforcing their embargo on white traffic, Great Britain took up the war-club against the French tribes. In 1763, as a result of its victory in the Seven Year's War with France—more commonly known as the French and Indian War—England fell heir to the St. Lawrence fur trade.

Within a year, Fort Cavagnolle, under constant harassment by the Shoshoni since its construction in 1743, was abandoned. As the occupants of the little outpost made a 260 mile dash for safety on the Mississippi River, Pierre La Clede, a nervy French trader accompanied by his 14 year old stepson, Augusti Chauteau, slipped across the Mississippi into Spanish hunting grounds. Taking over an abandoned Spanish mission on the south bank of the Missouri River, La Clede and Chauteau founded St. Louis in 1764. Established as a fur trading post, it became the supply depot for explorers of the west and the springboard into Oregon country.

Things were also heating up on the Shoshoni's Pacific front. Two nerve-wracking nightmares had jarred Spain out of its slumber, and it was once more on the prowl. The first jolt came from Russia. In 1728 the Danish navigator, Vitus Bering, flying the Russian flag, discovered and explored the strait which bears his name. On a second expedition in 1741 he laid the basis for Russian movement into Alaska. From then until the 1800's private subjects of the Czar crossed into Alaska and very actively and ruthlessly engaged in fur trade, moving down the Pacific coastline towards Mexico. The other disturbance concerned England's sweeping victory in the French and Indian War which, as confirmed by the Peace of Paris in 1763, drove the French from North America and upset the balance of power in the New World to the disadvantage of Spain.

Under the direction of Antonio Bucoreli, governor of Mexico, Spanish exploration was given renewed impetus. In 1769, the year Daniel Boone led settlers into Kentucky, causing further armed conflict between the Shoshoni and Sioux nations, imperial Spain lunged northward across Paiute territory, establishing missions, presidios and pueblos on the very edge of Snake possessions.

To further complicate Shoshoni foreign affairs Chief Evea, representing the Comanche tribes, began a courtship with the Spaniards. In June, 1772, he rode into San Antonio and signed a peace treaty with the colony of Texas, causing the first damaging split in the Shoshoni high command. Cuerno Verde (Green Horn), a tough Kotsotika dog soldier and high-ranking war chief in the Shoshoni alliance, refused to recognize the treaty and in so doing took command of the Comanche western division. While this rift was in progress, England became embroiled in an argument with her colonists, and by June, 1775, this quarrel had exploded into raw violence, setting the eastern seaboard aflame.

Taking advantage of this diversion, Juan de Anza slipped out of Santa Fe in the early spring of 1775 and jammed overland across nearly 1,000 miles of hostile desert into upper California. At the moment when British and Americans were slaughtering each other on the slopes of a Massachusetts knob called Breed's Hill, de Anza founded the city of San Francisco less than 500 miles southwest of the Snake's Ochoco stronghold.

Adding to the confusion, Cowlitz subjects of the Chinook nation claimed a party of white men landed on their shores, where they took on food and water. This was Bruno Heceta, sailing under orders of the Spanish crown in search of the elusive Northwest Passage, who entered Oregon coastal waters in 1775. He was the first European sailor to put a landing party onto the Oregon mainland. In 1776 Heceta and Lt. de Alyola anchored between the capes of the Columbia and concluded from the currents and eddies that they must be near "the mouth of some great river or some passage to another sea." Although they could never locate its exact position, Spanish charts named the river's mouth Heceta Inlet and the river behind it, St. Roc.[58]

While Heceta was making an assault on the Oregon coast and de Anza was marching overland to link Santa Fe with northern California, Ute warriors encountered soldiers of Christ in the Ruby Mountains of northern Nevada. Two Spanish padres, Silvestie Velz de Escalante and Francisco Antonio Dominquez, had made a push into Ute territory nearly to the present Idaho border. Hostilities were sufficient to convince the good fathers that Spain could never muster the resources to raise the red and gold banner among the Utes.

Within two summers of these visitations, the Chehalis, another tribe of the Chinook nation, claimed they traded animal skins for valuable merchandise with white men who had sailed across the Sundown Sea. They told the truth. In 1778 Captain James Cook in a British merchant vessel touched shore north of the Columbia. Here he purchased 1,500 beaver and sea otter pelts from the natives for what amounted to 90 dollars in trade articles. He sold these furs in China for 150,000 dollars. No longer would Oregon bask in anonymity.

As Cook closed his deal with the Chehalis, Mano Mocka—Maimed Hand—a Ute mercenary, sold out to de Anza for a gold medal, engraved with Charles III's profile, a Spanish uniform and a general's commission in the Spanish army. Then, de Anza proclaimed him head of the Ute tribe. General Maimed Hand got the idea.

Green Horn and Big Nose (Moitcha), leaders of the Snake war tribes, had successfully cut off direct communication between St. Louis and Santa Fe. In desperation in 1779 Spain mustered 600 troops to march on the Shoshoni, and Maimed Hand was right there at de Anza's side with 200 fighting Utes.[59] Green Horn in a savage raid against the Spanish was killed in the Colorado Rockies and Maimed Hand was instrumental in his defeat. The death of Green Horn was a decisive Spanish victory. The Comanche war chief Painted Man (Ecueracopa) became Green Horn's successor, but he lacked the support of Big Nose.

---

[58] The ship of discovery, Alyola's schooner, was only 36 feet long, 12 feet wide and 8 feet deep. Heceta was in a frigate which was a war vessel. (Mourelle's Journal from Barrington's *Miscellanies*, p. 473.)

[59] Sprague, *Massacre, the Tragedy at White River*, pp. 71-72.

Both Comanches and Snakes—and for that matter the Utes with the defection of Maimed Hand—would suffer from this lack of cooperation between the ranking war chiefs.

Three summers after Great Britain touched pen to the paper, bestowing upon the United States the awesome responsibility of a new nation, Painted Man grew weary of fighting. In 1786 he signed a truce with Juan de Anza, which in reality was more of an alliance.[60] Over the years as the two superpowers had slowly bled each other to death, the Apache had watched and waited. When both factions appeared sufficiently weak, the Apache struck, killing Shoshoni and Hispanic with equal fervor. To survive, the dog soldiers and the conquistadores had to join forces. By now Shoshoni solidarity was at a dangerously low ebb.

---

[60] Not all Comanche stopped raiding nor did the Spanish really expect them to. One of the objectives of the Comanche-Spanish alliance was to make use of the Comanches in fighting Apaches who were playing havoc with both nations. (American Heritage, *Book of Indians*, p. 378.)

CHAPTER 7

BROWN BESS

We obtained Misstutam—
Big Dogs—from the Snakes and
black guns from the British.
A man on horseback armed with a musket
could cause wonderful consternation among
the Shoshoni tribes..

Saukamappee (Young Man)
Blackfoot Medicine Man

By 1775 the estimated population of the American colonies stood at 2.8 million. Five years later a smallpox epidemic, which lasted for two plague ridden years, ravaged western America from Texas to the Yukon and the dwindling Indian population was further reduced. The Shoshoni were not spared. Death among his troops was one of the contributing factors in Painted Man's decision to call a halt to Spanish hostilities and smallpox would pave the way for the first invasion of Oyer'ungun.

In the late summer of 1785, while their hunting parties prowled the Dakota plains in pursuit of buffalo, Big Nose was killed during a raid against the Sioux. In the ensuing days Owitze (The Man With a Twisted Left Hand), a battle-scarred Lohim warrior, seized the reins of command of the powerful Snake tribes and with Painted Man on the verge of joining the Spaniards it made him the unspoken leader of the Shoshoni nation.[61]

---

[61] Twisted Hand (Owitze) is referred to by some historians, such as Judge in his *Half Alligator, Half Horse*, as Bad Left Hand. Some forty years later, French-Canadian trappers would call him Mauvais Gauche which literally meant bad left hand. (Vestal, *Joe Meek*, p. 95.)

The head chiefs' concerns were now centered on change within their own political structure and that of neighboring nations, for they were wise enough to realize that aspiring leaders, both domestic and foreign, could have far reaching ramifications. In the southern Ochoco a Snake teenager was being hailed as a youth "touched by God." Taking the name of Wuna Mucca, the Giver of Spiritual Gifts, he was gathering a huge following in the Snake, Ute and Paiute tribes. Many believed him to be a prophet of such magnitude as to challenge the power of the formidable Dakota medicine chief, Wabasha, the Glowing Man, who held the Sioux nation in the palm of his hand. He was the man the Shoshoni believed to be responsible for the death of Big Nose.[62]

On the north, internal strife was ripping the Nez Perce apart. One segment under the leadership of Wa'tiste Mene—Eat No Meat—formed their own nation soon to be recognized as the Cayuse. In this same sector the Snakes had broken off all trade relations with Sticky Mouth (Pahkia Kwayi), chief of the Blackfeet, so they could expect to be carrying on warfare in that direction. On the west a moody youth called Concomly was in line to inherit the throne of the Chinook nation. The Chinook posed no real threat, but a change of command could liven up the slave trade which would add little to the comfort of their horseless wards, the Paiutes.

Meanwhile, some 3,000 miles to the northeast the British, who had been momentarily detained from their plans to annihilate the Snakes, were taking a hard look at the distant Pacific slope. Thirty-two years

---

[62] There is an interesting story connected with Wuna Mucca's name. North West Company Journals state that in 1807 British traders in Columbia country were met by several natives. At the time, their leader was wearing only one moccasin, presumably too destitute to own another. The Nor'westers thought this quite humorous. Thereafter, when referring to the Indian, they called him "One Mucca," mucca being French for moccasin. This nickname evolved from One Mucca into Winnemucca and the name with which he entered American history. Family members such as his grand-daughter, Sarah Winnemucca Hopkins, say that Wuna' Muca is a Shoshoni word meaning Giver of Spiritual Gifts or the Gift Giver and that was his name long before contact with the Canadians. One Moccasin—of Snake parentage—married into a Paiute clan and thus became identified in later years as a Paiute.

had elapsed since Hudson's Bay had dispatched Anthony Henday into the interior to negotiate trade agreements with the Blackfeet and still they were not reaping any furs from the Oregon country. Obviously, it was only a matter of time before the Americans started casting yearning eyes in that direction and, to add to their concerns, a stubborn group of independent Canadian traders were challenging company authority in central Canada and in the process driving up the cost of furs to Hudson's Bay traders.

Company agents who had been working with the inland tribes consistently painted a gloomy picture. West of the Rockies in the unexplored Columbia drainage there existed a dangerous Indian nation, a people so hostile that they would be extremely detrimental to British expansion in that remote region. From what information they could gather, the Snakes were different from other inland tribes. . . in appearance, in wealth and in their excessively war-like nature. None of the tribes contacted had seen the interior of the Snake's hunting grounds, believed to be centered around a mountain range deep in the heart of Oregon country. All agreed the Snakes were a predatory group who preyed upon all other tribes. In fact, according to informants, these people were so antagonistic they would attack their own members just as viciously over real or imagined wrongs as they would an unrelated tribe. And thus, as the Honorable Caleb Cushing observed in a speech to the U.S. Senate Committee on Foreign Affairs. . . "occasionally an obstacle presents itself in some unproductive country or some Indian tribe. . . and the advancing column is momentarily checked."

Faced with this intelligence, British officials, including the sovereign head of England, deemed it prudent for the adventurers of the Hudson's Bay Company to bring the Snakes into submission quickly and by the simple expedient of arming the Blackfeet with muskets and plying them with liquor to bolster their courage. Thus encouraged, let the Blackfeet deplete the population of malcontents while the British reaped the rewards.

In this manner Bay Company officials were now to prove what the American states had always suspected, that being that Hudson's Bay represented one of the "more corrupt monopolies instituted during the reign of Charles II.''[63] Before the winter's blast of 1786 could choke off the St. Lawrence seaway, a shipment of whiskey, arms, powder and ball was dispatched with the Grande Brigade into the Canadian Rockies.

The liquor was rot-gut, but the armament was definitely not of the quality of the Carolina musket as Hudson's Bay called the ordinary trade weapon. This same weapon was referred to by Americans as the London fusile. The Shoshoni considered it safe to fire only if (1) you were an expert horseman (2) and you could, while galloping hell-bent, hand-pour powder into the barrel, disgorge from your mouth a bullet into that barrel and strike the butt smartly to place the bullet, (3) tip the gun horizontally, take accurate sight and fire and (4) do all this in that critical split second before the ball shifted forward. The dog soldiers knew from experience that if you made a mistake, a split or ringed barrel bloomed right in front of your face.[64] Small wonder the Snakes and Comanches were unimpressed with European technology when it came to firearms. Especially was this true with Twisted Hand, who received his name from a ruptured musket barrel.

Hudson's Bay was not about to supply their new allies with a weapon such as this. The corporate heads of Hudson's Bay Company meant business. The Blackfeet were given official British military muskets, fondly referred to as "the Brown Bess." These guns, weighing between 10½ and 12 pounds, shot a .75 calibre ball at an effective range of 100 yards, a rather sophisticated weapon for a tribe that had never before seen a firearm.

By spring of 1787, company officials were impatient to find out if their plan for destruction was being implemented. A British agent slipped out of St. Anne's Chapel on the southern tip of Montreal Island as a priest intoned, "the Lord be with you." A bound servant to the Hudson's Bay Company, this man was departing for the unknown interior of British America. His mission... to find his way into the Rocky

---

[63] As stated in the *House of Representatives Report No. 101*, 25th Congress, 3rd session, January 4, 1839.

[64] The London fusile was a highly inaccurate .58 calibre, smooth-bore, lightweight weapon, running from 46 to 64 inches in length. In the 1820s and 30s the United States government supplied them to the fur-trading posts under the name of North West guns.

Mountains, a journey that would place him some 2,300 miles closer to Oregon country, and to determine if company muskets were being put to the proper use.

David Thompson—soon to be known by the Indians as Koo Koo-Sint, the Man Who Watches Stars—had been chosen for this important job not because he had studied for seven years as a geographer but because he had an unusually winning way with the native girls, allowing him free passage where others dared not tread. With the priestly blessing and company orders spurring him on the 17-year-old clerk embarked up the Ottawa River into the waiting forest.

Far to the west, the balmy days of spring were warming the land. Deep within the misty valleys of the southern Blues, the Shoshoni were stirring from their winter camps in preparation for their annual trek to the east. . . hunting, fishing, trading and enjoying life to the fullest. By midsummer the various bands were separated by hundreds of miles, each in pursuit of its own desires. By late autumn their whole way of life would be changed. . . forever. They had no way of knowing what happened to family and friends, for where the Blackfeet struck there were no survivors. In their drunken stupor the Blackfeet were killing horses and dogs, oldsters and youngsters, women and babies—something which had never before happened in the annals of Indian warfare.

AUTHOR'S NOTE:

The following two chapters are drawn almost in their entirety on information obtained in interviews with Columbia Plateau and Great Basin Indians, including Tom Ochiho and Agnes Banning Philips, descendants of Old Deer Running; Dave Chocktote, descendant of Wolf Tail; Le Roy Saunders, Yakima tribe; John Wahsees, Umatilla tribe; George Winishut, Paiute tribe. These two chapters are based on history passed down from generation to generation. Who can say that their method of record keeping is any less accurate than the written history of the European tribes? Following the birth of the Shoshoni nation in the early 16th century, they had been fighting Spanish, French and British for nearly 250 years before the Americans arrived on the scene in 1805 and had maintained records of these events. Anthropologists have determined that Shoshoni pictographs tell a definite story of tribal events. There are caves in the Mill Creek Valley east of Prineville whose time-faded pictographs have defied archeologists in their attempts to solve an age-old mystery. Some of the clearest characters are found in Medicine Cave on the old Martin ranch. In this cave tribal history has been recorded as late as the 1880's.

Concerning the information given by Indian informants, what could be researched through Canadian and American records proved to be correct. The Lewis and Clark Journals of 1806, North West Company Journals of 1810 and Pacific Fur Company journals of 1811-12 describe the same events at Celilo Falls as those told by the Indians, which occurred by their reckoning some 20-25 years earlier. The event was placed at six summers before Captain Robert Gray put the *U.S.S. Columbia* across the river bar, or as the Indians put it. . . "a big war canoe carrying white men entered the river of the north" and approximately one year before the arms delivery to the Blackfeet. If nothing else, the reader will gain a better insight on those people called "Snakes." They possessed human traits, social habits, economic needs no different, no better and certainly no worse than their European counterparts.

CHAPTER 8

A' TRADING WE WILL GO

I see a dark-eyed copper maid
Beckon to her brave. . . .
I see the smoke from wigwams curl up
And mingle with the haze
to float above the river. . . .
I see the bold-faced cliff, the woodland
And the limitless reach of prairie
All untouched by paleskin hand. . . .
As the languorous days of Indian summer,
Gift of the Great Spirit,
Rest upon the land.

Marjorie W. Scott

The big Shoshoni encampment on the upper Ochoco River was alive with excitement. Men, women and children scurried about like a colony of ants, for with the return of the horse hunters they would begin their annual trek to the legendary trade market at Kwai An Tikwokets, the easternmost village of the Chinook nation.[65]

Far to the south a blazing sun arced across the smoldering highlands of the Pohoi Tuwiwa Gaiya.[66] Up near the head of a narrow canyon,

---

[65] Kwai An Tikwokets was the Shoshoni name for the mid-Columbian market area that spanned the Columbia River from Celilo on the south bank to Wishram on the northern shore. A literal translation means "on the other side of the river" and refers to the Deschutes boundary river separating Shoshoni hunting territory from alien lands.

[66] Pohoi Tuwiwa Gaiya is the Shoshoni name for the High Desert of Central Oregon. It means "where the wild sage grows." Classified as one of the major deserts of the world, it is referred to on early maps as the Rolling Sage Plains and the Great Sandy Desert.

where dozens of wildhorse trails merged into one, a huge oval corral was slowly taking shape. It encircled the main horse trail with widespread wings running from both sides of a single opening. Sagebrush and tree limbs were being heaped so high around the juniper poles which formed the main structure that a horse could neither see nor jump over them. This trap, which more resembled a stockade, would according to its builders stand until the sun toppled from the sky.[67]

The sweating workmen laboring on their brush corral were in a foul mood, especially Kwewa tai—the Wolf's Tail. Trapping wild horses was the last recourse for the Shoshoni. Being practical men, they could see no reason to risk their necks wrestling wild mustangs when they could steal from the Spanish horses that were already trained. Because of this aversion to capturing wild horses the Shoshoni had become the most accomplished horse thieves west of the Mississippi River. However, when it came to bartering, the Shoshoni held to their ancient practice of offering only the scrubby, inbred descendants of the pure blood Spanish herds. To trade a horse of better quality to an unrelated tribe was akin to selling your wife or eating your hunting dogs. It just wasn't done.

Everyone on the horse trapping party was fully aware of this time-honored custom, including Wolf Tail. Each was equally aware that Wolf Tail's bad temper stemmed from an act of his own doing, and they thought it was quite humorous. Only four suns ago, Wolf Tail had taken the daughter of the old Banattee warrior, Sits Under the Pine, as his wife. The wedding festivities were still in progress when Old Deer Running casually announced that he was looking for men to go after horses. Certain in his own mind that this was going to be a daring horse-raid on the Mexicans, Wolf Tail, hoping to impress his bride, volunteered to ride along.

Two days out of the big river encampment, Old Deer Running told him they were going after trade ponies. Were it not for the fact it would have made him the laughingstock of the entire Shoshoni nation, Wolf Tail would have deserted on the spot. As it was, he had little choice but

---

[67] Remnants of Shoshoni horse traps known to be over 100 years old can still be found on the High Desert. For further description of these corrals and how they were constructed see John Clark Hunt, "Wild Horses Fade from Scene," *Sunday Oregon Journal*, Portland, Oregon, June 22, 1958.

to continue on with the horse hunters and gripe. It didn't improve his frame of mind when Old Deer Running placed him in charge of the corral building, a back-breaking job which he thoroughly despised. It was Wolf Tail's opinion that trapping these miserable creatures, which roamed the desert in herds rivalling the buffalo of the Great Plains, was an insult to his manhood.

While Wolf Tail's group worked on the corral, the remainder headed into the desert in search of their quarry. They were not long in finding what they wanted, a cantankerous bunch of broom-tails which in no way resembled the warrior's powerful mounts. In fact, they more resembled the prehistoric horses, which once grazed on the high rims overlooking ancient Lake Ochoco. But they were ideal trading stock. Wolf Tail was just finishing the trap when the wild ones thundered into captivity.

Before the trade ponies could be moved back to camp, they had to be semi-broken. This was a brutal performance on both horse and man. Old Deer Running as group leader had earned the dubious honor of breaking the first horse. Riding into the corral, he roped one of the mustangs and choked it until it could no longer fight back. At this point he threw the animal to the ground. With split-second timing he and the horse hit the ground at the same instant. Before the horse could regain his wind and jump to his feet, Old Deer Running quickly slipped a rawhide noose around the horse's lower jaw and then looped the rope around its neck so he could hold it down. Careful to stay clear of its slashing hooves, which could cleave a man's skull as neatly as a war axe, he knelt by the animal's head and blew his breath into each nostril. While doing this he plucked the "wild hair" from around the horse's eyes with his free hand. At the end of this strange ceremony, which supposedly aided in the brute's subjection, the first harsh phase of training was completed.

Wolf Tail—as builder of the corral—was the next to break a wild one. At daybreak three days and 250 horses later the horse hunters headed for the Ochoco River with their rough string in tow.

Back at the river camp everyone was making last minute preparations for the coming trip. Chosro—the Blue Bird—hummed as her gifted hands molded the final contours to an exquisite clay jar. A work of art, it would be placed in the oven beside her other pottery items many of which had long, narrow necks complete with tapered stoppers. Only the flawless would pass her rigid inspection, for they were to be bartered for precious salt and other luxury items gleaned from the beaches of the Pacific Ocean by the Canoe Indians. Blue Bird knew from past experience that her jars were highly prized trade articles, for Shoshoni women had a reputation for being master craftsmen in the art of pottery.

Blue Bird smiled as her infant daughter played among the many baskets stacked in front of her lodge. These beautiful air-tight containers represented endless hours of tedious labor. . . patiently woven from hoc'tu (willow) twigs and tough psuc'see-que (ryegrass) stems, each carefully sealed on the inside with a layer of gum from the tu'vou (pine) tree. . . they too would bring a good return at the trading center, for the ancient art of basket weaving had reached the peak of perfection in the nimble hands of the women of the Ochoco.[68] Durable and strong, Blue Bird had no fear that little Lost Girl would harm the baskets in her play. At the moment she was more concerned about the dusty horseman who galloped into camp and reined in at the lodge of Twisted Hand.

Twisted Hand and his battle-weary troops had but recently returned to the Ochoco after an absence of more than seven summers. . . long years of fighting in the tortured canyons of the Colorado, the wind-swept plains of the Dakota and the dark forests of the Canadian Rockies. . . sad years during which many dog soldiers, including the great warrior Big Nose, had given their lives to protect the homeland. Now, any

---

[68] Some of the finest art work in the world, including baskets and pottery, has been found at Wakemap Mound between Spearfish and Wishram on the Washington shore of the Columbia a scant 50 miles northwest of the old Shoshoni land. Hundreds of fine carvings in stone and bone have been recovered from Wakemap Mound, some of them so delicate that they seem to have been worked with the aid of a microscope. In the words of Dr. B. Robert Butler, former editor of the Davidson Journal of Anthropology, founder and director of the Laboratory of Anthropology in the Dalles and archeologist in charge at the Wakemap project: "the same artistry done in marble would rival Greece and Rome." There is little doubt that some of this work was contributed by the Shoshoni for they were the only western Indians whose symbolic art told of a definite incident in the history of the old Oregon country. Also, these carvings coincide with a period of booming economic prosperity and religious resurgence which spread throughout the interior northwest, a cycle when the Shoshoni were at their very peak in productiveness, inspired and protected by their personal ta'mano'was—Guardian Spirits.

stranger entering the chief's lodge brought anxiety to the whole camp, for Twisted Hand was the heir to Big Nose's command.

But, curious as she was, Blue Bird had other thoughts to occupy her mind—not the least of which was the newly wed daughter of Sits Under the Pine, a girl who was beginning to wear on Blue Bird's nerves. Since her marriage, Rippling Voice had nearly driven Blue Bird out of her mind with constant questions. Rippling Voice had never been to the trade market and she was torn between joyous anticipation of seeing it and abject fear of making a fool of herself in public. She so wanted to make a good impression on her husband, but the poor girl was totally lacking any practical knowledge of how to manage a household. Although she was only two winters younger than Blue Bird, Rippling Voice had been left motherless from early childhood. Her doting father had taught her absolutely nothing in the way of domestic chores, mainly because he knew nothing about them himself. As a huntress, she excelled. As a tracker, no brave could equal her. As a horsewoman, she had no peer. As a homemaker, she fell short of the goal.

Only a couple of days ago Rippling Voice had been lamenting that she couldn't locate any tough neck-hide off a bull buffalo anywhere in camp. It seemed she had her heart set on making a small, round war-shield for Wolf Tail as a coming home present. Finally, Blue Bird took pity and taught her how to make one from the paper-thin hide of the antelope. This she did by taking many layers of the antelope's flimsy skin and cementing them together with pine pitch and river sand. Rippling Voice was ecstatic. She had made with her own hands a war-shield that was every bit as effective as the buffalo hide protector, for it would turn a lance in full charge. The betting around the campfires that night was whether she would give it to Wolf Tail or keep it for herself.

Now, Blue Bird heard someone approaching and deep in her heart she hoped it wasn't Rippling Voice, for she really didn't have time for any more lessons in homecraft. Fortunately, it was Burning Ember, the provocative young wife of Old Deer Running. Burning Ember grumbled as she passed Blue Bird's tipi, straining under the weight of a heavy buckskin bag filled with obsidian from the famed Arrowhead Land.[69] This raw material was in great demand, for it produced the finest knives, needles, awls, hide-scrapers and arrow points to be found in the western world. However, Burning Ember could care less what obsidian brought on the world market for she was pregnant and because of this would not be allowed to make the journey to the Other Side of the River, a fact she didn't let Old Deer Running forget.

At least, she wasn't required to prepare jerky or gather pine nuts which was something the other women didn't let her forget. Both of these were eaten; therefore, Burning Ember couldn't touch them because during her pregnancy she was considered unclean. Without thinking she passed by Wolf Tail's lodge and immediately thought, "Oh, no, now I have to talk to that crazy wife of his." Burning Ember didn't like Rippling Voice. Since her recent marriage Rippling Voice had been in constant tears over the departure of the horse trappers, certain that Wolf Tail would get lost or fall off his horse. The fact that Wolf Tail was as tough as any man in the Shoshoni nation and war-chief of the Banattee didn't seem to inspire much confidence in Rippling Voice.[70]

Burning Ember had no sympathy for Rippling Voice and was about to make a tart remark when a cloud of dust appeared and Rippling Voice took off in a happy trot to alert the camp that the men were approaching with the trade ponies. Blue Bird paused in her work as her husband rode by without speaking and disappeared into Twisted Hand's lodge. Old Deer Running playfully tousled Burning Ember's hair as he passed— only to get hit with a chunk of obsidian. He, too, reined in at the head

---

[69] Known to the Shoshoni as Utum Paints (the Arrowhead Land), this area would be renamed Glass Butte for the tons of volcanic glass found around it. Today, it attracts rock-hounds—collectors of semi-precious gem stone—from all major countries of the world. Within sight of its lightning-struck top lies an ancient Shoshoni burial ground.

[70] Wolf Tail and Rippling Voice were the paternal great-grandparents of Dave Chocktote. Old Deer Running and Burning Ember were the paternal great-grandparents and Weasel Lungs and Blue Bird were the maternal great-grand parents of Agnes Banning Philips and Tom Ochiho. Lost Girl, oldest daughter of Weasel Lungs and Blue Bird was the mother of Washakie, head chief of the eastern Snakes during the war-torn last decades of the 1800s.

chief's lodge. Wolf Tail charged Rippling Voice at a full gallop and she vaulted onto the back of his horse. They faded into the willows at the river's edge.

Inside Twisted Hand's lodge, the atmosphere was grim. He had waited until the arrival of the horse trappers before holding council. Pah'wuko—Big Water—gnarled leader of the Paiute tribe, had sent word that the treacherous Moat Koni were once again on the prowl and up to their old tricks.[71] Several Paiutes had disappeared singly and in pairs, giving suspicion that they had been kidnapped by the sneaking Southerners and were now bound for one of the slave markets along the Ogwa'pe-on. . . the river of the north.

Big Water knew that the Snakes would be making a ride to the Columbia for trade purposes, and he asked that they do the honorable thing, if they found any tribesmen in captivity. As the old Paiute had anticipated, the vote of the Snake council was heavily in favor of carrying out his wishes. This was a mission for the dog soldiers, the young men of the warrior societies. So, the trading party would become a highly mobile, deceptively dangerous war-party, unencumbered by women and children.

---

[71] Drifting up from the Klamath Lake region, the Moat Koni slavers or the southerners as the Shoshoni word indicates were in the English language the Modoc Indians, blood relatives of the Klamaths.

CHAPTER 9

THE DOG SOLDIERS

There's a race of men that don't fit in,
a race that can't stay still;
So they break the hearts of kith and kin
and they roam the world at will.

Robert W. Service

The dog soldiers were the shock troops of the Shoshoni nation. Known by their clan affiliations as the White Knives, Hungry Dogs, Pony Stealers and so on, they were the elite of the warrior class. Young, strong, many with wives and children, the dog soldiers enforced tribal law and when on the move acted as rear guards, advance guards and scouts for the main party. In battle they rode at the head of the attack column and would give their life rather than abandon a fallen comrade.

Dog soldiers formed their own war parties and attacked on their own initiative, often without the knowledge or consent of their head chiefs. They chose their own war chiefs, medicine chiefs and subordinate chiefs and to a great extent—more than the head chiefs cared to admit—influenced tribal policy. Without exception, from their ranks came the ruling chieftains of the Shoshoni nation.

Quickly, the lines of command were established. By unanimous decision the tough leader of the Tussawehee dog soldiers, Old Deer Running, would head up the brigade. To back him were Elk Tongue, war chief of the Bear Killer tribe, Swooping Eagle, war chief of the Big Lodge, and Wolf Tail, war chief of the Robber Snakes. On the slim chance these gentlemen should run into unforeseen trouble, Weasel Lungs, the White Knife medicine chief, would ride with them. The Paiute messenger could return word to Big Water that the Snake dog soldiers were riding. They now had until daybreak to bid their families good-bye.

At daybreak Weasel Lungs put on his moccasins and stepped down to the river's edge. Here he threw a handful of clear, cold water into his face and then plunged in. After the bath he stood erect before the advancing dawn, facing the sun as it rose on the horizon and offered an unspoken prayer.[72] Returning from the river, Weasel Lungs threw back the flap on his lodge and scowled as Blue Bird stepped forward to greet him. She laughed. Undoubtedly her husband was trying to keep up appearances as the most feared medicine man west of the Shining Mountains. Her gaiety soon faded when she heard the news. Of course, she was disappointed for not getting to make the trip, but she was also crying inside for her husband. Like many of the women she couldn't understand why the men must always make these dangerous raids in the name of honor.

A few lodges away, Koo'yah tuvu—the Burning Ember—secretly thought it poetic justice that no women were allowed to make this journey. Outwardly, she was fiercely proud that her man was to lead this risky mission. It never once entered Burning Ember's thoughts that Old Deer Running might never return. He was young. He was strong. His enemies could not prevail against him.

Rippling Voice was having her problems also. When Wolf Tail announced the council's decision, she quietly went out to her best horse and platted a war-club into its mane on one side and her own personal spiritual bag on the other. Wolf Tail was still trying to convince his stubborn wife that she did not qualify as a warrior when Old Deer Running gave the order to mount.

At the first light of dawn the merchant dog soldiers aimed their caravan into the west. Two days later, Old Deer Running nosed his horse into the treacherous current of the Hidden Water.[73] Following in his

---

[72] Charles Eastman would observe on this Shoshoni custom, that a man's wife may precede or follow him in his devotion but never accompany him. Each soul must meet the morning sun, the new earth and the Great Spirit alone. (Dr. Charles A. Eastman, *The Soul of the Indian*, pp. 45-46.)

[73] Known to the Shoshoni as Towahnakiooks (The Hidden Water), this river would be renamed Au Riviere des Chutes (River of the Falls) or the Deschutes River. The Deschutes was the first Oregon stream to be used as an inland waterway by the fur brigades. Heading deep in the Central Oregon Cascades, it formed the

wake were three war-chiefs, one medicine chief and upwards of seventy battle-scarred warriors of the Snake clans, many of whom were war-chiefs in their own right. These were men who, if one of their hunting parties was molested, would think nothing of riding from their Ochoco stronghold across the Great Basin, over the Continental Divide and into Texas territory to avenge this wrong. To them this mission was as necessary as breathing.

When the last trade horse pawed his way up the west river bank, Old Deer Running signaled to halt. The Shoshoni were now on alien ground and certain preparations must be made before continuing on. First in order was to make peace with the spirit world. Weasel Lungs took care of this matter. While offering a prayer to the Mighty Chief Above, he dipped the tail of a buffalo into the swirling Hidden Water and sprinkled each horse and rider in a purification ceremony. Next, Old Deer Running carefully circled his right eye with white paint, a performance which was repeated by Wolf Tail, Elk Tongue and Swooping Eagle. If the need should arise, this would serve as warning to the fish eaters that these warriors were the most deadly in battle. Each of the remaining braves traced a line of red paint around his mouth, telling the world. . . . "I have defeated my enemies in previous fights and, if necessary, I will do it again!" They were now ready to proceed.

To further prove his prowess Old Deer Running was mounted on a multi-colored stallion. The war horse was chosen for endurance and a level head under fire. Usually, the Shoshoni favored geldings for patrol or war-party work. Mares, if very well trained, were sometimes employed, but stallions almost never. The latter's eagerness to challenge or court as the sex of the enemy's mount might dictate was far too great a hazard for any but a very great warrior. Old Deer Running was of that calibre.

What this daring group had in mind could be considered as bravery at its very highest. . . or sheer madness. To the inhabitants of the Pacific

---

undisputed western boundary of the Shoshoni nation. The steep canyon walls of this river are composed of gravel and lava in alternating layers which absorb water during flood stage and release this stored up water when the stream drops to normal. The result is that the Deschutes River has a more uniform flow than any other river in the United States.

Northwest the great village which Old Deer Running was intending to invade was the hub of the universe. As far back as the memory of man this place was and it would continue into the future for all time. It was the ultimate city of an advanced civilization. The city—eight miles long from Spearfish to Wishram on the north shore and from Winquatt to Celilo a like distance on the south shore—was neutral ground where all nations met, laying aside ancient grudges to trade.[74] Here, Blackfeet, Nez Perce, Shoshoni and Flatheads mingled with Klamath, Chinook, Rogues and Yakimas. Now, the Snake dog soldiers intended to ride into this mecca and claim all Paiute hostages without payment. If need be, they were to start a battle within the confines of this non-partisan territory with the full knowledge they most likely would die along with their released prisoners. It is small wonder the tribesmen left in the Ochoco were filled with apprehension.

Ahead of the dog soldiers by 24 hours a pitiful group of naked, half-starved, vermin-infested people ranging in age from early teens to late twenties stumbled northward down the west bank of the Hidden Water. It was tortuous progress for these captives were lashed together ankle to ankle and neck to neck with rawhide ropes. The short-tempered Modocs prodded, stoned and goaded them to even greater efforts for their destination, the head of the dangerous narrows in the Columbia, was nearly in sight. The Modocs were eager to arrive, for they had an exceptionally good catch—a half-dozen Shasta braves, twice that many Umpqua men and women, some thirty Washoe tribesmen and five Paiute girls.

At the junction of the Hidden Water and the Columbia they were joined by Katchkin of the Wascos, who was also bringing in slaves captured in the middle Columbia Basin. . . Spokanes, Umatillas and Walla Wallas. All were young people for the old did not make good

---

[74] Wakemap (between Spearfish and Wishram on the Washington shore of the Columbia) and Celilo on the Oregon shore, represent the oldest continuously occupied center of prehistoric culture in the world. Older cities have been discovered but nowhere has such a record of uninterrupted occupation been found. The culture of this mid-Columbia area has been traced back 16,000 years. The ancient camp-sites were flooded by the backwaters of The Dalles Dam (Lake Celilo) in 1957, signalling another coup for the Army Corps of Engineers.

trading stock. They were either killed or kept by their captors as personal servants.

A short distance downstream the squalid Wasco long huts reeked in the afternoon sun as they sat imbedded in the south bank of the great river of the west. Like maggots on a dead carcass they defiled the otherwise serene beauty of the majestic canyon. Across the vast expanse of water the same conditions prevailed on the north bank for here clung the soiled metropolis of the Klickitat nation. Both sides of the river were a seething mass of confused activity. Traders and buyers from all points of the Pacific Northwest had been converging on this area for two weeks and were now scurrying in and out of the log cabins, peddling wares, arguing over prices and comparing merchandise.

Molalla and Clackamas long boats skillfully navigated the swift water as they shuttled trade goods and passengers from Wakemap to Celilo, the fabulous twin cities of the western world. Agile fishermen netted fish by the hundreds as the Columbia ran black with salmon in the long narrows and the dangerous falls area called Celilo. Chinook and Nootka war canoes beached at the lower rapids and disgorged shells, carved whalebone and other exotic articles gathered from the beaches of the Pacific Ocean. Moving overland from all directions, they came, Klamath and Modoc slavers from the south, Walla Walla and Kootenai buyers from the east, Yakima and Spokane peddlers from the north, Kalapooi and Nisqualli spectators from the west.

Old Stacona, chief of the Bowl Makers, was overjoyed as he haggled with Concomly, squat prince of the Chinook nation, for a hand-carved walrus tusk totem and made his price. Winap Snoot of the Peo Umatilla clan stalked through the main village, heading for the compound at the base of a high cliff, checking to see if any tribesmen were held captive in the slave market. Suddenly, a deathly quiet fell as hundreds of jabbering people froze in their tracks. A line of horsemen had appeared on the southeastern rim. Their arrival was viewed with mixed emotions. They would have superb trade articles, gold and silver, buffalo hides, jars and baskets, gaudy feathers, turquoise, obsidian and horses. But these dangerous Inland People could also trigger instant death, depending entirely upon their frame of mind.

Leisurely, almost arrogantly, the thin line of horsemen entered the sprawling market place. The crowd became noticeably nervous, for it was apparent there were no women, children or old people with this group. They became more shaky when they recognized the four war-chiefs, for these men's reputations were known throughout the west.

Eagle Wing, the Nez Perce war-chief, nervously fingered his war-axe as Good Man of the Umatillas sneaked off to Wenap Snoot's lodge to forewarn him of possible trouble. Whispers passed from ear to ear. The Shoshoni—warriors of the Ochoco—were riding into town. The Modocs were quick to drag the Paiute girls into one of the Wasco long huts, for they wished no argument from these men. Then, one of the girls cried out and had her head caved in with a club for her effort. Her body was hastily tossed into the murky waters of the Columbia.

Meanwhile, the Shoshoni rode cautiously into the city. Their plan was simple. Some would set up for trade while others mingled with the crowd, hoping to locate the captives. Under cover of darkness they would release the prisoners and by morning be headed back to the Ochoco. No fuss. No bother. But the best laid plans exploded into raw hell when Old Bull stumbled upon the body of the Paiute girl caught in an eddy. Like rabid wolves the Shoshoni rode their horses across fleeing Nootka, Tillamooks and Modocs alike. And in the strange manner of Indian outbursts the Nez Perce joined forces with the dog soldiers as Eagle Wing, screaming a war cry, charged into the fray and bludgeoned a Wasco chief whom he believed had cheated him in a gambling game. Old Deer Running roped and dragged a Modoc brave half the length of the Celilo village and threw his broken body on the door step of Stacona.

Eat No Meat of the Cayuse, excited by blood, rushed in on the side of the Modocs and took Wolf Tail's lance through both hips. Concomly downed a Shoshoni with a whale bone axe and got his left eye gouged out by an exuberant Klickitat brave, thus insuring he would become salmon bait if Concomly survived this battle.

During the confusion Weasel Lungs—with an unexpected ally in Good Man—was torching long houses in his search for captives. When the smoke of battle cleared, Weasel Lungs had the four girls in tow and an unwanted refugee, a Umatilla boy who had also been rounded up for slavery.[75] He most certainly didn't want him, but in view of Good Man's

---

[75] This boy would marry Weasel Lung's daughter and around 1804 they would become the parents of a son who would lead General Crook's army to victory over the Sioux after the Custer defeat and would be the only Snake warrior to be

assistance he couldn't very well leave the boy behind and he didn't have time to locate the Umatilla camp. Having gained their objective, the remnants of the war party beat a hasty retreat for the Ochoco.

It was the final days of August, 1786.

---

honored by the United States government. . . Chief Washakie, the Gourd Rattler. For his mixed Umatilla-Shoshoni parentage and approximate birthdate see *Handbook of American Indians North of Mexico*, Hodge, ed., Part II, pp. 919-20.

CHAPTER 10

BROWN BESS SPEAKS

Indian kids are so used to being handled gently, to getting away with things that they don't pay much attention to what grownups tell them. . . . Sometime I feel like yelling at one of these brash kids, "Hey, you little son of a bitch, listen to me!"

Lame Deer
Sioux Medicine Man

As the summer of 1787 drifted across North America, sowing the seeds of smallpox in its wake, David Thompson pushed steadily into the interior, visiting Indian encampments along the way. Past the mosquito-infested shores of Lake Winnipeg, across the grass-covered Manitoba plains, up the south Saskatchewan River. By late autumn and near the present Manitoba-Alberta border he reached the base of the Rocky Mountains in a swirling snowstorm. As he plotted his erratic course across the Canadian wilderness, a grim drama was being enacted some 500 miles to the west.

In the dying glow of a saffron sun a haggard Indian raised his eyes to the sky and cried, "Wuko tobats masi po'kunt massuu. . . Mighty Chief Above, why have you sent me to the realm of the dead?" Before him lay the smoldering ruins of a camp; at his feet sprawled the body of a dying child. Around him lay death and destruction. He had failed miserably. Out of nearly eighty Shoshoni he and this gasping shell at his feet remained alive, and at this moment he wouldn't give a rotten deer hide on the chances of this boy's survival. Nevertheless, he bent to the repellant, bloody task at hand.

As the days turned into weeks the shrill winds of winter took possession of the land. In the snug encampments of the Ochoco there was a sadness. One of their hunting parties had not returned and now it was certain they never would. Blue Bird, again pregnant, comforted her small daughter, while her own heart ached. Her husband was among the missing.

In the last cold days of the Snow Moon a weary rider rode into Twisted Hand's camp on Powder River and called for an immediate council with the clan chiefs of the Snake tribes. No time was lost in delivering this summons, for the gaunt horseman was Weasel Lungs, medicine chief of the White Knife dog soldiers and the most powerful medicine man in the Shoshoni nation.

By nightfall riders were packing the message across the Ochoco and Eldahow that Weasel Lungs was alive and requesting a hearing. Within two weeks most of the dignitaries had arrived at Twisted Hand's camp. Those who hadn't were conspicuous by their absence. Noticeable among the latter group were Elk Tongue, popular young war chief of the Bear Killer Snakes, who had ridden with Big Nose in the Sioux campaign and Singing Dog, chief of the Big Lodge and right hand man to Twisted Hand. When it seemed apparent that the gathering was complete, the council began. Twisted Hand's opening statement stunned all present. . . "the Pahkees have a weapon capable of destroying the Shoshoni tribes!" With this dire warning hanging over the council grounds like a halo of gunsmoke, he motioned Weasel Lungs to tell what had happened. This was his story.[76]

The summer of 1787 was fast fading into eternity when a small band of Big Lodge warriors worked some 200 ponies down the eastern face of the Flathead Mountains and came to rest on the south shore of Horse Lake. The women set up camp while the men watered the jaded livestock. It was rumored that Sticky Mouth, chief of the Piegon Blackfeet was encamped some eighty miles to the east on the Milk River.

Two suns later Weasel Lungs, Elk Tongue, Singing Dog, the Umatilla boy and twelve warriors moved cautiously into Canadian territory in search of the Piegon camp. Each of these men rode with a specific purpose in mind. Because of a strange disease, which mysteriously appeared seven summers in the past and which flared up periodically, killing Shoshoni by the dozens, Weasel Lungs joined the traders to

---

[76] As remembered by Tom Ochiho, direct descendant of Weasel Lungs.

negotiate a professional exchange of herbs, remedies and visions with Sauk'am-appee (Young Man), an aged Piegon medicine man who was thought to be travelling with Sticky Mouth. He had taken the Umatilla boy along to learn the fine art of horse trading. Singing Dog had ridden along to add dignity to the procession. Elk Tongue was there for the obvious reason that if something should go astray they had a war leader. The Big Lodge warriors rode solely to reap a nice profit on the horses Old Bull had talked them into stealing from the Dog Eaters. For most of these men it would be their last day on earth.

Some 2,000 miles to the east the Northwest Ordinance—which set the pattern for the creation of new American states by encouraging mass settlement of the Ohio Valley and causing further encroachment on Indian lands—was passed by Congress. Meanwhile, a diverse body of elder statesmen gathered at Philadelphia to draft a Constitution for the United States of America. As these gentlemen argued, the Big Lodge warriors arrived at Sticky Mouth's camp where everything seemed to go wrong.

The Blackfeet were acting very strangely. Many were seeing visions, talking to the spirit world and walking erratically. For those dog soldiers who had ridden with Big Nose and Twisted Hand on the Mexican front, the Blackfeet appeared to be acting the same as the Apache, who induced spiritual visitations by chewing peyote buttons from the mescal cactus. It made them very nervous. Adding to the tension, Elk Tongue traded ten horses for a Nez Perce slave woman only to grant her freedom, thus evoking the ire of their hosts. Whether Elk Tongue acted by design or accident made small difference. Sticky Mouth was convinced that the Snake war chief had singled him out for insult by accepting nothing in return for the horses.

A short time later Weasel Lungs lost his temper. He had imparted valid information to Young Man on symptoms and cures for the unexplained sickness that was raging across their hunting grounds only to receive an incoherent tale about a vision-producing liquid and glorious new weapons now in the hands of the Blackfeet. It had been given to them by their new-found allies, the "white men." However, Young Man made no effort to back up this claim by showing Weasel Lungs the spirit juice or one of the super arrows.

To further complicate matters Old Bull had accepted the favors of a Blackfoot girl only to find out she was promised to a white man, the man the Blackfeet had met two months earlier on the Saskatchewan River and whom they called Koo' koo-sint, the Man Who Watches Stars.

As a climax to an imperfect day the Umatilla boy counted coup on a Piegon brave in an argument over the price of a horse. Partly because it was a fair fight but largely due to Weasel Lung's reputation as a dangerous medicine man the Snakes were allowed to leave Sticky Mouth's camp in peace, although they rode out under strained relations. A few miles west of the Piegon camp the Snakes were congratulating themselves on their good fortune when thunder rent the air. Weasel Lung's horse collapsed like a Paiute tipi with a gaping hole in his side. In the terrifying seconds which followed Elk Tongue's head disintegrated like a rotten tree stump; the Nez Perce woman was thrown to the ground, her life snuffed out under the slashing hooves of her frenzied mount; Singing Dog's stomach opened like a lanced buffalo's paunch; Old Bull hung over his horse's neck like a freshly cased rabbit skin; and the remainder of the Big Lodge traders scattered like a covey of quail.

Umatilla Boy wheeled his mount toward the fallen Weasel Lungs and the latter watched in shock as Umatilla Boy's right leg turned backward at the knee and flopped like a weed in a hail storm. Scooping up the medicine chief, Umatilla Boy promptly fainted. Weasel Lungs, now thoroughly terrified, clasped the boy in his arms as he headed toward the Big Lodge camp at Horse Lake.

Upon arrival he found a nightmare. Men, women and children murdered; butchered dogs hanging from tree limbs; lodges put to the torch. In a strained voice Weasel Lungs told the assembled Shoshoni that he firmly believed that the Piegons had gained awesome strength from some potion brewed by the white men and that they possessed firearms vastly superior to the rusty flintlocks some of the dog soldiers were packing.

As evidence to this terrible carnage Weasel Lungs beckoned and Umatilla Boy limped into the council tent. There was no doubt in anyone's mind that his leg showed recent scars of having been nearly severed at the knee. The fact that he had any leg at all was proof that Weasel Lungs was still the most gifted healer in the Shoshoni nation.

The clan chiefs had witnessed too many strange things brought about by the European tribes to disbelieve Weasel Lungs. They were also quick to agree that this unprecedented Blackfoot attack on Snake women and children could not go unpunished. Messengers were dispatched to muster the faithful away from the traitorous Ute camps of Maimed Hand and the failing Comanche leadership of Painted Man. All loyal Shoshoni were to join with Twisted Hand on the Green River from whence on the first spring winds they would again scourge the Oyer'un-gun from the Cascades to the Big Horns and from the Yellowstone to the Colorado before the balance of power could change hands.

It was well known among the clan chiefs that dissension within the Shoshoni ranks could cause major problems. An overwhelming major-ity of the tribesmen were following the teachings of the pacifist vision-ary Wuna Mucca, and this movement was gathering strength daily, threatening the authority of the Shoshoni hierarchy. To the rank and file, softened by decades of easy living, protected from the realities of war and Europeans by the far-ranging dog soldiers, this latest warning of a Blackfoot invasion, backed by thunder clubs and men the color of snow, threw them into mirthful hysteria. It never occurred to them that Weasel Lungs might be telling the truth.

At the same time Weasel Lungs was holding council in the Ochoco, David Thompson fought his way against the icy blast of winter and slipped into the lodge of the Blackfoot medicine chief, Young Man. Sweet Grass was waiting. For the next few days they shared buffalo robes, where Sweet Grass did an excellent job of thawing out Man Who Watches Stars. This cozy flirtation was interrupted by the untimely arrival of Young Man. But the wrinkled medicine man was all smiles. He assured Thompson that the .75 calibre muskets the Piegons had received from the Hudson's Bay Company were ample payment for this interlude with his granddaughter.[77]

A few weeks after Thompson's meeting with the Blackfeet, families and friends of the warriors who chose to ride with Twisted Hand gathered for the blessing of their sacred bundles and the ceremony of the paint. This ceremony, held prior to departure of a war-party, was the big moment in a brave's life. The main purpose for marking his face

---

[77] For a full account of the arms agreement see Thompson, *Narrative*, Part I, Chapter XXII; Hodge, *Handbook of American Indians*, Part II, p. 556. A vivid description of the effects on the Shoshoni is given in Irving, *Astoria*, pp. 225-26. The North West Company shared in later guilt when they armed other Pacific Northwest tribes for the purpose of shooting Hudson's Bay Company employees.

was to gain the favor of the Great Spirit, showing him by these visible signs that the warrior had reason to seek revenge. Second, it would serve to discourage the enemy by showing the fury and intent with which he was going into battle.

To show that he intended to avenge the death of a family member the Shoshoni would paint a red or white stripe across his upper cheek-bone and over the bridge of his nose. White signifing his father, red a brother and the number of red stripes telling how many had been lost in former battle. Yellow stripes for a wife and white ones for a sister running from the eye to the jawbone meant the enemy had captured a woman dear to this brave's heart and that he was out to get her back or die in the attempt.

A tribesman who had lost many ponies would paint various stripes converging on his nose. Each pony's color would be represented on a stripe, letting one and all know that he would get them back. A red nose and yellow bars on the chin said that another tribe was trespassing on private ground, spoiling the hunting, and that this was soon coming to a bloody halt! All these various facial markings would be represented by the warriors joining Twisted Hand's command.

As an extra added precaution Shoshoni mothers, sisters, wives and sweethearts joined in this ritual by softly echoing the chilling war cry in their warrior's ears. It was their belief that by repeating this call to the braves before they went into battle it would make their hearts strong and their hands steady in winning victories and bringing home many scalps. Women of other Pacific Northwest tribes were never known to give the war whoop at any time. The Shoshoni war cry can best be described as sounding like a screeching "whoooo-whoooo-yaaaaaah," showing a marked resemblance to the battle cry of the plain's tribes.[78]

---

[78] With the exception of the Shoshoni, the war whoop of all north Pacific tribes sounded like "innnnnngha." Chiefs Allan Patawa, Umatilla; Max Quinn, Warm Springs; Tommy Thompson, Wasco; William Yallup, Yakima; and Warm Springs Charley, second in command of the Indian scouts who assisted in the capture of the Modocs in 1873, when asked by Robert Hendricks if this was the cry of all Northwest tribes, answered "yes." The Arapahoe used "whooo whooo"; the Sioux and all other plains Indians including the Blackfeet, "whoooo yaaaah"; Cheyenne and Apaches, "ouuuuie-ing-ing-ing" (Hendricks.)

Now the Shoshoni were ready for combat. They held no rancor that two-thirds of the population, acting like over-protected children, refused to join them. In glory they rode out of the Ochoco, bound for the southern Rockies and a reunion with the Ute and Comanche dog soldiers. By the white man's calendar it was May, 1788. Sixteen devastating summers would pass before those who did return again saw their ancient homeland, the Ochoco.

CHAPTER 11

PAY THE BILL

*Those who would give up
essential liberty to purchase a
little temporary safety deserve
neither liberty nor safety.*

Benjamin Franklin
American Statesman

By 1790 the population of the United States had swelled to nearly four million. The British, French, Russian and Spanish colonies could easily account for that many more. For the Shoshoni it was a different story. Individual families, small hunting parties and patrols were disappearing never to be seen again. It was as though the earth had swallowed them. More frightening, scores of tribesmen, covered with pustular sores, were dying in feverish, vomiting agony. A mystery to the Shoshoni, it was known to the French traders as the dreaded variola.

Whatever it may have been, it was making the Shoshoni very uneasy. Even the renowned Giver of Spiritual Gifts had no reasonable explanation. The great majority still refused to believe Weasel Lungs that it was the Blackfeet, working through Young Man. There was no tangible evidence that the Blackfeet or any neighboring nation for that matter were responsible. The only thing certain was that the Shoshoni were having trouble. The spirit world was on the loose and had singled out the Snakes for harassment.

While the Shoshoni were beset by confusion, Spain and Great Britain became embroiled over who held rights to Oregon country. The outcome was the signing of the Nootka Convention Treaty of October 28, 1790, which among other things allowed both nations to fish the Pacific coastal waters and carry on commerce with the natives without intervention from the other. Then on May 11, 1792, three centuries after the Spanish discovered North America, a daring American naval officer discovered the long-sought river of the west.

In defiance of the Chinook sea gods Captain Robert Gray sailed his merchant vessel over the treacherous Columbia bar, proving the river's actual existence. Cruising upstream for a distance of ten miles, Gray and the crew of the 220 ton *S.S. Columbia Redivivia* became the first recorded white men to see interior Oregon. But, as Gabreil Franchere, one of the Astorians, later observed... "it is certain that long before the voyage of Captains Gray and Vancouver they (the Spanish) knew at least a part of the course of that (the Columbia) river which was designated in their maps under the name of Oregon."[79] Captain Gray not only made friendly contact with Concomly's subjects but his sailors eagerly shared such wondrous white man's gifts as syphilis and gonorrhea with the Chinook ladies. Within the year the Chinooks were generously transmitting this favor to the mid-Columbian tribes. The seeds of destruction were now planted for all Oregon Indians.

American politicians viewed the discovery of the Columbia (named for the ship of discovery) as giving the United States first claim to Oregon. Since Mexican traders had navigated the river at the close of the 1600's, Spain thought otherwise. As the Americans were touting their premise, Spain and Great Britain reacted. Gray had barely cleared the Columbia when Don Fidalgo planted the Spanish banner on the Washington mainland and established the first European settlement in Oregon country on lands of the Makoh in 1792.[80] One year later an employee of the Northwest Fur Company, Sir Alexander Mackenzie, on his second attempt crossed the Canadian Rockies and reached the Pacific Ocean just north of Vancouver Island on July 20, 1793. He was the first white man to span the North American continent.

---

[79] Taken from the French Edition of Franchere's *Voyage to the North West Coast*, p. 113, published in Montreal, Canada in 1819 with English translations in 1854.

[80] This settlement was at the entrance of the Straits of Juan de Fuca at Cape Flattery. The straits were discovered by Apostalos Valerianos, a Greek ship's pilot employed by the Spaniards in 1592. Some historians claim that Don Fidalgo didn't arrive on the Washington coast until 1799. (*United States House Report No. 976*, 25th Congress, 3rd session.)

As early as 1745 the British Parliament offered a prize of twenty thousand pounds to any private navigator who would sail his vessel through a Northwest Passage into Hudson's Bay. The offer did not include a land discovery. In 1776 the act was amended to include any ship of the royal navy. Mackenzie's overland trek brought an end to the search for a passage to the western sea.[81]

In 1796, while the Chinooks, now as bewildered as the Shoshoni, puzzled over their dwindling numbers who were slowly rotting away;[82] and the United States government was excited over the first road grant of public lands for construction and maintenance of a wagon trail later known as Zane's Trace, the Snakes celebrated the birth of another daughter to Weasel Lungs. This baby girl would one day become the mother of the last great war chief of the Shoshoni nation. It was also rumored that his eldest daughter, Lost Woman, now approaching seventeen, was to become the bride of Crooked Leg.

Eight years had passed since Twisted Hand had taken to the field. Splitting into small units, the dog soldiers had ranged from the Gulf of California to the Arkansas River in an unsuccessful attempt to negotiate an arms trade with the Spaniards. Next, they took to the Great Plains, plundering the Sioux and what few white traders wandered into Indian territory, but the few arms they obtained were not sufficient to mount an effective campaign against the Blackfeet. Because of this they were at a decided disadvantage in their foray into the Canadian Rockies.

When riding into battle the dog soldiers used no "horse furniture" as the historian Bancroft so quaintly put it except for a small pad girthed on with a leather thong. One trick of horsemanship, which few white men were able to master, was the spectacular stunt of swinging over the

---

[81] *The Public Records Office, Colonials Office,* Case 323, Vol. 18, P. 327, London, England.

[82] The Europeans introduced diseases against which the Indians had no racial immunity. The ravages of smallpox, measles and venereal disease between 1789 and 1880 nearly wiped out some Indian groups in the old Oregon country. For example, the lower Columbia Chinooks numbering 22,000 in 1790 were reduced to a population of 2000 by 1830. (John W. Collins, "The Opening and Development of the Region," *Atlas of the Pacific Northwest,* p. 5; and "Indian Distribution in Oregon," *Atlas of Oregon,* p. 6.)

off-side of a mount in battle and using the horse's body as a shield. By hooking a leg over the horse's back and hanging in a rope plaited into his mane the Shoshoni had both hands free to operate bow or rifle or to pick up a wounded comrade.

The Shoshoni was utterly fearless, and there was absolutely no fun in a fight unless he could ride in close, elude the weapons of his enemy and chop him down with a heavy war club or skewer him on the end of a short battle lance. This was known as "counting coup" and the scalp went to the man who first struck the vanquished with a hand weapon. The main object of the Shoshoni in making war was to set the enemy afoot. This done, his destruction was rendered more easy if not certain. Also, ponies were the wealth of the conqueror; therefore, in dividing the spoils, each man claimed the animals first struck by his coup stick.

The bow and arrow was a weapon used primarily for the hunt and not as an instrument of war. The bows, made of seasoned juniper, varied in length from the mighty six-foot long bow to the tiny two and half foot short bow. Strangely enough, the short bow—dear to all warrior's hearts as the deadly "Awata" or medicine bow—became the ill-famed war bow. In battle this weapon was stoutly backed by the equally notorious war-club, a lethal bludgeon measuring two feet from tip to tip and supporting not less than a three pound stone axe head. To ensure that this weapon did not desert its owner in time of stress it was attached to the wrist by a leather thong.

In their early days the dog soldiers fought hand-to-hand, having nothing to outrange a lance or club in getting to an enemy. With the advent of firearms they still preferred this type of close combat. As opposed to the white man's concept of pitched battles carried out by massive armies, the Shoshoni's idea of warfare was conducted by small, highly efficient raiding parties depending upon the element of surprise. Raiders struck from the Pacific Coast to the Missouri River; from the Selkirk Mountains to the Sierra Madre. Any given raiding party could and most often did strike targets a thousand or more miles apart in a matter of months. In the 1860's the Snake raider, Paulina, in a span of 29 days struck Oregon settlements in a sweeping arc covering some 750 miles.

This is the way Twisted Hand's cavalry was now riding on the heavily armed Blackfeet. Occasionally, they met with families on the hunt but, more often, they were hundreds of miles from the main bands in their efforts to hold the Blackfeet and other intruders out of the Oyer'ungun. Meanwhile, the pacifists were being picked off one by one as sickness took its toll. Visitors to the coast brought syphilis and gonorrhea inland. Still others brought cholera and measles from the Spanish missions to the south. Disease, not the gun, was devastating the most war-like Indian tribe west of the Mississippi with hellish thoroughness.

CHAPTER 12

WUNA MUCCA'S VISION

Then suddenly the angry wind is loose
The storm king throws his flaming spear;
And, as the mighty drums of thunder roll,
The heavens weep torrential tears.

Milly Walton

By the end of 1794 the last of the British troops—holdovers from the Revolutionary War—had been evacuated from the few remaining western outposts in the Northwest territory. A new frontier was ready for American settlement and by 1800 the population of the United States exceeded five million.

With the war chiefs spread to the four winds Wuna Mucca—the Paiute visionary—was now in control of the Shoshoni homeland. The clan chiefs were little more than figureheads. Daily, The Giver performed feats of mystery, confirming his spiritual powers. This was not uncommon for shamans. Earlier, according to Shoshoni legend, Weasel Lungs, searching for spiritual power, went alone to the top of Lookout Mountain. Here he received the talon of an eagle for power above earth; the claw of a bear for power on earth; and the claw of a badger for power below earth. Another legend speaks of a man who during his vision quest learned a new way of making fire. Instead of rotating a wooden drill to create friction he showed the Shoshoni how to strike a spark from a stone.

It was never doubted by the rank and file that The Giver was in direct communication with the Great Spirit. This concept should be easy for Christians to understand, since it involves the conviction that the human soul can communicate with God and derive guidance from that contact. The Shoshoni considered those things which were revealed to Wuna Mucca in dreams and visions to be sent from the Man Above.

In 1798 Wuna Mucca was seized with a vision that would cause confusion and bewilderment among his disciples for years to come. Most of his current following was within the ranks of the downtrodden Earth Eaters, whom the white men ultimately defined as the Northern Paiute. According to his grand-daughter, Sarah Winnemucca Hopkins, this dream was based on an ancient legend that foretold the return of long-lost white brothers of the Earth Eaters.[83] It is believed this event took place northwest of Harney Valley near the headwaters of Twelvemile Creek. According to Paiute information, this revelation was preceded by a violent thunderstorm over the Ochoco Blue Mountains. Lightning-sparked fires rampaged through the forest and, as darkness fell, the sky was split by a fiery object. What happened is best told in the word pictures of the Shoshoni language.

In the early days of August (the Blood Moon) the Bird Eaters (Kuyuidika Paiutes) set up camp at the edge of the pines northwest of Harney Lake (tono wa'ma u'intaw gump). The next morning The Giver of Spiritual Gifts (Wuna Mucca) picked his way across a windswept slope, climbing to high ground. Below him the Kuyuidika lodges wilted in the sultry heat of the Southern Blues, yet a hundred campfires blazed and curling upwards with their grayish smoke came the monotonous roll of the medicine drums. A sickly, sodden beat, it settled upon the pine-studded ridgetops like the tolling of a death knell. Wuna Mucca, now 2000 feet in elevation above the encampment, entered a split in the weathered rim and climbed toward a tall pole driven into the battered mountain top. Upon reaching it, he silently faced the east and then slowly sank to his knees for atop this slender spire, gently swaying in the afternoon breeze, was a white buffalo head. . . the most sacred religious symbol of the Shoshoni nation. A prayer offered in the presence of this powerful totem was certain to receive the attention of Tobats, the Great Spirit and Wuna Mucca was definitely in need of divine guidance, for his people were dying of strange sicknesses which

---

[83] Sarah gave a vivid account of her grandfather's prophecy to General Howard in 1878. He recorded it in his *Famous Indian Chiefs I Have Known*, Chapter XIII. Also see Canfield, *Sarah Winnemucca*, p.4. Perhaps this legend of white brothers is a reference to the Spanish invasion of 1698, exactly a century before Wuna Mucca's vision.

baffled the greatest healers of the Shoshoni tribes. Voicing his appeal through the nerve-wracking intonation of the medicine chant, the tall, thin red man bared his soul to the Mighty Chief Above.

As the pagan ritual increased in tempo, Oyer'ungun became gripped in deathlike stillness. Overhead, towering cumulus clouds—dreaded thunderheads of the Ochoco—stood shoulder to shoulder on a shimmering field of blue, while far below on the sun splotched plateau, clumps of yellow sage awaited the coming onslaught with tired expectancy, their gnarled arms bared for battle. High above the desert floor sighing pines clung to the parched slopes of the Blue Mountains, their heads bowed in acceptance of nature's undeniable will. Within minutes after the medicine man had invoked the aid of the spirit world earth and sky gave vent to strained emotions through the hideous crackle of a dry lightning storm. Thunder rumbled along the knife-edged peaks, its deepthroated moan diminishing like a stifled sob in the pine congested valleys below. Lightning plowed angry furrows across the sky, its searing backlash stabbing viciously at the taunting rimrock plateau. Billowing columns of black smoke interspersed with orange flame leapt from a dozen separated spots. Wind, like the dying breath of a blast furnace, prowled the melancholy sands of the Great Basin, pausing now and then to poke inquisitive fingers into the cross-grained scars which marked the base of the Southern Blues, goading the lightning fires into uncontrollable rage.

This holocaust went unnoticed as the Kuyuidika prophet, absorbed in meditation, ignored the challenge of the elements. Without interruption his prayers climbed the storm-tossed heavens. Then, toward evening, the chanting suddenly stopped. Perspiration streaked his narrow shoulders as the lanky Indian, now outlined in the greenish glow of chain lightning, gave up to a higher power and pitched forward in a deep, unshakable trance. In the electrifying calm which followed Wuna Mucca fulfilled his rendezvous with destiny.

Beneath the grim-lipped mountain the steady throb of medicine drums continued. Darkness approached and with it the thunder faded away toward Crooked River Valley. Only the wind remained to switch back and forth across the heat-drenched prairie. Finding nothing of interest on the lowlands, it crept ever higher up the growling backbone of the inner mountain chain; stalked cautiously along the smoky edge of the relentless timber fires; hesitated as it sensed the cool defiance of

Snow Mountain; then back-tracked to the lonely figure it had passed on the battered crest of Mowich (Deer) Mountain.

Suddenly capricious, the breeze danced along Wuna Mucca's sweat-encrusted brow. Failing in this attempt to arouse the dreamer, it pirouetted to the ground, stirring up dust devils on the feverish earth which cushioned his head. . . coaxing, teasing until the gaunt body jerked erect. Involuntarily, the Indian reached out as though to clasp someone's hand and his voice, soft as eagle's down, uttered words so fantastic that the mountains seemed to quake in terror. Fervently, the holy man repeated his awesome message: "My white brothers, I welcome you. Oyer'ungun is yours!"

Dreadful understanding flooded the Indian's face with disbelief, as the full impact of those words were driven deeply into his mind. Like a soul doomed to hell the prophet cradled his head in trembling arms, while his heart cried out for relief. Haltingly, he raised his eyes to a blood-red sky which ominously transformed to midnight black. His whole body echoed the unspoken question locked on his quivering lips. . . . "Oh, Mighty Chief Above, what does this mean?"

With a terrifying roar a blinding light broke over the Ochoco and a heavenly body, glaring white in its brilliance, split the storm ridden firmament like a celestial war axe as it gouged a fiery path toward the Snake River Plateau. The frightened Paiute sank to his knees, knowing that he had witnessed a miracle.[84]

Packing his sacred bundle, Wuna Mucca trudged dejectedly downward toward the Paiute encampment. The medicine drums stopped in mid-beat as the weary chieftain passed the first circle of lodges. Excited voices greeted his arrival, voices which died in the early morning gloom

---

[84] It is possible that the object from outer space which Wuna Mucca sighted and interpreted as a message from heaven was Encke's Comet, a frequent visitor to earth. If so, it is one of the earliest references to this glowing body from outer space which was first sighted in 1786 and known to have reappeared in the Western Hemisphere in 1798. The German astronomer, Johann Encke placed its orbit of Earth at every 3.3 years. (*The American Educator*, Vol. II, p. 898; *Universal Standard Encyclopedia,* Vol. 5, pp. 1884-5, Vol. 8, p. 2782.) It is also possible that it was a meteorite on a collision course with Earth.

as the smashing blow of the shaman's awesome prophecy shook the entire village.

Gently he spoke, yet his words seemed to reverberate from the Cascade crest to the Wyoming plains. "Someday, my people, a tribe very different from what we know will come to visit us. This tribe will come out of the rising sun. They will be a finer people than any we have ever known, and their faces will be of white color... bright and beautiful as the sun. But do not fear them. In my dream I stretched out my hands to them and knew them as my White Brothers!"[85]

Wuna Mucca's latest revelation was not something he really wanted to know. Equally disturbing, he had been given a sign from the sky as to the reality of his dream. As a shaman he had to accept this vision as the truth. For the common folk it would be a different matter. The Shoshoni were gullible when it came to spiritual influence, but some things are beyond human understanding. Wuna Mucca's vision fell within this category and he knew it. Many of his followers did believe him. Others, specifically the Snakes who had fought in the wars against French, British and Spanish, were not so certain. The only "white brothers" they hadn't met on an equal basis were the newly born Americans. Perhaps they would be different.

Then again, legend passed down through the centuries recalled that far back into the distant past light-skinned warriors marched onto the lands of the Aztecs. Believing these men to be led by the great god, Quetzalcoatl, the people of Aztlan welcomed the divine visitors into heart and home. Overwhelmed by the Aztec's kindness, Quetzalcoatl, known in his native Spain as Hernando Cortez, slaughtered his children for their gold and silver trinkets. Now, the Aztecs were nothing more than grains of sand, drifting across the southern deserts.

The dog soldiers told still another story about Ishaui, a young Snake warrior. Ishaui was a fidgety, unsettled youth who was never satisfied with his lot. One day, while wandering around the forest, he met an old Shoshoni medicine woman, a very powerful figure in the pre-American west. Ishaui was a treacherous lad and, therefore, admired the cougar

---

[85] These are Wuna Mucca's own words as remembered by his granddaughter, Sarah Winnemucca. (See Howard, *Famous Indian Chiefs I Have Known*, pp. 208-09.

who was even more treacherous. He asked the medicine woman to change him into a cougar. The old woman did his bidding and for many weeks Ishaui terrorized the forest—until one day a coyote outwitted him. Back he went to the medicine woman and asked her to turn him into a coyote, because the coyote was even more cunning than the cougar; again she complied with his wish. As a coyote, Ishaui roamed the camps, killing all the dogs, until one fine day he met a snake which slithered from his grasp. Back to the medicine woman he went to become a snake. As a snake he was stung by a wasp and so he changed into a wasp. As a wasp he stung a man who was trying to steal his honey. The stinger, of course, remained in the man's flesh and the wasp died. Ishaui returned to human form as a human spirit must do when living in an animal body. Sadly, he went back to the medicine woman and asked her to make him into an animal more ferocious than a mountain lion, more crafty than a coyote, more loathsome and deceitful than a snake, more vicious than a wasp. So the medicine woman changed Ishaui into a white man!

Wuna Mucca was going to have trouble convincing the Shoshoni that a good tribe of white men were soon to grace their homeland. He did, however, gain one staunch convert. A young Snake boy—who was showing signs of developing into a holy man—became so obsessed with the idea of having a white brother that in a moment of good-natured mockery his friends christened him Tavibo, the White Man; a name he would carry to his deathbed; and a name that would be linked to the bloodiest mass murder of Indians by army personnel in United States history.

Another note of interest: five months before Wuna Mucca ascended Mowich Mountain for his interview with God, a rangy 27-year-old Virginian named John Day drifted into St. Louis. There on March 2, 1798, he petitioned the Spanish governor for "240 arpens of land on a river south of the Missouri." An arpen varied with local measurements between .84 and 1.04 acres and the river mentioned was probably the Osage in Comanche territory. Here, Day farmed 700 arpens until 1803, when the Comanches burned him out.[86] This was just the beginning of

---

[86] "The John Day Country: a Living Memorial," prepared by Connie Johnson,

Day's running battle with the Shoshoni for this "white brother" was also on a collision course with the Ochoco Snakes.

published by *Blue Mountain Eagle*; *The History of Baker, Grant, Malheur and Harney Counties*, published 1902 by the Western Historical Publishing Company.

CHAPTER 13

SUNSET

Success is failure turned inside out—
The silver tint of the clouds of doubt—
And you never can tell how close you are,
It may have been near, when it seemed so far.
So stick to the fight when you are hardest hit—
It's when things seem worst that you mustn't quit.

Author Unknown

Within a year of Wuna Mucca's prophecy word drifted in from the Dakota plains that Glowing Man (Wabasha), the great Santee warrior and medicine man believed to be invincible, had died.[87] This was a bad omen and did little to help the credibility of Wuna Mucca. This same year the Russian-American Fur Company was granted a charter, thus giving a certain degree of stability to the Muscovite operations on the north Pacific coast. Great Britain and the United States, far enough removed from the Oregon country, were unconcerned with this latest Russian strategy. It was a different story with Spain. The suspicious Spaniards were nervously wondering when the Russian bear would descend on California. It would happen sooner than they had anticipated.

Meanwhile, Snake raiders who had been gone for years in the far reaches of the west began straggling back into the Ochoco. One of the returning veterans was Twisted Hand, now being assisted by a rabid Hoonebooey brave in his late teens. Tattered remnants of the once

---

[87] This Sioux chief, an admitted friend of the Hudson's Bay Company, is sometimes referred to as Wapasha (Red Leaf); he was succeeded by his son Wapasha II. (See Hodge, *Handbook of American Indians*, Part II, p. 911.)

glorious dog soldiers who had returned told a chilling tale which explained the disappearance of Shoshoni, and it had nothing to do with the spirit world. Someone was supplying the Blackfeet with guns and ammunition. The Comanches, bogged down in heavy fighting with the Spanish and Apaches, could not cover their own needs for firearms let alone supply the Snakes. The Utes, led by the corrupt Mano Mocka and ripped from within by political strife, refused to help.

Protected by the far-ranging dog soldiers, easy living within the rank and file was now reaping its reward. The split-offs into small family groups and the blatant disregard for authority had caught up with the Shoshoni. The horse rustlers to the north were getting stronger and British military weapons were quickly closing the gap in supremacy. By 1802 the plans set into motion by Hudson's Bay Company twenty five years earlier were coagulating to bring destruction to the super power of western America.

In a two year period beginning in 1800 Hudson's Bay—and to a lesser extent the North West Company—plied the Blackfeet with 195,000 gallons of whiskey.[88] Thus primed, the once reluctant Blackfeet, now goaded into savage fury by the Hudson's Bay Company, took to the vengeance trail. Riding with them was that sallow horseman of the apocalypse. . . pestilence.

Before the Blackfoot cavalry broke free of the northern Rockies, smallpox struck in the lodges of the Omaha. One of the first to die was the tough Omaha war chief, Wasingu Saba—Black Bird. Holding no awe of the Snake dog soldiers, the epidemic quickly spread to the camps of the Shoshoni. Those who didn't die from small-pox were dispatched by the avenging Bloods. Their intent was to destroy and as every person, old or young, was a part of the present or future strength of the Shoshoni, neither age nor sex was spared. No noncombatants were recognized and mutilation of the dead became common practice. The destruction was complete as 1802 went down in Shoshoni folklore as the most devastating year in tribal history.

Hundreds of Shoshoni would never return to the Ochoco. Of those who did many would remain cripples for the rest of their lives. Their

---

[88] See Winther, *Great Northwest*, p. 35.

loss of supremacy was a dramatic change in the west. It was completely unknown to the advancing Americans, and the British perpetrators were not about to reveal it. In fact they were spreading tales that the Inland Horsemen were healthy, ready and willing to annihilate all comers, while priming their new allies to lay waste to any Americans fool-hardy enough to breach the Pacific slope. During this propaganda exchange between Canada and the United States, the Snakes and Flatheads in mutual desperation formed an alliance that would last for years.

By mid-winter of 1803—the year the Jefferson administration acquired more than 500 million acres of Indian lands west of the Mississippi from France for less than three cents an acre—a tragic number of Shoshoni women and children taken in battle were being sold in the Missouri slave markets to the highest bidders from the Sioux, Gros Ventres and Minnatree nations. With the arrival of spring the Blackfeet, backed by gun powder and rot-gut whiskey, continued their raids of pillage and death. The Ikumwhhahtsi (meaning All Comrades and the Blackfoot equivalent to the Snake dog soldiers) charged recklessly across the Snake River country, leaving burned lodges and charred bodies in their wake as they completed the rape of Oyer'ungun.[89] Showing no mercy, they drove the Snakes into the wildest and most desolate recesses of the Blue and Seven Devil Mountains. Simultaneously, the Spanish launched an attack on the south and within months Utes and Comanches were being sold in Mexico City, where a teenage Shoshoni boy in good physical condition brought as high as $100 in Spanish silver; a girl, if she were so unfortunate as to possess good breeding qualities, would command the unheard of price of $200 in Aztec gold.

By 1804 the arrogant Blackfeet were riding boldly across Shoshoni hunting grounds, demoralizing the weaker clans and plundering at will. Whole segments of the Shoshoni nation reverted into pitiful, half-starved groups so timid that they often hid from each other. These vanquished souls became Earth Eaters, never again to recover. A government official traveling through Nevada and Utah reported in 1858

---

[89] The "All Comrades" were a Blackfoot military and fraternal organization consisting of at least twelve orders or societies, most of which were extinct by 1890. (Hodge, *Handbook of American Indians*, Part II, p. 571.)

that he had visited a small tribe called "Go-sha-utes." "They are," he said, "without exception the most miserable looking set of human beings I ever beheld."[90]

The once mighty Shoshoni were split to the backbone and bleeding like a lanced buffalo. In a state of shock those who would not admit defeat pulled back into the protective shoulder of the southern Blues to lick their wounds. Here, rallied under Twisted Hand, now in his early forties, and the war-chief Red Wolf, they could think of nothing but revenge.

This same year Umatilla Boy, who had taken a .75 calibre ball in the leg, nearly severing it at the knee, changed his name to Crooked Leg. Son-in-law of Weasel Lungs, his wife, Lost Woman, presented him with a son. The proud mother named her baby Smells of Sugar. As a teenager this boy would change his name to Shoots the Buffalo Running. Because of his penchant for high-stakes gambling, which involved shaking a gourd filled with pebbles (something like dice), his friends renamed him Gourd Rattler. The Americans would know him as Washakie.[91]

Heralding Washakie's birth, Wuna Mucca's "white brothers" were on the move. By now the Giver of Spiritual Gifts was held in very little esteem by the Shoshonean clans and his popularity dropped to absolute zero when in the summer of 1805 came whisperings of a white expedition; murmurings which spread across the western mountains like wildfire, that a party of white men were pushing up the Missouri River bound ever closer to the Shoshoni hunting grounds. Known to the United States as the Corps of Discovery, this group was intercepted by Wuna Mucca on the Lemhi River. Here he discovered they were being guided through this part of the Eldahow by Pikeek Queenah, Swooping Eagle, who in the past had been one of the glorified dog soldiers of the Shoshoni nation. Swooping Eagle—named by his American employers and known to history as Tobe—was leading the Lewis and Clark

---

[90] This was Jacob Forney, Superintendent of Indian Affairs for Utah. (Hodge, *Handbook of American Indians*, Part I, pp. 494-95.)

[91] Unbelievable as it may seem, some historians claim this baby was half white. For more on Washakie, see Hodge, *Handbook of American Indians*, Part II, pp. 919-20.

Expedition to the Columbia River along the age-old Banatee Snake route now held by the Blackfeet.

Wuna Mucca felt that in the Blackfeet's present state of mind this was not the trail to send a party of white men on, and he believed that Swooping Eagle was plotting their death. Because of this, he offered to lead the white brothers to the Columbia over the ancient Shoshoni Trail through the Ochoco. Swooping Eagle, knowing the low esteem held for Wuna Mucca, was equally certain that the prophet was planning to redeem his lost prestige by luring the Americans into Twisted Hand's trap. He told not only of the hostile war tribes but also of the many other dangers to come if the white men should be so foolish as to follow the Gift Giver.[92]

In typical Shoshoni fashion Swooping Eagle painted a vivid word picture of the waiting Kim'ooenim Tuwiwa Gaiya (Snake River Plateau), the treacherous crossing of the Pohoi Tuwiwa Gaiya (the High Desert of Eastern Oregon), the back-breaking journey into the headwaters of the Paga Tubic (Crooked River) and, finally, the awesome descent over the ruptured rims of the Towahnokiooks (Deschutes River).

> . . . you will have to traverse a land of crashing waterfalls, boiling infernos, yawning chasm and deep gorges. You must cross areas of black desolation where there are caves deep within the earth and wild rivers that plunge into crevices and disappear never to be seen again. It is a land of horrors. If you go that way, you will have to climb sheer mountains of solid rocks. You will come to a nation of savage redmen who wear moccasins which always have holes in them because of the knife-edged rocks upon which they must constantly walk. Your horses will soon have raw and bleeding hooves. You will come to a waterless desert where the only moisture is a little rain caught in stone basins in the spring of the year. Then you will come to another nation of redmen. . . bad people who are expert horsemen and born killers. Here you will find a waterway to the western sea.

---

[92] Lewis and Clark were told that "Snakes lived in large numbers" on the Deschutes River. (Thwaites, *Original Journals of Lewis and Clark*, Vol. 3: 147-149.)

Being an ex-dog soldier, one would suspect that Swooping Eagle—although his information about the land ahead was accurate, knew that his comrades were in a very weakened condition and was trying to prevent the Corps of Discovery from seeing them. Whatever his motive, after such a description the Americans had no desire to attempt Wuna Mucca's route. Even when the medicine man assured them that if he and Grass Woman, now the wife of a white man, were leading the group no harm would befall them while crossing Snake hunting grounds it was not enough. Clark, who had done some erratic exploring to the south, did not believe that there were any rivers in that direction flowing to the western sea. He was wrong. On August 27, 1805, the dejected Wuna Mucca sadly watched as the Americans turned north into the Bitter Root Range.[93]

Prior to Wunna Mucca's interception of the Lewis and Clark Expedition, word drifted into Twisted Hand's camp that the Spaniards, stirred by some new force, were ripping across Ute territory, headed toward the Eldahow. Scraping together a fighting force, Red Wolf rode to intercept. The Utes, now in rebellion against the puppet government of Maimed Hand, supplied Red Wolf with more troops and badly needed firearms.

A year earlier on the insistence of Aaron Burr, President Jefferson had appointed General James Wilkinson civil governor and military commandant of the newly acquired Louisiana Territory. Acting as a double agent, Wilkinson informed the Spanish of Jefferson's plan to send an American expedition into the Louisiana country with intent to cross the Rockies to the Pacific Coast. Spain, anxious to keep the Americans out of Oregon country at any cost, had no intention of letting

---

[93] It is recorded that Clark consulted a visiting Shoshoni from "the Duck Valley country which lies somewhere in Oregon country—possibly between the forks of the Owyhee River." This Indian related the hardships which the party would encounter endeavoring to reach the Pacific by Tobe's (Swooping Eagle) route which swung them almost 200 miles north of the main line of travel. (*Idaho Yesterdays*, Vol. II, No. 2, 1958, pp. 12-13). Devoto, in his *Journals of Lewis and Clark,* pp. 210-12, has Lewis instead of Clark conferring with Wuna Mucca. The error comes from a very confusing, misleading arrangement of the *Journals* by Thwaites 2: 379-382 with the correction indicated obscurely in a footnote.

this happen. Lewis and Clark were apparently unaware that they were the target of international intrigue.

As a result, four military expeditions were sent out of Santa Fe by Spain to "arrest Capt. Merry and his followers and seize their papers and instruments."[94] Each attempt failed to get through.

Crossing the tracks of Zebulon Pike on his push to the Colorado Rockies, Red Wolf's raiders inadvertently ensured the success of the American Corps of Discovery when they blockaded the Spanish strike force. At the same time one of their kinsmen, Boi'naiv, the Grass Woman, was guiding the Lewis and Clark Expedition ever closer to the Pacific coast. Because of her they were the first white men to see the Snake River in whose murky waters swam fish twelve feet long. North of the Ochoco they saw large deer, which Lewis named "mule deer" and on the lower Columbia below Celilo Falls they saw sea otter described as being the size "of a mastive dog."

But Wilkinson's spies were apparently seeing more astonishing things. In December, 1805, General Wilkinson wrote a curious letter to President Jefferson in which he spoke casually of natural wonders in what is now Yellowstone Park, an area not even discovered until years later. He also hinted at financing an expedition to establish a post on the upper Missouri to exploit the resources. This strange letter was written a year before Lewis and Clark returned to civilization at a time when the expedition was believed lost!

At the time of this letter, Boi'naiv had just gotten the Corps of Discovery to the Pacific Coast. Few will recognize Boi'naiv, the Grass woman (a Saidyuka princess) by her Shoshoni name, but as Sacajawea, the Bird Woman, this intrepid Snake maiden changed the history of two nations when she guided the Lewis and Clark expedition into the Oregon country.[95]

To the memory of this gallant woman a bronze statue was erected in the Portland, Oregon City Park in 1905. Other monuments com-

---

[94] From a letter to Nemesis Salcedo from Casa Calvo, New Orleans, March 5, 1804. (Quoted in Cook's, *Flood Tide of Empire*, p. 455.)

[95] This mission, which suffered but one casualty during the entire journey, reached the Pacific Ocean on November 8, 1805, and set up winter camp north of Seaside, Oregon.

memorating her assistance to the advancement of white civilization are located in Montana, Wyoming and North Dakota.

Part II
THE GATHERING STORM

THE GATHERING STORM
(THE FUR TRADE ERA AND QUEST FOR EMPIRE)

Beyond there, in the trees, say can you see
If the Dark Angel walks? Or does this night
Primeval shroud another mystery—
The gulf eternal 'twixt red men and white?

Owen Wister
Western author

The young explorers, Meriwether Lewis and William Clark, with their 30-man Corps of Discovery changed the course of history. Now, tough British traders like David Thompson, Finan McDonald and Peter Ogden—after some botched and bloody forays with the Snakes— would send their brigades deep into Shoshoni country to turn fur trading into a cut-throat business. Soon grizzled American mountain men like John Day, Jim Bridger and Moses Harris would fill in the gaps on the western map in their eternal quest for beaver. Still others, outspoken visionaries like John Jacob Astor, Marcus Whitman and Joseph Lafayette Meek would extol Oregon as the fulfillment to a new nation's dream in an effort to lure civilization into the wilderness. And now, gaunt dog soldiers like Crooked Leg, The Horse and Red Wolf, their hunting grounds dwindling with each passing year, would be recognized by the advancing column.

It is the white man that has brought our troubles upon us. If he
had stayed in his own country, there would be no whiskey to
influence the passions of our young men, and the chiefs would
have retained their power. Take away the white man and give
us back our roots and fish and game, then we will be content.

Howlish Wampo
Umatilla Clan Chief

Companies Vying For Control of the Northwest Fur Trade
1600's - 1800's

COMPANY	PARTNERS	BASE	EST.
Hudson's Bay Company	British nobles & businessmen; leader: Lord Selkirk	Quebec	1670
North West Company	Previously independent English/Canadian trappers that banded together: Simon McTavish, Benjamin & Joseph Frobisher, Peter Pond, Alexander Mackenzie, David Thompson, Simon Fraser	Montreal	1775
Russian-American Fur Company	Georgi Sheilkov and Count Alexander Baranov, with the backing of the Russian government	Sitka, Alaska	1796
XY Company	Alexander Mackenzie		split off from NW Co. in 1796
Missouri Fur Company	Manuel Lisa, William Morrison, Pierre Menard, William Clark, Reuben Lewis, Andrew Henry, Pierre Chauteau	St. Louis, Missouri	1807
American Fur Company (South West Company)	John Jacob Astor	Fort Mackinac, Michigan	1809
Pacific Fur Company	John Jacob Astor, Alexander McKay, Donald McKenzie, Duncan McDougal, Wilson Hunt, David Stewart, Robert McLellan, John Clarke		1810
Rocky Mountain Fur	William Ashely, Andrew Henry	St. Louis, Missouri	1821

CHAPTER 14

A CARTEL OF ROGUES

Hell, there ain't no rules here!
We're tryin' to accomplish somethin'!

Thomas Edison
American Inventor

Less than 43 years after Great Britain gained control of the fur market an American expedition—traveling under the protection of a Shoshoni slave and only vaguely aware of the pelt industry—linked the Appalachian Trail to the Cascade Crest, and on its return to civilization the fur lords of the world geared for battle.

Because of Shoshoni interference half a continent of furs had been left untapped. For over 200 years the fur trade had been the only source of revenue of the American wilderness. As early as 1600 French traders paddled log canoes into the interior, where they built trading posts and collected furs. These pioneers of the North American fur industry controlled the market for 163 years. In the rich pelteries of the Mississippi Valley and Saskatchewan Plains they had found a source of wealth to rival the Spanish mines of Mexico and Peru. Then, the tri-color of France gave way to the Cross of St. George and Great Britain inherited this profitable commerce, exploiting it through two great Canadian monopolies: the Hudson's Bay Company, based at Quebec and glorying in the special patronage of the British Crown and the North West Company, based at Montreal, whose daring traders opened the Canadian West. By 1787 these companies were engaged in a violent struggle for supremacy of the North American fur trade.

The Hudson's Bay Company, organized by British nobles and business men in 1670, ruled Canada by the granted authority of King Charles II. Company officials had the exclusive right to "trade and commerce in all the waters and countries of Canada" and furthermore, Hudson's Bay could "make rules and govern according to the laws of

Great Britain." Even the British navy and army were at their command and by 1800, Lord Selkirk, leader of the Hudson's Bay Company, exercised this authority with vengeance. Not until 1869 did the company cede this right to the civil government of Canada.

The North West Company was organized on an informal basis in 1775 by powerful fur interests in the St. Lawrence Valley. In contrast to Hudson's Bay the North West Company was created as a partnership of twenty-three independent fur traders who had been carrying on their trading in defiance of the Hudson's Bay Company and in fierce competition among themselves. By 1788 North West was operating at full force, driven by the vicious and uncompromising Simon McTavish. Included in the organization were such well known men as Benjamin and Joseph Frobisher, Peter Pond, Alexander Mackenzie, David Thompson and Simon Fraser. Operating individually, these traders in an effort to get furs away from Hudson's Bay had been offering higher and higher prices to the Indians for pelts, which lowered profits to the independent merchants. Some began selling liquor to the natives and encouraged them to make war on competing traders. By organizing their own company they hoped to put a stop to such practices. The result was that while competition among the formerly independent traders ended, the new rivalry between North West and Hudson's Bay became a brutal one.

Within a short span of time armed conflict broke out between the two companies, including disruption within North West's own ranks. Following a bitter flair up with McTavish, Mackenzie broke away from North West in 1796 and formed the rival XY Company. He then contested McTavish for the fur empire of western Canada, seizing control in northern British Columbia where he then jammed northward to the Russian outposts in Alaska. Luckily for both Indians and whites, Simon McTavish died in 1804 and relations were not quite so strained between North West, Hudson's Bay and the XY Company.

Meanwhile, on the bleak northwest tip of the North American continent, separated only by a mountain range from the warring British companies, another cut-throat organization was in the making. For years Georgi Sheilkov, who planted the first Russian colony on Kodiak Island in 1780, had dreamed of a vast fur trading empire similar to that of Hudson's Bay. To accomplish this he needed new territory to conquer and a strong, resourceful leader to carry out his orders. Sheilkov found his man in Count Alexander Andreivich Baranov, cold, calculating trader from the frozen plains of Siberia. In 1789 Sheilkov and Baranov organized the powerful Russian-American Fur Company, based at Sitka, Alaska. To protect their interests in North America the Russian government incorporated Russian-American Fur in 1799, giving the company exclusive rights to expand operations on the Pacific Coast. To ensure success, imperial Russia advanced Sheilkov and Baranov $1,265,000 (260,000 pounds sterling) for operating capital.[96] They were now looking south to the Columbia country for more conquests.

The newly organized American Fur Company was also entering the scene. Based at Fort Mackinac on Lake Michigan, it was controlled by the New York industrial giant, John Jacob Astor. Prior to the formation of this company the people of the United States and the colonies before them had profited little, if at all, from the early fur boom. What trading they did was casual and part-time. Initially, their access to ready riches had been blocked by the French and later by the Canadian monopolies. But more importantly, the Americans were not interested in the fur trade. Their concerns were concentrated on nation building or, more specifically, land-clearing, religion and politics. American Fur was going to change their ideas on values.

A native of Germany, Astor arrived in the United States in 1784 and before a year had passed was shipping furs to England. Astor was irked by the knowledge that the North West Company and Hudson's Bay had powerful and strangling tentacles into the United States. He knew that American furs flowed into Canada and that at least 75% of the furs purchased in the U.S. came from British controlled Canada. By 1800 he had a monopoly on the Missouri fur trade, besides providing the

---

[96] All transactions at that time were in pounds sterling and it is interesting how the dollar—the U.S. standard of measure—arrived on the scene. The dollar originated in a small Bohemian town called Joachimithal, where in 1517 a local count minted a large silver coin. It was called the Joachimithaler, or just thaler. The English pronounced it dollar, a name they also gave to a popular Spanish coin of similar size and value. The dollar sign comes from the Spanish peso. In the late 1700s and early 1800s the peso circulated widely in the United States. The abbreviation for the peso was P, and for the plural, PS. The "P" and the "S" were eventually superimposed, emerging as "$."

North West Company an outlet for their furs, which didn't please the Hudson's Bay Company. Astor became even less popular with Hudson's Bay when the word got out that he planned to organize more American companies and hoped to extend the U.S. fur trade to the very shores of the Pacific Ocean. It was a grand-scale venture with factories to be located at New York City, New Orleans, St. Louis and the mouth of the Columbia. They would be connected by ocean, river and overland routes of staggering length. He made these plans known in part to President Jefferson with a view towards securing a charter which he did in 1808, working through the governor of New York State.

By 1809 Astor formed the American Fur Company with a capital stock of one million dollars, bought out the Mackinac Company, and formed the South West Company.[97] His next move was to form the Pacific Fur Company. Associated with him were Alexander McKay, Donald McKenzie, Duncan McDougal, Wilson Hunt, David Stewart, Robert McLellan and John Clarke. Astor was now ready to wrest the lucrative fur trade from British and Russian hands and place it under American control. More likely, as his biographer, Kenneth Porter, was to observe. . . "it was Astor's intent to concentrate the western fur trade in the hands of only such American citizens as had been born in Waldorf, Germany, in 1763 and had arrived in the United States from London in the spring of 1784." Whatever his motives, Astor tried to assert U.S. ownership of Oregon country thirty years before a lagging Congress made any serious effort to gain possession. Had the Pacific Fur Company been successful, it is quite likely British Columbia would be a part of the United States today.

To add spice to this cauldron of intrigue a swarthy trader of Spanish ancestry, backed by mysterious funds, arrived in St. Louis around 1795. His name was Manuel Lisa. Described as "a violent man of rare ruthlessness and few principles," Lisa could hold his own with Simon McTavish, Count Baranov, John Jacob Astor, Lord Selkirk or anyone else who crossed his path and in his own free-wheeling way would make unique contributions to both the United States fur business and to the exploration of Shoshoni territory. Months before the big syndicates

---

[97] Meacham, *The Old Oregon Trail*, p. 3.

moved on Oregon country, Lisa was probing the eastern Rockies making contact, mostly hostile, with the mountain tribesmen. In late November, 1807, he erected the first fur trading post in the American Rockies on the extreme northeast corner of Shoshoni hunting grounds at the confluence of the Big Horn and Yellowstone Rivers. When he returned to St. Louis in 1808 laden with prime furs, Lisa proved one thing; he might still be a scoundrel, charged with the murder of one of his traders, but, now, he was undisputedly a very rich scoundrel. Recognizing this, some of the shrewder businessmen of St. Louis were eager to become partners in Lisa's latest venture, out of which evolved that famous enterprise known as the Missouri Fur Company. Organized as the St. Louis Missouri Fur Company, it included William Morrison and Pierre Menard, both prosperous traders of Kaskaskia, Illinois; William Clark, co-leader of the Corps of Discovery; Rueben Lewis, brother of Meriwether; Andrew Henry and Pierre Chauteau, illegitimate son of the founder of St. Louis.

Then, while the organized companies were making intricate plans to play havoc with Oregon country, a new breed of exploiters entered the fray. In August 1806, Joseph Dickson and Forrest Hancock—suspected agents of Manuel Lisa—intercepted the returning Lewis and Clark party below the mouth of the Yellowstone River. Here, they persuaded one of the expedition members, John Colter, to guide them into the treacherous Shoshoni country he had just left. By their own admission, Dickson and Hancock were trappers, not Indian fur traders or explorers.

Prior to this time no white man had ever trapped animals for a living. That was beneath European standards of conduct. Natives caught the fur-bearing creatures and prepared the skins. White men traded gaudy trinkets for the catch. Everyone made a profit. Now, Hancock and Dickson planned to trap their own furs and in so doing pioneered a new and dramatically different phase in the fur industry of North America. Seen in this light the decision by Colter to become a trapper takes on special historical significance even though he was not consciously trying to place the United States in competition with Canada and Alaska for half a continent of unexplored land. All Colter had in mind was to make a few dollars trapping furs.

In one short winter Dickson and Hancock disappear from historical record as suspiciously as they had appeared. Not so with John Colter.

During the next four years he established an unshakable claim to being the forerunner of the famous American mountain men. . . those tough, wide-ranging fur trappers who opened the American West and made the world aware of what lay out yonder back of the setting sun.

And, finally, two more entities were to enter the scene briefly—perhaps with more impact than would be recognized for over 100 years into the future. One was Charles Courter, a French Canadian trader, who set up operations in St. Louis and became an American citizen in 1805. The other was General James Wilkinson, a known master of intrigue and military governor of the newly-acquired Louisiana Territory. . . an honor bestowed upon him by Vice-President Aaron Burr. Wilkinson, a counter-spy, had been selling confidential information to both Spain and the United States since 1786.[98] For his information to Spain, the Spanish governor of Louisiana had given Wilkinson a trade monopoly to run flour, tobacco and whiskey on the lower Mississippi River. Wilkinson, described as "handsome, brave, hard-drinking but everlastingly greedy" was the only one concerned with Spain's interest in Oregon country, for throughout all the four companies' schemings dying Spain, fighting tooth to toe with the Shoshoni, was being ignored.

The start of the Oregon fur war could not have happened at a more inopportune time for the Shoshoni who were destined to be the defenders. The Snake war tribes, decimated by smallpox and British muskets, had pulled back into the Ochoco, leaving everything from the Wyoming plains to the Columbia Plateau unguarded. During this critical period the fur brigades of every major world power were converging on Shoshoni hunting grounds.

Completely ignoring the fact that they had rejected all tribal authority, the people were blaming the ruling chieftains for their weakened position in foreign affairs. By 1807 many were looking to the young Hoonebooey warrior, Gotia, the Red Wolf, to rally the scattered tribes and once more unify them into the powerful war machine that in past decades swept the Oyer'ungun clean of enemies from the Cascade Mountains to the Mississippi Valley.[99] Ironically, it is believed that Red

---

[98] Jacobs, *Tarnished Warrior*, pp. 205-6.
[99] Historians have confused Red Wolf—Gotia—with Twisted Hand or Bad Left Hand—Goche. An example appears in Vestal's biography of Joe Meek where he

Wolf was born in 1786, the year the Hudson's Bay Company entered into a contract with the Blackfeet to eliminate Snake competition from the fur industry.

The tribal chiefs, painfully aware that the Shoshoni must react and do it quickly if they were to hold any chance for survival, put their backing behind Red Wolf. Twisted Hand, now advancing in years, would be acknowledged head chief of the war tribes while Red Wolf became the leader of the dog soldiers. The clan chiefs also realized that other western tribes would eagerly join forces with the white men, if for no other reason than to count coup on their old adversaries. Neither could the Snakes depend on help from the Comanches, who had all they could handle holding the Spanish in check, which actually would benefit the British, the Russians and the Americans in their determination to gain a foothold on the Snake's western flank. Not only did it split the Shoshoni fighting force in half, but it kept Spain from protecting its interests in the Oregon country.

And so the contenders in the coming struggle for empire—the Canadian monopolies representing the British Crown, the Russian-American Company, backed by imperial Russia, the American Fur Company, subsidized by the United States government, the Missouri Fur Company, financed by St. Louis merchants and the American free trappers, owing allegiance to no one—had the advantage. But the only characteristic these competitors held in common was a determination to deplete the Shoshoni fur supply. How this would be accomplished was of little consequence, just so long as the operation was complete.

---

states that Meek faced a "treacherous old man, Bad Left Hand, known also to the trappers as Goche or Gotia from the French translation of his name Mauvais Gauche." (Vestal, *Joe Meek, the Merry Mountain Man*, p. 95.) Twisted Hand was head chief of the Snake war tribes while Red Wolf was war-chief.

CHAPTER 15

INTRIGUE ON THE PACIFIC SLOPE

*History. . . includes detailed accounts of events
that never happened, wonderful biographies of persons
that never existed and graphic descriptions of places
that no geographer ever located, nor mortal eye had
ever seen. We thus seem to know more of what we
suppose had happened thousands of years ago than we do
of what is going on right now before our very eyes. . . . .*

William Galvoni
Northwest Historian

Official word of the Lewis and Clark success didn't reach Canada or Alaska until the late winter of 1807. Immediately, North West Company agents made covert plans to open the American West ahead of any competition, for they suspected that the United States would eventually realize that the Corps of Discovery had unlocked potential wealth.

Simultaneously, Hudson's Bay flexed its muscles for another go at the Pacific fur trade. In view of Hudson Bay's arms trade with the Blackfeet it was unlikely that the Snakes would welcome company arrival with horseloads of pelts. This would require some more courtship with the Blackfeet and a channelling of their efforts not only at the Shoshoni but the Americans as well. However, Lord Selkirk was more concerned about North West opposition than he was about any interference from the United States.

Meanwhile, Astor was losing no time in convincing President Jefferson, who in his second inaugural address solemnly stated, ". . . I fear not that any motives of interest may lead me astray. . . ," that it was time to be led astray. American Fur, trained in exceptional ruthlessness and backed by Astor's huge amounts of capital, was the logical stumbling block to Great Britain's dreams of expansion into the Pacific Northwest. But Astor's enterprise was getting off to a sluggish start.

While Canada and the United States shuffled for position, the Russians struck. In the spring of 1807 Nikolai Rezanov, tough brigade leader for Russian-American Fur, attempted to seize the lower Columbia. Like the others, Rezanov was operating in secrecy and no record was made as to why this spearhead failed. In all likelihood the Russians ran afoul of a Snake raiding party. During their conquest of Alaska these Cossacks in keeping with the prevailing Russian style of diplomacy blasted Aleut strongholds with grape-shot and after each slaughter would capture a number of hostages to insure the good behavior of the remaining natives. Where this might have impressed the Chinook and Salish warriors, it is doubtful that the Snakes would have avoided a clash with the traders from Sitka.

It is not speculation that a Snake war party could have been west of the Cascade Mountains. Lewis and Clark record in their journals that they encountered Lohim Snakes (called by them the Sho bar Boo'beer) as far west as the Willamette River in 1805.[100] They estimated their population at 1,600, no small number for a Shoshonean tribe. Pacific Fur Company traders also reported them ranging the Willamette Valley in 1811.[101] Lohim was the family tribe of Twisted Hand. . . hardly a

---

[100] (*The Original Journals of Lewis and Clark*, VI, p. 119). This Shoshonean band called Lohim or Juniper People never made a treaty with the United States and are generally spoken of as renegades belonging to the Umatilla Reservation. In 1870 their number was reported as 114. Ross, the fur hunter, mistook them for Nez Perce. (Hodge, *Handbook of American Indians*, Part I, p. 773.)

[101] In journals written in 1811-12, two Pacific Fur traders, Robert Stuart and William Price Hunt, refer to the Deschutes as the Shoshone River. Stuart mentions the river as "being thickly inhabited by the Shoshoni nation." (Rollins, *Discovery*, pp. 60, 70, 305, 326.) Lewis and Clark were told that "Snakes" lived in large numbers on the Deschutes. (Thwaites, *Original Journals*, Vol. 3: 147-149.) Elsewhere in his journals and "on excellent authority," Stuart mentions the "Shoshonos" as also being on the Willamette River. These Shoshonos whom Donald McKenzie, another Pacific Fur trader, met along the banks of the Willamette sometime prior to 1811 were "very numerous and went by the name of Shoshonos. . . they have no villages or stationary habitations but live in temporary huts along the river banks. . . and they were respectful and obliging in the extreme." (Rollins, *Discovery*, pp. 33, 44.)

group to be intimidated by some wandering Russians. Nor is it beyond possibility that the Russians made it east of the Cascade Range.

For whatever reasons Rezanov's assault was momentarily checked, but he soon formed a huge pincers which applied pressure from the south as well as from the north. By 1813 Ivan Kashov—another brigade leader who had been snooping around the Siskiyou Mountains, dealing Umpquas, Shasta and Rogue warriors misery—shouldered the weary Spanish aside and established a Russian outpost at Bodega Bay within shouting distance of de Anza's stronghold at San Francisco. From Fort Rossiza Russian brigades were inching relentlessly toward the southern Ochoco.

In the late summer of 1807 as Rezanov retreated to the mouth of the Columbia; while the U.S. federal court was occupied with the trial of Aaron Burr for treason—Gen. Wilkinson squealed on him; as Lisa's brigades were slinking around the Rockies, trying to get their bearings; and while Lord Selkirk and John Jacob Astor rattled their sabres in an attempt to frighten each other, North West agents were quietly paddling up the Towahnakiooks in the heart of the present state of Oregon. This silver wisp of river, ripping a channel 1,000 feet beneath the volcanic rims of the Columbia Plateau, formed the undisputed western boundary of the Shoshoni nation. A savage torrent, the Hidden Water (as named by the Shoshoni) plunged recklessly over cataracts, glanced sharply off submerged boulders and veered dangerously into underground caverns, posing many hazardous threats to inland navigation. The Canadians were not long in renaming it "Au Riviere des Chutes," the River of the Falls.[102]

Earlier in the year, as the other fur companies vied for position, David Thompson (now with North West Fur) rushed westward in an effort to grab the Oregon country before the Americans could capitalize on Lewis and Clark's discoveries. Working with Duncan McGillivary, nephew of Simon McTavish, they were pushing North West Company

---

[102] This is the Deschutes River, first Oregon stream to be used as an inland waterway to gain access to Shoshoni furs. Heading deep in the Oregon Cascades, it entered the Columbia from the south a few miles east of the grand rapids at The Dalles. By 1980 it was one of the most popular whitewater rivers in the United States.

field operations to the Pacific coast. Knifing across the crusted snow of the Continental Divide, Thompson reached the upper Columbia in June and established a trading post one mile below the outlet of Lake Windemere, a few miles north of the present Canadian-U.S. border. Called Kootenai House, this was the first white outpost within the area drained by the great Columbia since the abortive attempt made by the Spaniards some 110 years earlier. Thompson manned this post until spring of 1808.

Once over on the Pacific slope Thompson was to map the beaver streams of the entire Columbia drainage south of the 49th parallel. This was no small undertaking and Thompson was gambling that the Blackfeet would keep an eye on the Missouri drainage to ensure no American traders would hamper his movements. Traveling light and fast, for the North West Company wanted no one to know of this venture, Thompson and Finan McDonald with seven men slipped out of Kootenai House in mid-August and by September were moving up the Deschutes River into the heart of Shoshoni territory. It was not by accident that they were in this specific area.

On August 13, 1807, two Flathead braves, allies of the Snakes, trotted into Kootenai House and blandly announced that a party of Americans were wandering around the lower Columbia. On that day Thompson recorded this jolting news in his journal:

> The Indians inform me that about three weeks ago the Americans to the number of 42 arrived to settle a military post at the confluence of the two most southern and considerable branches of the Columbia and that they were preparing to make a small advance post lower down river. Two had been with Captain Lewis. The establishment of the Americans will give a new turn to our long delayed settling of the country on which we have entered, it seems, too late.[103]

---

[103] Herein lies a mystery not completely solved to this day. Historians speculate that one of Lewis' men was John Colter. The other could have been Peter Wiser or John Potts or possibly George Drouillard. All worked for Manuel Lisa. Potts was with Colter in 1808 when captured by the Blackfeet and was killed. Drouillard was killed by the Blackfeet in 1810. Not until Thompson's *Narrative of Expedition of 1807* was published in 1925 did historians learn just how close

They also packed a letter signed by Lt. Jeremy Pinch, stating that the Americans had established a military post, possibly on the Snake River where it breaks through the northern Blues, to keep the British out of Columbia country. Whoever he was and wherever he settled, Lt. Pinch had beat the far-ranging David Thompson into the Oregon country. At least, Thompson had no doubt in his mind that this had happened.[104]

During his plunge from the Flathead country, Thompson had engaged Nez Perce warriors to guide him into the lonesome land south of the Columbia River. All went well until at the confluence of the Deschutes and Crooked Rivers Thompson chose to follow the Crooked River into the foothills of the "Snake Mountains." At this point the Nez Perce deserted. They had no intention of travelling across Shoshoni hunting grounds. Before retreating to the Columbia, they gave the Nor'westers some of their best mounts and advised them to travel due south.

As yet Thompson had found no indication of an American military establishment which was his main objective, but equally as urgent was the survey of beaver streams. For two days the Canadians moved continuously up Crooked River, covering some ninety river miles. They were the first white men to see the lower Crooked River valley along whose headwaters sat the hidden camps of the Snake war tribes. At one point Crooked River—named "au Riviere de Toure" by the French Canadians because of its meandering course—divided, one fork disap-

---

the British came to occupying and establishing an unshakable claim to the entire Columbia drainage. The British suppressed this part of Thompson's Journals at the time of the Oregon boundary controversy in the 1830s and 1840s. (Thompson, *Narrative of Expedition of 1807, Oregon Historical Quarterly*, Vol. XXVI, p. 43.)

[104] The Lt. Pinch affair was considered only legend until Professor Robert Clark of the University of Oregon found two letters in the Public Records Office at London, England. One was from a Lt. Jeremy Pinch, dated Sept. 29, 1807, at "Politio Palton Lake" addressed to "British Merchants Trafficking with the Cabanows." The other was dated July 10, 1807, at "Fort Lewis, Yellow River, Columbia," and was signed by Lt. James Roseman. (Holms, "Who Was Oregon's Mystery Pioneer?" *The Sunday Oregonian*, December 26, 1965; Josephy, *The Great West*, pp. 86-7.)

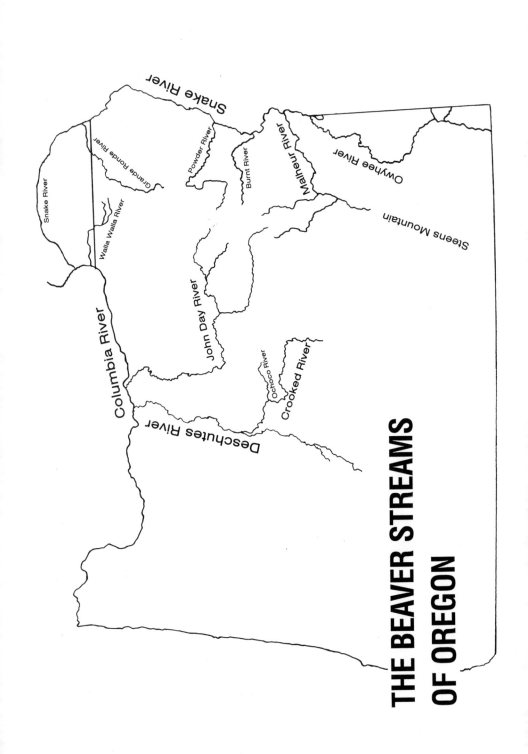

THE BEAVER STREAMS OF OREGON

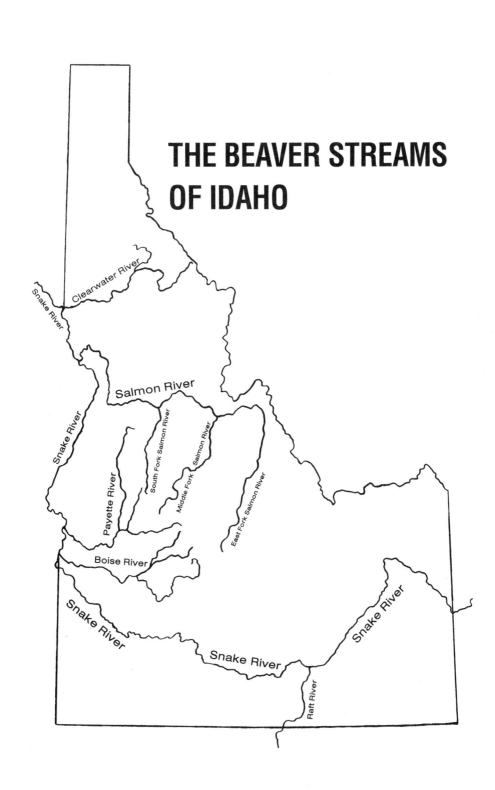

THE BEAVER STREAMS
OF IDAHO

pearing northward into a gap in the southern Blue Mountains and the other bearing eastward. Thompson pushed to the east.[105] Beaver signs were abundant and Ignace Shonowane, one of the Iroquois hunters, snared a huge one which served as the main dish for supper and whose pelt, if it had been in prime, would have been the finest the North West Company had yet taken in this remote corner of the world.

Normally, the Canadians would have encountered natives by the score in their wilderness wanderings. Here, they didn't expect to, but as the beaver sign increased, so did the Indian sign. Intelligence from Hudson's Bay claimed that the Blackfeet had wiped out the Snakes, yet it was obvious there were Indians in the area and Mike Bourcier, one of the scouts, was certain they had been under constant observation since passing the mouth of the Ochoco River. At the mouth of Camp Creek, Bourcier was sent out to scout. The following day he caught up with the main party and reported that this stream sluiced around the southern base of the "Snake Mountains" and headed on the edge of a barren, mountainous plateau. No Indians or Americans in evidence but the stream was well stocked with beaver, muskrat and mink. At what Thompson called the "beaver fork" of Crooked River, he split forces. Finan McDonald, Michael Boulard (interpreter), Etienne Lussier (scout), Bourcier and Shonowane proceeded up the south fork in an attempt to reach its headwaters. Thompson, Jacques Finlay (clerk), Nicholas Montour (scout) and Jules Quesnil (Iroquois hunter) worked up the Beaver Fork and northeast towards the Snake River, where they hoped to intercept McDonald's line of march.

On September 6, 1807, McDonald's party scouted the southern tip of the Ochoco without seeing a living thing. Two days later they reached the warm springs at the head of Crooked River. Still, they found no

---

[105] There is little doubt that David Thompson traveled up the Crooked River for the full course of the river appeared on Arrowsmith's *Maps of North America* published in London, England, as early as 1814. Thompson has become recognized as one of the greatest land geographers of the English race. He placed on the map the main routes of travel across 1.2 million square miles of Canadian territory and some 500,000 square miles of United States territory. Nevertheless, his important work went unrecognized until after the publication of his *Narrative of Explorations in Western America* in 1916.

evidence of the rumored American military encampment, but they did observe a lone horseman far out on the prairie. From the head of Crooked River McDonald wandered into the northern backwash of the Great Basin, searching for beaver streams in a land where he couldn't locate a decent drink of water. Bearing southeast through a "parched and treeless region," he was plotting a course which would eventually take him into Harney Valley. On this leg of the journey McDonald was visited by the high priest of the Shoshoni nation.[106]

The Snakes had kept close check on the Nor'westers progress, but more interesting things were happening to the north. Twisted Hand's main fighting force under the leadership of the Snake dog soldiers Red Wolf and Crooked Leg were operating in that area. Meanwhile, a messenger rode into the mounted Paiutes hideout in the southern Ochoco and told Wuna Mucca that white men were approaching. Elated over this news, Wuna Mucca was now going to prove to the Snakes that not all white men were bad.

In his frenzy to contact the Canadians, believing them to be the white brothers of his vision, a loosely tied moccasin fell to the ground and was ignored as The Gift Giver vaulted onto his horse and headed for the desert. In the vicinity of Silver Creek he caught up with McDonald's brigade and the fulfillment of his prophecy.

Knowing the reputation of the Shoshoni, the Canadians quickly dove behind some rocks and opened fire. Fifty yards from the North West traders Wuna Mucca reined in, hands weaponless, both arms raised in friendship. He shouted, "Te'yuwit nim wuna mucca no'koni tavibo!. . . Wandering white men, I am your friend!" Interpreting this as a Shoshoni war cry, Michael Boulard replied in kind, "Guerre a' mort!. . . war to the death!" Again Wuna Mucca shouted for peace, a cry lost on the desert wind as a second volley rent the air. The medicine man rode back to his lodge on Harney Lake nursing a gaping hole in his left shoulder, where a lead ball had torn through bone and muscle. Not only was Wuna

---

[106] According to the Paiutes, this meeting with white fur traders took place "some time before the great explorers, Lewis and Clark, crossed the plains and saw Chief Wuna Mucca's valley," which is unlikely. (Howard, *Famous Indian Chiefs I Have Known*, pp. 209-216.)

Mucca a badly disillusioned man, but forevermore he would be known to the whites as One Moccasin.[107]

Yet, as history bears out, for another half century One Moccasin, bewildered prophet of the Shoshoni nation, would believe that the whites were his friends. He never refused to help them in time of need and through his influence over the war chiefs saved countless lives. Some Shoshoni, mainly the down-trodden Paiutes, were willing to accept Wuna Mucca's stand on toleration and appeasement, but the majority were not so forgiving. Notable among this group were Wuna Mucca's protege, White Man, a dangerous Ayaihtikara warrior who was fast becoming a powerful medicine man in his own right, and Bad Face, Wuna Mucca's son-in-law, who inherited his name and the man who would become war chief of the Mounted Paiutes.

Having lived up to North West's dubious reputation of "inviting danger and fomenting trouble," McDonald lost no time heading for more friendly territory. While McDonald's party was stirring up trouble, Thompson was busy cementing relations. On his push across the Ochoco it became apparent the Blackfeet had lied to the British. Thompson was not happy. On the Grande Ronde River in the northeast corner of Snake holdings he was intercepted by Red Wolf and Fires Black Gun (Tooite Coon) who were moving south from the headwaters of the Umatilla River.[108] They were well armed, which didn't aid Thompson's peace of mind, and they also had beaver pelts. They

---

[107] Except for this slip-up and the fact that their movements were observed by someone other than the Shoshoni, North West Company had covered its activities in Central Oregon quite well. Thompson's journal spares all details on this chance meeting by McDonald and One Moccasin, choosing to portray Wuna Mucca as the poverty-stricken representative of an ignorant race of savages. To fill in the sparse details one must turn to the account of the incident as remembered by Sarah Winnemucca in *Life Among the Paiutes: Their Wrongs and Claims*, 1883.

[108] Fires Black Gun, brother to Sacajawea, was the Indian so frequently mentioned in the journals of Lewis and Clark as Comeah Wait, a name given him on the spur of the moment by his fellow tribesmen when questioned by Clark. (Thwaites, *Original Journals of Lewis and Clark*, 3:29.) Red Wolf became the father-in-law of such famous American mountain men as Milton Sublette and Joseph Meek.

managed to trade three muskets and a Hudson's Bay axe for their furs. Other trade articles had no appeal.

Thompson wisely decided to cultivate the Snake's friendship in keeping with British policy, for it was obvious the Blackfeet had defaulted on their contract. He promised Red Wolf that Jacques Finlay would return and establish a trading post on the Grande Ronde. By 1810 the Snakes were enjoying a very special trade agreement with the North West Company. Finlay provided first-class weapons and the Snakes flooded his post with prime beaver, otter, muskrat, ermine, marten or whatever else the Scot-Canadian trader desired.

By the time Thompson completed negotiations with Red Wolf, McDonald was well up the Snake River with his eyes on the distant Selkirk Mountains. Thompson had barely arrived at Kootenai House when in late October, 1807, a Kootenai brave stalked into the British outpost and tossed him a soiled letter. The trader was astonished in view of his push through the Snake mountains to find that it had come out of Oregon. The letter, dated July 10, 1807, was addressed to "foreigners who may at present be carrying on a traffic with the Indians within our territories." Since Thompson had not entered the lower Columbia until late August, the Nor'westers were not the guilty party. The only reasonable explanation was that Rezanov had made it east of the Cascades, placing the Russians in prime position to claim the Pacific Northwest. But, like the Spanish and the British, the men who governed Russia also systematically suppressed all accounts of their exploration in the Oregon country.[109]

---

[109] By 1711 the Russians, having subjugated the whole of north Asia, were looking for more lands to conquer—something beyond their recently fixed ocean boundary, something farther east in the direction of the Spanish, French and British settlements in North America. To this end were directed the efforts of Bering and Tchirikoff during the years 1728-29 and of Lt. Synd, Capts. Kremitz and Levascheff between 1766-74. In 1774, J. L. Stachlin, Councillar of State to Empress Catherine, prepared a circumstantial account of exploration from the original records in possession of the Russian government, but they throw very little light on Russian discoveries in North America. Later explorations were equally suppressed to keep Great Britain, Spain and the United States in ignorance of what was going on. (Greenhow, *History of Oregon and California*,

The letter further stated that the North West Company had been observed poaching in the area "under the military authority of General Braithwaite, Commandant of U.S. territory on the Columbia." In no uncertain terms it spelled out what was purported to be United States regulations governing that territory and with which the British must comply in their trading with the Indians. It was signed, "Captain Zachary Perch and Lt. James Roseman, Fort Lewis, Yellow River, Columbia Country." Later letters to the North West Company would refer to Yellow Lake (instead of river) and suggests the phonetic rendering of yelletpo or Waiilatpu—the Shoshoni name for the Cayuse Indians—which could mean that this outpost was on the Umatilla River within a day's ride of the Ochoco.

Having travelled from the Deschutes to the Snake River in the past six weeks, Thompson dismissed the October letter as a hoax—but by whom? Two months later on December 26, a Nez Perce delivered still another message. Dated September 29, 1807, and again signed by Lt. Pinch, it was a repeat of the previous letters only in a sterner vein. In this letter Lt. Pinch wrote that "the Pilchenes" (which could be either the Banattees or Tussawehees, two of the more dangerous Snake war tribes) and "their blood thirsty allies" had attacked the "friendly Polito Palton" (most likely the Palouse Indians) and wounded one of his soldiers. Pinch warned Thompson to stop trading arms to the Indians, a tip-off that the Snakes were definitely involved—and threatened expulsion from the country if the British traders did not obey American laws.

This time Thompson returned a reply with the Nez Perce messenger, haughtily stating he believed that "if prior discovery forms any right to a country, Lt. William Broughton of the British Royal Navy explored the lower Columbia for a distance of 120 miles in 1792." He neglected to mention that Lt. Broughton used a chart drawn by Yankee Captain Gray; but, Captain Gray used a chart drawn by the Spanish sea dog, Bruno Heceta, so everything turned out even.

Apparently three years prior to Major Andrew Henry's documented crossing of the Continental Divide someone besides the British was on

---

Chap. V, p. 138, published in 1845.)

the lower Columbia and knew exactly what David Thompson was doing.[110] Some believe it was Manuel Lisa, while others are equally certain that the messages were originated by Gen. James Wilkinson, "master of intrigue and the most amiable traitor in American history." No one blamed John Jacob Astor's agents.

It is very possible Wilkinson saw in the Oregon fur trade an opportunity for personal gain. Perhaps he and Lisa were working together to bluff the Canadians or, more likely, to gain the jump on Astor's American Fur Company. But the most logical guess is that this hoax—if it was indeed a hoax—was perpetrated by a former French Canadian trader from Michilimackinac named Charles Courter (called Curtin by the Americans), who drifted into St. Louis and became an American citizen in 1805.

In the fall of 1806 Courter organized a fur brigade, which most likely included members of the Corps of Discovery. They may even have been from the contingent sent back to civilization from the Mandan village in the spring of 1805 under the command of Corporal Richard War-fington. As soon as the ice broke up on the Missouri, Courter's brigade jumped off in the vanguard of the great fur trade rush to the Rockies and was the only group that could have reached the headwaters by July, 1807. Courter undoubtedly heard of Thompson's push to the Columbia from Indians at the Mandan village and may even have sent word ahead in an attempt to scare him out of the country. Perhaps the letters were simply a ruse used by Courter to eliminate British competition but, if so, this was an exceedingly mild and gentlemanly trick in an era noted for its vicious, cut-throat opposition to rival companies.

One could also wonder as to where Colter, Dickson and Hancock spent the winter of 1806-1807. Some historians believe it was in the vicinity of Billings, Montana, but this is only speculation. Colter, noted

---

[110] Investigation by many a curious historian (including the writer) has turned up nothing in connection with this bit of history in United States records. Yet, North West Company records bear them out. So far as U.S. records are concerned, the first American to cross the Continental Divide after Lewis and Clark was Manuel Lisa's Missouri Fur partner, Major Andrew Henry, who constructed a short-lived trading post on the Henry's Fork of the Snake River in 1810.

for spinning yarns of his interior travels, never told. Dickson and Hancock were never seen again. It is possible that they died at the hands of the Snakes in Columbia country while Colter was spared.

John Colter enjoyed a very special immunity from the Snake war tribes because, through no fault of his own, he was a sworn enemy of the Blackfeet. In the late spring of 1806 Colter had been with Lewis when expedition members became involved in a skirmish with the Blackfeet. . . the expedition's only armed conflict with a western tribe in its memorable two year journey to the Pacific coast. In the ensuing battle a Blackfoot brave was stabbed to death and another one shot. Any hope for peaceful American relations with the Blackfeet was shattered forever. Within months they captured, tortured and attempted to kill Colter.[111] Following this incident, Colter was accepted without question as a Snake ally and given free passport anywhere upon Shoshoni soil.

As proof, it is now known that Colter blazed most of the trails through Shoshoni country. Yet at the time he received no recognition for his discoveries, mainly because he drew no maps nor did he keep any journals. By contrast written tales circulated by those who had never been farther west than the Iowa prairies set American imagination aflame. Public opinion was eager to accept the possibility of western mountains composed of pure crystal and inhabited by man-hating, arrow-shooting Amazons, each of whom had her right breast amputated, because it got in the way of the bowstring. . . or exotic dwarfs 18 inches tall who lived in piney bluffs along the intermountain rivers. . . or even the possibility of pre-historic animals roaming between the Blues and the Rockies.

But when Colter tried to describe the wonders he had seen, first to other trappers and later to the well-bred society of St. Louis, they refused to believe him. It was bad enough when he told of standing in a high mountain glade where three great streams began their separate journeys into different oceans. But his report of steam-filled mountain valleys, covered with seething hot-springs, rent by spewing geysers and whose ground trembled beneath boiling mud basins was sheer nonsense. No

---

[111] Colter's capture and subsequent flight from the Blackfeet during which his partner, William Potts—also an ex-member of the Corps of Discovery—was killed is graphically described in John Bradbury's *Travels In America*, p. 17.

way would a well-informed public accept that God's inferno was located out west. No one other than "crazy" John Colter had seen such a devilish place. And so the discovery of Yellowstone Park was given the derisive name of "Colter's Hell."

True, no one—not the far-ranging Spanish, the equally well-traveled French, the map-making British or even the nomadic plains tribes—had heard about, let alone seen, this natural wonder or any of the other marvels Colter was to describe. Colter had been in the ancient homeland of the Saydocarah. In the early 1800's only the Shoshoni were aware that within their territorial boundaries lay the awesome Yellowstone thermal region, regarded by them as "the land where the Mighty One Above had not yet completed the work of creation." Neither were they afraid of the area's vapor-filled valleys and sulfurous cauldrons, for Yellowstone was the hunting ground of the Tookarikha Snakes.[112] They also knew that within their borders lay the highest land west of the Appalachian Mountains. In this high country, soon to be known as the Wind River Range, stood the most unusual peak on the North American continent. Here was the source of three very large rivers, for the waters off Triple Divide Peak flow into the Colorado, the Mississippi and the Columbia. Since no one would believe Colter on discoveries of this magnitude, would they believe he had been a member of the first military outpost in Oregon?

Like Dickson and Hancock, after disappearing into the Rockies in 1806, Courter's brigade was never seen again. And therein lies a real mystery. If they made it into the Blues or beyond, it seems incredible that a party of 42 men would leave no trace of entry, particularly a

---

[112] During extensive research into western Indian culture, John Rees determined that at the start of the 19th century only the Shoshoni knew what lay between the Rockies and the southern Blues. They alone knew intimately the great Rocky Mountain system extending from Mexico to Canada, a mountain range which divided the waters of a continent. (See *Oregon Historical Quarterly*, Vol. XXI, No. 4, December, 1920, p. 321; also Hodge, *Handbook of American Indians*, Part II, p. 835.) Following Ferdinand Hayden's impressive reports, highlighted by the remarkable pictures of Henry Jackson and the paintings of Thomas Moran, Congress designated Yellowstone as the first national park in 1872, some 65 years after Colter reported its existence.

quasi-military expedition. But they disappeared as though the mountains had swallowed them.

Bear in mind, David Thompson met Red Wolf, the ranking Snake war chief, somewhere between the Umatilla and Grande Ronde rivers in the present state of Oregon. His warriors were well armed and the implication was that they were military weapons, not the inferior trade articles. Also, Thompson quickly set up an arms agreement as indicated in the American correspondence to the Canadians, which suggests that Thompson, contrary to his earlier negotiations with the Blackfeet, deemed the Snakes to be adversaries worth bringing into the British alliance. It seems reasonable that this second white expedition to attempt settlement on or near the Ochoco had also become another ghost battalion. No one will ever know. The two men who might have answered that question, John Colter and Charles Courter, were soon eliminated from the scene.

Courter was killed by the Blackfeet in 1810, the same year Colter again escaped death while five men were shot down around him. Making it over the Rockies to Lisa's fort on the Missouri, Colter solemnly swore ". . . if God will only forgive me this time and let me off, I will leave the country and be damned if I ever come into it again!" With that he climbed into his canoe and in a month paddled 2,000 miles down river to St. Louis never to return—for he died (some say of a broken heart longing to go back to the Shoshoni country he loved) in 1812.

While all of this was taking place, American Fur was gearing up to stage an overland assault on Shoshoni country from the east to coincide with a sea attack from the west. But for a moment, let's digress to get a better understanding of the land that had now become a battle ground for three major world powers.

CHAPTER 16

WHAT MANNER OF CREATOR?

*. . . for every problem the Lord has made
He also has a solution. If you and I can't
find the solution, then let's honestly admit
that you and I are damned fools. . . .*

Thomas Edison
American Inventor

It is not likely that the Shoshoni gave much thought to the origin of their homeland. It was here, always had been, always would be and that was enough to satisfy their curiosity. The Europeans would be more questioning and the first white men to stumble upon the pyroclastic awesomeness of the Crooked River Gorge would certainly be no exception.

The sun, a blazing ember smoldering upon a blanket of glowing blue, branded an unwavering line towards the zenith. Beneath its glaring eye a minute speck toiled up the scorched slope of a treeless plateau. It was late August, 1807, a year slated to go down in Pacific Northwest history as the summer of intrigue. Two weeks earlier, canoes had drifted down the dwindling Columbia River, crossed the long dead trail of the American explorers, Lewis and Clark, beached at the mouth of an unnamed tributary and disgorged a group of bearded traders into the fractured ravines of the southern Columbia Plateau. Now, deep within Oregon territory, the cautious travelers came to rest on the seared lip of a twisted chasm. One thousand feet below two silvery ribbons of water met in moral combat. The Nez Perce guide, who had directed these men into the Oyer'ungun from the Flathead country to the north informed them that this was the junction of the Towahnokiooks (Deschutes) and Paga Tubic (Crooked) rivers. They could continue up the Towahnokiooks in comparative safety but travel up the Paga Tubic would only bring death.

David Thompson, leader of this North West Company detachment and a highly trained land geographer, wiped the sweat from his piercing grey eyes and gazed at the broken, forbidding land to the east. . . the Indian had called it the Ochoco. As Thompson stared across the miles of dipping plateau, studded with ruptured basalt, he could but wonder what manner of Creator had fashioned this tortured terrain.

Perhaps, the geographer juggled a chunk of volcanic glass in his hand and thought. . . "if only this rock could talk, what a tale it could tell." Thompson would little realize how near to the truth he actually was, for the answer, cloaked in the dust of antiquity, lay in the overlapping formations at his feet. Three-quarters of a century later another man would stand on this promontory and muse much the same as Thompson. In his hand there would also be a rock, and that rock would reveal its secret to Dr. Condon, unravelling the mysteries of an age gone by, taking him back. . . back. . . back into the dim eternity of the long dead past.[113]

---

[113] Thomas Condon, scientist, clergyman, author, discovered the fossil beds of the John Day Valley and through succeeding years made many important geological discoveries in eastern Oregon. Professor of Geology and Natural History at the University of Oregon from 1876 to 1907, he was Oregon's foremost geologist and paleontologist. In later life he was known as "Oregon's Grand Old Man of Science." (see "Thomas Condon, Pioneer Geologist of Oregon," *Oregon Historical Quarterly* VI: 201-14.)

CHAPTER 17

UP FROM THE DEPTHS

The Sundown Sea now shone mobile,
Translucent, flaming, molten steel!
The Sundown Sea all sudden then,
Lay argent, pallid, white as death;
As when some great thing dies. . . . .

Joaquin Miller
Poet of the Ochoco

Slowly, the glaring Proterozoic sun traced its endless arc across the ancient sea, a daily ritual it had been observing for more than 650 million years. Sometimes the water churned as if in agony but most often it lay in glassy stillness, shielding from the rays of the curious sun its mysterious submerged floor, a land which in the far distant future would be known as Central Oregon. Another 350 million years came and went while a cold Paleozoic moon aided the solar star in its eternal watch over this vast expanse of salt water. Then, in the early Mesozoic Era the floor of the prehistoric ocean quietly folded into one of the great mountain ranges of ancient times, the Triassic Alps, which ruled the Central Oregon skyline for 20 million years.[114]

A lonely island surrounded by reptile-infested waters, this gigantic upthrust towered 16,000 feet above the Donovan Sea. Ichthyosaurs, giant fish-killing lizards, sporting the head of a dolphin and the body of

---

[114] Lookout Mountain, Mount Pisgah and Snow Mountain are remnants of the Triassic Alps which were discovered by the paleontologist, Dr. E.L. Packard in the early 1900s. Evidence that they were covered by water can be told from the eroded stumps of this vanished mountain range which are heavily deposited with marine sediments.

a huge fish, cruised the coastline of the Triassic Alps.[115] Cradled in its bosom lay the Mowich Sea and across its murky depths were etched the first faint traces of a primordial Crooked River. A restless body of water, covering 2,000 square miles of Central Oregon mud flats, the Mowich Sea was constantly probing its bays and inlets, seeking to escape. For 20 million years it gnawed at the gripping slime in an effort to join the parent sea and eventually the three-mile high Triassic Alps—bombarded from without and within—were reduced once more to water level and the Donovan Sea crashed over the land, depositing 2,500 feet of marine sediment over one of the most imposing landmarks of the Mesozoic Era.

Thirty million years of upper Mesozoic rains lashed the victorious sea to a white-capped frenzy, as its murky water rolled across the Triassic Alps, grinding them ever lower into the Jurassic muck. A brutal captor, the sea was making certain that the land would never rise again, but a thousand miles to the east its main line of defense was treading on dangerous ground. With a powerful surge the Rocky Mountains broke through a hundred fathoms of crushing water at last to be free from the sunless depths and in so doing broke the 200 million year reign of the Donovan Sea. It was now the Pacific Ocean. Nursing this defeat, the ruptured waves became more cautious and for 50 million years land and water were locked in stalemate.

One quiet afternoon mid-way of the Cretaceous Period, the thoughtful Pacific lay at rest. Not so much as a ripple stirred its mirror-like surface. It seemed unlikely that either side would make a gain this day. What transpired can best be told in the descriptive words of Robert Frost:

---

[115] Remains of these gigantic marine reptiles were first located in the southern Blues by prospectors in the 1860s who were seeking gold, not bones. They left the massive skeletons undisturbed in the rock which long eons ago had been crushed into mountains. The sea-going saurians found in the Mitchell hills overlooking Bridge Creek, were the first ever discovered in a Cretaceous formation in the Pacific Northwest. A state park has been set aside in the Shoshoni Mountains of Nevada honoring the ichthyosaur, whose cousins ruled Oregon seas for millions of years in the Mesozoic era and left their bones in the marine ooze of the Mitchell country.

The shattered water made a misty din.
Great waves looked over others coming in,
    and thought of doing something to the shore
    that water never did to land before.
The clouds were low and hairy in the skies
Like locks blown forward in the gleam of eyes.
You could not tell and yet it looked as if
The shore was lucky in being backed by cliff,
The cliff in being backed by continent;
It looked as if a night of dark intent
    was coming, and not only a night, an age.
Someone had better be prepared for rage.
There would be more than ocean—water broken
Before God's last *Put Out the Light* was spoken.[116]

Without warning, thunder jarred the sky; bolt after bolt of chain lightning scorched the sleeping waters and two hundred miles from the nearest land, the sea shrank back, voicing a defiant roar as Shoshoni Land erupted from the depths of the Pacific Ocean.[117] A young and vigorous up-thrust that wasn't content until it had shoved a granite arm upward and eastward to grasp the jagged shoulder of the Rocky Moun-

---

[116] "Once By the Pacific" from *The Complete Poems of Robert Frost*, copyrighted 1928 and 1949 by Henry Holt & Co., Inc.

[117] Shoshoni Land is the geologic name given to the ancient Blue Mountain range which included the present Bitter Root range in northern Idaho. In the beginning the Blues were considered a single mountain chain. Then as explorers got to reviewing the situation, they divided the Blues into the Blue Wallowa range northeast of the main John Day River and the Blue Ochoco range west of the John Day. The Wallowas, the only mountains in Oregon which are granite in origin, derive their name from the Nez Perce word "wallowa" meaning winding waters. The Ochocos, the fiery product of volcanism, derive their name from the Shoshoni word "ohoctu" meaning red willow tree. Not satisfied with this arrangement, the geodetic survey has further divided the Blues into three independent ranges: the Wallowas, running from the Snake River to the Powder River; the Blues, sandwiched between the Powder River and the south fork of the John Day River and the Ochocos, reaching west from the south fork of the John Day to the High Desert and Columbia plateaus of Central Oregon.

tain barrier. During the initial upheaval the Wallowa blockade was the first to appear.

Following this unexpected reversal, the Pacific rallied its battered forces and assailed the Wallowa obstruction with renewed vigor as the continental plate, straining against the Pacific plate, gave a spasmodic jerk. Suddenly, pounding waves disintegrated in twitching agony. Scalding steam arose from their boiling surface, enveloping the northern hemisphere in an eerie mist. A shattering roar—one hundred times more deafening and a thousandfold more terrible than that which preceded the first land attack—shook the planet to its very core. Illuminated in a halo of hell-fire, the Ochoco ripped the ocean floor and exploded into seething existence. Nature had given birth to the Blues. . . the oldest exposed land mass west of the Rocky Mountains.[118]

During the final collapse of the Cretaceous Period, when petroleum was in the process of being formed, Shoshoni Land ceased to be a part of the Pacific coastline. With a deafening roar a section of the great Pacific dike rose out of the ocean from southern California to the Aleutian Islands, forming the Cascade Barrier. These mountains were low at first but even so another major battle had been won. Trapped

---

[118] Evidence that the Blues were a promontory shoved far out into the Pacific Ocean can be found in southwestern Grant County and southeastern Crook County. Beds of fossilized clams and other sea creatures are found in the dark shales of the Izee-Suplee region which was once covered by the ancient Mowich Sea. (Mowich is the Indian name for mule deer.) Early records of exploration in this area are found in the letters of Dr. Condon. In them he also makes reference to the discovery of Cretaceous fossils along Beaver Creek, a tributary of Crooked River, and along the headwaters of West Branch and O'Kelly Creeks, tributaries of the John Day River. Further studies of the Ochoco dealing extensively with rocks and their formation were carried out by Russell and Calkins in 1902. In 1927 R.W. Chaney made paleobotanical and stratigraphic studies of the upper Crooked River basin which has become a training ground for young geologists. These scientists found the Ochoco to be composed of six different formations dating from Cretaceous conglomerates (120 million B.C.) to the geologically recent Ochoco lava flows (12 million B.C.) The oldest Paleozoic fossil beds in Oregon, discovered in 1961, lie near the Berger ranch in southeastern Crook County. For further information see Ewart M. Baldwin, *Geology of Oregon*, University of Oregon Press.

between this up-thrust and the Rocky Mountain barrier—with Shoshoni Land jutting out as a 400 mile long peninsula—was the enormous Mesozoic Inland Sea.

Throughout the Paleocene and Eocene Epochs, an age which lasted 30 million years, the imprisoned sea was constantly on the prowl, searching for an outlet. Over the eons its strength began to ebb and it became very shallow. Each century in passing saw more water evaporate. Finally, in frenzied desperation, the Mesozoic Sea ripped through the Cascade barrier, forming the spectacular Bridge of the Gods. Known to the Indians as "Wauna," this natural stone arch spanning the yet unborn Columbia River, held a prominent position in tribal folklore. To them it represented the rise and decline of the Indian empire. So long as the Bridge of the Gods connected the Cascade Mountains, the Indians would rule supreme over North America.

Century upon century melted into the past as the victorious inland sea transformed into a system of fresh-water lakes which eventually became one great stream, the Columbia and its tributaries. But still one section of the dying sea was ensnared by a low arm of the Blues. Feverishly, it hammered at this stony blockade while its sunken floor, the High Desert of Central Oregon, lay in watery obscurity. Then in a moment of weakness during the Oligocene Epoch, Shoshoni Land allowed the sea to escape. Nearly 55 million years ago the forsaken orphan of the once huge Mesozoic Sea gouged an opening through a spur of the Blues, forming the channel of Dry River. . . now a twisted, dusty, rattlesnake-infested crevasse, separating the farming communities of Alfalfa and Powell Butte from the High Desert on the east and the metropolitan areas of Bend and Redmond on the west.

In a fit of rage over this sea victory, Shoshoni Land began reinforcement of its fortifications with destructive power beyond imagination. Throughout this cataclysm the Cascade barrier, now struggling to hold off the rabid Pacific, and the Rocky Mountain barrier, smug in its remoteness from the battlefront, let the Blues do all the work. Early in the Miocene age, the Ochoco was consumed by molten lava.[119] But this

---

[119] This can be determined from deposits bearing Oligocene flora which directly underlie the Ochoco lava. The name "Clarno" is applied to the rocks of this early volcanic origin because they were first exposed at Clarno's Ferry on the

was only the beginning. By late Miocene wave upon wave of glowing magma spread across the land, destroying everything within its fiery path. During this violent action the Steens Mountains uprooted from the floor of Harney Valley and jammed skyward to give support to the fighting Blues. Lava spewed from fissures and vents which ruptured the earth's crust from Crooked River to the Snake, spreading in white-hot sheets over the Ochocos at the rate of 50 miles per hour. Each successive layer added another 20 to 80 feet of molten rock to the bastions of Shoshoni Land. Now known as the Columbia River basalts, they intended to stop for all time any intrusion from the Pacific Ocean. The Columbia flow—some 250,000 square miles of volcanic matter—represents one of the largest bodies of lava on earth, covering the greater part of Washington, eastern Oregon, northern California and southern Idaho.

There were periods of relative quiescence and times of violent explosive action since both flows and pyroclastics of varying thickness occur. This volcanic activity produced tremendous earthquakes, which are expressed in the faults and folds found in all of the older formations of the Ochoco. In the early Tertiary age, these intrusions were heavily charged with mineralizing solutions which collected under favorable conditions. Precipitation occurred to form the cinnabar deposits for which Central Oregon is famous. One of the major faults—the Ochoco fault—occurs near the headwaters of Ochoco Creek on the north side of Mount Pisgah and extends eastward to the Snake River. At various points this fault is charged with gold, cinnabar, silver and agate. Agate, a semi-precious stone, has made Central Oregon the rock hound capital of the world.

One exceptional cross-section of the huge Columbia flow can be seen on the rims of the lower Ochoco and Crooked River valleys. Especially in the Crooked River Gorge is this phenomenon in evidence. Here, the palisades rising 1,000 feet above the winding river give proof to the region's seething past. They tell a story of broad ancestral canyons into which flowed streams of molten rock, blocking the Deschutes and Crooked Rivers, while choking off the mouth of the Metolius.

John Day River. In places the Clarno formation contains fossil leaves indicating Eocene age of the Ochoco flow.

There were sometimes intervals of centuries between flows, for they are separated by soil deposits in which are found trees that had time to grow to a considerable size. One of these giants which may have been uprooted by a hurricane-force wind some 20 million years ago and claims the distinction of being the largest petrified tree in existence was discovered five miles north of Prineville in the spring of 1950.[120]

Fresh, unaltered specimens of the Columbia lava, black in color and having a flinty or glossy luster are found in abundance around Glass Butte on the southern border of the Ochoco country. It was from this volcanic glass, called obsidian, that the Shoshoni made many of their cutting implements. Because of the distinct conchoidal fracture of this rock, it was very easy to chip a sharp cutting edge on a knife, axe or arrowpoint. The superior workmanship of this material was found to bring a good price on the foreign market and soon developed into a paying business for the Shoshoni, becoming the first major export to leave the Ochoco.

Before the lava floods Shoshoni Land had been a broken country made up of lakes and wooded mountains, a land sweltering in tropical heat as dinosaurs fed beneath waving palms. When the basalt poured into this mold, it became a plain with only the summits of Pisgah, Strawberry, Lookout and Snow Mountains showing as low hills. These flows choked Crooked River with steaming lava from Smith Rock to the Cove, creating the Island at the junction of the Deschutes and Crooked Rivers. The Island, a solid block of basalt some 800 feet high and just short of a mile long, once glowed in fiery splendor as it oozed into the Crooked River Gorge.

Thermal rock piled up in the Deschutes and Crooked River valleys to a depth of 1,000 feet, forming one of the most spectacular intracanyon lava flows on earth. Crooked River, first to be attacked by this glowing, twisting mass—which came from a single vent just north of the Ochoco—was struck just below the mouth of the Ochoco River. Moving

---

[120] Ernest and Van Moore partially uncovered this tree when building a road across their property on McKay Creek. The exposed part of this gigantic redwood measures sixteen feet long and weighs approximately 500 tons. Other petrified logs are found throughout Crook County. These chunks of wood turned to stone, bearing traces of uranium, are found to be highly radioactive.

slowly westward, the fluid rock spilled over into the Deschutes Canyon, where it inched its way sluggishly downstream to the mouth of the Metolius. When the lava chilled, Crooked River was dammed. Behind this lava plug formed a huge inland reservoir—Lake Ochoco. This body of water covered the present site of Prineville and lapped the beaches of Lookout, Grizzly and the Maury mountains. Into this lake flowed streams carrying reworked material from The Dalles Formation. The ultimate result was some of the finest gravel in the region now massed in the valley once occupied by the vast reservoir of the Pleistocene age.

Along the shores of Lake Ochoco grazed camels, horses, elephants and bison, animals which lived in the world's Ice Age and may possibly have existed into late pluvial times, when heavy rain drenched Shoshoni Land.[121] Ancestors of the Snake war tribes fished this lake. The waters of Lake Ochoco, as the Mowich Sea before it, were not idle. Tirelessly they worked, sluicing around the lava enclosure and in places sawing directly through solid rock. Once more the water escaped, but in going it left the story of Miocene life stamped forever in the sediments of the Mascall Formation.[122]

---

[121] In 1956 Dr. Arnold Shotwell, University of Oregon paleontologist, began studies of the Crooked River gravel deposits. Horse and camel remains were definitely identified from gravel deposits south of Smith Rock. Some of the ice-age horses were as large as those of today. Fossils found include teeth and the one-toed hoof of a horse. Camels that lived in the Crooked River basin are believed similar to those found earlier in the ancient lake areas of Lake County studied by Dr. Condon. Elephant finds made in a gully near Smith Rock include tusks and bones. Other elephant finds were made in the late 1970s at the site of the Prineville railroad depot on North Main Street and on Bridge Creek west of Mitchell in the late 1980s.

[122] Named for W.R. Mascall, a Dayville rancher who played a prominent role in the 1890 sheep and cattle wars and on whose property this outcrop was first identified, the name "Mascall" designates the upper Miocene cream-colored tuff beds lying over the Columbia basalts. Composed of interfingering layers of tuffaceous sandstones, conglomerates and volcanic ash, it reaches a maximum thickness of 200 feet in the southeast quarter of Crook County, making its best showing on Logan Butte, not far from the first Spanish settlement. Throughout the years many animal remains have been discovered on this barren knob. Because of the extensive deposit of bones of extinct creatures it is believed this

Perhaps nowhere in North America does a representative portion of the past history of mammals unfold so clearly and impressively as in the Mascall beds of the Clarno region in north-central Oregon. Here also are found the bones of the three-toe horse, sabre toothed tiger and prehistoric rhinoceros. Here are the bones of dinosaurs, preserved since the dawn of time in a tertiary marsh. Scientists from many parts of the world come to study these fossil remains so well preserved in this ancient graveyard. In the area between Spray and Picture Gorge can be found the skeletons of bear-like dogs, giant pigs with cud-chewing teeth, camels and mastodons.[123]

In the first period of the Quarternary Epoch, the Glacial Age, the ice advanced upon the Columbia Basin from several directions but probably never reached the Ochoco. As the polar ice drew near, the Ochoco lavas spewed up from the John Day Basin to the High Desert Plateau, covering all of the older formations. They were first observed along the flanks of Wolf Mountain in eastern Crook County, but the structure of the Ochoco flows are most pronounced along the south rim of Lookout Mountain. The main course of destruction lay down the North Fork of Crooked River, passing about two miles north of Rabbit Valley through to Arrow Wood Point in the southern Blues. The last volcanic action in the Ochoco occurred one million years ago.

Volcanic activity continued in the Cascade Range throughout the Ice Age. In the earth's long winter of the cold Pleistocene Epoch, Hood, Jefferson, South Sister and other of the younger Cascade volcanoes had not yet taken their position astride the roof of Oregon. Only the older peaks, created by late Pliocene volcanism showed. Such volcanoes as Broken Top, Mt. Washington, Three Fingered Jack and, far to the south, Mounts Howlock and Thielson. The North Sister, oldest of the sisterly volcanoes overlooking Central Oregon, lost about half of its ancestral volume when the glaciers gouged down its rugged sides.

---

butte—six miles due south of Tower Point in the Maury Mountains—was a promontory which caused a backwash in prehistoric Lake Ochoco. It has not been possible to trace the Mascall Formation across the Ochoco Mountains.
[123] In the 1970s the Clarno-Picture Gorge area was designated the John Day Fossil Beds National Monument.

Then, only five to ten thousand years ago Mount Mazama went on the rampage and literally blew its top over all of Eastern Oregon, scattering pumice over an area of 5,000 square miles. The eruption of this Cascade monarch formed the caldera now holding Crater Lake, one of the natural wonders of the world. Wizard Island is believed to be the top of old Mount Mazama. Gradually, all volcanic action in the Cascade Range ceased, but as late as 1882 people in the Prineville area could witness the sight of black smoke belching from the peak of Mount Jefferson.[124] Nearly 100 years later, citizens of the Pacific Northwest were shaken to their toes when Mount St. Helens, which had been giving warning since the early 1800s, belched ash and steam on March 27, 1980, and two months later on May 18th exploded, leaving 63 people dead or missing in an age when it was believed that it couldn't happen.

Except for a small amount of Cretaceous sediment, the geologic history of the Ochoco is one of violent volcanism, beginning in the Eocene age some 40 million years ago and continuing until late Pliocene or early Pleistocene. In this manner the Ochoco in a time lapse covering more than a billion years was raised from the depths of the Pacific Ocean and eroded into the familiar outlines we know today. This is a never-ending change. Slowly over the years this process will continue until someday in perhaps the not-so-far-distant future the mountains we call the Blues may once again become the floor of a raging sea.

And now, back to the flood of fur brigades inundating Shoshoni Land with all the viciousness of the ancient Mowich Sea.

---

[124] "The sight from here (Prineville) was a grand spectacle. . ." so stated an article in the *Central Oregonian, Old Timer's Edition*, August 4, 1939, reprinted from the files of 1882.

CHAPTER 18

DECLARATION OF INTENT

Columbus and John Jacob Astor!
I daresay Irving will make the last
the greatest man.[125]

James Fenimore Cooper
Writer of adventure stories

As 1809 began, the headlines were filled with forecasts of doom. Napoleon was on the march across Europe and no nation seemed safe from his power-hungry grasp. In the midst of this preoccupation with political happenings other events would pass unnoticed. In the forecasts for 1809 everyone worried about the European battles but forgot about the Pacific Northwest—all that is but John Jacob Astor.

The Snakes, now secure in their commerce with the world market, little realized that the end was near. At the start of the fur war the United States population stood at five million and by 1810 it would swell to more than seven million. During this period there were perhaps 4,000 native Americans left in the huge rectangle between the Appalachian Mountains, the Ohio River, the Mississippi River and the Canadian border. Between 1795 and 1809 the eastern tribes had been forced to part with 48 million acres of prime hunting grounds. This land-grab was only momentarily checked by the two great Shawnee warriors, Tecumseh and his brother, the Prophet.

---

[125] Remark made by Cooper when he was told that Washington Irving had accepted a commission to write the epic struggle of Astor's assault on Oregon country. At the time Irving was the nation's most eminent author and Cooper believed he had sold his literary integrity down the river for a rumored $5,000 plus free room and board at Astor's Hell Gate mansion.

By the time of the Louisiana Purchase John Jacob Astor was ruler supreme of the Missouri fur trade, where his power surpassed that of the United States government. The old trader's system of getting furs cheaply by debauching the Indians with whiskey had been followed on a larger scale and, if possible, in a more scandalous way by the great Astor. His predatory methods were notorious and his financial strength was such—at a time when wages in the eastern factories ranged from 12 to 25 cents a day—that he could order his London bankers to make a single investment of half a million dollars out of his idle balance. When Astor spoke, Congress, now located in the new city of Washington, listened. Now, Astor was out to secure exclusive control of the Pacific fur market, which would place the entire western fur trade under his command.

Supported by the governor of New York, Astor presented his plan to the Madison administration where he was successful in enlisting government aid to form a Pacific fur company. . . aid in the form of a charter giving American Fur Company exclusive trade rights on the Pacific slope and backed by low-interest government loans.

This scheme included the founding of a trading post at the mouth of the Columbia River, which would become the main factory of the entire Pacific Coast. His agents, who now saturated the country east of the Rockies, would hit the Pacific slope with instructions to secure most if not all of the furs the natives could produce. The Columbia factory would be connected with St. Louis by a string of posts across Oregon and Louisiana territories and connected to New York City by shipping routes around the Horn with yearly supplies flowing into Oregon from New York. It also called for trade connections with the prime fur market in the Orient, a market closed to North West and Hudson's Bay by reason of a monopoly enjoyed by the East India Company, also British-controlled. It arranged for commercial trade relations with the Russian-American Fur Company by which Pacific Fur would ship in supplies in return for Alaskan fur. Astor's plan was good, but his agents were hamstrung from the start by Astor's complete lack of guidance in how they were to accomplish this monumental task.[126] Had he paid more

---

[126] For a complete insight to Astor's indifference to his Pacific enterprise, and often

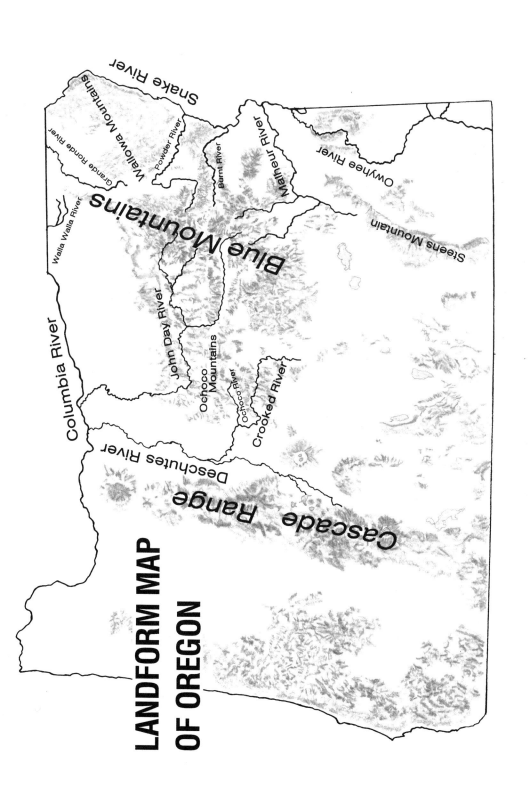

LANDFORM MAP
OF OREGON

Columbia River

Walla Walla River

Grande Ronde River

Wallowa Mountains

Snake River

Powder River

Blue Mountains

Burnt River

Malheur River

Owyhee River

Steens Mountain

John Day River

Ochoco Mountains

Ochoco River

Crooked River

Deschutes River

Cascade Range

attention to his partners, all capable men, Astor might have won the entire Pacific Northwest from Alaska to California for the United States.

Perhaps Red Wolf and his beleaguered nation could take comfort in Madison's first inaugural address in which he stated that the Americans would be "indulging no passions which trespass on the rights or the repose of other nations. It has been the true glory of the United States to cultivate peace by observing justice." He further emphasized that the United States would "exclude foreign intrigue" from its policy and that the federal government was "too just to invade the rights of others." Time would tell.

Moving into Canada, Astor attempted a merger with the North West Company, mainly to bring it under his command thus ensuring no trouble from that quarter. The disciples of Simon McTavish were not buying into this venture. They suspected treachery on the part of American Fur for the Blackfeet were getting extremely belligerent. The truth was that the Blackfeet, finding out that the Nor'westers were supplying the Snakes with weapons, had turned on the British. In 1810 the energetic Thompson, whose domain now embraced the entire Columbia watershed, including the Snake River with the northern part of Utah and Nevada tossed in for good measure, was disconcerted by the news that the Piegons had blocked Horse Pass through the northern Rockies, the route over which his supplies were being sent. Company officials, worried that the Columbia district had become too big for one man to control, slipped in John McDonald, brother to the red-haired giant, Finan McDonald, to share the responsibility.

Unlike the Americans to the south the Canadians sought to convert the Indians to capitalism, not Christianity. Working out of the newly-constructed Spokane House, a trading post on the middle Columbia, Fin McDonald and Jacques Finaly moved down on the Grande Ronde River in the present state of Oregon. Here, guns, ammunition and iron-headed arrow points which could pierce the thick-skinned buffalo were dispensed to the Snakes for hides and furs. They were also trading iron awls and needles which were in great demand by the Shoshoni women.

---

actual pettiness to their very survival, see Ross, *Adventures of the First Settlers on the Oregon or Columbia River*, 1810-1813.

Thompson's journals for 1809-10 refer to constant trading of North West merchandise for furs, horses, fresh and dried meats.[127]

The Grande Ronde operation was placed under the direction of Jacques Raphael Finaly, an amiable Scot-Canadian trader known to all as Jaco. Finaly became the Shoshoni savior. Perhaps he felt an affinity to the Snake's plight for in his veins ran the blood of the Chippewa nation. This he inherited from his mother who had a passing acquaintance with James Finaly, a charter member of the famous and exclusive Beaver Club of Montreal. Jaco was to supply the Snakes with arms and ammunition for nearly 20 years, dying in the northern Blues in 1829.

While Thompson was secure in the belief that he had the Columbia tied up and Astor was equally certain he could wrench it away, the Winship brothers, Abiel, Jonathan and Nathan, tough sea-going traders who knew Pacific waters like Thompson knew the land and Astor knew finances, were about to bid for the Oregon fur trade. Loading their sailing vessel, the *Albatross,* with trade goods, they slipped out of Boston Harbor in 1809 and headed for the Columbia. On May 26, 1810, Captain Nathan Winship put the *Albatross* over the Columbia bar and sailed up river about 45 miles, where at an inviting meadow on the south bank they lashed the *Albatross* to a tree and began construction of a two-story log fortress. It took just eight days for the Chinooks to convince the Winship brothers this was not the sensible thing to do. The sea gods attacked with torrential rains, driving the Columbia to white-capped fury as it overflowed its banks and inundated the Winship settlement. They then attempted to move farther inland only to be permanently stopped by Concomly's warriors. Both Jonathan and Nathan continued to operate trading ships in northern Pacific waters until 1812, when British men-of-war ousted all shipping other than for British and Russian trading vessels.

Meantime, Astor, having failed in his attempted merger with the North West Company, offered to bear all expenses for the first two years,

---

[127] Fur trading was not limited to beaver. John Hoskin, who sailed with Captain Gray in 1791, noted in his narrative: "the skins are bears, wolves, foxes, rein, fallow and moose deers, land otters, raccoons, brown minks, marten, beavers, wildcats, grey rabbits, the large grey and small brown squirrels and mice." (Winther, *Great Northwest*, p. 29.)

while retaining 50% of the stock in his name, to enlist membership in Pacific Fur, a subsidiary of America Fur Company. Apparently this was a paying proposition for when Astor died in 1848 he left a 20 million dollar legacy to set a milestone in American financial history.

On Thursday, June 12, 1810 (the same day the Winships were run out of the Columbia) Pacific Fur Company was formed at Montreal, Canada, with Astor as president and William Price Hunt, the sole American partner, second in command. In what proved to be a fatal mistake the other partners were Canadians formerly employed by the North West Company. Among these were Ramsay Crooks, Robert Stuart, Alexander McKay and Donald McKenzie, all men in their twenties. Strangely enough, many of the partners were loyal to Pacific Fur.

With rumors running rampant concerning west coast activities, Astor lost no time in setting up his defense and by late summer the hide war on the Pacific slope had been declared. In accordance with the Montreal meeting two expeditions started simultaneously for the Columbia, one by land and the other by sea. Hunt, a 27-year-old merchant tempered in the forge of the St. Louis fur market, knew little to nothing about running a fur brigade and even less about what lay out yonder across the wide Missouri. Yet it was he who would lead the overland party. The wilderness-wise Donald McKenzie and Ramsay Crooks were relegated to second and third in command. The 64-man expedition— made up of guides, trappers and hunters—was to time its line of march so as to arrive at the mouth of the Columbia at the same time as the supply ship, an ambitious undertaking. Although given no publicity, the crossing of the continent by the Astorians was in complexity and courage equal to the Lewis and Clark expedition.

This band of adventurers, hand-picked by the partners from every riverfront dive between Fort Mackinac and St. Louis, was to execute a threefold mission. First, they would spearhead a cross-country attack from the Missouri River to the Snake mountains. . . a broken escarpment forming the western stronghold of the Shoshoni nation, which before the end of another year would go down in history as "the Blues."[128] It

---

[128] Kaiba Uin'karets, Shoshoni name for the Blue Mountains, gained recognition in

was said by those who had been there that if the Shoshoni didn't get you, the Snake mountains would. Second, they would attempt a permanent American settlement in Oregon country. Third, they would monopolize the Pacific fur trade.

At the same time the northwest corner of Shoshoni territory raged in the grasp of a devastating forest fire which laid waste from the upper reaches of Burnt River to Hell's Canyon, Hunt shoved off from St. Anne's Chapel, bound for St. Louis. This old church on the extreme southern tip of Montreal Island was the departure point for all grand brigades into the unknown west, and it was from here almost a quarter of a century earlier that David Thompson embarked to check on Hudson Bay's arms shipments to the Blackfeet. St. Anne was the patroness of western explorers. At the chapel the devout hunters, Indian scouts, traders and river boatmen made their confessions and offered up their vows to St. Anne prior to departing into the interior. It was the custom, too, of these vagabonds—after leaving the chapel—to have a grande carouse in honor of the saint. In this part of their devotion Hunt's crew proved themselves by no means deficient.

Hunt arrived in St. Louis on September 3, 1810—five days before the sailing of the supply ship—where he immediately locked horns with

---

1811. Although he gives them no name, Gabreil Franchere, one of the Astorians, makes first reference to the Blues in his statement: "They were visible southwest of the Walla Walla River, 60 miles off." On July 19, 1811, David Thompson refers to them as the Shawpatin Mountains. But on August 8 he writes: Beginning to see the Blue Mountains between the Shawpatin and the Snake Indians." This is the first known record of their being called "The Blues." Two days later on August 10, 1811, Alexander Ross—another Astorian—at the mouth of the Umatilla River would note: "This river takes rise in a long range of blue mountains which runs nearly east and west and forms the northern boundary of the great Snake nation." Rev. Gustavis Hines describes the range in this manner: "As you approach the mountains on the south, the hills disappear and you find yourself passing over a beautiful and level country about 25 or 30 miles broad on the farther borders of which rise with undescribable beauty and grandeur that range which from its azurelike appearance has been called the Blue Mountains." Unknown to most travelers who saw them from a distance, the Blues appeared this way from smoke of constant forest fires which crept beneath the towering pines from late spring until snowfall.

Manuel Lisa. From the outset there would be no love lost between the leaders of Pacific Fur and Missouri Fur. Lisa had tried without success to get two of the Pacific Fur partners, Crooks and McClellan, scalped by the Sioux when they were working for the Canadians in 1807. It was common knowledge that McClellan had sworn to shoot Lisa the minute he caught him on Indian soil. Hunt was well known along Front Street and when the word got out that he was back in town offering high pay to accompany him to the Pacific coast, every trapper, guide and trader on the border was eager to follow him. It just so happened that at this same time Lisa was trying desperately to outfit an expedition to go in search of his partner, Major Andrew Henry, who was believed to be cut off by the Blackfeet somewhere in Oregon country. Both brigades were amply staffed with border riff-raff. What they needed now was experienced mountain men, and Hunt counted first coup when he snatched Joseph Miller away from Lisa. Miller, ex-U.S. Army officer, gentleman trapper and educated trader, was a welcome addition to the Astorians. To insure against Miller's being tempted by a more lucrative offer, Hunt signed him on as a full partner in the Pacific Fur Company.

On October 10, 1810, after obtaining the services of a gabby little Irish carpenter named Patrick Gass—Indian scout, Snake country guide and former sergeant in the Corps of Discovery—Hunt headed up the Missouri. The overland party had barely gotten up a head of steam when it was forced into winter retirement at the confluence of the Missouri and Nodaway rivers. During all this North West was doing little on the Pacific coast. Thompson had been recalled to Fort William to explain American activities on the west slope, while John McDonald had moved north to check on the Russians. This left 28-year-old Finan McDonald in charge of the operation. Finan, snug and cozy in a Spokane lodge, was doing little to improve North West's position in Snake country. His sole interest in the Columbia region was his newly acquired partner, Margaret Chin'chay Naywhey.

On September 8, 1810, four Pacific Fur partners, ten clerks and nineteen mechanics, hunters and laborers boarded the Astor brig, *Tonquin,* in New York harbor. All were British subjects sworn to establish an American fur-trading post in a region disputed by the United States and Great Britain. There were foreseeable inner conflicts of loyalty. While McDonald played, the *Tonquin* plowed through the stormy Atlantic on its 18,000 mile journey, bound for the most hazardous ocean currents in the world—the frigid passage around Cape Horn. At the helm was a headstrong former naval officer, Captain Jonathan Thorn, described as a "rigid commander with a reckless crew."

Lt. Thorn had served in the war against the Barbary pirates and was cited by Stephen Decatur, U.S. Naval Commander, for conspicuous gallantry. When given furlough for the purpose of commanding Astor's ship, it was implicit that the U.S. was supplying a valuable man for an establishment that would strengthen America's claim to the Columbia country.

Gallant or not, the Astorians soon found Captain Thorn to be a tyrant who at least in part was responsible for the eventual downfall of their mission. A graphic example of his strange behavior happened at the Falkland Islands. Among others, David Stuart and Gabriel Franchere were given permission to go ashore. Shortly after they reached land Captain Thorn weighed anchor and under full sail put out to sea with all intent to abandon them. As a last resort Robert Stuart—a partner in the company and David's nephew—held a pistol to Thorn's head and gave him the choice of waiting for the passengers or having his brains blown out.[129] Thus went the pleasant sea journey to the Columbia.

Back at the god-forsaken Nodaway winter camp, Hunt was joined by Robert McClellan. McClellan, ex-army officer who had fought under the command of "Mad Anthony" Wayne blew in from the Dakota plains just one puff ahead of a Sioux war party. With him was John Day, who had been burned out by the Comanches seven years earlier and had probed the high plains with Ramsay Crooks since 1805. Day signed on with the Astorians as ramrod of the company hunters. He proved to be a dead shot and that in itself was enough to make him an important man on the frontier. Soon after arriving at the Nodaway winter camp he won the everlasting gratitude of Hunt quite by accident. While on guard duty, Day discovered and helped discourage a mass desertion of Hunt's "hand-picked" crew, thus proving that he was one of the few dependable men in the outfit which was to face the dangers of Shoshoni country together.[130]

---

[129] Ross, *Adventures of the First Settlers on the Oregon or Columbia River, 1810-1813*, Chapter II: 49-53.

[130] At the time of planned mutiny, besides company officials, the Astorians at the

On New Year's Day, 1811, Hunt with eight men set off on foot for St. Louis, 450 miles downriver, to recruit more trappers. No sooner had they hit the frontier town than Patrick Gass, the only man who had been in Oregon country, mysteriously acquired enough credit to get staggering drunk. During the erratic course of this binge Gass quit Hunt and joined up with Missouri Fur, leaving Hunt without a guide.[131] Hunt, far from being a greenhorn, suspected where the source of supply was coming from and decided to slug it out with Lisa on his own terms.

A little roaming around at the local pubs revealed that Lisa's halfbreed Sioux guide, a young man who held the dubious distinction of having attempted to scalp his father, was ripe for the picking. This warrior was the son of Pierre Dorion, the French interpreter who accompanied Lewis and Clark on their trek to the Pacific Ocean. Old Dorion had married, among others, a Yankton-Sioux maiden and by her had a hopeful brood of half-breed sons one of whom was Pierre Jr.[132]

According to a Creole trader, "Wild Pierre" Dorion's love of liquor had got him into bad trouble with Missouri Fur. Going on a grand and glorious toot at Fort Mandan the previous winter, he sobered up to find he had consumed enough whiskey at ten dollars a quart to put him everlastingly in debt to Manuel Lisa. Dorion had refused to work without pay and no other outfit would touch him for fear of retaliation

---

Nodaway camp included 11 American hunters and 40 Canadian trappers. Five men had already deserted. John Day, a Virginian of Irish descent, was born in Culpepper County in 1771. . . the actual birthdate being uncertain. At the time of his entry into the Ochoco, Washington Irving described him as "a man around 40 years of age, 6'2" high, straight as an Indian with an elastic step as if he trod on springs and having a handsome, open, manly countenance." By 1810 he had already joined several North West fur trading expeditions up the Missouri under the leadership of Ramsay Crooks. (Timmens, *Who Was John Day?*)

[131] Gass left Missouri Fur to fight in the War of 1812 and was wounded at the Battle of Lundy's Lane. For a time he became a drunkard, then got religion, sobered up and at the age of sixty married and sired seven children.

[132] Young Dorion had also been acquainted with the Corps of Discovery for in Lewis's Journals for August 27, 1804, he states that they sent Pierre Dorion a trader familiar with the area, to invite the Yankton-Sioux to a council. Dorion returned two days later with his half-breed son (Pierre Jr.), five chiefs and seventy warriors. (Irving, *Astoria*, p. 117.)

from the tough Missouri Company. Likewise, the mere mention of this awkward position was enough to goad the excitable Dorion into a war dance.

Hunt ferreted out Dorion and made an offer. . . 150 dollars in gold to serve as interpreter and guide to the Pacific. Word leaked out to Lisa that Hunt was out to hire his man and overnight Dorion received more attention than he had ever gotten in his whole misspent life. Lisa had Dorion brought into his quarters where he explained things to the hot-tempered half-breed. He tried threats, promises and bribery in an effort to prevent Dorion from teaming up with Pacific Fur, but all this accomplished was to convince Dorion that he was indispensable to the fur trade. During the time Lisa was making his pitch Hunt started back up river, but he had barely gotten out of sight of St. Louis when here came Dorion, his undernourished wife and two sad-eyed children. The young half-breed informed Hunt that he was willing to listen to further offers. Dorion drove a hard bargain. After two weeks of negotiations he finally accepted 300 dollars in gold. . . 200 of which was to be paid in advance.

In the midst of this bargaining Hunt ran into Daniel Boone, who at 85 was returning from a trapping expedition deep into Sioux territory and was packing 59 beaver skins as trophies of his skill. Hunt tried to get Boone to join Pacific Fur. The old frontiersman was tempted, but after giving Hunt's offer some serious thought decided he best not risk Shoshoni country because of his advanced years. This meeting took place on January 17, 1811. Boone flourished for several years after this encounter, dying in 1818 at the age of 92.

The morning after Boone's departure Hunt was visited by John Colter. Colter who less than a month before had sworn never to return to Oregon country followed Hunt for half a day before continuing down river. He died 22 months later.

Arriving at Fort Osage on April 14, Hunt was met by Ramsay Crooks who had been holed up for the winter at Fort Mackinac. Picking up McClellan, Miller and McKenzie at the Nodaway winter camp, the Astorians braved the swollen crest of the Missouri and grimly paddled westward, led by a gun boat mounting a swivel gun comprised of two 4-pound howitzers. It was now May, 1811, almost two months past their scheduled meeting with the sea party and they still had almost two thousand miles to go.

As the overland party fought its way up the Missouri, the sea-thrust knifed through northern Pacific waters. Amid pounding waves, the *Tonquin*—following a journey filled with bickering and feuding between Captain Thorn, his crew and his passengers—reached the treacherous Columbia on March 22, 1811, and the Chinook sea gods were waiting. Despite high seas and approaching darkness. . . "damn the pagan deities, full sails ahead". . . Thorn made a run over the Columbia bar. In two attempts during which seven men were drowned a landing party finally reached shore. Pacific Fur had arrived in Oregon.

CHAPTER 19

WELCOME TO OYER'UNGUN

What would you have me do?
Would you have me stay at home and weep
for what I cannot help?

John Jacob Astor
Fate of the Tonquin

Operations at the mouth of the Columbia were still in a state of confusion when Captain Thorn decided to fire his first mate and ship out, leaving the Astor trading post unprotected and destitute of trade articles. Alexander McKay, Astor's partner in charge of Fort Astoria, was requested to accompany him. Knowing the disposition of the erratic naval officer, McKay sensed danger ahead and placed his 14-year-old son, Tom, in the care of Alex Ross, commenting. . . "the captain in one of his frantic fits has now discharged the only officer on board. If you ever see us safe back, it will be a miracle."[133] On June 5, 1811, Captain Thorn and McKay, leaving less than half the party behind to construct a trading post, sailed up the Washington coast to begin immediate trade operations with the coastal tribes.

By early summer the outlook was desperate at Fort Astoria. Not only did the *Tonquin* fail to return on schedule, but the overland party which was due in March had yet to arrive. It was now believed they had perished enroute.

Back on the Atlantic slope of the Rockies the overland party was being guided by an ex-Mississippi river pirate, Ed Rose, who came in out of nowhere and departed the same way, leaving the Astorians to the mercy of the land. To make matters worse McKenzie was not speaking

---

[133] Ross, *Adventures of the First Settlers on the Columbia River*, p. 98.

to Hunt. When he signed on as second in command, McKenzie believed that he and Hunt would share equally in the giving of orders, but that had been changed. When Crooks arrived from Fort Mackinac, he bore a message from Astor placing Hunt in full command. To McKenzie this amounted to a personal slap in the face and he swore that one day Astor would pay for this insult.

As the Astorians moved into Sioux country, they met Ben Jones and Alex Carson. For the past two years, these hardy souls had been trapping Shoshoni hunting grounds and in the course of their wanderings had traversed most of the beaver streams between the Blues and the Wind River Range. Hunt added them to his collection. Within the week he intercepted another canoe headed downriver and manned by Ed Robinson, John Hoback and Jacob Rizner, employees of Missouri Fur. Robinson—66 years old and one of the first settlers in Kentucky— had been scalped and had to wear a handkerchief on his head to protect it from the elements. These men convinced Hunt that the route of Lewis and Clark which he intended taking was not the best. They had discovered a better route to the south in what in the future would be known as the Great Divide Basin. With this information Hunt decided to leave the Missouri River when he reached the Arikara village— 1,430 miles inside Indian territory in central south Dakota—and find his way overland to the Pacific.

He also learned from them that they had been with Major Henry when he was routed by the Blackfeet at the forks of the Missouri and had followed him over the divide into Shoshoni country, where he was now forted up on a stream that flowed into the Pacific. Robinson, Hoback and Rizner were fed up with dodging Snake war parties now armed with modern weapons and were returning to Kentucky. But the sight of this grand brigade with its glamorous promise of riches stirred them to return to the Pacific trapping grounds. By now Hunt had a formidable array of riflemen, trappers and voyageurs.

Manuel Lisa had been dogging Hunt's back trail for 1,400 miles in an attempt to beat him into Oregon country. With twenty stout oarsmen pushing his canoe, Lisa caught up with Hunt just short of the Arikara village on July 3. Immediately, Lisa and Dorion got into an argument over the whiskey debt. It was a short-lived discussion. The half-breed slugged Lisa in the teeth and the fiery Spaniard with blood dribbling from his mouth dashed for a weapon. In a matter of seconds he returned with a skinning knife to find Dorion armed with a brace of pistols. At the first war whoop, McClellan headed for the battle and attempted to blow Lisa's brains out but Hunt jerked the rifle away before McClellan could inflict any damage. At this point Lisa accused Hunt of being a "double-dealing son-of-a-bitch." The outcome was that Hunt challenged Lisa to a duel and was joyfully accepted. They stalked off to get their respective weapons and the situation was fast shaping into a free-for-all when more sober heads intervened.

One was John Bradbury, who was acting as publicity man for the Astor expedition. Bradbury, an Englishman in his forties, had been sent to America to collect plants for the Liverpool Botanic Garden and in terms of natural history his journey with Hunt might be likened to the first voyage of Columbus. The other was Henry Breckenridge, a young pleasure-seeker and journalist who was writing up the Missouri Fur Company story for the New York press. They persuaded Hunt and Lisa to listen to reason by the simple expedient of calling upon the awesome assistance of the 6'6", 330 pound, Donald McKenzie and for the moment bloodshed was spared. Having settled this mess, Bradbury and Breckenridge hopped into a canoe and headed downstream for a more genteel society, happy to be still alive.

The two parties continued on in mutual distrust, a feeling transmitted to the crew. At the Arikara village John Day warned Crooks the Astorians were again plotting mutiny. Three of the partners were encouraging the men to revolt and the voyageurs were more than willing to desert at the prospect of having to ride a horse or walk to the Blue Mountains instead of gliding over the water. According to Day's report the laborers had stolen several weapons and a barrel of gun-powder and buried them in the river bank in readiness to seize one of the boats and head back to St. Louis. Again, Hunt whipped a desperate situation and on July 18 headed for the elusive Continental Divide. By now the expedition had been slashed to 65. . . including six partners, eleven hunters, interpreters and guides, Marie Dorion and her two children and forty-five French-Canadian laborers mounted on Indian ponies.

For the next two months they followed a route generally southwest, some of the time using a trail the Snakes had beaten out on their periodic visits to trade horses to the Arikaras, Mandans and Hidatsas. At the foot of the Big Horn Mountains they traded for more horses with the Crows and majestically entered the ancestral homeland of the Shoshoni. They reached the Wind River (already named by Robinson), on September 8 and journeyed up river, traveling a broad-beaten Shoshoni trail. On September 15 Hunt entered in his diary. . . "one of our hunters who had been on the shores of the Columbia showed us three immensely high and snow-covered peaks which, he said, were situated on the banks of that river." And thus, the magnificent Tetons—the glamour girls of the Rocky Mountain chain—called by Hunt "the Pilot Knobs" rose up on history's skyline.

Not certain as to where they could reach the Snake River, Hunt sent Day, Dorion and John Reed, the company clerk, on an exploratory tour to find those puzzling waters. While awaiting their return, he cast loose his first trappers into the maw of Shoshoni Land. Sending them out in pairs, the Pacific Fur partners began with their most experienced men. Alex Carson and Louis St. Michael were one team, Pierre de Taye and Pierre de Launey the other. They were outfitted with traps, arms, ammunition and horses with orders to trap the upper Snake until spring and then head for the mouth of the Columbia.

Hunt then took a bearing on the highest peak in the Teton range, called simply and appropriately "The Grand." Unknown to Hunt, he was heading towards sacred and therefore dangerous ground. High on the western slope of The Grand—known to the Shoshoni as "Big Brother"—is the Enclosure, a small, positioned rock circle where the Shoshoni made solitary visits to offer special prayers to the Great Spirit.[134]

Because of a scarcity of game Hunt could not head directly for Jackson's Hole through Togwatee Pass, the route Henry's men had taken in coming east. Instead, he took his men across Union Pass and down the Green River (which they called the Spanish River), correctly believing it to be a source of the Colorado. From the upper Green, taking the Shoshoni trail via the Hoback River, Jackson Hole and Teton Pass, they found their way to Pierre's Hole on October 8 and found the abandoned Pacific slope fort of Major Henry.

---

[134] Information given by the Shoshoni to the St. Stephens Indian Mission, St. Stephens, Wyoming.

While Hunt was trying to outmaneuver Lisa on the Atlantic side of the Rockies, Duncan McGillivray dispatched James Hugh, John McDonald and George McTavish with 30 men and 5 canoes out of British Columbia to release Thompson so he could continue exploration of the Blues and trade with the Snakes. Thompson headed into the Ochoco with an illustrious group, guided by Pierre Michael who had been working out of Grande Ronde with Finaly.[135] Also accompanying Thompson was Charolette Small, his 26-year-old Chippewa wife. Charolette was well aware that Snake maidens were considered by the fur men as the most beautiful and therefore the most desirable of all the western Indian ladies. Being of a suspicious nature, she was not about to trust David in their presence and for good reason. Having borne five children by March 28, 1811, Charolette was to produce eleven more for a total of sixteen Thompsons during her lifetime.

She also knew that there were probably a few more little Thompsons chasing around between the Blues and the Selkirks. It is fortunate she never lived to see this statement made by Duncan McDonald and released by the Montana News Association May 21, 1934: "David Thompson was a great man. He lived among my people (the Spokanes). . . he had a woman among the Salish and a daughter by a Pend Oreille woman. . . his descendants still live on the reservation." No mention was made of his romance at age seventeen with Sweet Grass, the Blackfoot temptress.

Curious as to what the Americans were up to, Thompson swooped down the Columbia to the mouth. On his downward plunge he drove a post at the mouth of the Snake River and attached a sign:

---

[135] This brigade was made up of: Francois Rivet, father-in-law to Peter Skene Ogden; Jaco Finaly and his Snake girlfriend who were to act as interpreters; Michael Boulard who shared in the shooting of Wuna Mucca; Nicholas Montour whose daughter married Tom McKay; Michael Bourdeaux, interpreter; Pierre La Gasse; Louis Le Blanc and Michael Kinville. (Masion, *Les Bourgeois de la Compagnie du Nord-quest*, Vol II, pp. 37.)

> Know hereby that this country is claimed by Great Britain as part of its territories and that the North West Company of Merchants from Canada do hereby intend to erect a factory in this place for the commerce of the country around.
>
> **D. Thompson**
> *Junction of the Shawpatin River*
> *with the Columbia, July 9, 1811*

Six days later Thompson's brigade moved into Fort Astoria, throwing the already dejected Pacific Fur partners into a state of frenzy. Just a few days before Thompson's unwelcome arrival they had received word of the fate of the *Tonquin.*

Lamay'sie, a Chinook warrior, stumbled into Fort Astoria and told a grim tale. As the *Tonquin* sailed up the Washington coast, Captain Thorn took Lamay'sie aboard to serve as an interpreter. A few miles south of Nootka Sound the *Tonquin* lay at anchor in Templar Channel and the first bargaining session began. In an argument over prices Thorn lost his patience and struck a Salish chief, one of the royalty of the Pacific Coast. A few days later as the *Tonquin* lay at anchor the Salish returned and butchered nearly everyone on board.

Alexander McKay was knocked down with a war-club and tossed into the Pacific, where he was finished by women in canoes. He was the second man to die. Thorn, opening Indian paunches with a whaling knife, soon followed McKay. Later believed to have been driven by suicidal tendencies, the ship's clerk touched off the powder magazine and the 290 ton *Tonquin* along with hundreds of Indians was blown to splinters. The Chinook interpreter was the sole survivor. He reported that arms, legs and torsos washed onto the Washington shore for days.

The Astorians were still in a state of shock when David Thompson arrived on July 15, bringing the competition of a company which had fought the mighty Hudson's Bay and the equally powerful Russian-American Company to a standstill in western Canada. Their senior partner and financier was not so disturbed. Astor was enroute to a New York theater when he received the shocking news of the loss of the company ship, *Tonquin.* He calmly proceeded to enjoy the evening out.

Back at Fort Astoria Thompson and his men coldly weighed the situation and bided their time. Perhaps with tongue in cheek Mike

Boulard tried to get David Stewart to switch alliance in exchange for title to an island in the Hawaiian group. Seven days after his arrival Thompson headed back up the river to plunge into the fur-rich Ochoco, followed by nine Astorians. The Nor'westers soon outdistanced them, but the hide war was now officially declared.

CHAPTER 20

AN ANGRY RIVER

*A short cut is often the quickest way to
some place you weren't going.*

Author Unknown

The overland Astorians didn't arrive upon Shoshoni soil unannounced. Word of their progress across the Dakota plains into the Eldahow had sifted up river via the Sioux, where it was picked up by the Crows and finally dribbled down to the Snakes, who were keeping a wary eye on British activities in the northern Blues. Their patrols also kept track of the Pacific Fur traders who attempted to follow Thompson on his thrust into the Ochoco. As it turned out, the Astorians missed Thompson's trail and continued northward up the Columbia where on August 31, 1811, they founded Fort Okanogan as a countermove against North West's factory on the Spokane River, which posed no problem to the Shoshoni.[136] While construction of Fort Okanogan was in progress, small war-parties slipped across the Snake River Plateau and watched the Americans progress with little concern. These warriors sensed that it was only a matter of time before Pacific Fur would be broken by the harsh embrace of their homeland.

Meanwhile, the overlanders had barely crossed Teton Pass when two well-armed Snake warriors rode into their camp. Earlier, Hoback,

---

[136] The Astorians hounding Thompson's back-trail included David and Robert Stuart; Ovide de Montigny; Francois Payette; Donald McLennon; Alexander Ross; three French-Canadian voyageurs and two Hawaiian Islanders. They took the first shipment of Pacific Fur supplies and trade goods up the Columbia in 1811 and founded the first American settlement in what is now the state of Washington.

speaking as a veteran of Shoshoni country, warned Hunt that he was treading on quicksand. Hunt found this information hard to accept, because the first Indians encountered on the Pacific slope, a mixed party of Earth Eaters and displaced Flatheads, had been cautiously identified by Dorion as Shoshoni. At the time Rizner had voiced his doubt as to the accuracy of Dorion's deductions but was generally ignored by all concerned. This chance meeting with the Earth Eaters, which culminated in a community buffalo hunt complete with mutual exchange of trade goods and beaver skins left the company partners jubilant. If these were Shoshoni, then the North West Company had been lying and Pacific Fur had little to fear in the Columbia operation.

Now, two braves rode arrogantly into camp and proceeded to watch activities with idle curiosity. At this time Hunt believed he could take to river travel once again. Observing the voyageurs busily making canoes in preparation, the Snakes offered Hunt a little friendly advice. The Kim'ooenim, their name for Snake River, would become angry if people attempted to ride upon its waters. Harm would befall those foolish enough to do so. This information brought forth a loud laugh from the boatmen. Louis la Bonte, his brother-in-law Joe Gervais, and Antoine Clappine—three of the best whitewater men on the North American continent—calmly announced that the Snakes were stupid even to suggest that Canadian oarsmen couldn't navigate this Oregon stream. Joe Miller was quick to agree with the voyageurs only because he was so saddle-galled he could barely walk let alone ride a horse for another 800 miles.

Hunt was not so sure. His own guides didn't seem to know for certain where they were and they were definitely confused as to the location of the Henry's fork of the elusive Snake River; Robinson's short cut to the Pacific Ocean. At the mention of Henry, the Snake visitors became quite interested and explained they knew the exact location of the white man's stockade. On October 8, 1811, the Astorians arrived at Fort Henry in a swirling snowstorm only to find it deserted, which came as no surprise to the Shoshoni guides. Missouri Fur had fared no better with the Shoshoni than they had with the Blackfeet. At least, there was shelter from the storm so Hunt holed up for some badly needed repairs on his equipment and again cast adrift a party of trappers into the wilderness. Because of their knowledge of the land these teams were made up of Robinson, Hoback and Rizner. To complete the set they took Bill Cannon, an ex-soldier who by his own admission was "a damn poor shot." As the trappers made preparations to shove off into the Lost River Range, Joe Miller gave up his partnership in Pacific Fur and voiced his intention to join Rizner. The partners argued that Miller, a man of education and cultured habits, was not suited to the harsh life of a free trapper. Miller was a stubborn man and his course of action was settled. Amply supplied with rifles, traps and ammunition, Miller slipped into the waiting mountains with the Snake warriors and Hunt was certain he would never be seen again.

Seven days later with a sodden snow covering the ground the Astorians completed work on 15 log canoes and, disregarding the Snake's warning, took to the waiting river. Following their customary prayers when challenging new waters, the boatmen made the sign of the cross and before embarking entrusted their horseherd to some bedraggled Earth Eaters who had wandered into camp the previous afternoon. In three days the brigade covered 280 river miles without seeing a living thing and the Snake's dire prediction of trouble seemed at best a premeditated bit of misinformation. Among the Canadians it became an increasingly hilarious topic, inspiring some of the more witty rascals to compose silly and impromptu verses about "les maudite riviere enragee."

With such joyous melodies as this reverberating across the barren Craters of the Moon the Astorians entered the ninth day of river travel intent upon making 100 miles before the sallow sun died in the western sky. Without warning the lead boats were being ground up in a whirling vortex of tortured water where the massive Snake River was compressed into a jagged basalt split 200 feet high and less than thirty feet wide, which Hunt later identified as "Cauldron Linn. . . the boiling waterfall." The canoe in which Crooks was riding and whose steersman was Antoine Clappine careened into a boulder and overturned in mid-channel. By some whim of fate Crooks, Day and Etienne Lucier were swept to shore. Clappine's luck had run its course. The old boatman who had seen America's wildest rivers from the deck of a pirogue was dashed into the rocks and his body strained through the wreckage of the splintered canoe. The cruel and unrelenting Snake had claimed its first white victim. The date was Tuesday, October 22, 1811. Only a few days before, the 480-ton *Beaver* sailed out of New York harbor, bound for the mouth of the Columbia with supplies and a reinforcement of men aboard.

With Clappine's death scream hanging like an omen of doom over the Snake River plateau Hunt ordered a halt. The following morning scouts were dispatched to check the river's course. For forty miles it got progressively worse as it crashed through two hundred foot gorges and over the terrible cataracts of Shoshoni and Twin Falls, aptly named by Hunt "the devil's shuttle hole" and accurately described to Lewis and Clark by the old Snake dog soldier, Swooping Eagle. On a last ditch gamble, for time was running out, McClellan took sixteen men with four of the sturdiest canoes and again took to the river six miles downstream from Clappine's watery grave. In less than five hours they lost all canoes, their weapons, furs and all personal effects. The Snake River was in no mood to be tampered with.

Hunt then dispatched Reed and Day south into Ute country with orders to bring back horses at any cost, for their position was now extremely critical. In an area never before traversed by white men they had no idea which way to go to reach the Columbia and no Indians to ask. They had but five days of provisions. . . after that only God knew what would happen for they hadn't seen any game in over 300 miles.

Now seven months overdue in their scheduled arrival at Fort Astoria, the company officials went into conference and decided to take off in different directions, each party to be led by one of the partners. Should any of them contact friendly Indians or obtain food, they would return to the main party; otherwise, they would shift for themselves and make their way as best as possible toward the Columbia River.

On October 24 the Pacific Fur brigade split into four units. Ramsay Crooks with five men started back up river to Henry's deserted fort to retrieve the horses. Robert McClellan with three men headed down river in hopes of finding quiet waters. Donald McKenzie with six men headed northwest across the lava beds toward the glistening Blues. Wilson Hunt with the main party set up camp at Shoshoni Falls. While the other partners searched for an avenue of escape, Hunt kept the men busy trapping beaver and building a cache in which to hide their extra blankets, trapping gear, trade goods and pelts they had traded for thus far.

Three days after his departure Crooks returned to Shoshoni Falls, defeated by the barren lava of the Snake Plateau. Four more days passed as Crooks and Hunt hopefully awaited word from either Reed or McClellan, while their men lived on sturgeon, which they speared at night by torchlight. On the eve of the fifth day, Ben Jones and Giles LaClerc staggered into camp and reported the Indians hostile, no game, the river impassable. On that bleak intelligence Hunt, Dorion and eighteen men struck down the north bank of the Snake, swinging into the desert in an effort to locate food. Crooks, Jones and seventeen men plodded down the south side of the river with the same thought in mind.

For 27 days Hunt's group straggled across the dismal Snake Plateau, begging what food they could from the Earth Eaters, which was precious little for these tribesmen had scarcely enough to keep body and soul together. Nevertheless, they generously shared fish rations and sold the Americans two horses. On their 58 mile push from the mouth of the Bruneau River to the Boise River, Hunt's party crossed one of the more desolate stretches of Shoshoni country. Until relieved by a driving rain, the thirst-crazed Canadians took to drinking their own urine.

Moving down the Boise River, the Astorians wandered into Crooked Leg's camp among whose lodges grazed close to 600 horses. While not unfriendly, the Snakes were very reserved and not only did Crooked Leg refuse to sell Hunt any horses, but he was not anxious to feed the trappers. Here, Crooked Leg's young son, Washakie, met his first white men. Finally, to get rid of the unwelcome visitors, Crooked Leg consented to sell them some dried fish, a few camas roots and four dogs.

The Astorians settled down to a hearty meal when a scowling brave stamped into camp, leading one of the horses Hunt had purchased from the Earth Eaters. Without fanfare, the Snake flatly stated that the horse belonged to him. Hunt had sense enough not to argue this matter, for he believed he could retain ownership in exchange for a couple of iron kettles. This amounted to nothing less than an insult. Hoping to avoid further trouble, Hunt, minus one horse, made ready to retreat down the Boise River. It was now November 22, 1811.

In leaving, the Pacific Fur men were again completely astonished by the behavior of the strange, aloof Indians. As they broke camp, a grim looking group of Snake dog soldiers stalked into camp and Hunt expected the worst. To everyone's amazement they presented Dorion's wife with a pinto pony and with no comment left camp.

Even Dorion realized that his Sioux blood hadn't aided in this transaction. Most likely it was held against him. But the sight of a hollow-cheeked, scrawny Iowa maiden—eight months pregnant—who was trying so valiantly to keep abreast of the line of march, packing all of her husband's worldly belongings on her back, struck a responsive chord in these tough warriors' hearts. Above all the Shoshoni admired anyone who could display raw courage in the face of hardship.

Five days after this episode the Astorians were forced to kill Hunt's saddle horse. Hunt refused to be a party to this sacrilege. In his journal he penned this observation. "The men find the meat very good and, indeed, so should I were it not for the attachment I have to the animal. . . November 27, 1811." The next day being Thanksgiving, this admirable loyalty fell by the wayside. Hunt lunched upon his faithful pony, pronouncing him. . . "fat and tender."

One hundred miles to the southwest in the bleak Ruby Mountains— the southeastern division between the Ochoco and the Eldahow— Crooks' emaciated group bore north, pushing ever closer towards the brooding headland of the Blues. Near the mouth of Malheur River, Crooks caught up with Reed and Day, who had veered west looking for horses and wandered into the Strawberry range of the Blues. They were now camped on the Ochoco side of the Snake, living on bear meat. These two had been dodging Utes, Snakes and Paiute hunting parties ever since leaving the main expedition at Shoshoni Falls and had killed very little game for fear their rifle shots would attract the Shoshoni. Their windfall of bear meat had come quite by accident.

Just before their union with Crooks, Day and Reed, while sneaking through a lodgepole thicket, ran head on into a big grizzly, who was hunting a place to hibernate. Although the bear showed signs of fight, Day forbid Reed to shoot for fear of alerting the Snakes, but the grizzly had other ideas. With a snarl it reared up on its hind legs and stalked towards the trappers. Again Day warned Reed to stand still and not shoot. For a moment it worked. The bear retreated some twenty yards, then turned back, rumbling deep in his throat. This was too much for Day and a rifle ball slapped into the enemy. Surprised, Reed asked Day why he broke the silence. "Why boy," replied the old hunter calmly, "caution is caution, but one must not put up with too much even from a bear. Would you have me suffer myself to be bullied all day by a varmint?"[137] Crooks could sympathize with Day for near Henry's Fort he, too, had gotten into trouble with a grizzly when he wandered from camp without his rifle and couldn't find a tree to climb.

Six days before Crooks' arrival Reed and Day had met with McClellan, who was traveling light and fast. He and his men were in excellent shape and were heading due north up the Snake River into the Seven Devil Mountains, home of the Banattee (Robber) Snakes. In sharp contrast to Crooks and Hunt, McClellan had encountered friendly but starving Indians along the east side of the river, which brought forth a lively discussion. If Dorion was correct and these were all Shoshoni, why was it that "some had horses to ride, weapons to bear and were openly belligerent, while others had worn moccasins for transportation, no weapons and were overly accommodating?" It didn't make sense to the Pacific Fur men. They would not be alone for this issue was to confuse the white race into the 20th century.

For the present Crooks had more pressing problems to ponder. His men were facing starvation. No longer did they encounter any Shoshoni, hostile or friendly. Neither could they find game along the dreary, wind-swept river, for the deer, elk and buffalo had pulled back into the protected valleys of the Ochoco. At the mouth of a stream which eight years in the future Peter Ogden would name Burnt River they found McKenzie. McKenzie was in no better condition than Crooks' party. Normally weighing over 300 pounds, he was now reduced to a hide-covered skeleton.

Under a snow-laden pine a few yards from Burnt River, McKenzie and the fever-ridden Crooks held council. They decided McKenzie would head north into Cayuse country in the hopes of intercepting McClellan. Reed, who was in the best physical condition of all, would accompany McKenzie's unit as a hunter. Crooks and Day would continue into the maw of Hell's Canyon—1,800 feet deeper than the Grand Canyon and the narrowest and deepest gorge on the North American continent.

---

[137] A full account of this episode can be found in Irving's *Astoria*, pp. 211-12. A complete description of the Astorians struggle across the Snake River Plateau to the Columbia can be found in Irving's *Astoria*, Chapters XXX-XXXVI.

On December 6, where the Blues and Seven Devils merge, Hunt and Crooks, although on opposite sides of the Snake, united. Hunt sent a boat made from the hide of a recently killed horse over to pick up Crooks. By now Crooks and Jean Baptiste Dubreuil were so burned out with malaria that further progress into Hell's Canyon was suicide. Unknown to them, McKenzie had united with McClellan on the head-waters of the Grande Ronde, both parties being unaware of North West's trading post farther downstream. From here, McKenzie and McClellan's group battered their way across the Blues, keeping alive by eating boiled strips of beaver skins and one mountain sheep, killed by McClellan. They found the Umatilla River and on January 18, 1812, this vanguard of the overland expedition arrived at Fort Astoria almost a year behind schedule.

Back on the Snake, Hunt had little hope for the survival of the Astor Expedition. He had left the main party some 130 miles up river at the mouth of the Weiser River. He and Crooks having scouted both sides of the Snake to Hell's Canyon decided that the Weiser camp would be the best spot to attempt a crossing of the Snake. Crooks took the horsehide boat back to the west side and they headed back, each party on his own side of the river. On the return trip Dorion spotted a lone Shoshoni lodge, which he estimated to hold five inhabitants. Hunt ordered an attack. The Shoshoni, thoroughly addled by the first blood-curdling shriek, took off without even catching their horses. With a little maneuvering Hunt managed to capture five of the animals of which one was killed and consumed on the spot. Now well supplied with horse meat Hunt set up a cheery night camp.

Crooks, moving up the west side, made a cold camp. The next morning he was furious when he looked across the river to see Hunt's men dining on horse flesh while his men starved. Crooks tried but was too weak to take the horse hide boat across the Snake and his voyageurs were so terrified of the "mad river" they refused to cross, even with the promise of roast meat. Finally, Ben Jones and John Day arrived from an unsuccessful hunt and Jones took the canoe across. During this interlude Jean Prevost went insane.

Jones, who was as weak as the rest of Crooks' men, stayed with Hunt and Joe De Launey brought some meat over to Crooks. No sooner had he beached than Prevost was on top of him, screaming for food. In his unhinged condition Prevost wouldn't wait for the meat to be cooked, yet refused to eat it raw. Lunging into the canoe, he and De Launey got into a violent fight and in the process the canoe swamped and the Snake swallowed another Astorian.

The next morning Hunt decided to get his group together on the east shore and began ferrying Crooks' men across the Snake. By afternoon Day, who had been strong enough to man the canoe, came down with malaria and by evening was too weak to move. At the same time Dubreuil was "having fits." Crooks, still mad at Hunt, told him to go on, that he would stay with his men, and so Crooks, Day and Dubreuil were left to die.

On the morning of December 10, Hunt headed upriver and reached the Weiser camp on December 12. It took him eleven days to get the frightened Canadians across to the Ochoco side, but the operation was finally completed on December 23. During this period the mighty Kim'ooenim had iced over and the back-breaking labor of packing supplies over the frozen Blues now faced him. To attempt the mountains without a guide would be certain death. . . to remain in hostile Shoshoni territory without food was equal to two deaths!

Hunt and the overland expedition spent Christmas eve 1811 in Lone Pine Valley at the eastern base of the Blues. After more than 800 miles of unbelievable hardships they were finally leaving the Snake, a river which the Canadian boatmen always spoke of as "les maudite riviere enragee. . ." the accursed "mad" river, a name bestowed in unbridled merriment was now held in abject fear.

CHAPTER 21

WOLF TAIL'S CAMP

. . . . . a proud-spirited race and
uncommonly clean. . . . .

Wilson Price Hunt
Pacific Fur Trader

On December 30, 1811—in the extreme northeast corner of the snow-stifled Ochoco—a new member joined the Astor overland expedition. Marie Dorion in her 25th year staggered into a frozen windfall on the Powder River and gave birth to her third child.[138] This first native Oregonian in whose veins flowed the blood of the white race was born on the ancestral hunting grounds of the Bear Killer Snakes.

Her tiny son may have been an extra burden to the Iowa woman, but his appearance didn't slow Hunt down for a single minute. Doggedly he wallowed through knee-deep snow, pushing onward and upward toward the summit of the Blues. Four hours behind him, the exhausted Iowa woman clasped a shivering baby to her breast, painfully mounted a weary horse and pushed him to the utmost in an effort to catch up. In the gloom of evening she unknowingly passed within feet of Michael Carriere, who was about to take his last sleep in the gently sifting snows of the northern Blues.

Ahead of her the main party clawed over an icy divide and beheld a sight which to them resembled the garden of Eden. Before them lay a long, narrow valley unexplainably bare of snow. Yet around its outer

---

[138] Marie Aioe L'Aguivoise Dorion, daughter of an XY Company fur trader and an Iowa Indian woman, was the first woman to cross the western plains and settle in Oregon. Married three times to white men, she died September 3, 1850, and is buried in the old Catholic cemetery at St. Louis, Oregon.

rim lay four-foot snow drifts and its bubbling stream was fed by frozen creeks. In the head of this "pleasant valley" sat the main lodges of the Banattee Snakes. To complete the idyllic setting hundreds of fat, juicy horses grazed along the valley floor. With whoops of joy the Astorians descended into the valley and were greeted with another pleasant surprise. These Shoshoni under the leadership of Wolf Tail were willing to trade horses for rifles and ammunition. Hunt, priding himself on being a shrewd trader, little realized how desperately the war tribes wanted weapons. For a rifle, one smooth-bore musket, an iron hatchet and a few boxes of lead balls, he bought four horses, three dogs and some camas roots. Beside the lodges of the Snakes, Pacific Fur celebrated New Year's Eve, 1812, complete with dog chops and horse steak. No doubt the German partner was faring somewhat better at a New York banquet room.

However, all was not smooth. No one wanted to leave Pleasant Valley. Following a bitter flare-up, Wilson Hunt and Ben Jones split forces. Many of the men mutinied, striking out on their own. On January 6 those who remained loyal to Hunt crossed the summit of the Blues. . . and high on the gaunt side of the Elk Horn Range a sad little depression in the frozen ground marked the final cradle of Marie Dorion's infant son who died of starvation January 7, 1812.

Moving down Granite Creek toward the north fork of the yet unnamed John Day River, Hunt noted in his journal. . . "dropped down onto the headwaters of a large river which led through a deep, narrow defile between stupendous ridges. Here among the rocks and precipices we saw game of that mountain-loving animal the blacktailed deer and came to where tracks of horses were to be seen in all directions, made by Indian hunters. Below the mouth of a sizeable stream adding to this river we found a large winter encampment of the Sciatogsa (Saidyuka) and Tuschepas (Tussawehee) tribes around whose camp there were grazing upwards to 2,000 horses.[139] These people speak of knowing and

---

[139] These were the Buffalo Killer (Saidyuka) and White Knife (Tussawehee) Snakes under the leadership of Lake Hunter and Old Deer Running.

trading with Jacques Finaly." Hunt describes the Snakes as:

> . . . being as well clad as the generality of the wild hunter tribes. In fact, they are better clothed than any of the wandering tribes I have yet met west of the Rocky mountains. Each has a good buffalo or deerskin robe and a deerskin hunting shirt and leggings. This tribe of Indians, who are a proud-spirited race and uncommonly clean never eat horses or dogs, nor will they permit the raw flesh of either to be brought into their huts. They have a small quantity of venison in each lodge but set so high a price upon it that we could not afford to purchase it. They hunted the deer on horseback and they are admirable horsemen and their weapons are bows and arrows which they manage with great dexterity. They are altogether primitive in their habits and seem to cling to the usages of savage life even when possessed of the aids of civilization. They have axes among them, yet they generally make use of a stone mallet wrought into the shape of a bottle and wedges of elk horn in splitting wood. Though they might have two or three brass kettles in their lodge, they frequently use vessels made of willows for carrying water and even boil their meat in them by means of hot stones. Their women wear caps of willow neatly worked and figured.

From the Shoshoni camp Hunt moved over onto Butler Creek and followed it to the Umatilla River, reaching the Columbia on January 21. On February 15, 1812, the main overland party arrived in a driving rain at Fort Astoria to find company morale in shambles. Hunt immediately took over command of the operation and just as quickly shipped out to Hawaii on company business.

CHAPTER 22

TERROR IN THE OCHOCO

Now John Day lies brittle as ice,
with snow tucked up to his Jaws,
Somewhere tonight where the hemlocks moan,
and crack in the wind like straws.

Lew Sarett

Hunt's decision to forsake Crooks, Day and Dubreuil most likely saved their lives. Watching Hunt tramp up river, leaving the half-dead trappers to starve, the Snakes were unimpressed. They held no respect for a chief who would desert sick men in the heart of enemy territory.

On the afternoon of December 10, 1811, as the three headed south to intercept Hunt's line of march they were met by the noted Snake medical doctor, Weasel Lungs.[140] For nearly a week he stayed with the feverish trappers, providing food, medication and tending to their needs. During this time he moved them to the Powder River where he gave instructions on how to reach the Columbia. Crooks and Dubreuil quickly recovered under Weasel Lung's care but Day, pushed to the brink of complete exhaustion, failed to respond.

---

[140] Besides being priests many of the so-called medicine men were also gifted physicians. Alexander Ross, one of the Astorians, witnessed what a Shoshoni doctor could accomplish: "I once saw an Indian who had been nearly devoured by a grizzly bear and had his skull split open in several places and several pieces of the bone taken out just above the brain and measuring three-fourths of an inch in length, cured so effectually by one of these doctors, that in less than two months after he was riding on his horse again at the chase." (Ross, *Adventures of the First Settlers on the Oregon or Columbia River, 1810-1813*, Chapter XIX, p. 290.)

On the sixth day his fever broke and Weasel Lungs abruptly left. Next morning Crooks headed up the Powder in hopes of uniting with the main expedition, unaware that Hunt was still bogged down on the east side of the Snake, trying to convince his boatmen to attempt a river crossing. Covering less than fifteen miles, Crooks was forced into early camp at the mouth of Eagle Creek, for Day was still too weak to travel under his own power. For the next twenty days Crooks and Dubreuil suffered in this snow-encrusted canyon, fighting to keep Day alive and in the process again succumbing to malaria.

Unable to hunt for game, Crooks dug a few frozen roots and was attempting to cook them when he fell into the fire, smothering it with his body. Lurching to his knees in a near state of panic, he was too feeble to rekindle the fire and so the Astorians lay in a stupor, awaiting death, when two Snake hunters drifted into camp.

These hardened warriors, accustomed to the harshness of their native land, couldn't ignore this suffering. Quickly they kindled a fresh fire, cooked food, carried water and constructed a suitable camp. Within three days the Americans were feeling quite cheerful. The Snakes assured them that their luck was much better than they realized. The roots which Crooks had so painstakingly dug and had been unable to cook were those of the deadly, poisonous water hemlock.

Day especially thrived under the Shoshoni's care and the day after they left was able to shoulder his rifle. Wolves, which had been silently watching this Oregon frontier drama unfold, were due for a surprise. "Mad John," every bit as savage as his four-legged enemies, coldly took aim and that evening the convalescents dined on wolf cutlets. Before leaving Eagle Creek, Crooks boiled the wolfskin into a pungent broth, which gave the trappers the needed strength to resume their journey. The remaining wolf meat was sliced and dried and the bones pounded into powder and mixed with camas roots to provide more broth material. Day strung the teeth on a rawhide thong around his neck to insure good hunting on their perilous jaunt across the northern Blues.

They had hardly broken camp when they were joined by Jean Baptiste Turcotte, Francis Landry and Andre La Chapelle, Canadian deserters from Hunt's brigade. These men told a harrowing tale of how the Blues stripped Hunt's command of any semblance of order, leaving a pitiful shell of the once glorious grande brigade which was to have captured the Shoshoni fur trade.

Crooks, still the voice of authority, ordered the deserters to return with him to the Columbia and in late January, six frost-bitten trappers hounded Hunt's fading trail into the raw north wind, guided by Chapelle. Moving away from the Powder River, they became lost in a blizzard and wandered into a desolate wasteland of tree skeletons. . . memorial of the 1810 Burnt River forest fire. Starkly etched against an eerie backdrop of ghostly mountains, their blackened limbs seemed to point into eternal damnation instead of the easy route Weasel Lungs had spoken of and the snow-free valley Chapelle had been babbling about since joining Crooks.

Chapelle, missing Pleasant Valley by 50 miles, found himself on the frozen crest of the middle Blues. February, engulfed in a mountain white-out, whistled through Dixie Pass, stampeding Chapelle, Turcotte and Landry into another revolt. Cursing Crooks for being a madman, they disappeared onto the Snake River slope. Hopelessly confused, Crooks, Day and Dubreuil continued down what they believed was the Columbia slope, taking a southwesterly course deeper into the glowering ridges of the inner Blues. On the headwaters of the John Day River, they stumbled across the tracks of hundreds of horses heading west into the southern Blues. Drifting along this trail, they came upon an old Indian hunter who told them that the tracks they followed were those of a Shoshoni movement to better grass in the southern Ochoco.

This was the migration of the big Snake encampment Hunt had visited on January 6. The Shoshoni hunter also told Crooks that he was a friend of Jaco Finaly and that the North West Company had a trading post less than two days ride to the north.[141] As proof he proudly

---

[141] When an Indian spoke of distance, he meant the shortest and most direct route for that is the way he traveled. For a better understanding of this measurement we again turn to Ross, the Pacific Fur trader. "In traveling, the distance of places is always calculated according to time. If on horseback, a day's ride is estimated at about seventy of our miles; if on foot, at half that distance. This mode of calculating distance is, however, very erroneous and not to be depended upon by the whites, as the natives seldom take into consideration either the good or bad state of the roads. But interruptions which are grievous obstacles to us are nothing in their way; for where a rabbit can pass, an Indian horse will pass, and where a horse can pass, the savage who sticks on his back

displayed his North West rifle. That night a mountain blizzard obliterated all sign of the migration and their Snake informant had disappeared.

Completely lost, the Astorians wandered aimlessly down the backbone of a trapper's paradise, vainly searching for trails concealed beneath six feet of snow. The cold stabbed like a driven arrow as they sank deeper into the frozen jaws of the Ochoco. It was a winter hell of frosted pines whose brittle arms clutched menacingly as each gasping man passed by. . . a frigid torture chamber whose wind-swept ridges promised escape only to lure them into an intricate maze of storm-lashed canyons each more foreboding than the last. . . a sub-zero temptress who allowed them just enough roots and wood mice to thwart the Snow Spirit's design for death.

On this journey, they saw beaver to defy the imagination, huge animals measuring five feet from nose to tail and weighing upwards to 100 pounds. But the knowledge that such animals existed held no charm for the starving, frightened trappers. Week upon week of absolute confusion was taking its toll. The brutal effects of their rigorous efforts became more evident each day. Search for the Columbia trail was forsaken; fur became a thing of no consequence; all desire to locate Hunt was lost in the fight for survival. More beast than human, the Astorians only thought was to break free of the crushing forest.

Crazed by hunger, cold and fear they staggered into a Snake hunting party on the headwaters of the Ochoco River.[142] Instead of rejoicing, Crooks and Dubreuil scurried into the dense thickets but not the gaunt Irishman. Cackling like a demon, Day lunged toward the Indians.

---

like a crab passes over hill and dale, rock and ravine at full speed; so that good roads or bad roads, rugged or smooth, all is alike to him. (Ross, *Oregon Settlers*, Chapter XX, p. 309.)

[142] The time of this encounter corresponds with tribal legend that with the arrival of white men in eastern Oregon, spirits took possession of the area between Mount Pisgah and Slide Mountain in the Ochoco range of the Blues. No Shoshoni would enter that area other than to conduct burial services. Most accounts claim Crooks, Day and Dubreuil never reached present Crook, Wheeler or Grant counties. Then again, they also claim Day died in 1812. John Day trapped the Ochoco and Eldahow for at least seven years before his death, and there is evidence that he may be buried in the heart of the Ochoco.

Seeing this, his companions, now fired with reckless bravery, came out of hiding to shake their fists threateningly and mouth animal-like snarls. The startled Snakes knew beyond doubt they were set upon by evil wood spirits and abandoned the area in speechless terror, leaving the demented white men to rant at will. Watching the Shoshoni ride off brought some return of sanity to the Astorians, for, too late, they realized their sole chance for survival was melting into a blinding snowstorm.

Through the glittering eyes of a mad-man, John Day chose the avenue of escape. Back they staggered across the frozen John Day River, pawed over the frigid middle Blues and, finally, emerged on the frozen Umatilla plains. The shock was too much for Dubreuil and on the wind-torn breaks of the Columbia, he collapsed, unable to move any farther. Within a few hours some Walla Walla hunters, led by the war-chief, Eagle, found the emaciated Astorians and took Dubreuil into their camp where they nursed him back to health.[143] Day and Crooks shoved on to the Columbia, reaching the river near the present site of Umatilla, Oregon. It was now mid-April, 1812.

Back on the eastern seaboard a harassed government was also suffering grave hardships. . . what to do with all the ill-gotten Indian lands the United States was accumulating by the millions of acres? Why not, reasoned an inspired Congress, create a new bureau? In that manner they could also pay off some political debts to those who had been faithful to the Madison Administration. And so, while Congress wrestled with a solution to the Indian land problem in Washington, D.C., Crooks and Day on the banks of the Umatilla River made the acquaintance of Zeck'a Tapam, head chief of the Walla Walla nation, who

---

[143] Eagle is the same man who in 1825 elected to have himself buried alive in the same grave with his dead son as so graphically related by Peter Skene Ogden in *Traits of American Indian Life and Character*, published in 1853 "By a Fur Trader." Jean Baptiste Dubreuil eventually recovered from his trek through the Ochoco and trudged on to Fort Astoria, pledging his support to Pacific Fur. In 1814 he became a North West Company trapper and later was engaged by Hudson's Bay. In 1840 he settled in the Willamette Valley where his name appears on the Oregon tax lists from 1840 to 1844. Thereafter, his name vanishes from the records and from Oregon history. (*The Washington Historical Quarterly*, Vol. XXIV, p. 230.)

clothed and fed them. At the end of three days rest they mounted Indian ponies and started down the Columbia, still expecting to catch up with Hunt at any moment.

Many miles downstream a Snake war party wandered its course up the river of the West, heading toward Crooks and Day. These Hoone-booey raiders—after a week of trading, gambling and bordello hopping—had stirred up plenty of trouble in the great Wasco village of Celilo and were now beating a hasty retreat to the Kosípa Tu-wiwa Gaiya, age-old northern route into the Ochoco.[144]

The warriors were in a jovial mood after this impromptu raid, staged for no other reason than to let the river tribesmen know that the Shoshoni had survived the long winter of 1811-12. In so doing they unwittingly played another important role in Pacific Northwest history. Slashing their way through Wasco long huts, they ran head-on into John Reed's brigade which had left Fort Astoria on March 22 with dispatches to John Jacob Astor in faraway New York City. Showing no partiality between Wascos and Americans, Reed was clouted with a war club and left for dead. His dispatches, unimportant to the Shoshoni, disappeared into a Wasco long hut and a dizzy, disgusted Reed headed up river for Fort Okanogan. Astor was not to find out the fate of his fur venture for another year.

Now some twenty miles up the Columbia, the Bear Killer dog soldiers laughingly goaded their jaded mounts into a half-hearted trot, for they planned to camp at the mouth of the Muddy Water and dusk

---

[144] The Kosípa Tu-wiwa Gaiya is known today as the John Day River. On October 21, 1805, Lewis and Clark named it the Lepages River to honor one of the men in the Corps of Discovery. John Work in his journal entry dated June 25, 1825, first used the name "Day's River." Two years later on November 29, 1827, Peter Skene Ogden writes of crossing "John Day's River." With four major watersheds—North Fork, Middle Fork, Main Channel and South Fork—the John Day River drains a large area of very little rainfall. The amount of suspended material it carries away from its drainage basin each year equals 198 tons per square mile or a total of more than one and a half million tons of earth and debris floated away annually. Its Shoshoni name translates to "Muddy Waters."

was near at hand. Swinging around a rocky bluff which marked their goal, the Bear Killers came to a surprised halt.

On the east bank a brush fire crackled in the chill air. Within its circle of warmth two men were engrossed in laying out camp. Curiously, the Shoshoni studied this new situation. Black Coal, leader of the pack, watched in stony silence. Eyes hard as chilled lava caught each movement as the unwary strangers prepared to eat. Then he made a decision. The dog soldiers would slip up stream a few miles, ford the Muddy Water and pay these intruders a visit at daybreak. With that the raiders melted into the night.

The following morning the Pacific Fur traders relinquished all claim to property rights, including saddle ponies, food, rifles, blankets, flint and steel. Then they were stripped of clothing. Had Black Coal not intervened, the saga of Crooks and Day would have played its final scene on the banks of the Muddy Water. As was, when the revelry appeared to be getting out of hand, the stoic chief interrupted with a curt command, ordering the white men's release.[145] Later, Crooks would give this account of their misfortune:

> One morning as we were sitting near the river, gazing on the beautiful stream before us, the Indians in considerable numbers collected round us in the usual friendly way. They then told us some of their people had been killed by whites and threatened to kill us in turn. In this critical situation John Day prepared to draw his knife. It would have instantly proved fatal for us and he desisted. The Indians then closed in upon us with guns pointed and bows drawn on all sides and by force stripped us of our clothes, ammunition, knives and everything else. . . by their movements and gestures it appeared evident that there was disposition on their part to kill us. But after a

---

[145] Most historians, including Bancroft, Carey, McArthur and Scott, say that the Astorians were protected by "an old Snake Indian" who saved them from death and helped them to escape. Black Coal (Tovuveh) was not an old man. As nearly as can be determined from historical records, Black Coal was approximately 25 years old in 1812. Old men did not ride with Dog Soldiers.

long and angry debate in which two or three old men seemed
to befriend us, they made signs for us to be off.[146]

Thankful to be alive, Crooks and Day headed back for the Walla
Walla encampment on the Umatilla River.

For two days they stayed inland on top of the Columbia bluffs,
making as fast time as was possible on bare and bleeding feet. Their
only food in four days was the pounded bones of a long-dead fish. On
the fifth day they begged scanty rations from some more kindly
Wishram Indians and two days later safely reached the camp of Zecka'
Tapam.

During their move back up river, Congress had solved its problem.
On April 25, 1812, it created the General Land Office as a bureau of the
Treasury Department with Edward Tiffen, an Ohio politician and former
Indian land surveyor, as Commissioner of the newly established bureau.
Too add dignity to this enterprise every land patent issued would be
personally signed by the President of the United States. This practice
would continue until 1833 when a full time secretary was authorized by
Congress to sign the President's name. By the close of 1812 sixteen
district land offices were in full operation, dispensing Indian lands.

Meantime, several warm meals, skin clothing and two saddle horse
livened the spirits of Crooks and Day, but not to the extent that they
wished to see more of Oregon country. Both agreed that returning to St.
Louis would be far easier and considerably safer than facing the
Shoshoni again. They were turning their backs on the Columbia when
a flotilla of canoes bound from Fort Okanogan to Fort Astoria hove into
sight. Hailed from the shore, John Reed saw "standing like two spec-
ters" Crooks and John Day.[147] And thus, one year, seven months and
two days from the date of their St. Louis departure, Crooks and Day
completed the hazardous journey across Shoshoni Land.

It was May 12, 1812. Three days earlier with the clouds of war
hanging heavy on the horizon, the company ship *Beaver* crossed the
Columbia bar and lay at anchor opposite Fort Astoria.

---

[146] Ross, *Oregon Settlers*, Chapter XI, pp. 191-92.

[147] Grinnell, *Beyond the Old Frontier*, p. 25; Ross, *Oregon Settlers*, Chapter XI, p.
188.

CHAPTER 23

DEATH BLOW

Too often the struggle's been given up,
When he might have captured the victor's cup.
And he learned too late, when the night slipped down,
How close he had been to the golden crown.

Author Unknown

After months of privation in the Ochoco it was difficult for Crooks and Day to adjust to life at Fort Astoria. Day, normally an outgoing person, became increasingly moody and uncommunicative, while Crooks' dislike for Hunt seemed to increase daily. When Hunt assigned Robert Stuart to pack similar dispatches to Astor which John Reed had lost at Celilo, Crooks and McClellan gave up their partnerships in Pacific Fur and accompanied him back to the states. Day was entrusted to Stuart to serve as a messenger. It was his job to elude Snake war parties and carry dispatches between Stuart's eastbound party and Fort Astoria. Although he said nothing at the time this apparently weighed heavily on Day's mind.

Stuart's brigade, made up of four Canadians and four Americans, left Fort Astoria on June 29, 1812, unaware that England and the United States were at war. During Hunt's push to the Columbia, England—at odds with France—issued the unpalatable Orders in Council, which prevented the United States from trading with either country. Madison, who had been the patron saint of Pacific Fur, was now struggling with the international situation, trying to get George III and Napoleon to listen to reason and rescind the obnoxious orders on foreign shipping which were playing havoc with American trading vessels. Out on the high seas they were being kicked about by both nations and it was not easy to tell which was kicking harder. Meanwhile, Baranov's Russian kayak fleets ranged the Pacific Coast from Alaska to Baja California for sea otter, fur seal and salt.

Tired of arguing with Madison, Parliament repealed the Orders in Council on June 23, 1812. It was too late. There was no Atlantic cable to bear the news to Madison. Hotheads in Congress, shouting how Canada could be conquered in six weeks, inflamed the public with the war-cry of "sailor's rights" and on June 18—five days before repeal—Congress declared war on Great Britain; a war which proved nothing for either side other than wiping out the Pacific Fur Company. The United States was unprepared for war and England had her hands so full elsewhere that one more small enemy was not worth bothering with. U.S. troops jammed north into Canada and were soundly thrashed but in so doing goaded the fur trade into a scorched earth policy.

Earlier, both British and Americans had tried to scuttle the Russian fur trade by supplying arms and ammunition to the Alaskan Tlingits. In fact, the Indians were even aided in this armed conflict by American sailors. Now their sights would be set on each other and the battle ground would be Oregon country.

Stuart had barely gotten started to St. Louis when on July 1 near the mouth of the Willamette River he noted in his journal: ". . . between the hour we stopped and dusk evident symptoms of mental derangement made their appearance in John Day." That night Day went to bed "gloomy and churlish." The following evening Day grabbed a pair of loaded pistols from Ben Jones both of which he put to his head and fired. His aim was high and all he succeeded in doing was parting his scalp. Stuart had him instantly secured and placed under guard in one of the boats. He now had a problem.

On July 3, Stuart diagnosed that "John Day's insanity amounted to real madness" and that "it would be highly improvident to suffer him to proceed any farther, for in a moment when not sufficiently watched he might embroil us with the natives." This was true for whenever they met any Indians, Day would curse them and try to get into a fight. So Stuart negotiated with a Chinook chief to take him back to Fort Astoria.

It was a stroke of luck that Stuart got rid of Day when he did for three days later his party ran into the backwash of a Shoshoni raid. At the dalles in the Columbia (see footnote 153 on page 214), a Snake war party under command of the Tussawehee dog soldier, Crooked Leg, had ripped the Celilo village to shreds. These notorious river pirates got a taste of their own medicine when they lost most of the valuables they had looted from the Americans. Four of the more foolhardy Wascos put up a fight and at Stuart's arrival were still twitching in a bloody heap on the south bank of the river. Caught in this quick slaughter were two women who had been keeping Paiute slave girls. The Astorians prepared for battle. Had Day been present to shout insults at the raiders, they would have gotten it. As was, Crooked Leg had what he came after and left Stuart's party alone.

Heaving a sigh of relief, Stuart continued up Hunt's back trail. His most impressive accomplishment on this jaunt east—for which he received no credit—was the discovery of South Pass just a half mile north of the Great Divide Basin, known to the Shoshoni as the place "where God ran out of mountains." Twelve years later Ashley's fur brigade, led by Tom Fitzpatrick, was given the honor of discovery. Here it was difficult to tell that they were crossing the mighty Rockies for the ascent from Sweetwater Valley was so slight as to be hardly noticed. In the summer of 1842, Kit Carson had to inform Fremont that they were riding through South Pass. Unimpressed, Fremont compared the crossing to "the ascent of the Capitol Hill from the avenue at Washington."

Back on the Columbia, Day, trussed up like a Christmas ham, arrived at Fort Astoria a raving madman and was chained in a log hut. Hunt was not impressed with Stuart's decision. Only John Reed treated the old veteran with kindness and through his efforts Day regained sanity, although rumor was that he died soon after his delivery to the fort.

By 1813, the rawboned Virginian had returned from the realm of cobwebs and gloom, stoutly insisting that the hardships encountered in the Ochoco were in no way responsible for his "lapse of memory." He blamed it on rot-gut whiskey and women or as he put it, "I lived a mite too fast and injured my constitution by too many excesses." Having regained full possession of his senses, Day realized that Pacific Fur was a doomed venture. Once word trickled down from the Canadians in the spring of 1813 that England and the United States were at war, panic and treachery ripped the company to shreds.

Early in the year Hunt took command of the *Beaver* to trade with Count Baranov, leaving Astoria in the hands of McKenzie and Duncan McDougal. This proved to be a fatal blunder for McKenzie's brother, Roderick, was one of the main stockholders in the North West Company and McKenzie had never forgiven Astor for placing Hunt in command of the overland expeditions. He knew that trouble was imminent and bided his time. Meanwhile, he took charge of the inland fur brigades, which were already meeting Astor's greatest expectations. On May 25, John Clarke, whose brigade had been working from the Spokane River to the lower Snake during the winter of 1812-13, sent twenty-eight horse loads of pelts to Fort Astoria. He then proceeded to the Weiser River where he had cached the company barge and some canoes on hunting grounds of the Robber Snakes. To his surprise nothing had been stolen.

Clarke, another Canadian partner, was somewhat of an arrogant dandy who thoroughly enjoyed the luxuries of life even when traveling the wilderness trails of the raw Oregon country. Alex Ross—chief Pacific fur trader at Fort Okanogan, which was in direct competition with North West's Spokane House—had little respect for Clarke's trading abilities. Although he referred to him as "the brightest star in Astor's constellation" and a "man of nerve on most occasions," Ross believed Clarke was afraid when it came to dealing with Indians.[148] Clarke may have been cautious, lacking in judgment and self-indulgent but he certainly wasn't intimidated. Hudson's Bay could vouch for that. Company records would describe Clarke in this manner:

> Farther up the table the fearless, actor-like John Clarke and the swarthy, shifty-eyed William McIntosh, an old Northwester, faced each other across a few feet of board. For years the two had led opposing forces in their district, keeping as close to each other as flint and steel and striking sparks of violence. Their latest meeting had been in the winter when they marched all day on snow shoes on parallel courses a few feet apart, cursing each other. In the evening, by agreement, they had made one campfire and then emptied their pistols at each other with only the flames separating them. Clarke had cheered him on, sympathizing with him for his bad shots and proposing that they keep loading and firing until one or both was dead and gone to hell in their campfire.

Now, Clarke's gratification of the inner man would reap a lasting reward. Among other delights, he packed a silver goblet, which he treated like a relic and from which he drank imported rum with the air of a statesman. This expensive goblet had originally been presented to

---

[148] Ross, *Oregon Settlers*, Chapter XII, pp. 195-96.

Alexander McKay by Astor. When McKay was killed on the *Tonquin,* Clarke immediately snatched the chalice, which rightfully belonged to young Tom McKay, and considered it his personal property from that day forward. After drinking, he would lock this rare vessel in a large iron box which accompanied him wherever he went. Naturally, this sensitiveness aroused the curiosity of the Shoshoni no end and its silvery brilliance was far too much in the way of temptation to be ignored.

On the night of May 30, 1813, while camped on the Weiser River, Clarke was somewhat befuddled by the appearance of an extremely shapely Banattee wench and during the course of the evening he forgot to lock his strong box. . . an oversight he would soon regret. The next morning a wild-eyed, tousle-haired Clarke aroused half the Oregon territory, yelling that his precious goblet was missing. Before anyone realized what was taking place, he posted guards all around camp and was searching anyone and everyone he could lay hands on.

During this intermission the Banattee temptress disappeared. By late afternoon Clarke was in an exceptionally foul mood when a simple young Dog Rib (Shirrydika) brave sneaked into camp to find out what all the commotion was about and got caught by Etienne Lucier.[149] Gloating over this catch, Clarke decided to make an example of this "bold renegade." At daybreak he sentenced the Shoshoni to death. Don McLennan, second in command of the brigade, attempted to reason with Clarke, but he would not be side-tracked even if it meant war with the "whole damn Snake nation!"

Amid confusion, a gallows of canoe oars was erected as a motley crew of curious Robber and Dog Rib Snakes crowded around to see what the crazy white men were up to this time. All were overjoyed when Clarke painstakingly explained how good he had been to them and how dastardly their actions had been toward him. He went on to tell how

---

[149] Lucier, who was one of the original members of the Hunt Overland party, became the first farmer in the Willamette Valley in 1829. On the 1844 tax roll he is listed as having hogs valued at $100; horses worth $450; Cattle $1,295 and clocks worth $12. His farm was situated on the east side of the Willamette River on the present site of Portland, Oregon. Lucier was present at both the first and second "wolf meetings." (*Washington Historical Quarterly*, XXIV, October, 1933, p. 286.)

"this skulking scoundrel" had been apprehended in the act of a gross crime and now he must be punished. The Snakes, understanding nothing, were in full agreement.

Tom Farnham, a Green Mountain boy from Vermont who had been robbed of a pistol, would act as executioner. When the Dog Rib brave was brought forth, he, if none of his tribesmen, suddenly realized that this was the end. He made a frantic effort to escape only to be launched into the land of his fathers. The gathered Snakes, now stunned into reality, gazed at the jerking body in mute awe. Aside from that no emotion flickered across their now stoic faces, but in their hearts a terrible, unrelenting hatred was mounting like the rising surf on a storm-lashed sea.[150]

Clarke, his ruffled ego now salved, moved back across the Blues toward Fort Astoria, feeling in all honesty that he had taught the Snakes never to tamper with white men again. Long before he reached the mouth of the Columbia horsemen packed the word to the war camps and the courtship for American arms was over.

Adding to the unrest, word had filtered across the Rockies that Black Gun's young sister had died at a fur company outpost on the upper reaches of the Missouri. Her premature death was blamed on the "white man's curse." If the rumor was true, it would place current accounts of Sacajawea's long life in jeopardy, and there is substantial evidence to support her early death. Five months before Clarke's fatal blunder with the Shoshoni, John Luttig, a Missouri Fur Company trader at Fort Manuel in present-day South Dakota, would note in his journal on December 20, 1812: ". . . this evening the wife of Charbonneau, a Snake squaw, died of a putrid fever. She was a good wife and the best woman in the fort, age about 25 years. . . ."[151]

---

[150] Alexander Ross would later note: "If you offend or even assault an Indian, he seldom resents at the moment or shows any sign of violence or passion; but, on the contrary, he remains sullen, mute and thoughtful. This forbearance, however, forebodes no good; for he broods over the insult or injury and meditates revenge. Years may elapse, but the injury is still fresh in the savage breast; and there is but one way left for you to ward off the meditated blow and that is by a peace-offering. . ." (Ross, *Oregon Settlers*, Chapter XXI, p. 307.)

[151] Luttig, John C. *Journal of a Fur-Trading Expedition on the Upper Missouri,*

Shortly after Clarke arrived back at Fort Astoria, Hunt ordered John Reed to trap the Ochoco and in August, Reed headed up river with the first fur brigade to string traps solely within the boundaries of the ancestral hunting grounds of the Shoshoni. Unknown to Reed, he was to lead a Pacific Fur brigade into the interior, but before it strung its first traps it would become a North West brigade.

As Reed approached the Ochoco, Hunt—leaving Duncan McDougal in command of the fort and Don McKenzie in charge of inland fur operations—boarded the company ship *Beaver.* Dodging British men o' war, he sailed up the Pacific coast for the Russian outposts of New Archangel and St. Paul, where he intended to complete a deal he had negotiated with Baranov involving a cargo of seal skins. Hunt had barely gotten out of sight when on October 16, 1813, McDougal and McKenzie—acting in spite of the protests of John Clarke and David Stuart—sold the Pacific Fur post to the North West Company for $42,000, which amounted to nothing less than an outright gift to the Canadian company. Immediately, Russell Farnham, brother to the Snake executioner, hailed a trade vessel and sailed to Kamkatcha in an attempt to overtake Hunt. He carried with him all the company records and the bill of sale for Fort Astoria. Failing in his search for Hunt, Farnham then struck out on foot across the frozen plains of Siberia and nearly three years later tramped into Denmark where he caught a ship at Copenhagen bound for New York harbor. Hunt wouldn't learn of the sell-out until he returned from Alaska in February, 1814. In April, he abandoned the post and returned to St. Louis.

Less than two months after McDougal and McKenzie transferred ownership of Fort Astoria to the North West Company, the *Raccoon,* a British sloop of war under the command of Captain William Black, escorted the merchant vessel *Isaac Todd* to the mouth of the Columbia

---

1812-1813. Confirming Luttig's entry for Dec. 12, 1812, William Clark would note in his *Cash Book* that Sacajawea was dead by the 1825-28 period. The misconception of long life occurred when Grace R. Hebard published her *Sacajawea* in 1933, claiming that the Indian woman had lived at the Wind River Reservation in Wyoming under the name Porivo until her death in 1884. For further information see "Probing the Riddle of the Bird Woman" *Montana: The Magazine of Western History,* Vol. 23, 1973, pp. 2-17.

where it continued up the north Pacific coast on a trade mission. On November 30, 1813, Captain Black jammed his 26-gun war ship over the Columbia bar to claim Fort Astoria as a prize of war. His first comment on seeing the Pacific Fur post was: "Is this the fort I have heard so much of? Great God, I could batter it down with a four-pounder in two hours!"

In an effort to wrest the trading post away from the Canadian company, Captain Black formally seized Fort Astoria in the name of his Britannic Majesty on December 13. This proved to be a costly mistake, which may have been the deciding factor in Great Britain's loss of Oregon to the United States. However, with the Union Jack flying over her ramparts, Fort Astoria became Fort George.

Following this transformation, the Ochoco came under British control for a period of five years and the Eldahow—under the influence of Fort Henry—flew the Union Jack until 1826. On Christmas Eve, 1814, President Adams signed the Treaty of Ghent and Fort Astoria again came under the Stars and Stripes, but it was a barren restoration. Astor's Pacific Fur Company which, to use his words was to "have annihilated the XY Company; rivalled the North West Company; extinguished the Hudson's Bay Company; driven the Russians into the frozen ocean; and with its trade with China to have enriched America". . . was dead.[152]

---

[152] Ross, *Oregon Settlers*, Chapter XVII, p. 270.

CHAPTER 24

THE FIRST SNAKE BRIGADE

Each man is born to one possession
which outvalues all others—
his last breath.

Mark Twain
Nevada News Reporter

The collapse of the Astor enterprise left control of the Pacific Northwest entirely in the hands of the Canadian North West Company and by April, 1814, it began expanding into the heart of Shoshoni country with Alexander Henry in charge of inland operations. Throughout all this, Red Wolf had been keeping a low profile and was thoroughly disgusted with the Earth Eaters—Snake, Ute and Paiute alike. With word of Clarke's hanging of the Dog Rib brave, it was time for the dog soldiers to ride and they eagerly awaited the arrival of the next American Fur brigade, unaware that it would come as a North West brigade, a group they did not wish—just yet—to antagonize.

Meantime, expecting John Reed to return at any moment, Henry had already appointed him as brigade leader of the North West Snake country operation. As for the remainder of the Astorians, those who wished to return to the United States were free to do so. On April 4, 1814, the famous Grand Brigade under the leadership of Don McKenzie and John Clarke left Fort George for Montreal. It was composed of ten bateaux, each of which was designed to carry fifty 90 pound bales of fur plus provisions for the eight-man crew.

To give an idea how the fur men traveled, Frederick Merk in his *Fur Trade and Empire* describes it thusly. . .

> When enroute the voyageurs were at their paddles 18 hours a day. The general travel routine was to rise at 2:00 a.m. With tents struck and canoes loaded they were away in a half hour.

Around 8:00 a.m. a place would be located for breakfast. Forty-five minutes was allotted for this meal, including un-packing, cooking, washing, shaving, packing again and away. At 2:00 p.m. a stop was made for dinner. Only 20 or 30 minutes allowed for this as no cooking was involved. After 18 hours of such, camp was pitched for the night and six hours allowed for sleep. On a portage (such as the dalles of the Columbia) each man carried two pieces of ninety pounds each in a leather sling across his forehead, leaving his hands free to clear the way.[153] All this incredible toil the voyageurs bore without murmur and generally in great glee.

Among the passengers in the Grande Brigade were John Day, Alexander Carson and William Cannon.[154] They had entered a contract with Henry to trap the area between Crooked River and Spanish (Green) River in southwestern Wyoming for 50 percent of whatever they caught and delivered to Fort George. Following in the Grande Brigade's wake came Henry's North West Brigade, which was to strike eastward from Fort George, stripping the streams as they went from the Coast Range to the Blues in an effort to close out Baranov's Russian brigades and to discourage any undue interest from the American fur companies. It was Henry's belief that these rival outfits would present the only competi-tion, but he was soon informed by his Cayuse and Nez Perce scouts that the Russians and the Americans were not the ones that North West had to worry about. Nurturing a healthy respect for their inland neighbors,

---

[153] The word "dalles" signified to voyageurs river rapids flowing swiftly through a narrow channel over flat rocks. The Dalles derived its name from this French word and was applied to the narrows of the Columbia River—La Grande Dalle de la Columbia. The name first appeared in print on April 12, 1814, in Franchere's *Narrative* to describe the long narrows.

[154] It is obvious from this entry in the diary of Alexander Henry, dated March 20, 1814, at Fort George, that John Day was still alive: ". . .the last of the free Americans, John Day, Alexander Carson and William Cannon, arrived from the Willamette. . . ." A few days later Henry made this entry, ". . .arrangements made with John Day, Carson and other freemen on halves for Spanish River. . . ." It is almost certain that he was the "Joshua" Day who, with David Stuart, were canoe passengers in the Grand Brigade which left Fort George for the east on April 4, 1814.

the Columbia tribesmen cautioned Henry to tread cautiously when he entered the hunting grounds of the Shoshoni. The proof of this warning would come much sooner than anyone expected.

The Shoshoni had learned through bitter experience with the Black-feet that muskets were the latest fashion in modern warfare. Without one, you were a dead duck. All in all, this was not a pleasant thought even to a heathen savage, so the Shoshoni painstakingly began to amass a small arsenal and by 1813 they were successful in obtaining firearms from Canadian, Russian and American fur trappers by trade, by theft or by force. . . to them it made little difference just so long as they secured weapons. However, it didn't take long to figure out that trade weapons (with the exception of North West guns) made especially for the fur trade and more commonly called "Indian guns" were of an inferior quality. No less a man than Sir George Simpson, governor of western Canada, confirmed this belief. Writing to the Hudson's Bay Company on May 18, 1821, he assured them that. . . "the trading guns (marked Wilson) are not to be compared with those of Barnet's make which the North West Company imports. The Wilson's locks are badly finished, soft in the hammer, the tumbler and shear not properly tempered and the pan loses the powder. . . . "[155] Small wonder the Indians chose to steal or kill for their weapons for they reasoned and rightfully so that if the white man was packing it, it must be a better weapon.

Once again armed bandits of the western mountains, the dog soldiers were riding the vengeance trail when in the last gray days of 1813 their path crossed that of John Reed's Snake brigade. Despite a grim warning that he was trespassing, Reed proceeded to string traps throughout the hunting grounds of the Buffalo Killer and Robber Snakes, two of the more unpredictable tribes of the Shoshoni nation. This was a fatal mistake for the war tribes were already seething over Clarke's hanging of a Dog Rib brave. Because of this and the flaunting of tribal rights the Snakes flew into sudden rage and in the first murderous attack launched by one of the sixteen war tribes which later formed the Paviotso Confederacy, slaughtered every man in the North West fur brigade.[156]

---

[155] Hudson's Bay Record Section, Publication VI, p. 408.

[156] Alexander Ross, who studied the different tribes of Shoshonean stock, identified Reed's killers as Banattee. For some reason, perhaps because they couldn't

The full impact of this sudden explosion was not to reach the Canadians until the spring of 1814.

While this was taking place, Congress on February 10, 1814, granted 875 acres of Indian lands in northern Louisiana to the old warrior, Daniel Boone, now in his 88th year. Some two months later and three thousand miles to the west, the Grande Brigade beached at the mouth of the Walla Walla River. Don McKenzie was dumbfounded to hear a woman calling to him in French. It was the bony Iowa woman, Marie Dorion. Sobbing with relief, she finally blurted out what had transpired during the terrible winter of 1813-14.

Having trapped through the middle Blues, Reed set up base camp in September on the Ochoco side of the Snake opposite the mouth of the Boise River. He was now poaching on hunting grounds claimed by the Robber Snakes. The Earth Eaters were friendly and willing to trade furs for any trinket available. But when the dog soldiers rode into camp, they demanded guns and ammunition in exchange for furs which Reed refused to do. In view of their threatening nature Reed abandoned his log trading post and moved a few miles north, where he constructed a fortified log cabin near the present site of Nyssa, Oregon. At this site Reed was joined by Hoback, Robinson and Rizner who two years before had left the overland expedition to trap the middle Snake. Fifteen days before their arrival at Reed's outpost, they had been robbed of horses, furs, guns and ammunition by the Snakes and left to starve.

Reed re-outfitted the trio and from the Nyssa position started stringing traps in all directions. The next warning that he was treading on dangerous ground came when Francois Landry on a scout up the

---

understand the Shoshoni dialect, all other white men of that period referred to the Banattees as "Bannocks," a name that would stick. According to other Snake tribes, the Banattees to date had caused most of the disturbance between the whites and the Snakes. (Grinnell, *Beyond the Old Frontier*, pp. 88 and 111). Ross would further state, ". . .this Shoshonean tribe (the Banattees) lived mostly by plunder and had a long career in crime." They perpetrated the unprovoked murder of John Reed's hunting party from Fort Astoria in 1814 and in the year following, they added to their score many acts of savage violence. (Ghent, *Road to Oregon*, p. 218.) Marie Dorion claimed the Dog Ribs (often called Dog Eaters) were also involved and she was an eyewitness to the affair.

Owyhee River ran head-on into a Shoshoni bullet. Thrown from his horse, Landry managed to remount and made it back to Reed's cabin where he died. Immediately thereafter, Reed and Joe De Launey got into an argument over the sensibility of trapping the Ochoco and De Launey on advice of his Earth Eater wife headed back for Astoria. Five days later on a small stream in the middle Blues, Robinson found the Earth Eater girl staring at a rock mound which covered the last remains of her departed husband. Later, Dorion saw De Launey's scalp dangling from a Snake war lance. The news of this second killing didn't deter the hot-tempered Reed one bit. If anything, it only served to make him more determined to trap Shoshoni soil.

In November, Reed dispatched Jake Rizner, Giles LeClerc, Andy La Chapelle and Pierre Dorion up the Riviere au Malheur, so named by them and meaning "a bad hour or bad time of day." Trapping as they went, these men by mid-December had worked their way into the southern Blues, moving across the hunting grounds of the Buffalo Killer Snakes onto the winter camp grounds of the Bear Killers. Here, they set up camp at the forks of the Malheur River. Finding an abundance of beaver, they built a log cabin in preparation for an all-season's work, for they were taking pelts "with great success." They were also killing any game that came within sight.

While the trappers worked the feeder streams, Marie Dorion, who had remained at Reed's cabin with her two children, stretched the skins and cooked meals. She was thus employed on a late evening about January 10, 1814, when a friendly Indian came running to Reed's cabin "in great fright" and told him that a band of Dog Rib Snakes had burned the first outpost built and were now headed for the Nyssa house "whooping and singing the war song."[157] Upon hearing this dire warning, Marie with her two children left for the Malheur camp in a night snowstorm to alert her husband of danger.

For three days the Iowa woman slipped up the Malheur, dodging Snake patrols. Late in the evening of the third day and within sight of the trapper's cabin, Le Clerc staggered out of the brush and collapsed, his buckskin jacket soaked with blood. In a rasping voice he told Marie

---

[157] *Oregon Settlers*, Chapter XVII, p. 266.

that her husband was dead. Early that morning the four men had been stringing traps up a small feeder stream—now called Calamity Creek—when they were ambushed by a Snake war party. Rizner shot one dog soldier and dropped another with his clubbed rifle before he went down with a buffalo lance jabbed through his chest. Dorion, who never fired a shot, departed the Ochoco with a war axe buried in his skull. The last La Chapelle was seen, he was headed toward the Malheur River at the end of a rawhide rope. LeClerc, his huge carcass so full of holes he looked like a sieve, was left for dead.

Marie Dorion did not approach the trapper's log cabin for fear of being detected. Common sense told the terrified Iowa woman that her only chance for survival was instant flight. With super-human effort she got the dying LeClerc on her horse. Then, placing her oldest child with LeClerc, packing the youngest in her arms and leading the horse, she headed for Reed's base camp, travelling all night.

The following evening she encountered a Snake war party which was heavily armed and riding east toward the Snake River. Immediately, the Iowa woman hid her children in the rocks, then dragged Le Clerc to the ground and led the horse into a ravine. That night the four fugitives slept without food or fire. Huddling her children to her small body, Marie kept them alive through the sub-zero night, but Le Clerc with blood freezing to his chilled body died before morning.

At the first streak of gray in the eastern sky the woman cut across the northern face of Double Mountain and slipped into Reed's camp in a softly falling snow storm. Splotches of fresh blood were seen in the snow. Stumbling over a new-blown drift, the frightened Indian gasped as she stared down on the bald head of Ed Robinson. This survivor of one scalping by the Wyandotte in the dark and bloody ground of Kentucky had not been so lucky on the Oregon frontier. Horror-stricken, she burst into the cabin and there sat John Reed with a bullet hole in his head and both arms missing. Running blindly out of the cabin, the young widow Dorion hurried up the Snake River, praying she might find Hoback and Turcotte. A half mile from the violent Reed massacre she found Jean Baptiste Turcotte. . . as well preserved as a chunk of marble. A few yards away John Hoback formed an eddy in the gently drifting snow. This was the legacy of John Clarke. . . "an old Nor'wester who should have known better than to commit the grave indiscretion of hanging an

Indian who had stolen a silver goblet but later returned it."[158]

Numb with fear the Indian woman headed toward the sullen hump of the Blues, travelling for two days and nights without food or sleep. Moving ever upward across the headwaters of the John Day, she went into hiding in a lonely ravine in the middle Blues where she spent the winter in a lodge of pine bark and fir branches pitched beside a mountain spring. Here, she killed her horse and smoked him for food. Marie Dorion and Nannette De Launey, a terrified Earth Eater girl who quickly joined her tribesmen, were the sole survivors of the first ill-fated Snake brigade.

Now, at the mouth of the Walla Walla River in the arms of Don McKenzie, Marie Dorion allowed her emotions to give way. At last her lonely ordeal was at an end and the senseless hanging of a Dog Rib brave had been avenged in true Shoshoni style.

A few hundred miles down river new indiscretions were in the making. They, too, would add little good to North West's reputation in the Oregon country.

---

[158] Grinnell, *Beyond the Old Frontier*, p. 31.

CHAPTER 25

INTERMISSION AT FORT GEORGE

The girl whose tailored jeans reveal
Her ultimate dimension
Is basically, one can't but feel,
Just panting for attention.

Mo Nugent
A Posteriori Reasoning

The slaughter of the North West fur brigade threw Alexander Henry's plans for advancement into the Ochoco off schedule. He immediately retreated to Fort George only to find administrative activities in a miserable mess. Before the messenger bearing the grisly fate of Reed's party reached company officials in Montreal, North West suffered another loss.

Following the signing of the bill of sale turning Astoria over to the North West Company, Henry had taken charge as acting governor of the Columbia district. As Henry was rushing back to Fort George from the interior, his replacement, an iron-willed Scot who believed in the creature comforts of life had arrived at the post aboard the *Isaac Todd* on April 17, 1814. Donald McTavish (of the McTavishes who helped form the North West Company) had been appointed governor of the Columbia district at the purchase of Fort Astoria; an appointment he viewed as being tantamount to exile among the savages of the Pacific Northwest. Prudently, he stocked his stateroom on the *Isaac Todd* with some of the comforts of home—bottled wine, prime tinned English beef, cheese and. . . a curvaceous blonde Portsmouth barmaid. Jane Barnes to McTavish's practical eyes definitely spelled comforts of home. He lost little time in convincing her that an ocean voyage was just what she needed to broaden her outlook.

When they arrived at Fort George thirteen months later, Jane's sole broadening experience had consisted of a prolonged scamper around

McTavish's stateroom. That would soon change. When they arrived in the ship's longboat, the astonished clerks and lonely fur hunters swore that flaxen-haired Jane with eyes of blue had a figure that ". . .would founder a man o' war in full rig."

Before the month of April had passed McTavish's wandering eye latched onto a Kathlamet girl fondly referred to by the trappers as "young Madame Clapp." A headstrong member of Indian royalty, she was the unstable wife of the extremely jealous Chief Calpo, second in command of the Chinook nation. The chief took an exceedingly unsportsmanlike view of this current love affair. Earlier, he had upped the price on furs when he caught his wife playing around with the traders. Now, Calpo refused to trade with the Nor'westers at any price, which was not good for company profits.

Suspecting that business matters were in a decline since their trade for Fort Astoria, a dispatch arrived ordering McTavish to report immediately to company headquarters at Montreal. Obviously, Miss Barnes—although she was such a comfort—would be no asset to him at that august body, so McTavish adroitly decided the overland trip would be too arduous for a lady of her genteel upbringing. He made arrangements for her to return to England. But the *Isaac Todd* wasn't scheduled to sail for three months for it was awaiting fur shipments from the upper Columbia. As McTavish explained it, "to protect Miss Barnes from the love-struck clerks and lecherous trappers" he formally and publicly turned Jane's safe-keeping over to Alexander Henry. Henry quickly disclaimed all emotional considerations in this deal, admitting Jane was rather nice to have around but noting in his diary that the transaction was "more an act of necessity than anything else." Perhaps it was.

While the Montreal brigade was being outfitted, McTavish now had free rein to play house with Madame Clapp while Henry—now without responsibilities with the disbandment of the Snake brigade—took to roaming the beach with Jane Barnes. On one of these jaunts they were spotted by Cassakas and the chase was on. Cassakas—son of old one-eyed Concomly, chief of the Chinook nation—was no poverty-stricken suitor and his offers for Jane's companionship were hard to compete with.

To bring things into perspective, Fort George, situated on the main north Pacific sea-lanes and capital of the Columbian district, was fast becoming the Babylon of the west coast. Having first priority on

European delicacies brought by merchant vessels around the Horn, it was an important port of call. Sailors and passengers flooded ashore where slavery, gambling and prostitution flourished. The Anglo-American acceptance of this free-wheeling lifestyle would soon court disaster in their business relations with the Snakes. As noted by Meriwether Lewis in Journals of 1805 ". . . the Shoshoni were extremely rigid in their morals and especially did this code hold true for women. By contrast the sexual standards of the women of the Columbia River tribes were unusually lax. . . . " By 1814 venereal disease—introduced by fur hunters and sailors of the fur-trading ships—had spread like wildfire, reaching epidemic proportions among the fur traders from their contact with these women.[159]

Chinook concubines were a mixed blessing at Fort George. Successive chief factors made no progress against prostitution. Added to the low state of morale and bickering there was disease. Nine out of ten white men at the fort had to undergo "a course of mercury."

Now, to add to the love web of McTavish, Madame Clapp, Henry, Barnes and Cassakas, young Alex McKenzie brought Chief Concomly's daughter, the Princess of Wales, into the fort. Accompanying the Princess were ten female slaves whom she rented out to sailors on shore leave and visiting traders from the interior. This did not set well with jealous Chinook concubines of other North West employees. The Princess and her slaves interfered with their chief source of revenue and they were seriously plotting to end the reign of Her Royal Highness.

Luckily for North West Company, this farce was drawing to a close. At 5:00 p.m. on the wind-lashed afternoon of May 22, 1814, Henry and McTavish—well-supplied with rum—started across the Columbia to the *Isaac Todd* in a long boat. Within the hour, Jane and Madame Clapp began a weeping session that was to last far into the night. Their gallant lovers—now floating face down in the churning breakers off Ilwaco Head—would never return.

The minute Cassakas heard that Jane had become a double-widow so to speak, he borrowed his father's best war canoe, loaded it down

---

[159] For more on this subject see, *Surgery, Genealogy and Obstetrics*, 85: 663-669, November, 1947.

with 100 prime sea otter pelts and boldly dashed to the fort in full courting array with painted face and body glistening with whale oil. In an impassioned voice he told Jane that on her acceptance, he would ship the otter pelts to her relatives in England. In a moment of weakness he promised he would never ask her to draw water, carry wood, dig for roots or hunt game. Further, he would make her mistress over his other four wives. Jane could wear her own clothing rather than the scanty bark garments of the Chinook women and she . . . "would always have an abundance of fat salmon, anchovies and elk and be allowed to smoke as many pipes of tobacco during the day as she thought proper." Cassakas was smitten but, tempting as his offer was, Jane turned him down and slipped off for Canton, China, aboard the *Columbia.* Or was it the *Isaac Todd?* It has never been known which sailors were lucky— the Yankees or the Limeys—and they never told. Probably of no significance but shortly after Jane's departure from Fort George, British troops burned the U.S. Capitol in Washington, D.C. Also, during her journey, John Quincy Adams signed the Treaty of Ghent, providing for restoration of Fort George to a U.S. possession under control of the Canadian North West Company.

On her return to England Jane sought an annuity from the North West Company, contending it was her due as a legitimate member of the party sent out to occupy Fort Astoria. The Company turned her down, but Jane Barnes now occupies a firm and unique niche in Oregon history. She is now recognized—among a lot of other things—as the first white woman to enter Oregon.

CHAPTER 26

A POWDER KEG

Has the white man become a child, that he should recklessly kill and not eat? When the red men slay game, they do so that they may live and not starve.

White Bear
Kiowa Chief

Taking heed from this tragi-comedy, company officials at Montreal took a long look at their Columbia district and before winter set in, their brigades were being pushed by some of the best in the fur business. When Don McKenzie arrived in New York City in the summer of 1814, North West representatives were on hand to greet him. McKenzie, still in the employ of Astor's American Fur, jumped ship when North West increased his salary to 500 pounds sterling annually to take charge of the Snake brigades. McKenzie would be chief trader in charge of inland operations while another tough Nor'wester, Douglas James, would take over coastal operations. To back up McKenzie, his brigade leaders would be Finan McDonald and George McTavish. John McLoughlin— a 30-year-old physician turned fur trader—and Peter Skene Ogden would cover his northern flank in the upper Columbia region.

McKenzie knew he would earn his salary. To date, sixty-one Astorians had paid with their lives in the conquest of Oregon and the surface had not even been scratched. McKenzie had no desire to add to this list with North West brigades. It would take nearly three years to get his operation up to full capacity. First, with the aid of Jaco Finaly, he began a search for John Day, who agreed to serve as a link between the North West Company and the Shoshoni. By 1816, Day had set up a profitable fur trade with the Snakes, who were willing to do business only so long as the white traders did not abuse their hospitality. For the next year, with Day and Finaly as arbitrators, McKenzie worked the most acces-

Courtesy of the Oregon Historical Society, OrHi 707.

Peter Skene Ogden.

sible and most profitable trapping grounds, skimming the cream of Oregon beaver.

During this initial contact all hell broke loose between Hudson's Bay and the North West Company. Overnight, or so it seemed to the frontline troops, the battle had gotten out of hand. The civil war between the two companies had invoked the ire of Governor General Sherbrooke, who appointed a commission to investigate and stop the bloodshed. The warriors of the fur companies had changed from half-breed riflemen to lawyers and with the shift of warfare into the courts nearly everyone of importance on both sides had been arrested or indicted on charges ranging from theft to murder. Even Lord Selkirk, dying of consumption, was fined 2,000 lb. sterling for false imprisonment of North West employees and Pete Ogden, one of the most bitter opponents of Hudson's Bay, was running from a murder charge.

The Snake chiefs were also getting nervous and under guidance of the elder statesmen called for a council. Careless traders were burning off the grass; game was being killed wantonly and left to rot; women were being molested; and most importantly, the quality of trade weapons was getting progressively inferior. Some stability had to be enforced and the best place to do it was on alien ground before the damage could spread farther into the Ochoco. Accordingly, they developed a plan of defense.

During the spring break-up, dog soldiers under the command of the Big Lodge war chief, Lost Arrow, (Paia 'Koni) and the White Knife war chief Horse (Po'have) rode across Cayuse country and borrowed four canoes from the Walla Walla chief, Yellow Serpent, known to the fur traders as Serpent Jaune. Leaving their horses at Yellow Serpent's camp, the dog soldiers floated down to the mouth of the Walla Walla River and patiently waited for some Nor'westers to drift by. They didn't have long to wait.

Descending on the flood waters of the Columbia in the spring of 1818 in a bateau mounting six swivel guns and oarsmen armed with cutlasses, hand grenades and hand knives, Ogden's brigade beached just north of the mouth of the Walla Walla. The dog soldiers, hidden under their overturned canoes, watched as the Nor'westers cleared a spot from rattlesnakes which the voyageurs skinned, spitted and began roasting over a brush fire. They were thus engaged when bullets and arrows whistled into camp. The Canadians took to the river, strategically putting them in their own element and the fight was on.

Powerful oarsmen headed down stream with Lost Arrow and Horse in hot pursuit. Just below the mouth of the Walla Walla was an island in the main Columbia channel and with two of the Shoshoni canoes standing in close and coming down fast, Ogden's bateau swung around the island, pulled to the shore and waited in ambush. The lead canoes were caught by a blast of gunfire, killing half the paddlers. As they veered off crippled, the other two canoes, more wary, stayed in the main current out of bullet range. If nothing else, Lost Arrow and Horse learned a hard lesson. . . they were much better cavalrymen than they were marines.

During this show of arms Ogden was completely confused. Hostility was not a typical introduction to the Columbia. As he later wrote, "white travelers on the river are seldom molested and the Walla Walla in whose territory the attack occurred are particularly friendly." Nonetheless, Yellow Serpent got saddled with the blame. Attempted murder was only the start of Ogden's bad luck. Before the year was over, he ended up having to marry a Cowlitz girl just to keep up trade relations with the Chinook nation.

Prompted by the Shoshoni attack, McKenzie began construction of Fort Nez Perce on the east bank of the Columbia a short distance north of the Walla Walla River. This project gave McKenzie the distinction of doing the first boom logging in the Pacific northwest when he moved into the northern Blues and floated logs down to the new outpost. It also kept him out of the Ochoco for most of the summer.

In late August of 1818, at the head of a cutthroat crew, McKenzie moved into Shoshoni country. His force included William Kittson—a man who hated him—as second in command; his brother, Alexander McKenzie, Jr.—accompanied by the Princess of Wales and her stable of slave girls—was brigade leader. There were also some Iroquois trappers who earlier had been robbed of horses, guns and traps by the Snakes and in retaliation had killed twelve men, women and children of the peaceful Cowlitz tribe. It was shaping up for a lively winter.

As the main brigade crossed the northern Blues, McKenzie with a party of Iroquois made a scout into the heart of the Ochoco. What he saw made a deep impression:

> . . . animals of every class rove about undisturbed; wherever there was a little plain, the red deer (elk) were seen grazing in herds about the rivers; around every bend ingenious and industrious beaver were at work. Otters sported in the eddies; the wolf and the fox were seen sauntering in quest of prey; now and then a few cypresses or stunted pine were met with and in their spreading tops raccoon sat secure. In the woods the marten and black fox were numerous; the badger sat quietly, looking from his mound; and in the numberless ravines, among bushes laden with fruits, the black, the brown and the grizzly bear were seen. The mountain sheep and goats white as snow browsed on the rocks and ridges; and the big horn ran among the lofty cliffs. Eagles and vultures of uncommon size flew about the rivers. When approached, most of the animals stood motionless; they would move off a little distance but soon came anew to satisfy a curiosity that often proved fatal to them. The report of a gun did not alarm them. Hordes of wild horses were seen and of all the animals seen on our journey they were the wildest and at anytime never came within gun shot.[160]

With the Iroquois killing animals for sport, McKenzie wandered across the John Day canyon into Ochoco Valley; thence up Crooked River and across Harney Basin to the Malheur. During this tour of eastern Oregon strange things were happening on the international scene. McKenzie had barely strung his first traps when George III and John Quincy Adams agreed to share the Oregon country, signing the Treaty of Joint Occupation on October 20, 1818, promising stiff competition from the American fur companies. By canoe, horse and foot dispatches were rushed from Fort William to the Pacific slope reinforcing North West's order to strip the country as they went and that meant all animals, fur bearing and meat bearing alike.

Two days ride south of the Ochoco, Spain—intimidated by Russian presence in northern California—would also suffer another blow to its

---

[160] Grinnell, *Beyond the Old Frontier*, pp. 73-75.

dignity. Argentina, after declaring its independence from the mother country in 1816, was looking for other Spanish-American colonies to join its campaign against Spanish imperialism. On November 20, 1818, two captains of Argentine men o' war, French privateer Hippolyte de Bouchard of the 38-gun *Argentina* and Englishman Peter Corndry, commanding the smaller *Santa Rosa,* dropped anchor opposite the Spanish garrison at Monterey. There, they commanded Spanish colonial governor, Pablo Vicente de Sala, to surrender. With barely 100 men, eight small field guns and little ammunition, the governor couldn't match the Argentine forces which numbered 360 soldiers. After a brief engagement de Sala abandoned the garrison. The foreign invaders hoisted the Argentine colors, looted the town, set it aflame and departed never to return.

Thus in a matter of hours, the Shoshoni gained and lost a colorful neighbor, but their Canadian brothers would make up for the lack of excitement. Armed with official orders from Fort William, the Nor'westers gave their all to lay waste to the Oyer'ungun. Red Wolf reacted in kind. The threat of Shoshoni attack became so bad that there was increasing talk of mutiny among the company trappers. During this critical period Kittson, a new man in the service, was serving as a link between Fort Nez Perce and McKenzie in his base camp on the Malheur.

In late October, Kittson with fifteen men crossed the Blues, taking supplies and reinforcements to McKenzie. He was full of confidence that he could handle and defeat all the Indians on the continent. He had good luck until the party got into the debatable land in Snake territory. First, a dozen company horses were stolen and then a little later all of them. He finally reached the Malheur camp, handed over what supplies he had left, received McKenzie's furs and set out again for Fort Nez Perce. Enroute, Kittson blundered into a squabble between the Nez Perce and the Mountain (Walpapi) Snakes. Two of Kittson's men were killed along with several Snakes. The Mountain dog soldiers with blood in their eyes routed the Nez Perce but before overtaking them rode into a Walla Walla camp less than three miles from Fort Nez Perce. Accusing the Walla Wallas of collaborating with the enemy, they killed seven and took three captives. The next day the whole Walla Walla camp, carrying their dead, moved into the North West outpost for protection and they couldn't be dislodged.[161]

When McKenzie and Kittson separated, McKenzie only had three men, the rest being spread to the four winds stringing traps. While waiting for these trappers to report back to camp, a Snake war party rode in. They didn't look friendly, but McKenzie was big and he was tough. Grabbing up a keg of gun-powder, he walked toward the advancing line of raiders. The sight of this giant with a barrel of destruction on his shoulder and a burning torch in his hand brought the horsemen to a halt. McKenzie quietly informed them if they came a step closer he'd blow them all to hell, himself included. Taken by surprise, the dog soldiers hesitated, then suddenly without a word took flight. . . not from fear of McKenzie's threat but because of the sudden appearance of a large Nez Perce war party on the other side of the river. Fortunately for McKenzie, they couldn't cross the Malheur because of high water.

Following this reprieve, McKenzie, now rejoined by his trappers, holed up on an island in the Snake River for twenty two days, waiting for the return of Kittson's supply train. The Nor'westers situation was not agreeable. On one side were the Nez Perce, on the other the Blackfeet and around all of them were the Snakes. All these tribes were hostile to one another and all were "more or less ill-disposed towards the whites." So the winter was an anxious one.

Losing men daily, the Iroquois and Abenaki trappers became so panicstricken they plotted to murder McKenzie. He forestalled this mutiny by flattening two of the would-be-assassins with a tent pole. Moving out of the Ochoco into the Eldahow, he set up camp on the Boise River only to discover his trappers had swapped all their horses, traps and guns for a choice group of Earth Eater girls. This treachery also irked brother Alex's mistress, the Princess of Wales, for she felt she had been slighted in the transaction. Thoroughly disgusted, McKenzie gave up for the season and let John Day work Shoshoni country in his own fashion.

---

[161] Ibid, pp. 81-82.

CHAPTER 27

WHERE IS JOHN DAY?

*Remove from Idaho's Highway 28 any and
all reference to the grave of John Day!*

Jack Holliwell, Jr.
Idaho President S.A.R.

By 1819, North West had shoved the Russians into northern California and slapped Lisa's American brigades back over the Continental Divide. They were now settling down to enjoy the spoils of a hard-won victory when Hudson's Bay moved in for the kill.

Colin Robertson, following a severe reprimand for his foul-up at the Red River settlement (Lord Selkirk's pet project) deftly removed all enjoyment from North West's beaver operation when he swooped down out of Athabasca, Canada, and stationed his brigades on the Columbia along North West's main water route into the interior. Waging a war of nerves, Robertson chose to ignore all North West activities north of the Columbia for the sole target of his trappers was the unknown wilderness of the Ochoco.

North West was fully aware of what lay there but they didn't deem it necessary to warn Hudson's Bay. Robertson dispatched William Kittson into the land below the Columbia on an exploratory trip which was to carry him deep into Shoshoni soil. What bribery Robertson had to resort to in order to obtain Kittson for this job will never be known but it was probably very little. Kittson, McKenzie's brigade lieutenant in 1818-19, should have known to tread softly in this area. He and McKenzie had clashed frequently on how to handle the Snakes for Kittson, an arrogant young man, believed he could ride rough-shod over the Shoshoni and make them like it. Because of this tendency, McKenzie reprimanded him and Kittson developed a hatred for McKenzie, branding him as a weakling.

Kittson's thrust, now famous as H.B.C.'s First Snake Country Expedition, left Fort Nez Perce on May 22, 1819. Kittson plowed over the Blues and headed straight for Snake hunting grounds, entering them near the headwaters of the John Day River. At this point he was working on a course south by southeast which led him directly across the tribal holdings of the Walpapi Snakes. After an uneventful trip, Kittson arrived at a stream which Ogden later referred to as the Sandwich Island River. Here, Kittson ordered his men to set out traps and if they were bothered by local Indians to shoot them. Bent on destruction, the Bay men became overzealous. When a band of peaceful Paiutes led by One Moccasin drifted into camp to see what was taking place, they were promptly fired upon. This was Monday, June 14, 1819. Before June 15 had settled into darkness, Red Wolf's warriors raided Kittson's camp in a slashing attack which left two trappers dead and three wounded in its wake. Taking this notice at face value, Kittson aborted his plan to march on Central Oregon and moved hurriedly back to the Columbia.

During this excursion, Spain—with the U.S. State Department applying pressure—ceded Florida to the United States and made drastic adjustments to its boundaries west of the Mississippi River. Three years before by act of March 25, 1816, Congress, expressing official sympathy toward squatters on unreserved public lands—their name for Indian holdings—authorized these settlers to remain as "tenants at will." Now, with the Spanish addition, the tenants at will had another 46 million acres of public domain to overrun. At least by act of April 24, 1820, the government abandoned the give-away system and fixed a minimum price of $1.25 an acre and the minimum unit of sale at 80 acres.

Back in Oregon country with the powerful Bear Killer and Mountain Snake tribes setting the example, the dog soldiers of the Shoshoni nation were girding for war. Even so, during the winter of 1819-20, Mike Bourdon, in charge of the upper Snake River operation, took one of North West's biggest catches. In the late spring of 1820, dodging Selkirk's Hudson's Bay patrols, Bourdon started for Fort Nez Perce with 154 horse loads of prime pelts. On the middle Snake he received word that John Day, North West's important link with the Snake war tribes, had died. Whether this time it was fact or some more gossip, Bourdon couldn't take the chance. If true, the crossing of the Blues would be extremely dangerous. But cross he must, so Don McKenzie was dispatched with reinforcements adding 500 armed Cayuse warriors to

Bourdon's sizeable force. With this escort, the fortune in furs arrived at Fort Nez Perce without mishap.

Hard on the heels of the Snake's open hostility, rumors circulated that John Day had been killed. The first report came in October, 1819, four months after Kittson's party had been attacked on the Owyhee River. According to this account, Day had given up his spirit in Day's Defile, a high valley in the Salmon River range. Whether he died of natural causes or had his life snuffed out by the Robber Snakes was never explained. But for a dead man Day was mighty active, even going so far as to pen his last will and testament four months later on February 15, 1820.

Fur prices had been on the increase since 1815 and Day, believing he could bargain with the White Knife Snakes, headed for the inner Ochoco in the late winter of 1820. It was here when he was hopelessly lost in 1812 that he had seen the largest beaver in the Pacific northwest and pelts like that made any risks involved worthwhile. Despite his reckless nature, Day had a premonition that he might not return for he asked Alex Carson to deliver his will to Donald McKenzie who was then trapping the northern Blues. It may well have been the first will executed within the present limits of the state of Idaho. This will named Donald McKenzie as probate petitioner.

That attended to, Day picked up a saddle pony and two pack horses from his Banattee friends; loaded his traps; and answered the call of the Ochoco. . . its veiled promise enticing as a lover's kiss, luring him ever closer to destruction. On February 16, 1820, he left the Snake River headed west never to be seen again. And so passed one of the most shadowy yet imposing figures to have appeared in the history of the Pacific Northwest. He gave his name to a river, a city, a town and a region all within the boundaries of the Shoshoni Ochoco.

In 1836 Day's will was filed by McKenzie at Mayville, Chautauqua County, New York. Today, it is filed at the John Day, Oregon, Chamber of Commerce office. McKenzie and his daughter Rachael—grand-daughter of Chief Concomly—were the sole beneficiaries. Rachael inherited all of Day's money and Donald all of his property.

Legend has it that John Day's body lies in a grave marked by a large stone inscribed "J. Day" near the headwaters of Ochoco River and the

legend may be more factual than recorded history.[162] If true, the
Ochoco had claimed its fifteenth white victim since the start of the
Pacific fur trade.

---

[162] The state of Idaho would dearly love to claim John Day's last resting place for
historical reasons. In 1953 the Idaho Falls Eagle Rock Chapter of the Sons of
the American Revolution erected a monument near "John Day's Grave" on
Birch Creek along southern Idaho's Highway 28. There is only one flaw to
such a commendable gesture . . . . John Day is not buried there. Members of
this group were certain that the grave contained the body of the explorer who
tramped through Oregon and Idaho from 1811 to 1820. They were equally
convinced that Day was a soldier in the Revolutionary War. John Day, the
northwest trapper, was only five years old at the signing of the Declaration of
Independence. As for proof that the grave does not contain the body of John
Day, officials of the Old Fort Hall Chapter of the SAR cite four months of
research to support this claim. A resolution signed by Jack Halliwell, Jr.,
chapter president, Pocatello, Idaho, states that Day's body is not in the grave.
Among other things the resolution asks the Idaho State Highway Commission
to "remove from its road maps any reference to the grave of John Day." This
resolution climaxed an investigation that began in July 1955 when a party led
by J.A. Harrington of Boise opened the disputed grave and found that the
skeleton did not correspond with the known dimensions of Day's body.

CHAPTER 28

OREGON MADNESS

Are they ashamed of their loathsome
conduct? No, they have no shame at all; they
do not even know how to blush.

Jeremiah 6:15

"No other country or age has produced a land system so sublime in principle, so perfect in practice, so magnificent in prospect. . . Greece in its wisdom, Rome in its grandeur, Europe in its glory never realized a system so deserving the admiration and applause of human kind." Thus did the editor of the *National Intelligencer* express his views following the acquisition of more Spanish lands in 1819. Maybe so, but immediately after John Day's disappearance less than a year later, everyone in Oregon country and for that matter in North America went berserk.

Laying aside ancient grudges, the Shoshoni and Blackfeet stopped killing one another long enough to set up an effective fur blockade. Then to ensure some stability along the Blue Mountain border the Nez Perce and Snakes agreed to a temporary truce. During these peace negotiations, Lord Selkirk, leader of Hudson's Bay, gasped his last breath. Not to be outdone by his arch enemy, old Alexander McKenzie, head chief of North West, followed Selkirk up the Sun Down Trail. This so shocked the companies that before they regained their senses the new department heads were plotting a merger. Adding to the confusion, Manuel Lisa, hit-man for Missouri Fur, miraculously died in bed while relaxing at a mineral health spring. By 1821 William Ashley—newly elected Lieutenant Governor of Missouri—snapped up the pieces of Lisa's fur empire and with Andrew Henry, Lisa's former partner, organized the Rocky Mountain Fur Company.

Without doubt, 1820 was shaping up to be a year of derangement. The U.S. population had jumped to over nine million—nearly equal to the 16th century Aztecs—and the citizens were getting restless. They weren't alone. The western Spanish colonies, disturbed by the latest indiscretion of Mother Spain, plotted revenge on the homeland, giving the Utes and Comanches some breathing room. These gentlemen could now send supplies to their beleaguered northern brothers.

Other forces were also adding to the turmoil. Not by accident, Russell Farnham—who in 1813 began a three-year walk across Asia carrying Pacific Fur Company records—checked into a Washington, D.C. hotel in 1820. Ramsay Crooks, now second in command of Astor's American Fur Company, and John Floyd, newly elected congressman from Virginia, were staying in the same hotel. It just so happened that Farnham was general manager of American Fur operations on the upper Mississippi. Between them, Farnham and Crooks persuaded Floyd to introduce legislation in Congress which would begin the political agitation for Oregon statehood.

Meanwhile Hudson's Bay, now led by the fiery 28-year-old George Simpson, lashed out in blind fury at anything that moved. Simpson—the illegitimate child of a Scottish minister's son—was being groomed for the governorship of western Canada and he was out to prove his worth. Within a matter of weeks, North West as the ardent suitor for Shoshoni pelts found itself pitted against Hudson's Bay, the jealous admirer of same. To further complicate matters, the Shoshoni-Blackfoot alliance to which all affection was being denied, took an unexpected interest in the hide scandal. Between the Bay Company's frontal assaults and the Indian's rapier-like thrusts the Nor'westers had to devote more time to saving their own hides than snaring those of the beaver. In the end, the Bay Company proved to be the more ruthless opponent. Not only were they shooting North West employees on sight but they soon concentrated on destroying their fur supply and in so doing won the everlasting hatred of the Snake war tribes.

The year 1821 would be just as chaotic. In July, tired of Spain's inattention and spurred by introduction of liberal political ideas from Europe, the western colonies which had been in revolt for years, declared their independence from Spain. In doing so the lands south of the Maury Mountains in Central Oregon technically became a part of the republic of Estado Unidos Mexicanos. . . the United States of Mexico. As this new political entity was being formed, Thomas Hart Benton, a youngster from Missouri who had picked off a seat in the U.S.

Senate, launched a campaign for the establishment of "a U.S. territory of Origone."[163] While Benton goaded Congress, the British Crown ordered North West and Hudson's Bay to form a merger under the name of Hudson's Bay Company. On that day, John Jacob Astor who had masterminded the assault on Shoshoni Land, saw his dream come true; only it was not he but his bitter Canadian rivals who secured a complete monopoly of the Pacific Northwest fur trade.

---

[163] For more on the Oregon controversy see Cushing's *Report on Territory of Oregon*, House of Representatives Doc. No. 101, 25th Congress, 3rd session, Jan. 4, 1839.

CHAPTER 29

VALLEY OF TROUBLES

*East of The Dalles and south of Fort Nez
Perce lay the country claimed by the Snake
tribes. Bounded on the east by the Rocky
Mountains, on the west by the Cascade
Range and encircling the western spur of the
Blue Mountains, it was thereafter named the
Valley of Troubles.*

Alexander Ross
Fur Brigade Leader

Fur prices sky-rocketed and with their meteor-like rise, the Americans who had been shoved out of Oregon by the Nor 'westers, re-entered the scene. Working for such companies as Missouri Fur, American Fur and Rocky Mountain Fur, these free trappers engaged in a breakneck race with the Canadians to determine who could exterminate the most beaver in the shortest possible time. In the elimination bout Hudson's Bay was slowly forging ahead. This was due in part to the strict British code of trapping. Composed of cold-blooded, professional hide-hunters, the Bay Company confined the fur industry to monopoly control while the romantic American companies permitted the free competition of anyone who had the nerve to take part. British trappers were employees of the company, serving for a monthly salary; whereas the thrill-seeking American trappers worked either for themselves or as partners of the company which they represented.

Names like John Day, Jim Bridger, Peg-leg Smith and Joe Meek are but typical in their suggestion of adventure and achievement of the Americans who combed the west in the search for pelts. American mountain men opened the unknown triangle between the Columbia River and the Santa Fe Trail and it was they who met Hudson's Bay trappers in the western Rockies in fierce contests reminiscent of the war between the Bay Company and North West.

These free trappers scattered into the wilds and then came together at such well-known rendezvous as Ogden's Hole where they met the traders of all companies—Canadian, Russian and American—to exchange their catch for gold. At these meetings, the American trappers usually gave vent ·to a yearly binge which left them penniless but, nevertheless, they were a dangerous threat so far as Hudson's Bay was concerned. . . more so even than the Shoshoni war tribes. So dangerous that Hudson's Bay in an effort to maintain the slim lead which it had gained during the initial onslaught was forced into trapping the dreaded Ochoco. These thrusts, known as the Hudson's Bay Company's "Snake Country Expeditions," were the most profitable and the most colorful fur trading ventures in the Pacific Northwest. . . they were also the most fatal. Although the Bay Company was reaping a fat return from these excursions, they were definitely no road to riches for the trappers who were executing them.[164]

Under the leadership of British bourgeois, parties of French-Canadian laborers; American free trappers; Iroquois, Abenaki and Delaware hunters; half-breed interpreters; and west coast Indian slaves (property of the trapper's Indian wives) roamed Shoshoni hunting grounds in pursuit of furbearing animals. Not only was it a hard life but the only sure reward was a violent end for the Ochoco dog soldiers were ever ready to kill the unwary. It was during this period that the Ochoco received a new name—the Valley of Troubles—a title which would soon encompass all Shoshoni territory.

Using Fort Nez Perce at the mouth of the Walla Walla River as a base of operations, the Snake Country expeditions would start out in early August to trap the rivers of Shoshoni country. Hudson's Bay

---

[164] During this period, chief factors received 2/85 of 40% of company profit; chief traders received 1/85 of 40% of company profits; clerks received 40 to 150 lbs. sterling per month (equivalent to 195 to 730 American dollars); apprentice clerks received 20 to 50 lbs. sterling per month; engages (first rank beneath a gentleman) 40 lbs. sterling; interpreters 25 lbs. sterling; mechanics, voyaguers, steermen, guides, laborers, hunters and trappers where in a class alone, getting whatever the company deemed proper at that time. The most popular trade goods were in order: guns, gun locks, gun balls, gun powder, blankets, beads and least of all, tobacco.

entered this area along two main routes of travel. One paralleled the Deschutes River into Central Oregon; the other crossed the northern Blues over Hunt's old trail into Central Idaho. The brigades coming in by way of Central Oregon worked on an easterly course through the southern Blues to the Bear River in southeastern Idaho. The Idaho trapper's path of destruction lay on a westbound course which eventually brought them into the Crooked River basin where they would trap until warm weather or the Shoshoni drove them out.

Few survived these rigors for any length of time. On New Year's Day, 1829, Ogden made this notation in his journal: "There remains now only one man of all the Snake men of 1819. All have been killed with the exception of two who died a natural death and are scattered over Snake country. It is incredible the number that have fallen in this country." Yet, the trappers were willing to risk life and limb to join one of the Bay Company's death marches. And the reason was obvious. Fur became cold, hard cash on the international market. . . gold with which a man could procure all the joys or griefs he so desired. Shoshoni fur was the king of pelts on the world exchange; therefore, it was a magic unto itself. The motives which drove the trappers to obtain this fur were as varied as the men themselves. The Americans were the reckless gamblers. . . the mountain men who loved the wandering life of the hide-hunter. The French-Canadians were the carefree drifters and to them the fur trade was a way of life. The Iroquois, Delaware and Abenakis chose the life of a trapper as the only feasible way of continuing their traditional life of the hunt. To the British, fur was a calculated business risk.

Most of the pelts taken from Shoshoni country were transported to Fort George where they were loaded aboard American merchant vessels bound for Canton, China, the leading market for the Pacific fur trade.[165] Prices for these pelts fluctuated from 15 to 30 dollars for a single hide and an average of 36,000 furs annually were being sent to the Orient by the competing companies. Cook had set the pace in 1778.

---

[165] Hudson's Bay, by virtue of the East India Company's monopoly, was barred from trading with China. Therefore, they either had to sell to the American trade vessels or make a deal with the ship's captain to secretly deliver company furs to the Chinese market. They were also finding an outlet through Russia.

Russia, the ranking contender for that trade, was taking up the slack. Although China's ports were closed to Russian shipping and open only under bothersome restrictions to other foreign vessels, Russia had her inlets. A lively trade was carried on by Chinese merchants through such border towns as Irkutsk and Petrovsk from whence the furs eventually found their way to St. Petersburg and Moscow. Other pelts were being packed across the high desert to be sold at Fort Ross, Baranov's factory on the southwest corner of Shoshoni holdings, and from this California outpost were being shipped directly into Siberia.

This traffic in furs between Oregon and the Orient was a perfect setup for the hide hunters and they would stop at nothing to preserve it. Individual trappers became wealthy overnight while company officials became millionaires. Men who were basically honest reverted into swindlers, thieves and murderers to obtain furs from the natives. Hudson's Bay frowned upon and tried to discourage such methods but British traders strolled hand-in-hand with their American competitors, taking by force what they could not steal. Well-versed in the art of deception, the British worked the old confidence game on the Shoshoni, playing them for suckers on every opportunity. An iron file in exchange for 500 dollars in prime mink or beaver was considered an overpayment for goods received; if the Indian objected to such a deal, a bullet was the next offering. Another method practiced by the Americans (Hudson's Bay had learned the hard way from the Blackfeet) was to keep the Shoshoni constantly debauched with liquor to secure their furs.

Prior to the trader's open warfare, the majority of the Shoshoni had made an honest effort to get along with the white brothers. At times it was exasperating, especially when the white men made no attempt to understand their needs or their problems. Much of the guilt for this attitude can be placed on the explorer-ethnologists of the period. As a result of their dubious opinions, fur traders lunged in where the warriors of western America feared to tread. . . and a deadly noose which had taken shape was slowly beginning to tighten.

CHAPTER 30

THE WHITE HEADED EAGLE

Stand, stand to your glasses, steady!
'tis all we have left to prize:
One cup to the dead already—
Hurrah for the next that dies!

Bartholomew Dowling

Hudson's Bay entered the Columbia battlefield blindfolded. The company would have to depend on its old enemies, the Nor'westers, if it was to succeed in this venture. Company officials were quick to retain the services of such men as Mike Bourdon, who had led the last North West brigade out of Snake country in the winter of 1820-21. Following Bourdon out of Snake country was a Canadian trapper, Joseph Delore, accompanied by his Spokane wife. On New Year's Day, 1821, where the Oregon town of La Grande now stands, a son, Peter, was born to the Delores. . . an infant who in manhood would play a key role in the final destruction of the Snake war tribes.

Another old Nor'wester, Finan McDonald was retained as a brigade leader and dispatched into Snake country in the late summer of 1822. The Company gambled on making a profit and lost. Red Wolf's border guard saw to that. But McDonald, a graduate of the North West's school of diplomacy, built up a fighting force of half-breed riflemen and struck back, dealing a harsh defeat to the Snake war lords. "68," he reported, "remain in the Plains as pray for the wolves. . . they will not be so ready to attack people another time." On the other hand McDonald wasn't ready to tackle the dog soldiers again either.

This fracas convinced company stockholders that they needed improved management on the Pacific slope. Other Nor'westers were having no trouble being placed in company ranks but Pete Ogden, one of the best traders in the business, was being ignored. His well-documented hostility toward Hudson's Bay had placed him on the blacklist.

Courtesy of the Oregon Historical
Society, OrHi 248.

Dr. John McLoughlin.

After much trouble which included a trip to England and high recommendations from Governor George Simpson, Ogden was finally accepted. In the winter of 1822-23, he was made a trader for the Spokane district which included all Oregon territory east of the Cascade range and south to the Mexican border. While Ogden was outfitting for his trip to the Columbia, President James Monroe in his annual message to Congress set forth the doctrine that the American continents were no longer "subject for future colonization by any European powers." This declaration wouldn't interrupt U.S. colonization of Indian lands.

On his plunge from Canada, Ogden ran into Alexander Ross camped with fourteen men at the mouth of Wood River. Ross, whom Ogden described as "looking and talking like a schoolmaster," was accompanied by his Flathead wife and children. After years on the Columbia, the old Astorian was heading east to rejoin civilization. It so happened that among the dispatches Ogden packed was one from Governor Simpson asking Ross to replace Finan McDonald and take charge of the Snake expeditions. By his own admission, McDonald had lost "Seviril Battils" with the Indians and had his fill of Snake Country. "When that Cuntre will see me agine the Beaver will have Gould Skins."

Ross was torn between his desire to leave Oregon forever and the high and dangerous honor of leading a fur brigade into the wild Shoshoni country. After several hours of debate, Ogden persuaded him to accept the challenge. The first would come in the form of Finan McDonald. Apparently in McDonald's mind the beaver began growing golden hides for he was soon back in Shoshoni country stirring up more trouble. Because of these indiscretions, Ross would suffer a heart-breaking loss. His wife would never see the eastern cities which he had promised to show her. She was kidnapped by a Snake war party and never seen again.

Ross would blame this outrage on the Blackfeet and the Shoshoni were ecstatic. They could now plunder at will and the Blackfeet would reap the consequences. With this new decoy to cover their tracks, Snake dog soldiers were raging across Hudson's Bay trapping grounds in Montana striking into the headwaters of the Missouri. Ute raiders were scourging the beaver streams along the Bear River while the Comanches, led by the war chief Shaved Head, were discouraging American advances into the eastern Rockies.

Back on the Pacific slope, with the problem of inland trader and Snake Expedition leader solved, Hudson's Bay was searching for a general manager. They found their man in John McLoughlin, Ogden's old North West partner now in charge of Fort William on Lake Superior. As Chief Factor, McLoughlin would have absolute authority over the entire Pacific operation. Charged with a three-fold mission, he was to monopolize the Pacific fur trade; impose permanent peace upon the Indians; and finally, prevent agricultural settlement of the region.

In childhood Ogden had seen God pictured as an angry old man. McLoughlin could have served as the model. Governor Simpson saw him in somewhat of a different light. He would note on September 26, 1824, his initial impression of Dr. McLoughlin. "He was such a figure as I should not like to meet on a dark night in one of the bye lanes in the neighborhood of London. . . his beard would do honor to the chin of a grizzly Bear. . . " The Indians saw him as a great "white headed eagle."

Some historians paint McLoughlin—standing 6'4" and weighing 230 pounds—as a ruthless competitor, driving rival American fur companies to the wall. Other depict him as a virtual dictator of a vast wilderness empire, demanding implicit and unquestioning obedience from Indians and employees alike. Still others portray him as a veritable saint, ministering to the sick, feeding the starving American immigrants even at the risk of his job with Hudson's Bay. In short they present him as the great Christian gentleman, the great doctor, the great teacher, the great friend of Protestant missionaries, the great philanthropist and the faithful husband of his Indian wife.[166] Perhaps all were right.

At age 37, McLoughlin—an experienced trader and fur company administrator—assumed command of HBC's outpost at Fort George in 1824. By 1826, he had established Fort Vancouver—a lonely outpost in the midst of 50,000 hostile Indians—making that his headquarters.

Personally escorted by Sir George Simpson, governor of western Canada, McLoughlin arrived on the Columbia October 27, 1824. Trailing along in his footsteps came the half-breed daughter of a Swiss trader

---

[166] For more on Dr. John McLoughlin see American Council of Learned Societies, *Dictionary of American Biography*, Vol. XII: 134-35.

and a Cree Indian woman. She was better known to history as Marguerite McKay McLoughlin, widow of the Astor fur partner, Alexander McKay, and wife of Dr. John McLoughlin. . . a regal woman who began living with McLoughlin several months before word of McKay's death on the *Tonquin* could possibly have reached them. Their guide from York factory to Fort George was Tom McKay, Marguerite's son who at the age of 14 was with Pacific Fur at the time of his father's death.

For Alex Ross, their arrival at Spokane House was ill-timed. In August McDonald, operating out of Fort Nez Perce, was supposed to meet Ross at the foot of the Rocky mountains. Enroute, six of his trappers were killed in a mutinous uprising staged by some Shoshoni captives held as slaves. The Bay men followed the escapees who joined a camp of Piegon Blackfeet. In typical McDonald fashion, he ordered a forest fire to be torched around the encampment and when the half-roasted Indians tried to get out of the flames blasted them down with buck-shot.[167] Then, instead of continuing to a union with Ross, he disobeyed orders and returned to Spokane House fully aware that both Snakes and Blackfeet would be seeking revenge. They did.

Meantime, Ross' brigade—undermanned and made up in part by men in their sixties and seventies—was facing a new threat. Major Andrew Henry had taken up the scent and at this moment Rocky Mountain Company trappers were working their way down the broad valley of the Snake. Two years earlier a want-ad in a Missouri newspaper had alerted Hudson's Bay as to what they might expect in the near future. Inserted by Major William Ashley in the *St. Louis Missouri Republican* on March 20, 1822, it read:

---

[167] McDonald ordered the oldest man in camp—"a hunter on the wrong side of seventy"—to set the deadly brush fire. (Grinnell, *Beyond the Old Frontier*, p. 99)

To enterprising young men. The subscriber wishes to engage one hundred young men to ascend the Missouri River to its source, there to be employed for one, two or three years. For particulars enquire of Maj. Andrew Henry near the lead mines in the County of Washington, who will ascend with and command the party; or of the subscriber near St. Louis.[168]

(signed) William H. Ashley

Among those who answered the ad were such worthies as Jim Bridger, Tom Fitzpatrick and Jedediah Smith. The following year, 1823, a group of Ashley's trappers (including some ex-Astorians) made what historians call the "effective" discovery of South Pass, later the route of the wagon trains to Oregon. It was effective because they publicized it. Astor's men had not. Now in the fall of 1824, these men were knocking on Hudson Bay's door.

As the Rocky Mountain trappers led by the Yankee trader Jedediah Smith closed the gap between them and Ross' Snake Brigade, killing game as they advanced, a Shoshoni war party was homeward bound for the Ochoco.[169]

With fresh Sioux, Blackfoot and Arapaho scalps dangling from their bloody coup sticks and spirits at a feverish pitch the dog soldiers were hardly what one would invite to a friendly social gathering. Drunk with power over their recent victories, they were about as unpredictable as a wounded grizzly and every bit as dangerous. Moving slowly across the Snake River basin, they were following a course that was bringing them ever closer to Alexander Ross' line of march.

In the camps of the Earth Eaters, the dog soldiers learned of McDonald's latest transgression. A retaliatory blow was in order and it was quick in coming. Swerving north, they attacked one of Ross' brigades robbing them of everything including his Flathead wife who

---

[168] Vestal, *Jim Bridger, Mountain Man*, p. 8.

[169] Major James McLoughlin would comment on this wanton killing of game: "I have never known an Indian to kill a game animal that he did not require for his needs. And I have known few white hunters to stop while there was game to kill." (McLoughlin, *My Friend the Indian*, p. 114.)

had been preparing hides for the detachment. During this skirmish Etienne Provost, working for Rocky Mountain Fur, moved into the line of fire and got hit. Seven men from his brigade fled with the Hudson's Bay trappers and joined Ross' column. Provost made it back to Smith's main party, blaming Hudson's Bay for the Snake attack. With this information, Smith decided to hound Ross' line of march and wipe out all beaver in his path.

Ironically, shortly before the Snake attack on his Iroquois trappers Ross had encountered a Blackfoot war party who claimed to be on a peace mission to the Snakes.[170] This was startling news, but Ross had more pressing matters to occupy his mind. Not only could be find no trace of his missing wife, but another discouraging situation had developed. In his offer of employment, Simpson had particularly cautioned Ross against opening any communication with the Americans. Now, his Iroquois trappers rushed into camp with seven American refugees. Knowing that a Rocky Mountain fur brigade was nearby, Ross—with the displaced Yankees sticking to him like pine resin—tried to shake Smith from his trail by heading south into the big Shoshoni trade village located where five major rivers—the Boise, Malheur, Payette, Owyhee and Weiser—emptied into the Snake.

Like Celilo on the Columbia this market place was neutral ground. Here, the middle Columbia tribes gathered to do business with Snake traders loaded with buffalo hides and dried meat; Ute exporters from Spanish country with turquoise and horses; and Paiute merchants from the desolate Great Basin with rabbit skins and obsidian.[171] In this crossroads of the interior Ross hoped to cover his tracks and elude the pursuing Jed Smith. He was only partially successful.

Weaving across the numerous trails leading to the trade market, Ross slipped across the Snake River and headed north on the eastern boundary of the Ochoco still unaware of McDonald's attack on the Shoshoni-Blackfoot camp and equally unaware of the Snake's declaration of war.

---

[170] Grinnell, *Beyond the Old Frontier*, p. 106.

[171] This market flourished until the early 1860s. Then the gold-seekers moved in and for some unknown reason (perhaps it was placer mining) the salmon ceased to run in the Boise, Owyhee and Malheur rivers. (Liljeblad, *The Idaho Indians in Transition 1805-1960.*)

On Sunday morning, November 28, 1824, Lady Luck took pity on her wayward children and intervened in what could have been a very touchy situation. Ross, some twelve miles south of the Malheur, decided to hole up for a few hours and repair equipment. Almost to the hour a large Snake party returning from the summer's hunt turned up the Malheur and headed for the southern Blues. That afternoon Ross crossed the Malheur and complacently noted in his journal. . . "found evidence of a sizeable Indian migration. The Nez Perce scout says it is but a few hours old. Making good progress. Weather fair."

With this happy thought Ross, still plagued with Provost's trappers—who he believed to be American spies—continued north toward Fort Nez Perce. The Snakes plowed west into the southern Blues and Smith, following Ross' confused trail, turned up the Malheur. Afraid of the Snakes, Smith followed Ross northward to Flathead House. Here, he did obtain valuable information on HBC's Snake Country operations The most important being that the British had 60 trappers in the country claimed by the Shoshoni and within the past four years had taken 80,000 beaver hides weighing approximately 160,000 lbs.[172]

When Ross arrived at Spokane House in early December, Simpson and McLoughlin were waiting. McDonald's account of his irresponsible attack on the inland tribes was worrisome, but when a Nez Perce messenger came into the post twenty-four hours ahead of Ross with news that Americans were stringing traps on the Malheur River, they were rabid. When Ross marched in with the adopted seven, his fate was decided. Simpson in a burst of anger relieved Ross of command and offered the job to Ogden, who was not overjoyed with the prospect but was in debt to Simpson for bringing him into the company. McLoughlin quickly sweetened the pot by offering Ogden the position of Chief Trader of the Pacific operation. Having little choice, Ogden accepted.

The relief of command probably didn't bother Ross to any great extent for by now he was speaking of the Shoshoni country as a theater of war. Being a keen observer of Indian character, he also deduced—given their lack of weapons to conduct modern warfare—what others

---

[172] Harrison C. Dale, *The Ashley-Smith Explorations and Discovery of a Central Route to the Pacific, pp. 157-58.*

252

had failed to recognize up to this time. For nearly a century their enemies had been receiving weapons of war from the white man, while the Snakes had to defend their country and protect themselves with the simple bow and arrow against the destructive muskets of their numerous enemies. Ross reasoned, and rightly so:

> Arm the Shoshones and put them upon an equal footing with their adversaries and I will venture to say from what I have seen of them that few Indians surpass them in boldness or moral courage; my only wonder is that they have been able, under so many discouraging circumstances, to exist as a nation and preserve their freedom and independence for so long.[173]

At this time the Shoshoni were gathering an arsenal to prove him correct.

The rumor that Jed Smith with sixty men was trapping the Malheur was no laughing matter. Hudson's Bay was faced with an immediate decision. Either it trapped the treacherous interior of the Ochoco or abandoned it to the Americans. Neither alternative was very enticing but it was clearly a case of act now or lose out completely. As Simpson saw it, the golden fleece hung within reach of the Snake country expeditions if placed under proper management. He was also aware that leadership of the Snake brigades was the most hazardous and disagreeable assignment in Indian country.

With this in mind, Simpson met with his lieutenants and within the week word spread like wildfire across the Columbia basin that Hudson's Bay was to begin a campaign to destroy all fur-bearing animals in the land south of the Columbia River. They would create a beaver desert in what would become eastern Oregon, southern Idaho, northern Utah, northern Nevada and northern California. The weapon Simpson aimed at the American fur companies was the Snake Country Brigades forged by Donald McKenzie ten years earlier. Starting in 1825, the Snake brigades took 10,000 pelts annually and they continued at this pace until 1836.

---

[173] Alexander Rose, *The Fur Hunters of the Far West*, I, pp. 249-55.

The Snake country expedition would get off to a late start in 1824, but from 1825 on it would leave in November, proceed directly to the heart of Snake country, spend the winter and spring there and trap its way out to Fort George in the summer. Governor Simpson made it clear that his greatest pleasure in life was saving the company money, a pleasure which he was eager to share with others. Therefore, the Snake expedition would pay for its own travel and save the company heavy expenses by delivering its pack train of furs directly to the annual ship for London.

Simpson was convinced that earlier expeditions had fallen short only because of bad planning. Nothing the governor said made the Snake country more attractive to the listening men, least of all the prospect of wintering in that desolate, hostile land. Nevertheless, on December 20, 1824, Ogden headed for Shoshoni country with a brigade made up mainly of free men who had no loyalty to the Hudson's Bay Company and no aversion to Americans who were waiting to tempt them with better offers. As Ogden put it, he didn't mind "going to hell but why take the devil with you?" He had good reason for misgivings. Among others, his second in command was "Wild Bill" Kittson, branded as a murderer by the war tribes. Three of the party—Alex Carson, serving as guide, Louie La Bonte and Michael La Fromboise, acting as interpreters—were ex-Astorians. Jean Toupin, another interpreter, was married to an Earth Eater girl, which inspired no respect from the Shoshoni and Dedron Senecal with his wife Lucy Du Sart were French nationals who held little liking for the British. Ogden, the tough, barrel-chested Scotsman who became a chief trader at the age of 30, was going to earn his pay. Ironically, Ogden himself, was an ex-employee of Astor's American Fur Company.

As Ogden and his misfit crew outfitted at Flathead House, the White Headed Eagle swooped down the Columbia to Fort George and made some more drastic changes. He moved his command post up river to a point on the Washington shore opposite the mouth of the Willamette. During construction, representatives of Great Britain and Russia met at St. Petersburg and on February 28, 1825, Russia agreed to make no more settlements on the Pacific coast south of Alaska. Three weeks later on March 19, 1825, McLoughlin christened his new stronghold on the Columbia "Vancouver" by breaking a rum bottle over the flagstaff. Later, the U.S. Committee on Foreign Affairs would describe Fort

Vancouver ". . . in all respects a military post though the garrison consists of servants of the company, not officers and men bearing the Queen's commission." The Committee would also charge that "other establishments of the company" among them Fort George, Fort Nez Perce and Fort Boise "are in fact military posts." They would also complain: "It has at all times been the policy of Great Britain—a policy little in keeping with her ostentation of humanity in regard to the black race—to keep the red men under such subsidy to her, so as to have them always ready to bring into the field against the United States."[174]

Apparently this august body didn't realize the tension which existed between the Hudson's Bay Company and the Shoshoni nation. Be that as it may, the war smoke between American free enterprise and Canadian monopoly was beginning to thicken. The catalyst for this added mistrust had jelled in the summer of 1824 during McLoughlin's push to the Columbia and would explain the Blackfeet's comment to Ross about a Shoshoni peace mission and the hiding of McDonald's escaped Snake slaves in a supposedly hostile Blackfoot camp.

---

[174] Report of the Committee on Foreign Affairs, House Executive Doc. No. 101 25th Congress, 3rd session, Territory of Oregon, January 4, 1839.

CHAPTER 31

CEASE FIRE!

I cut my hair above him. I gash my arms for sorrow.
My cries shall follow—follow. . . . .
Wailings and flute and drum—
Call to the Dead.

Lilian White Spencer
Shoes of Death

In 1824 Hudson's Bay officials would have sneered at the mere mention of a western Indian alliance. That was the least of their problems or so they thought, but the unexpected can happen. The summer of 1824 found the Shoshoni nation on the move and with good reasons, for each year in passing gave mute testimony that the buffalo were disappearing from the winding valleys of the Ochoco. In 1823 the last of the great herds left the bunchgrass prairies of the southern Blues never again to return to their ancient feed grounds. What caused this mass migration no one knows, but it coincided with the slaughter brought on by the fur hunters. Whatever the reason, in the minds of the Shoshoni this was the contributing factor. . . and hunger breeds a special kind of anger.

Being thrifty men, the Shoshoni once again reverted to their age-old custom of leaving game animals near their home camps strictly alone. With rifles to back up the war club, they began ranging deep into their former hunting grounds in search of buffalo. Aside from a mangy assortment of dogs, some oldsters and a few pregnant women, the camps of the Ochoco were deserted, for every able-bodied man, woman and child was trailing the migratory herds. Not only were they killing buffalo but any other large game which wandered across their path. Elk, mountain sheep, deer, bear and antelope were adding their share to a nation's survival.

As the game moved northward so did the Shoshoni and by mid-August they were high in the Montana Rockies and well within the southern boundary of the Blackfoot nation. Despite the fact that Fires Black Gun and the Piegon chief Ugly Head had negotiated a shaky truce in the summer of 1820, this was an open invitation to trouble and the Blackfeet were quick to accommodate.

On the Boulder River a Piegon war party under the leadership of Large Kidney and Four Horns hit the hunting camp of Twisted Hand. With him was the war-chief Red Wolf and the wildly popular young chief of the White Knife dog soldiers, The Horse. Wolf Dog and another young hot-blood, Gourd Rattler, moving north out of Wyoming country—where they had picked up a shipment of Mexican arms from the Comanche chief Shaved Head—heard the ruckus and arrived in time to join the fray.[175] The battle had barely started when Gourd Rattler packed word to his father, Crooked Leg who was camped a few miles upstream. Cooked Leg arrived in time to get killed.[176]

This mutual exchange of blood fanned the smoldering hatred of the Snake warriors into a searing flame. Backed by reinforcements led by the Comanche war chief Red Sleeves, buffalo hunting was forgotten as the dog soldiers took to the war trail, sweeping the Boulder, the Yellowstone and the Musselshell for the kill.[177] When the smoke of

---

[175] Shaved Head, a man of much influence with his own people and with neighboring tribes, became a great friend of the whites. He wore the left side of his head shaved close, while the hair on the right side was long, hanging down to his waist. (Grinnell, *Beyond the Old Frontier*, p. 138).

[176] Many historians claim that Crooked Leg—Passego—was killed by the Blackfeet when Gourd Rattler was five years old [W.F. Lander Report, Sen. Exe. Doc. #142, 36 Congress, 1st Session, pp. 121-39; Hebard, *Washakie*, pp. 48-51]. This doesn't fit with the historical record. The Shoshoni-Blackfoot alliance occurred in 1824 and according to Hodge [*American Indians*, p. 919], Washakie—Gourd Rattler—was born about 1804. This date also conforms with Washakie's age at the time of his death on February 20, 1900, as being nearly 90 years old. Therefore, Gourd Rattler at the time of this skirmish would have been in his latter teens and riding with the dog soldiers as claimed by Indian informants.

[177] In 1847 Red Sleeves was killed during a wagon train attack near Bent's Fort on the Santa Fe Trail. (Grinnell, *Beyond the Old Frontier*, p. 176). Shortly

battle drifted away there was black paint smeared across the face of the Blackfoot nation. During this upheaval Big Rumbling Belly (Kwoki Tsaup), father of the Snake prophet White Man (Tavibo) and grandfather of The Cutter (Wovoka) died of natural causes.

After twenty-two years of disgrace the Shoshoni were once more members in good standing in the warrior societies of western America. To celebrate this victory the Shoshoni in a move so typical of the red men called for a council with the Blackfeet tribes and voted to join forces against the increasing encroachment of the fur traders. This agreement by no stretch of the imagination guaranteed that they would not fight among themselves, but it did assure the participants that they would quit any private squabbles to make life miserable for the hidehunters. This truce, negotiated by Twisted Hand, Red Wolf, Fires Black Gun and The Horse, representing the Shoshoni tribes; and Old Bull's Head, Heavy Breast, Deceitful Dog and Four Horns of the Blackfoot tribes, was to spell nothing but disaster for the fur companies. It would also give the Snakes license to kill with the cause being laid at the doorstep of "Bugs Boy's," the American trappers name for the Blackfeet.

Three weeks after this peace-parley, the medicine chief Bear Skin was killed in an Arapahoe raid. As if to commemorate the event, the Office of Indian Affairs was established and placed under the War Department, perhaps in anticipation of trouble yet to come. With winter approaching the far-flung Shoshoni hunting parties began to reunite for their long trek home. It was the tracks of this migration into the Ochoco that Alexander Ross recorded in his journal of November 28, 1824.

---

thereafter a Snake war-party came down from the mountains and tried to break into Bent's Fort with one dog soldier being killed. (ibid, p. 178).

CHAPTER 32

FREEMEN ARE A CURSE

*There is certainly a fatality attending the
Snake country and all Snake Expeditions for
without exception no voyage to that country
has been undertaken without serious
accidents ensuing. Thus, we are only on the
outset of our voyage and have already lost a
man and 18 horses. . . . .*

Peter Skene Ogden
February 7, 1825

During his tour with North West Fur, Ogden had tangled with the
Snakes and he wasn't about to make the same mistake twice, especially
with the disgruntled crew under his command. Simpson in his mis-
guided effort to increase company profits was charging scalper's prices
for supplies, while paying less than 50 cents a pound for hides delivered
to Fort George. Because of this the free trappers attached to Ogden's
brigade held no allegiance to Hudson's Bay and Ogden was well aware
of their resentment toward company policy.

Therefore, ignoring Simpson's orders, Ogden made no attempt to
trap the Ochoco. Instead, he headed south into the Salmon River Valley
where he ran afoul of the Rocky Mountain Brigade led by Jed Smith.
Described by Kittson as a "sly, cunning Yankee," Smith dogged Ogden's line of march and no amount of trickery could dislodge him from
the trail. In the process Smith was filling in some blank spaces on the
American map.

Adding further disruption to sagging spirits, January 1, 1825, was
not to be celebrated in the normal carousing fashion. Watchful of the
ammunition Ogden asked the men not to open fire in their usual salute
to the New Year. Worse yet, Simpson had abolished liquor from the
brigade, successfully stopping the drunken revels of the old North West
days. Although Ogden was smart enough not to mention it in his journal,

Kittson noted that each man received a dram of spirits—apparently a token of good will from the brigade leader's private stock.

In an effort to shake Smith's brigade, Ogden moved into the Seven Devil mountains, hideout of the Sheep Killer and Robber Snakes, where caution was an absolute must. It was not forthcoming. Other than Bill Kittson, about the only men Ogden could depend on were Francois Rivet, his father-in-law, and Charles McKay, company clerk and Blackfoot interpreter. Enroute, his free trappers were killing buffalo for sport and leaving them lie; yet for much of the journey, they were faced with starvation. In disgust Ogden would note on January 27. . . "altho' the Freemen complain that their horses are poor, still they cannot withstand the temptation of running buffalo. Thirty were killed and not more than the meat of three were brought into camp. (At that time Ogden had 124 people to feed). This is not only a sinful waste of meat but of ammunition." It was also a waste of company time. That day the trappers took only four beaver.

This open invitation to hostile attack continued as the Snake brigade moved deeper into the mountains. Again Ogden notes on February 10, ". . . the freemen in their glory in pursuit of buffalo. Many were killed this day, not less than 30, but not more than 300 weight of meat came to camp." A few days later, ". . .buffalo and antelope everywhere; the day filled with the crackle of gunfire; in the evening wolves feasted along the trail; but the camp was low on food; the freemen had been too tired from killing to bring in more than a little meat for themselves."

Although Ogden was successful in losing Smith's brigade, this detour into the danger zone, coupled with his men's blatant disregard of orders, was taking its toll. Disrupting camp routine, one trapper in a fit of anger attempted to murder his Indian wife then committed suicide. According to Kittson's journal, this happened on January 13, 1825. On February 6, Louis Kamitagan was shot and killed by his wife, causing Ogden to remark with foreboding that "there is certainly a fatality attending the Snake Country and all Snake Expeditions." Losing men daily to Shoshoni snipers, Ogden made a terse observation. . . "the war tribes appear determined that we shall not want for their company this year." He was right.

Driven out of the Seven Devils, the Snake Expedition on Easter Sunday entered the great Snake plain, described by Ogden as "300 miles from east to west and sixty from north to south." And here, Nick

Montour with twenty-two out of the forty-four free trappers attached to the brigade, deserted taking horses, traps and 700 pelts worth more than four thousand dollars in American mountain prices. Montour—Tom McKay's future father-in-law—intended to join forces with Smith's Rocky Mountain fur brigade, if he could locate them, and sell the Hudson's Bay pelts for a big profit.

Forging steadily southward, Ogden traced a course toward Bear River and equally hostile Ute country. By April 30, Ogden had moved onto Ute hunting grounds and was trapping the headwaters of Bear River. Without knowing it, he had also crossed into Mexico. On his push from Snake River to Bear River Ogden saw thousands of seagulls and presumed he was near a large body of water. Although Jim Bridger takes credit for the discovery of Great Salt Lake some five months before Ogden's arrival, Ogden made the first recorded sighting. On Sunday, May 22, 1825, Ogden would note that two of his trappers informed him that Bear River discharged into a large lake equal in size to Lake Winnipeg.[178] However, a flock of seagulls held little interest when he met a Blackfoot war party who blandly told McKay, his interpreter, that they were searching for the camp of Iron Wristbands, a well-known Snake war chief. Ogden wisely got out of their way.

In what became known as Ogden's Hole, the Bay men had their first and only good luck. Ogden was elated. "Trapping excellent," he would write, "no whites have ever been here before." Joyfully, he advanced down river only to run into deserters from McDonald's 1822 Snake Expedition. These gentlemen informed Ogden that he was within fifteen day's march of the Spanish village of Taos.[179] A known supply post for American trappers, Taos could spell trouble and it did.

During Ogden's push from Flat Head House, Rocky Mountain Fur had selected a new target, not by accident but through necessity. In the wake of the Snake-Blackfoot alliance all hell had broken loose in the later summer of 1824. Their relentless attacks on Missouri Fur and American Fur had forced these companies to abandon the mountains

---

[178] (Binns, *Peter Skene Ogden: Fur Trader*, pp. 139-40). Actually, the first white man to see Great Salt Lake was a Franciscan priest, Father Escalante, who discovered it in 1776.

[179] Ogden, *Snake Country Journals*, 1824-1825, entry dated Sunday, May 22, 1825.

and go back to the Missouri River trade, while Rocky Mountain Fur, suffering heavy casualties, was driven south to the Colorado Rockies. To overcome these setbacks, the Ashley-Henry brigades were pouring through South Pass into southern Oregon country. The American companies as well as Hudson's Bay knew at least two-thirds of Oregon country, meaning all the land south of the Columbia to Mexico, was disputed property. Now, the Americans intended to reap their share of the fur reward. In the spring of 1825, as Hudson's Bay prepared for a profitable season, Major Ashley with brigades led by Jim Bridger, Jedidiah Smith and Johnson Gardner, were closing in from the east and other brigades out of Taos led by Etienne Provost were approaching from the south.

As Ogden progressed down river, he found Americans under foot everywhere, cleaning out the country ahead of him. All hope for a big catch as Ogden put it "was blasted." The Americans were not happy with Ogden's competition either. When they heard from his deserters that Ogden had crossed the Blues flying the British flag to take beaver in what the Americans considered to be U.S. territory, they were ready to fight. Unfortunately for Hudson's Bay, the Americans found their deadliest weapon before Ogden himself arrived. . . disloyalty, desertion and rot-gut whiskey.

Descending from Cache Valley to Great Salt Lake, Ogden found Provost camped on the north shore. With Provost were deserters from the 1823 Snake Expedition, a Russian trader, some Canadian free trappers and an old Spaniard who was serving as guide. Shortly after Ogden's arrival, a cavalcade thundered into Provost's camp with American flags flying and fourteen of Ogden's missing trappers, including Nick Montour and Alex Carson, in tow. The battle lines were now drawn.

Before Ogden's arrival, Provost had fallen in with a band of Snakes camped on the shore of Salt Lake where he had a disastrous encounter with Twisted Hand whom he referred to as the "evil-minded Shoshoni Chief, Mauvis Gauche."[180] After being invited to smoke the pipe, Twisted Hand said it was contrary to his medicine to have anything

---

[180] J. Cecil Alter, *James Bridger*, p. 45.

Courtesy of the Oregon Historical Society, OrHi 297.

Jim Bridger.

metallic nearby while a council was in progress, so he asked the trappers to remove their weapons and place them outside the council ring.

Provost, in no position to argue, did as he was directed. After placing their guns to one side, the trappers sat down in the circle to smoke. Suddenly at a prearranged signal the Indians seized knives and war clubs concealed under their blankets and attacked the unsuspecting trappers, seven of whom were killed. Provost, a powerful man, managed to fight his way out and, with three others, escaped. This unwarranted attack made a deep impression on the mountain men who vowed vengeance but the wily chief escaped. When Ogden arrived, the Americans were not in the best of humor.

The newcomer's leader, Johnson Gardner, rode into Ogden's camp carrying the Stars and Stripes and informed all hands that they were in U.S. territory. Ogden disagreed, believing he was in Oregon territory where British and Americans had equal rights. It is almost certain that Gardner knew that both parties were in trespass on Mexican soil. Whatever, he ran his bluff, explaining to the Hudson's Bay trappers that they were now all free to do as they chose, whether indebted to the company or not, and whoever wished could desert Ogden and join the Americans. He also stated he would pay $3.50 a pound for any beaver skins they brought with them, no questions asked. He then left.

With mutiny staring him in the eye and outnumbered by American guns, Ogden was caught in a dangerous situation. As the Americans plied his rebellious crew with liquor, Ogden's only hope for survival was to place a tight guard to keep defectors from smuggling furs into the enemy camp. It didn't work. How many pelts were stolen will never be known, but it was later claimed that Ashley got back to St. Louis with furs valued at 70,000 dollars—some claimed 200,000 dollars—which Ogden had harvested. Some thought Ashley had "lifted" these furs from Ogden's cache in Cache Valley north of Great Salt Lake. Others believed

---

[181] Chitterden, *The History of the American Fur Trade of the Far West*, Vol. 1, p. 276.

that he had somehow compelled Ogden to sell them dirt cheap.[182] Surprisingly, the men who held the most potential for causing trouble backed Ogden when the chips were down.

In the frantic moments when the Americans tried to provoke the Canadians into firing on them, Julia Ogden—Pete's wife—was looking down the muzzle of a gun. Their eight month old son was tied to the saddle of Julia's pony when deserters stampeded the company horses. Julia ran to the American camp where she found a shaken-up Michael crying in his pack board. Mounting and spurring out, Julia was almost in the clear when she noticed a company horse loaded with furs. She paused long enough to seize its halter rope.

Mountain-man Joe Meek, who recorded the one-woman raid, observed that his fellow Americans were glad to get rid of the baby but went after the furs.[183] When Julia grabbed the pack horse, guns were leveled and voices yelled "shoot the squaw." Most of the trappers, however, admired the woman's courage and when she charged out of their camp, no guns were fired, which was a stroke of luck for both sides. That night Ogden wrote in his journal: "I cannot but consider it a fortunate circumstance I did not fire, for had I, I have not the least doubt all was gone. . . indeed this was their plan that I should fire and assuredly they did all they could to make me. . . . "[184]

In all, twenty-nine of Ogden's men deserted to the Americans. A few years later Ogden would acknowledge that it was no mystery as to why his men were defecting. It would take ten years "with the strictest economy, barring accident" working for Hudson's Bay Company to make what they could in one year working for the Americans.[185]

The next morning Ogden broke camp and pushed north, reaching the swollen Snake River on June 5. A week later two Flatheads delivered a five month old message from Gov. Simpson urging Ogden to "pursue your hunt diligently and trap your way to Fort George by way of the

---

[182] Vestal, *Joe Meek*, p. 83.

[183] Meek could not have made a first hand observation of this incident as he didn't come to the mountains until the spring of 1829. (Vestal, *Joe Meek*, P. 19).

[184] Ogden, *Snake Country Journals*, 1824-1825, entry dated Tuesday, May 24, 1825.

[185] Ogden, *Snake Country Journal* entry for February 16, 1828.

Umpqua River." This order was based on Simpson's belief that the Umpqua drained out of Great Salt Lake. Actually, its headwaters are in the Cascade Mountains seven hundred miles to the west. Since this route was impossible and the attempt itself with his skeleton crew would have led to disaster crossing Shoshoni lands, Ogden continued north. Dodging Snake patrols, he finally reached the Boise River in October. On Sunday, October 30, almost a year since he left Spokane House, Ogden made the last entry in his journal. "We left Burnt River. . . am now three days march from Fort Nez Perce. . . 4 beaver." He had left the Snake River by the valleys of Burnt, Powder and Grande Ronde to the Walla Walla valley and Fort Nez Perce. This same route, blazed by Donald McKenzie in 1812, would eventually become a part of the Oregon Trail.

It was a tough year. After his heavy loss of fur to the Rocky Mountain Fur Company, Ogden had only 4,000 beaver pelts to deliver to Fort George. In his official report to Gov. Simpson he noted that the entry of the Columbia region by the Americans was reducing the catch to almost nothing. He would close his report with a heart-felt promise: "You may rely on my exertions to find beaver. . . . " In less than a month, Ogden would get the chance to prove it.

His failure to create a beaver desert in southeast Oregon territory caused little concern on the Atlantic seaboard, where some more pressing things were taking place. As Ogden made his retreat from Great Salt Lake to Fort Nez Perce, the Erie Canal linking the Hudson River to Lake Erie was opened to traffic. At the same time Fulton's steam engine was stirring up speculation on a steam-driven locomotive. This caused the *New York Quarterly Review* to wonder "what can be more palpably absurd than the prospect held out of locomotives traveling twice as fast as stagecoaches?" While the *Review* pondered such intriguing questions, Ogden embarked down the Columbia for his next assignment. It would not make him happy.

The defeat he had suffered at the hands of Johnson Gardner, the loss of his freemen and—important to a man of Ogden's temperament—the torments he had been forced to endure, left him with memories that rankled. One might expect that this would have led to an implacable hatred of the Americans but it didn't. Ogden's reaction is more complicated than hatred. He was an intelligent man and "seems to have become allergic to them" or so the editor of his journals, E.E. Rich thought. A month after his encounter with Gardner, Ogden had written to George

Simpson with unprecedented fury: "You need not anticipate another expedition ensuing year to this country for not a freeman will return, and should they, it would be to join the Americans."

For this outburst and an error in his letter of July 10, 1825, to the Hudson's Bay Company governing committee in Canada—mistakenly dated "East Fork of the Missouri," indisputably American territory—he got a stiff reprimand from his superiors and it did not set well with the tough partisan.

Because of this error and his clash with Gardner, the committee informed Governor Simpson—rather stiffly—that Ogden should have avoided the area as he had been repeatedly given direction not to collide with the Americans and furthermore, "any more inattention to instructions will be attended to with our serious displeasure." The confusion as to whether Ogden was at Great Salt Lake or the East Fork of the Missouri River was eventually straightened out but for the time being, Ogden was deeply humiliated and in the bad graces of the Hudson's Bay Company. His punishment—trap the Ochoco!

Above and below: The Guardian Spirit of the Ochoco Valley (Tamanawis) who stood guard over the Gateway of the Warriors which was destroyed by the construction of the Ochoco Dam in 1918.

CHAPTER 33

BREACHING THE OCHOCO

And, when the second morning shone
We looked upon a world unknown,
On nothing we could call our own.
No cloud above, no earth below,
A universe of sky and snow!

John Greenleaf Whittier
Snowbound

Days ahead of Ogden, word reached Fort Nez Perce that the 1825 rendezvous produced 191 fur packs each worth 1,000 dollars brought in by American trappers from Shoshoni country. Included in that shipment was. . . . "a valuable cache of furs taken from the Hudson's Bay Company in such a mysterious manner that not even Ashley attempted to account for them."[186]

Within hours after his arrival at the fort, Ogden was ordered to trap the Ochoco "as quickly and economically as possible." The last time Ogden had attempted to run Red Wolf's blockade as a North West Company brigade leader in 1819, he had lost two company men and carried three cripples back to the Columbia. He was not looking forward to a rematch with the dog soldiers and Simpson was not inclined to ease the pain.

In August during Ogden's retreat from the Eldahow, McLoughlin dispatched his step-son Tom McKay and Finan McDonald with thirty men into the Klamath Lake region on rumors it was rich in beaver. What they found was anyone's guess but Ogden was supposed to try and make contact with them. While men and supplies were being

---

[186] Chittenden, *American Fur Trade,* Vol. 1, p. 277.

organized, McLoughlin and his immediate staff studied maps of interior Oregon. . . pitifully inadequate charts labelled "Indian territory, western America, Unclaimed." A tremendous wilderness sprawled across the ancient Columbia lava flow. In 29 fleeting years it would be designated on U.S. military maps as Wasco County, Oregon Territory. After hours of checking all possibilities, the White Headed Eagle decided upon the ancient Klamath Indian trail as being the most logical and least hazardous route to be taken into the high country known to his Indian informants as the Ochoco.

Over the centuries, the moccasined feet of Klamath and Modoc slavers had worn a definite path across Oregon country on their semi-annual migrations to the great trade center at Celilo. This trail, running due south, left the Columbia a few miles east of the rocky flat named Kaklasko by the Chinook, meaning "the place of the springs" and known to the Shoshoni as Winquatt, "the place encircled by rock cliffs." Here, in 1838, the Dalles City, first American settlement east of the Cascade mountains was to get its start as a Methodist mission. But in 1825, the place encircled by rock cliffs was to become Ogden's passport into central Oregon.

Shortly before Ogden's arrival at Fort Nez Perce, Chief Concomly cruised upriver to Fort Vancouver where he honored Sir George Simpson with his royal presence. As was his custom, Concomly—preceded by 300 slaves—had the several hundred feet of ground that he had to traverse from the main fort entrance to the governor's door carpeted with beaver and otter skins.[187] This had the desired effect for Simpson appreciated any contribution to company efforts. However, it didn't pave the way for Ogden to convince him that stabilization of company loyalty through more equitable pay, manpower and supplies, would be a welcome relief toward reentry into Snake Country. Quite to the contrary. In accordance with Simpson's stubborn belief that previous Snake country expeditions had been extravagant in both personnel and supplies Ogden's brigade would include no more than fifty, including gentlemen, laborers, freemen and McDonald's thirty man crew if and when he found him. As a further economy no women were to accom-

---

[187] Hodge, *Handbook of Indians*, p. 329.

pany the expedition and so Julia Ogden—now seven months pregnant—remained at Fort Nez Perce with the children. To further emphasize his prudent use of resources, the governor dispatched Ogden into the Ochoco with the same horses that had limped into Fort Nez Perce three weeks before.

The men who would back Ogden on this dangerous venture—Finan McDonald, Thomas McKay, Baptiste Dubreuil, Joseph Delore, Alexander Carson, Antoine Sylville and Dedron Senecal—represented a cross-section of every major fur company which had tramped across the Pacific Northwest. The red-headed giant, McDonald—who had sworn beaver would have to grow pelts of gold before he went back into Snake Country—would take charge of the advance column into the interior. An old Nor'wester who had helped survey the Flathead, Spokane and Crooked river basins between 1807-1810, McDonald knew where he was going.

Tom McKay, son of Alexander McKay, the American Fur Company partner blown up with the Astor ship *Tonquin* and son-in-law of Concomly, would serve as second in command of the main expedition. Governor Simpson described Tom McKay as ". . . a half-breed, lame, very active. One of the best shots in Oregon country and very cool and resolute among the Indians. The more dangerous his job the better he likes it. Possesses very little judgment and a confirmed liar. Not a particle of feeling or humanity in his composition. . . . " He would not be intimidated by the Snake dog soldiers.

Bat Dubreuil, survivor of the Astor-Hunt Overland expedition and the only living man in the Pacific Northwest who had actually set foot in the heart of the Ochoco would act as the main expedition guide. Alex Carson, an American free trapper, had proven his allegiance to Hudson's Bay. Less than seven months ago he had been a deserter from Ogden's ill-fated thrust into Snake country but later rejoined the Hudson's Bay brigade at Great Salt Lake and in the face of Americans guns backed Ogden at the risk of his own life. Another survivor of the Hunt overland expedition, Carson along with John Day had opened the Eldahow to fur trade. His experience in dealing with the Shoshoni was vital to the success of this undertaking.

Antoine Sylvaille, who had accompanied Ogden on the North West Company's Snake brigade, would be chief of scouts. Since Simpson had not specifically excluded scouts from his manpower allotment,

Ogden recruited 100 Indian scouts to serve as hunters. These scouts, led by Jimmy Rabbit, were chosen from the Nez Perce warrior class for other than the Blackfeet, the Nez Perce were the only western tribe on speaking terms with the Shoshoni having negotiated one of their numerous peace agreements with Red Wolf and Twisted Hand in 1821.

In mid-November of 1825, this motley group made up of the toughest element south of the Saskatchewan River started on the first leg of their journey. By the time they arrived at the Klamath trail Ogden was already facing trouble. Two of the company horses "could scarcely crawl" and for Simpson's benefit Ogden would note that "it is truly distressing to undertake a long journey with such miserable creatures and I seriously apprehend, if the winter is severe, two thirds will die." Fortunately, the worst weather he had encountered was rain. Neither would his men give him any comfort. Three weeks from departure Joe Dupard got into a fight with an Indian laborer and beat him to death with his bare fists.

December 1 found the main party camped on the Deschutes River in an area untouched by white men and their orders were to "trap close." Not only did Ogden find the river already trapped but that afternoon a Snake warrior slipped into camp and stole a horse loaded with traps and ammunition. Ogden could understand the theft of the traps. The way he put it this was about the only way the Indians could get them. It was against company policy to trade traps to the Indians. Their only alternative was to rent them and turn over their catch to the company or steal them, which was the preferred choice. Then to add to his woes some of the free trapper's women mysteriously showed up in camp. Among them was Timmee McKay, the plump little offspring of Concomly and a Cayuse slave girl, who was looking for her "Toam."

Three days after this disruption McDonald and McKay—now on the middle Deschutes—met one of Ogden's scouts and sent word ahead that they would wait for his arrival. Among other information forwarded, the advance party would report that they only had 460 beaver to show for four months of dodging Snake patrols in the Klamath region now known as the Winema National Forest. Other than that ". . . all was well and starving."[188] McDonald's comment held no intended sarcasm. On a Snake country expedition starvation uncomplicated by other griefs was relatively good fortune. Five days after receiving this message the main party tramped into McDonald's camp on the Warm Springs River near where Kahneeta Resort now stands. Much to Ogden's disappointment McDonald had been unable to hire a Shoshoni to serve as a local guide, which placed him in an unpleasant situation for it was now obvious that the Nez Perce scouts didn't know the country.

Red Wolf, fully aware of Ogden's movements, obliged by sending in a spy. Two days after contact with McDonald and while ferrying supplies across the Deschutes, a lone Snake warrior rode out of Frog Canyon and offered his services as a guide. Ogden was overjoyed. "A more fit person could not have been selected. If he doesn't desert us, we may consider ourselves fortunate." On this happy note Ogden began his march on the Ochoco. It was now Tuesday, December 13, and bad luck was on his trail.

The lower Ochoco River valley nestled beneath the sullen rims of the ancient Columbia basalts was called the Unkatuwa Gaiya—the red sand gap—or more literally translated, the bloody ground. This inviting passage afforded the main breach into Snake hunting grounds from the west. Shaped like a wandering half moon with Grizzly Mountain holding down the northern point, Grey Butte like a blunted battle lance jutting up in the center and Powell Butte balanced on the southern tip, this notch presented an open front twenty miles wide with nothing to stop an invader but the fickle winds of the Crooked River plateau. . . and Ogden was moving toward this opening, his footsteps touching the earth where no white man had trod before.

Immediately upon crossing the Deschutes Ogden split the command. McDonald would trap Crooked River from mouth to source on a bearing toward the Malheur. Ogden with the main party would strike due east into the southern Blues, trapping his way to the Snake River. Ogden had barely cleared the Deschutes rim when Jimmy Rabbit

---

[188] Unless otherwise noted, all direct quotations are taken from Ogden, *Snake Country Journals*, 1824-1825 and 1825-1826. Entries dated from November 21, 1825 through February 10, 1826. Reprinted by the Hudson's Bay Record Society, London, England, 1950.

reported that a party of Cayuse were on their way to warn Red Wolf that Hudson's Bay was coming. Stringing traps up Willow Creek, the Bay men crossed over the high backbone of Lone Pine ridge, described as "four miles of high mountains well stocked in wood of the fir tree" and descended into a large plain twelve miles west of the confluence of the Ochoco and Crooked Rivers.

Setting up camp at Forest Crossing on Crooked River, they saw where forty Indian lodges had been recently abandoned, a bad omen for as Ogden reasoned, "they resembled in form and shape those I saw last fall in the lower Snake country." Therefore, he concluded, that "they must be Snake Indians." His newly hired guide offered no comment. Shortly thereafter, a Snake warrior appeared on the skyline and quickly disappeared when approached. On December 17, Ogden cautiously wrote. . . "being now I presume on the borders of the Snake Lands, we require to watch our horses by day and night." It was also becoming obvious that the Snakes were in no mood to trade with Hudson's Bay. Apparently, the free-wheeling Americans with their generous deals in arms, traps and whiskey were cornering the market. About the only favorable aspect Ogden had encountered since leaving Fort Nez Perce was "the weather is still very mild. God grant it may remain so. . . . " It was now seven days before Christmas.

In the hope of catching a few beaver nearly 100 traps were strung up present Jap Creek. No luck but that evening—to stave off starvation—the Nez Perce hunters did manage to kill three deer and found the tracks of two elk. Oddly, from the time the trappers had entered Willow Creek, they had seen large herds of mountain sheep in the rims along Willow Creek leading into Grizzly Mountain. Today, this seems unbelievable.[189] The following morning the main party advanced up Crooked River and though the river banks were lined with willows and grass "not more than 200 yards out, nothing to be seen but sand," thus explaining the Shoshoni name of "red sand gap." Of more importance the weather was still more like summer than late fall. For three days Hudson's Bay

---

[189] In 1978 the author found the skull of a rimrock bighorn (now extinct) in the lava beds north of highway 126 between Redmond, Oregon, and the community of Powell Butte. The place of discovery was only about 25 miles south of the rims of Willow Creek.

worked eastward, trapping the river, Lytle and McKay creeks and spirits were rising for they caught 73 beaver. The Shoshoni had trapped the river but it was Ogden's belief that if Hudson's Bay had reached it first, Crooked River would have yielded from 400-500 beaver in the eight miles they had travelled. On December 20, Joe Delore caught a raccoon which caused Canadian eyes to pop. "Big as an Indian dog. Biggest animal of that species we had ever seen." The best was yet to come.

On the first day of winter commenting on the "really warm weather," Ogden reached the mouth of the Ochoco River and set up camp within the present city limits of Prineville. If Ogden realized that he was making the first recorded entry into interior Oregon since Thompson's rapid crossing 18 years earlier, there is no indication of it in his journal. Scouting the two river bottoms, they found "grass seven feet high" growing in the Ochoco valley. "The Crooked River at this point turns into a deep canyon with high rocks on both sides which prevent setting of more traps." The Shoshoni guide told Ogden that by heading east he would again see Crooked River. Ogden was skeptical. . . "if so it must make a considerable bend." The Shoshoni—which McDonald later confirmed—had accurately described the big bend in Crooked River which runs due south from Prineville for twenty miles and then turns northward for fifteen miles to reach a point only fifteen miles distant from Prineville.

Stringing traps up the Ochoco River, Ogden's men snared 39 beaver and 2 otter before nightfall of December 21. The beaver defied the imagination—mammoth animals measuring five feet in length and weighing upwards to 100 pounds. Years before, Dubreuil and Day had boasted of seeing such animals in the inner Ochoco and they were ridiculed into silence. Now, Ogden would verify their claim. Even after the Shoshoni had worked the stream and the beaver catch was slim, the Ochoco River was yielding more than 1,000 dollars a day. In ten days of trapping—from December 21 to January 1—Ogden netted the company over twelve thousand dollars in prime beaver pelts.[190] He later said that the beaver caught "were certainly far from what we have a right to expect."

---

[190] Hudson's Bay Company records list the value at 2,533 pounds sterling at the U.S. dollar exchange rate of $4.8665 per pound sterling.

As unbelievable as beaver this size may seem, the Ochoco beaver often measured five feet from tip to tip. Overtrapping so exhausted the supply that for the past 170 years few have been seen. One of the few survivors of this breed was trapped as late as 1957 on Ochoco Creek. The following account is taken from the *Central Oregonian* of January 3, 1957:

> A big beaver that has been living in Ochoco Creek near Prineville Golf and Country Club was trapped last weekend by W.I. Mallery. The huge fellow measured an even 44 inches from nose to tail and weighed 52 pounds. This was not the largest beaver taken by Mallery, who until four years ago, worked as a government trapper in this area. He recalled one beaver taken on the Ochoco that measured 58 inches and weighed 82 pounds. . . .

Apparently, neither Dubreuil nor Ogden was exaggerating about gigantic beaver working the streams of the Ochoco.

On the evening of December 21, McDonald's party reunited with Ogden. That night they noted a "considerable change in temperature" and by morning the Ochoco and Crooked rivers were locked in two inches of ice. Leaving McDonald to trap Crooked River, Ogden moved up the Ochoco into a raging storm where the Kouse Eaters (Thoigarik-hos)—as the Snake guide called the Nez Perce hunters —threatened to leave, prompting Ogden to write. . . "one has no idea the trouble and anxiety an Indian gives particularly as is the case at present when the fellows know you are depending on them. . . . " Six miles upriver Ogden was surprised to find that the Ochoco disappeared into a narrow, boulder-strewn channel. For a distance of two tormented miles the steep canyon walls ended in sheer basalt cliffs towering 600 feet above the valley floor. This narrow passage was the Shoshoni nimma wuko gaiyu, meaning the Gateway of the Warriors.

High on a ledge above the entrance to this foreboding corridor stood a unique rock formation. The Snake guide called it Tamanawis, the guardian spirit who maintained a lonely, eternal watch over the homeland of his people. Tamanawis is a lava spire carved by wind and rain in the image of an Indian brave standing erect, arms folded, facing eastward into the depths of Shoshoni hunting grounds. According to Shoshoni legend, this natural rock formation was once a Snake war chief, undefeated in battle, fair in judgment and wise in council, who was placed on the ledge below Mesa Rim by the Great Spirit to protect his people against all forces of evil. Because his soul, living in this lofty pinnacle, was the strongest medicine which they possessed it became the personal totem of the Snake war tribes.[191]

On December 23, 1825, working through Ogden's Snake guide, Tamanawis proved his worth. Bogged down at the entrance to the upper Ochoco River valley, his traps buried in ice and snow, Ogden was facing mutiny. Told that Red Wolf's war camps were close at hand, Sylvaille's scouts refused to go one step farther and Dubreuil, now as nervous as the Nez Perce, told Ogden that east of this barrier lay the tortuous country where he, Crooks and Day had spent the winter of 1812. Stubborn as the Kouse Eaters, he rebelled at the idea of pushing ahead. Ogden, having faced his share of Snake hostiles, was reluctant to go on now that he knew the Nez Perce were "as ignorant of the country beyond this point" as he was. Still undecided, he retreated to McDonald's base camp at the confluence of the Ochoco and Crooked Rivers.

The Canadians spent Christmas eve on short rations, their traps locked in six inches of ice; and snow engulfing their camp. On Christmas Day 1825 a cold, hungry Ogden—a man who had spent winters on the Continental Divide, the crest of the northern Blues and the frigid Snake River plateau—penned these words in his journal: "It is hard to believe. Nowhere in Oregon country have we encountered weather such as this." Referring to the Ochoco River, he continues: "the ice is regrettable as I figured to take at least 300 to 400 more beaver and I strongly doubt if we should find another river equal to it in any part of the country. The wolves are moving in on us and two of the Nez Perce left in the storm. Starving didn't agree with them."

---

[191] Here, under the brooding gaze of Tamanawis, the Ochoco Reservoir was constructed in 1918. The dirt filled dam—at that time one of the largest in the United States—completely covered the Gateway of the Warriors, flooding the historic entrance to the Ochoco under 46,500 acre feet of water known as Lake Ochoco. The great stone warrior still stands above the lake hopefully awaiting the return of his children.

By now one third of their horses were lame and others so weak they couldn't stand up. For the next five days hunters battled the storm searching for deer or elk while those starving in camp would sneak out before daylight to steal beaver out of their partner's traps for food if they found nothing in their own. As Ogden put it. . . "if this cold weather should not soon pass away my situation with so many men will not be pleasant. . . it will alone depend on the success of our hunters if we escape starvation. . . may God preserve us."

To make matters worse Red Wolf's agent refused to show Ogden a way out of this trap. Aware that Ogden wished to proceed up the Ochoco River, his reasons for non-compliance were hard to ignore. In keeping with the war-chief's orders, he discouraged any probe into the southern Blues explaining that deep snow would make it impossible to cross the mountains. Furthermore, there were no animals of any kind in the Ochoco not even a beaver and the horses would die for lack of grass. Ogden was convinced. Finally, on the promise of a gun and ammunition when they reached Fort Nez Perce, the Snake warrior consented to guide them back to the northern Blues and the following morning struck a course for the barren hills east of Stephenson Mountain—an area which years later would be described as hell with the fire out.

This compromise between a representative of the Hudson's Bay Company and the Shoshoni nation took place on New Year's Eve and the Snake brigade had now been without food for three days. On January 1, 1826, after giving all hands a dram of liquor, Ogden turned his back on the Ochoco River valley and pushed northeast through a mountain blizzard toward the John Day basin. It was the first New Year's Day since Ogden first came to Indian country in the summer of 1819 that his men were without food of any kind. On this day, as Ogden struggled up McKay Creek toward the Bear Creek drainage, Sarah Julia Ogden was born at Fort Nez Perce—a daughter he would not know about until six months later.

On January 6 the horses—some with hoofs completely worn off—could scarcely crawl over the frozen ground and there was no chance of turning south for McKay, who had been on scout, reported four to six feet of snow in the Ochoco Blues and not a track of an animal to be found. By now the free trappers had resorted to killing their saddle horses for food and even so with this large of a group they were averaging only one meal every two days. On January 11 Ogden entered the John Day valley only to find that Shoshoni trappers had preceded the expedition. Apparently word had gotten to the Shoshoni camps that Hudson's Bay trappers were approaching and they saw to it that even if they didn't catch all the beaver and otter, their attempts would leave the animals wary and difficult to snare. During this trek five trappers disappeared and it was believed they had been ambushed by the Snakes. As it turned out, they had gotten lost.

As they progressed up the main fork of the John Day River, the snow disappeared, the grass was green and the frogs croaking as merrily as in May. This, too, would change. While hunting, McKay found an Earth Eater hidden in the rocks and brought him at gun-point to camp. This unwilling guide told Ogden if he stayed on this fork of the river it would take him into the Snake River drainage. Open to any suggestion, Ogden headed for the gap between the 7,000' peaks of Baldy and Little Baldy mountains in the middle Blues. Two days after bringing in the Earth Eater, five Snake warriors rode into Ogden's camp. They offered no advice on how to get out of the Ochoco but did trade eight beaver pelts for knives and beads. Ogden acknowledged that "they were fine, tall men, well-dressed, and for so barren a country in good condition." In short, they were not starving like the trappers.

By January 31 Ogden was again "swimming in snow." During this passage Ogden suspected what would confuse the military some thirty-five years into the future in their effort to locate the Snake war camps. As Ogden noted. . . "all this country (from Crooked River to the head of the John Day) appears to be well inhabited in the summer season. . . but where they resort at this season I cannot learn, but no doubt are concealed in the mountains. . . . " He was right. It took the army nearly four years of heavy fighting to figure this out.

On February 2, Ogden reached the crest of the middle Blues with men and horses looking like skeletons. On this wind-swept summit he dejectedly wrote: "This surely is the Snake country; as far as the eye can reach, nothing but lofty mountains. A more gloomy country I never yet saw." On this sad note he dispatched a Nez Perce messenger with a report to Governor Simpson at Fort Vancouver. . . "I truly wish it were in my power to give you more favorable accounts. . . we have now traveled upwards of 200 miles and not a track of animals to be seen. We have endured privation greater than I am willing to relate. . . the men suffer still more so for want of shoes in this cold weather. . . none but ignorant Canadians would have consented to such a long voyage. . . . "

CHAPTER 34

WHO ARE THESE PEOPLE?

March 9, 1826
> *They (a Snake family) had nothing in their*
> *hut but a small stock of ants and a few prickly pears—*
> *more wretched looking beings I never beheld. . . .*

March 11, 1826
> *. . . two of my hunting party had fallen in*
> *with two Snake Indians with two horses*
> *loaded with buffalo meat. . .*

Peter Skene Ogden
Journal entries, Second Snake Expedition

The following morning they dropped down onto the head of the Burnt River.[192] Now they were finding Snake camps well supplied with buffalo meat but offering no furs to trade. By the time Ogden's brigade reached the Snake River on February 11, men and horses were reduced to skeletons. On February 14, they camped on the Malheur and here Ogden again divided the brigade. Jean Gervais was sent back into the Ochoco with seven men on orders to trap until mid-July. Sylvaille with five men was to trap the Malheur and continue west until he heard from

---

[192] This appears to be the first recorded use of the name "Burnt River." In the fall of 1825 Ogden had referred to it as the "River Brule" which is the French form of "burnt." It is likely that the name was common among the French-Canadian trappers because of the burned timber along its banks. The river drains a southeast area in Oregon's Blue Mountains and flows into the Snake River near Huntington. On this same foray Ogden also named the Owyhee River due to the murder of two Hawaiians there in 1819. Owyhee was the old English name for Hawaii. No native Indian tribes ever bore the name of Owyhee Indians. (Hodge, *Handbook of American Indians*, part II, p. 177).

Ogden again. The remainder of the brigade headed for the Owyhee. Enroute, Ogden would lay the groundwork for the false impression of the Shoshoni that would dog them to their final destruction. It was a contradictory observation which he knew from his own experience could not be true of the Snakes, but his journal entry for February 26, 1826, would travel down through history as an accurate description of the Ochoco Shoshoni to the detriment of Indian and white alike.

> . . . on our travels this day we saw a Snake Indian and as it so happened, his hut being near the road, curiosity induced me to enter. I had often heard these wretches subsisted on ants, locusts and small fish, in size not larger than minnies and I was determined to find out if it was not an exaggeration of late travelers, but to my surprise I found it was the case, for one of their dishes, not of small size, was filled with ants and on inquiring in what manner they collected them: 'in the morning early before the thaw commences.' The locusts they collect in summer and store up for winter. In eating they give the preference to the former, being oily and the latter not. On this food, if such it may be called, these poor wretches drag out an existence nearly four months in the year. They however, so far as we can judge from appearances, live contented and happy and this is all they require. It appeared rather strange, and the only reason I can give for it is, from the poverty of their food on which they subsist that few or no children are to be seen among them. We have now seen upwards of 30 families and only three children among them, so from this, before many years, not many will be living and ants and locusts will again increase.

Mr. Ogden had just been royally entertained in a Hohandika household. He might not have dined so lavishly in a Tussawehee (White Knife) Snake war camp.

If, as Ogden now puzzled, the Snakes were so destitute, he was still in no mood to tempt fate. By the first of March, the main expedition had abandoned the Ochoco and was headed east toward Shoshoni Falls. Moving into the Eldahow, the trappers were now afraid to eat the beaver which were feeding on poison parsnip. For anyone so unfortunate as to eat one the accepted cure was to drink a cup of river water laced with a mixture of pepper and gunpowder. If the tainted meat didn't get you, the medication most certainly would.

Bearing down on Shoshoni Falls, Ogden again found the timid Earth Eaters subsisting on ants and prickly pears. Yet two days later his hunters discovered two Snake Indians riding toward camp with two pack-horse loads of buffalo meat in tow. These businessmen, seeing little of value in Ogden's trade articles, offered only enough meat to feed four men. During negotiations three horses and a colt drifted into camp and the trappers were in the act of killing them when Ogden wisely intervened. The next morning a heavily armed Snake warrior rode into camp in search of the horses. Since Ogden had dealt fairly with him, he returned with his wife and family, traded a bale of dried elk meat for two scalp knives and offered his services as a guide.

The following day, Ogden's benefactor along with the two Snake merchants took McDonald and McKay on a hunt. When they returned that evening the hunters had thirteen elk and famine changed to feast. Three days later another Snake hunter joined the camp with news that buffalo were grazing nearby. The expedition's horses were too weak for buffalo running, but with the aid of the Indians two buffalo were killed. The same day Tom McKay killed four elk within sight of camp.

That evening the weather which had been exceptionally warm turned cold and a violent snowstorm raged all night and all the next day. During this interruption the Snake hunter who had appeared the day before took his departure. Almost immediately some trappers who had braved the blizzard to set out traps reappeared, driven back by the storm and bringing with them the Snake. At the edge of camp he had found one of the women gathering wood and as a farewell gesture he had thrown her down in the snow and torn the beads and other ornaments from her leather dress. Ogden observed tersely, "this fellow we shall not see again."[193]

By now Ogden was beginning to recognize, if not openly at least subconsciously, that the Snakes were no different than their European cousins—some honorable, some treacherous, some very rich, some very

---

[193] All direct quotations and historical data for this chapter are taken from Ogden's *Snake Country Journals* 1825-1826, entries dated from February 11, 1826 through July 17, 1826.

poor and between the elite and the welfare recipients lay the vast middle class who kept the nation alive. It is too bad that those who reflected upon his journals did not gain this insight.

On Sunday March 19, one day after the execution of the Snake thief, with the horses struggling in snow drifts up to their bellies the expedition reached Raft River only to receive more unfortunate news. Thirty Snake dog soldiers rode into camp well-supplied with American made goods and reported that a party of Ashley's trappers were only three day's march from Ogden's camp. Equally disconcerting, the Canadians had blundered into a Shoshoni migration headed for the Spanish settlements to trade and steal horses. The Snake warriors promised to trade but it appeared they were independent of the Canadian goods, being well armed and well stocked in ammunition, knives and iron. There was not a beaver skin among them thus giving mute testimony that they had indeed met the Americans.

At this time it was believed that the Shoshoni migration numbered some 2,500 men plus women and children. Ogden in amazement would write ". . . I had no idea the Snakes were so numerous." One small stream west of the Raft River was lined with Shoshoni lodges whose occupants, according to Ogden, "were preparing to descend to avoid the Blackfeet Indians." How he arrived at this conclusion is hard to understand. By his own observation this Snake encampment was armed with at least 150 American guns.

On March 29, 1826, the expedition had encountered a party of Blackfeet who had left the Saskatchewan plains in December 1825, and were, according to Ogden "in quest of the Snakes to steal horses." At this point Mr. Ogden reverts to the popular Anglo conviction that the Shoshoni were incapable of defending their rights. Writing in all honesty, Ogden describes the Blackfeet horse thieves as . . . "this party consists of 80 men. They are poorly armed, only 15 guns, scarcely any ammunition, bows and arrows scarce among them. If rascals deserve reward, they do for the distance they came in quest of horses and scalps. Well may the Snakes dread."

This particular group of Snakes Ogden refers to numbered 200 with 60 guns and plenty of ammunition. It is unlikely they had cause to "dread" the Blackfeet. In view of the unadvertised Shoshoni-Blackfoot alliance it is more reasonable that these distant travelers had come to join a Snake raid on the Spanish settlements for badly needed supplies.

During Ogden's winter push through the Ochoco, the Robber Snakes had stolen some 350 horses belonging to a detachment of Ashley's men. When the loss was discovered, forty trappers on foot—half led by Fitzpatrick and half by Bridger—took to the trail and attacked the Snake camp. The trappers without the loss of a man not only recovered their horses but returned to their base with forty Indian ponies.

Shortly thereafter Jim Beckwourth paid for this transgression while he and some Crow companions were trading for horses with the Robbers. After trading, the Shoshoni told them they better get out of the country fast as the Utes were nearby and out to make trouble. The Crow horse traders soon discovered the Snakes had not sold them their swiftest mounts. They were soon overtaken by the Utes and, according to Beckwourth, "six of our noble young warriors were killed and scalped."[194] This is the kind of trouble Ogden's trappers were riding into.

Three days after the expedition's encounter with the Blackfeet, seven Nez Perce warriors who had wintered with the Flatheads, rode into camp looking for the Snakes. This led Ogden to the conclusion that they too were out to steal horses and would be quite disappointed to find the Piegons before them." Had the Canadians been aware of the Nez Perce-Shoshoni truce, they might have been more concerned about their own miserable mounts. As was, within a week the Snakes did cause them considerable alarm.

Prior to this immediate threat some 400 mounted Snakes passed their camp with nearly 800 horse-loads of buffalo meat. Ogden could not restrain the wishful thought that "the Blackfeet tribe, however, are fast diminishing their numbers." Nevertheless, he prudently moved camp across the Snake River only to encounter another Snake encampment of about two hundred lodges. This group—representing the Robber, Dog Rib and Bear Killer tribes—was flying the Stars and Stripes and packing American knives. When a group of head men led by Twisted Hand (Mauvais Gauche) and his two ranking war chiefs, Red Wolf (Roux Chien) and Iron Wristband visited his tent, Ogden identified them as the Indians responsible for the destruction of Reed's Pacific brigade

---

[194] Bonner, T.D., (ed.) *The Life and Adventures of James P. Beckwourth*, pp. 197-98.

on the Malheur in 1814; the murder of North West's Hawaiian trappers on the Owyhee in 1819; the pillage of Hudson's Bay Company's free trappers in 1824; and the deaths of ten Americans in the same vicinity in 1825.

The Americans, at their winter quarters near Salt Lake, would report that a large band of Snakes moved in on them. So many in fact that their encampment surrounded the trappers. Salt Lake had long been a favorite campsite of the Snakes who saw no reason for changing their plan even though the white barbarians had reached the lake first. According to Beckwourth, their leader was Ohamagwaya [Yellow Hand], the Crow name for Twisted Hand. It was also his belief that Twisted Hand was an oracle "resembling a prophet in the Old Testament."[195] Whatever, Twisted Hand told the Americans they would be wise to stay alert as "there is blood in your path" and he didn't lie.

The passing of this group did not insure safety for either the Americans or the Canadians. Now, on a Saturday morning, April 8, upwards of 100 Snakes converged on Ogden's camp. Most of the chiefs were unknown to Ogden and this alone made him nervous, especially when he could see they were well armed. However, they were low on ammunition and when Ogden refused to trade or allow them to come close to his camp, they passed peacefully.

This joy was short-lived for the following day the "dreaded Americans" arrived in force, but to Ogden's pleasant surprise they paid off their debt to Hudson's Bay from the previous year and the rival fur companies separated amicably. Although one threat had been removed, the Canadians were still near naked and destitute of shoes. Most were without blankets or shelter and the snow was still falling, so Ogden turned west toward the Ochoco in an attempt to locate Gervais and Sylvaille whom he had left on the Malheur in February.

Again the Earth Eaters added their imprint to Snake folklore. Crossing the bleak Snake River plateau, Ogden was in bad need of information about the country, but the few Snake Indians he saw faded into the landscape and ". . . will not come near us without we surround them as wild beasts and prevent their escape." Here Ogden would

---

[195] Bonner, *Beckwourth*, pp. 94-96.

witness another odd custom practiced by the bankrupt citizens of the Shoshoni nation. On May 23 he wrote, "We saw the corpse of an Indian lying in the plain. The Snake Indians have a mode of burying their dead different from all other natives I know of." (Here again Ogden blends the life-styles of the impoverished Shoshoni with those of the affluent Snake war tribes). He continues, "Where he falls he is allowed to remain, without a grave or covering—a feast for the wolves and crows, nor is there any ceremony observed or their grief of long duration. How pleasant it must be to part with our friends without regretting them. . . . "

June dawned on the main expedition, now suffering from desert heat and dust, as it struggled toward the hazy outline of the distant Blues. On June 2, the dejected Canadians blundered into a Snake hunting party led by Twisted Hand or as Ogden put it. . . "it was Mauvais Gauche, the rascal who headed the party who pillaged our party two years since." Finding the "outlaw less sinister than the desolate land," the expedition traveled with him to the Snake camp. There among the Indian horses Ogden found and claimed two company horses. Twisted Hand cheerfully admitted to having stolen one of the horses but insisted that he traded for the other. Ogden—in no position to argue—paid for its release.

Ogden had noted in an earlier meeting with Twisted Hand and Red Wolf in March that. . . "they are well dressed and comport themselves decently. . . " and so it was on this visit. In fact—for reasons known only to himself—Twisted Hand was downright friendly. Perhaps he thought the hostile environment of the Ochoco would complete the breakdown of this miserable group or maybe he was laying the groundwork for future trade in guns and ammunition with Hudson's Bay Company. Whatever the motive, according to Ogden. . . "he was very communicative in regard to the route we were taking and gave us every information we required: 'In three days you will find beaver. Do not attempt to cross the (Owyhee) mountains or you will perish from want of water.' This account agreed with the information we have received from other Snakes, also with information McDonald had received from the Clamuthe (Klamath) nation the previous fall. . . ."

Although Ogden believed that Twisted Hand was being truthful, he also believed the war chief was withholding vital information. Ogden was convinced in his own mind that out there in the great high desert basin south of the Blues. . . "there is certainly some fine streams that discharge into the Gulf of California." But he also reasoned that to reach these beaver streams across a country similar to the one they were now in with the expedition destitute of resources and the trappers without provisions would be a foolish attempt. Besides. . . "from the accounts we have received from the Indians here, the Americans have made the attempt to reach it but starvation has driven them back."

The next morning (June 3, 1826), ignoring Twisted Hand's advice, Ogden plowed into the Owyhee Mountains in the hope of intercepting Sylvaille in Malheur country. Ironically, it wasn't for "want of water" that the Bay men nearly perished. Twenty four hours into the boulder-strewn area the trappers who had suffered from heat, thirst, dust and blowing sand were treated to a change of weather. An arctic express arrived, accompanied by sub-zero temperatures and a raging blizzard. By mid-day it was so cold that the Canadians were forced to halt and light a fire to keep from freezing. In this winter wonderland they noticed an Earth Eater camp whose unconscious inhabitants were near death, causing Ogden to reflect. . . "more starving wretched-looking beings I have never beheld. . . indeed for some time I was at a loss to discover if they were dead or alive. . . " This uncertainty was quickly solved when one of the free trappers tried to steal their only horse.

Continuing northward through three-foot snow drifts, the expedition crossed into the Owyhee drainage in a drenching rain. Along the river they encountered two Snake maidens out for an evening stroll "whom," according to Ogden, "the freemen eyed lustfully" but the tough brigade leader was smart enough to allow the ladies to pass "without the least molestation." This was fortunate for all concerned for within a short time Red Wolf—undoubtedly checking on the hide-hunters progress—paid Ogden a visit. Amiable as the war chief appeared, Ogden could not refrain from noting in his journal that he was justifiably apprehensive: "Friday, June 8, 1826, had a visit from the Snakes. Within the last 10 months they have plundered 180 traps from the Americans and guns, knives and other articles. This with 13 men murdered in 1825 is sufficient to make them independent of trade. The Americans swear to make an example of them; I do hope from my soul they may."

Six days after this visitation the Snake brigade entered the Ochoco greeted by severe heat, hordes of mosquitoes and two well-armed Snake dog soldiers who rode boldly into camp. They gave some idea of the route into the headwaters of the John Day and Crooked rivers but bore no tidings of the fourteen men Ogden had dispatched six months before to trap the inner Ochoco. The only good news on this day was that the trappers had snared their two thousandth beaver for the season.

By June 27, Ogden had trapped Burnt River and from here sent McDonald and McKay on to Fort Nez Perce with the furs while he veered into the Ochoco looking for Sylvaille and Gervais. Within nine days, Ogden had stripped the north and middle forks of the John Day of beaver. On the middle fork, he found an old encampment with beaver frames which convinced him that Gervais and his party had passed that way. Hanging on to the tails of their swimming horses, Ogden's brigade forded the main John Day and headed for the summit of the Ochoco Blues which were as deep under snow as they had been in January.

While Ogden occupied his time in creating a beaver desert in the John Day country, the Americans celebrated their 50th-year of independence from British rule; and Thomas Jefferson, who started the conflict in Oregon, honored the occasion by dying, leaving his offspring a $107,000 debt which took them 52 years to pay off.

Unhampered by this nonsense, Ogden faced more serious obstacles. On the high divide between the John Day and Crooked Rivers he found the trail blocked by eight feet of snow, necessitating an eighteen mile detour. Wandering in the purgatory of Snake country from parched Eldahow deserts to frozen Ochoco snowfields, Ogden was beginning to wonder if he was doing penance for his youthful cruelties to Indians. Laying that disheartening thought aside, he dropped into the Crooked River valley and found fresh horse tracks, raising his expectations of finding Sylvaille's party. All hope was lost when he found a remnant of Spanish blanket beside the trail which led him to conclude this was the path of the Snakes—most likely those he had encountered in March—who were heading south to trade in the Spanish settlements.

Crossing the Cascades over hard-packed snow six feet deep, the expedition reached the Willamette River on July 16. A short distance upstream from Willamette Falls—which within three years would become the site of Oregon City, the first capital of organized government in the west—Ogden met an Iroquois trapper who told him Sylvaille had arrived safely at the newly constructed Fort Vancouver loaded with furs. This gentleman had no word on the missing Gervais.

At sunset the following day, the Snake brigade trudged wearily into Fort Vancouver ending nearly eight months of suffering and privation in the dreaded hunting grounds of the Snake war tribes. Upon his arrival chief trader Ogden was met by Dr. McLoughlin who received him "with every mark of attention." And well he should have, for Ogden's second Snake expedition had produced 3,800 beaver skins and a tidy profit for the Adventurers of the Hudson's Bay Company.

A few days after Ogden's arrival at Fort Vancouver, Gervais and his party slipped in with 800 beaver pelts. On their way, too loaded with furs to trap more, Gervais's brigade had passed through the heart of the Ochoco and the richest beaver country any of the trappers had ever seen. This news sealed Ogden's fate for another plunge into the unknown.

During Ogden's crossing of the Cascades, the 1826 rendezvous was in full swing. Jim Bridger would recall: "Several hundred Shoshoni Indians came down from Snake Country for the rendezvous. Some of the men called them Snakes because of the sensuousness of their finger movements when they talked sign language. They were good Indians, maybe the best. A man could trust the critters."

As a climax to the rendezvous, General Ashley—after selling his interests in Rocky Mountain Fur to Smith, Jackson and Sublette—gave a farewell speech. On July 26, 1826, using a whiskey keg for a speaker's stand, Ashley expressed his indebtedness to the loyal trappers who had raped the beaver streams but not one word of appreciation did he extend to the Shoshoni whose land they had ravished.

CHAPTER 35

IT WAS A GALLING EXPERIENCE

*This life makes a young man sixty in a
few years. . . a convict at Botany Bay is a
gentleman at ease compared to my trappers. . .
only the fit survive and not all of them.*

Peter Skene Ogden
Third Snake Expedition

By 1826 Hudson's Bay Company was operating in British Columbia, Montana, Idaho, Washington, Oregon and the northern sections of Utah, Nevada and California. The annual take was 50,000 pelts with one-fifth of the catch coming out of the Ochoco. With only a two month rest, Ogden's third Snake Expedition was outfitted and by early September was headed into the Ochoco before cold weather set in.

In Ogden's mind the only redeeming feature of this latest probe was that Gov. Simpson allowed Julia to accompany him, although in his journal Ogden would never acknowledge the woman and little children who were sharing in the ultimate of human endurance. Since his journal was a business record for the company, there was little reason to mention Julia, but there is also evidence Peter harbored a guilt complex stemming from his youth. As a boy in Montreal he had promised his aristocrat mother never to marry less than a white woman of good social standing, a pledge he renewed as a man in England. Now, by any standards of a loving relationship he was married to a Flathead Indian woman. As one biographer would put it: "He accepted the fact in life but could not face it in his own handwriting."[196]

---

[196] Binns, *Peter Skene Ogden: Fur Trader*, p. 197.

Even with Tom McKay serving as second in command; François Payette as chief of scouts; experienced trappers such as Joe Delore and Dedron Senecal acting as brigade leaders; and his faithful Julia tending to his personal needs, Ogden's third expedition was doomed to suffering, starvation and death. Leaving the Columbia September 11, 1826, the main party made it to Sherar's Falls on the Deschutes in ten days with their usual load of aggravation. In attempting to use the Wasco's fishing platform as a bridge, the flimsy structure collapsed and five horses loaded with supplies fell to their death.

Traveling at break-neck speed the expedition entered Crooked River basin under a leaden sky, made camp at the mouth of the Ochoco River and commenced to string out traps. As Ogden later reported by Nez Perce messenger to McLoughlin, "beaver not scarce. We have now three hundred." But it wasn't the number that amazed the veteran trader so much as their size. These were not beaver but cub bear. Joe Delore had one beaver that weighed 100 pounds. Expecting to make a record catch in a short span of time, small parties were dispatched in all directions.

On September 29 Jean Gervais—who would abandon the Ochoco to become a partner in Rocky Mountain Fur—joined the expedition with horses, pack mules and eight experienced trappers. Even so this would not alter the cycle of misfortune. That night a frigid north wind struck as the temperature dropped lower and lower. Less than four months ago the second Snake expedition on the breaks of the Owyhee River had witnessed such a weather change in Oregon territory, but they couldn't believe it was happening again. Morning found the trappers in frostbitten agony, their traps locked in ice. To make matters worse ice in Crooked River loosened by the mid-day sun ripped traps from their moorings and ground them to pieces on jagged boulders jutting up from the river bed.

The Ochoco River, equally unforgiving, locked hundreds of fine steel snares in an icy grip that defied every attempt to free them. On the evening of September 30 hoar-frost fell like driven snow and boulders along the rims overlooking the lower Ochoco-Crooked river valleys cracked like musket fire throughout the night. It was like winter on the Continental Divide. A party of Iroquois who had been working the upper Crooked River had escaped the cold front, but their Nez Perce guide, knowing the changing moods of the Ochoco, warned them of the approaching storm. Jerking their traps, they attempted to reach Ogden's main camp at the mouth of the Ochoco before the storm hit by crossing the ridge between the Ochoco and Crooked rivers, thus saving miles of river travel. Wind and sleet slashed across the highlands, buffeting the half-frozen group to the edge of the treacherous Ochoco River rims where the packhorses, loaded with pelts and traps, were last seen plunging over a sheer sixty-foot drop. Once again defeated in his assault on the Ochoco valley, Ogden headed up Crooked River in search of warmer climate. That is all he found.

About the same time Ogden moved up Crooked River, Rocky Mountain Fur was making sure this would be a dangerous season. Supposedly some Banattees, who the mountain man Jim Beckwourth called "Pun-naks" and described as "a discarded band of the Snakes," had fired upon three trappers, killing one and wounding the other two.[197] The outcome being that Sublette sent Jim Bridger with 215 volunteers to avenge the wrong. However, the Robber Snakes were already on the move.

The trappers followed their trail for 45 miles, catching up with them on Green River where they had taken refuge on an island. Blocking all escape, Bridger's militia open-fired. According to Beckwourth, the "withering" fire continued until there was "not one Pun-nak left of either sex or any age." It was his boast that they had taken "488 scalps" and had "annihilated the Pun-nak band." All they really did was set the stage for revenge.

Eight Banattee women were captured and turned over to the Earth Eaters who "were exuberant at the defeat of their kinsmen calling them very bad Indians." How bad, they would soon find out. Once tolerated and even protected by the war tribes their fate was now sealed. As for annihilating the Robber Snakes it must have been but very few. A year later, Ogden found 300 lodges [1,500 people] of the same tribe riding with The Horse a few miles east of the Ochoco on Camas Prairie.

Meanwhile, Odgen's expedition reached upper Crooked River on October 4, finding it blessed with sunshine and settled in for some profitable trapping. They were barely established when a party of Bear Killer Snakes arrived the next day and set up camp on the opposite side

---

[197] Bonner, T.D. (ed), *The Life and Adventures of James P. Beckwourth*, pp. 124-25.

of the river. In an effort to preserve good relations Ogden sent over some trinkets and food. It didn't work. That night some of the warriors swam the river and set fire to the grass within thirty feet of the sleeping Canadians. Fortunately the night guards were alert and gave the alarm. "All that saved everything from being lost," Ogden would write, "was a stand of willows which slowed the fire down; a gale blowing at the time. . . this is Indian gratitude." He also firmly believed. . . "if ever Indians deserved to be punished, these do."

Perhaps, but Ogden wasn't going to be the one to attempt it. Taking the hint, the expedition pulled stakes and rode toward Snow Mountain, looking for Sylvaille's "fabulous beaver river." On this day, October 6, 1826, the Franklin, Missouri, *Intelligencer* carried an interesting advertisement, marking the first appearance, or more correctly the first disappearance, in history of Kit Carson who would find the trail to Oregon for the celebrated "Pathfinder," Lt. John Charles Fremont. Said notice, addressed "to whom it may concern," stated in essence that about the first day of September, Christopher Carson, a boy about 16 years old and small for his age ran away from David Workman to whom he had been bound to learn the saddler's trade. Furthermore, all persons were notified not to harbor said boy under penalty of the law. Apparently Mr. Workman was not overly eager to have young Carson returned as the offered reward was only one cent. Had Peter Ogden stumbled onto the runaway in his wanderings he most likely would have considered Carson just another link in the chain of bad luck that dogged his footsteps.

By October 7, while crossing the high country dividing the headwaters of Crooked River from those of the John Day, McKay was dispatched with twenty five trappers and fifty horses loaded with traps to deplete the beaver colonies of the inner Ochoco.[198] The next morning Antoine Sylvaille with an advance party knifed across Snake hunting

---

[198] All dates (which have been corrected for this chapter according to 1826 and 1827 calendars) in Ogden's original Journal from September through February are one day early. This happened when Ogden incorrectly dated his day of departure which fell on Monday, September 11, 1826 as the 12th. The date was corrected the following February when he entered 29 days. 1827 was not a leap year.

Courtesy of the Oregon Historical Society,
OrHi 74366.

Christopher "Kit" Carson.

grounds to his beaver bonanza of the previous spring. Two days later at high noon Ogden with the main party reached Sylvaille's river.[199] Five days after Ogden's arrival, McKay galloped into camp to report they were in big trouble with the Snakes.

On October 13, three Bear Killer braves had raided McKay's base camp and made off with seven horses loaded with traps. Crossing over the mountains west of McKay's outpost, the Snake warriors were seen by Francois Payette and Baptiste Tyguauriche, an Iroquois hunter. Both of these were freemen, meaning they were not salaried employees of the company. These hotbloods took to the trail and just before daylight on the fourteenth, they located the horse thieves camped on the South Fork of the John Day River. Basing their strategy on past experience with the Earth Eaters, Payette reluctantly decided to stage an attack. Overjoyed at the prospect of teaching his western cousins a lesson they wouldn't soon forget, the Iroquois gave vent to a New England war whoop and charged the startled Snakes.

Evidently it produced the desired effect for the Snakes, offering no resistance, cheerfully returned the horses. After all, being honorable men, they had been caught in a somewhat shady business deal. This peaceful reaction fired Payette and Baptiste to greater endeavors. Making up his mind to cause real trouble, Payette demanded a little interest on the loan. The Bear Killers obliged by giving him two canoes which they had cached in the willows. This didn't satisfy Baptiste. Nothing less than "a sound beating short of killing them" could rectify the Indian's transgression and with that happy thought Baptiste struck one of the Snakes a vicious blow with a shot-loaded whip handle, crushing his skull. This was a grave mistake. The fallen warrior's comrades exploded. Besides being severely beaten, Payette and the Iroquois suffered numerous knife and arrow wounds in their escape.

---

[199] The river that now bears Antoine Sylvaille's name has been corrupted to Silvies River. (*Oregon Historical Quarterly*, Vol. X, p. 35ll; *Oregon Historical Quarterly*, Vol. XI, p. 202). The Arrowsmith maps published in London between 1830-50 show the stream as Sylvaille's River. In 1860 Major Steen named it the Cricket River because of swarms of the insects. (*Oregon Historical Quarterly*, Vol. XXXIII, p. 113).

Luckily for them, another trapper hearing the ruckus arrived on the scene. Seeing this man coming, the Bear Killers, now in possession of ten horses, killed four of the stolen mounts and rode off with the rest, taking with them the pistols, rifles, hatchets, skinning knives and traps of the wounded men. One brave was also defiantly waving the shot-loaded whip as a trophy of war. When found by McKay, Payette and Baptiste were in such bad shape they could not be moved for three days. All Ogden could say on this latest clash with the local citizens was, "It was a galling experience and the whole thing is disgraceful to us."

In a dispatch to McLoughlin, the chief trader would comment: "I have the disagreeable information to communicate that two of my trappers, Payette and Baptiste Tyguauriche, have been severely wounded. The latter received two wounds, one in the ribs and one in the back which has been extracted but one still remains in the ribs. . . Payette received his wounds under the ribs on the right side in a slanting direction and may be considered already out of danger—both suffer great pain and cannot be conveyed to the camp. . . . "

Fully aware that his tenuous truce with the Snake war tribes had been undone "by the childish savagery" of his freemen, Ogden dispatched McKay to the south in search of more friendly hunting grounds. On this thrust into the unknown McKay discovered Harney Lake but would later report there were no signs of beaver or any other living animals in that barren region, although both he and Ogden found buffalo skulls from herds that once roamed there.

Meanwhile, with the wounded men barely able to travel and Sylvaille's river looted of beaver skins, Ogden deemed it prudent to get out of the Ochoco. On the last day of October, tired and thirsty, Ogden's main party reunited with McKay at Harney Lake. Much to their disgust, they found both Malheur and Harney lakes to be heavily charged with alkali. In the first written description of Harney Lake, which he called Salt Lake, Ogden lamented, "all hands gave it a try but none could drink it." Emigrants would know both lakes as the Bitter Lakes.

The only happy note was that McKay had not found any Indians in that desolate country and Ogden didn't expect to find any. Then, while stumbling around in a November blizzard three days after his reunion with McKay, Ogden found himself in the middle of an Indian city! ". . . it is incredible the number of Indians in this quarter. We cannot go 10 yards without finding them. Huts generally of grass of a size to hold 6 or 8 persons. No nation so numerous as these in all North America. I include both Upper and Lower Snakes (in short the whole Shoshoni nation)." Wild as deer, Ogden believed them to be "fit subjects for the missionary who could twist them in any forms he pleased." And they were slowly starving. In fact according to an Indian woman who camped with the trappers these people during the winter of 1825-26 were reduced to subsisting on the bodies of their less fortunate comrades. She herself had fed on two of her own children who died through weakness. Ogden wondered if this had an impact on his own men who presently were "loudly and grievously" complaining about one meal a day. Ogden also learned that these people were afraid to venture out of this barren region because of the powerful Snake war tribes who would soon annihilate them if they pursued big game in the mountains to the north (the Blues).

Unfortunately, Ogden would identify this wretched multitude as being "Snakes," adding more confusion to the Anglo-American mystery concerning the Shoshoni. Unknown to Ogden, he had stumbled upon the Washoes, a poor tribe unrelated to any Indian family in North America. They were a distinct linguistic group within themselves. Resembling the Modocs, the Washoes were first found in southeastern Oregon, ranging across the high desert to the Truckee River in northern Nevada. Tribal holdings included the Carson River down to the first large canyon south of Carson City; west to the borders of Lake Tahoe; and the Sierra Nevada valleys as far south as Honey Lake, California. They had been driven into this area by the Snakes who knew them as W'asiu—Inferior Persons—and here existed in a state of chronic ill feelings against their oppressors, breaking out occasionally into open hostility.[200]

November found the trappers wandering aimlessly about the high desert east of Wagontire Mountain as they slowly starved. McKay, who had assumed Payette's scouting duties, slipped westward in a desert blizzard finding nothing but small alkaline lakes devoid of beaver and, equally unsettling, unfit to drink. Those foolish enough to try became

---

[200] Keane, in his *Ethnography and Philology of America*, mistakenly classified the Washoe as being of Shoshonean descent, thus among others—notably Ogden in his Journals—establishing the basis on which the Caucasians derived their misconception of the Shoshoni Indians.

deathly sick. In a ten day period—struggling through the wind-blasted Hampton area in an attempt to reach the headwaters of Crooked River—the main party had eaten only six meals. Confused by the murky expanse of desert, they passed caves of ice and in mid-November, while pawing across lava fields covered with bear tracks, Ogden with his men now plotting mutiny, entered Newberry Crater. Here, he discovered Paulina and East lakes. He would joyfully write: "these lakes are a God-send" because his exhausted horses, dying of thirst, had refused to drink melted snow water in beaver skins.

Two days after discovering the lakes, he reached the Little Deschutes River on November 17 at the point where McDonald the previous fall had hollowed out canoes to descend the Deschutes for his fateful meeting with Ogden's second Snake expedition at the mouth of the Warm Springs River. At this remote spot Ogden was expecting to intercept a message from McLoughlin. Instead, he received information that Snake war parties "were at this moment" breaking out onto the desert in search of the hidehunters.

Four days after receiving this intelligence the Bay men were galvanized into action when one of the trappers discovered "four Snake Indians like snakes crawling on their bellies within fifteen yards of camp." When apprehended and ushered into camp under armed guard, these lusty warriors had sense enough to appear friendly and offered to surrender their weapons. Ogden, likewise showing good judgment, treated them kindly whereupon they departed with no damage suffered by either party.

Following this scare, Ogden headed for Klamath country, plagued by his usual run of bad luck. Killing horses along the way just to survive, this advance through perpetual snow was an agonizing process. With provisions exhausted and one of the hunters "suffering greatly from the loss of a forefinger and part of a thumb" blown off when his gun barrel ruptured on discharge, the Snake Expedition arrived at Williamson River on the twenty eighth of November.

To their astonishment, they found a fortified town, composed of twenty large structures shaped liked log block-houses and set on pilings in the river and surrounded by water. The defenders were not happy with Ogden's arrival. According to them, the Nez Perce and Cayuse had made several attempts to reach the village but did not succeed. . . "now they will have your road to follow." Since the guardians were worried about a Nez Perce invasion rather than a Snake assault, it is a good bet that this village was a stronghold of the so-called Yahuskin Snakes, allies of the Snake war tribes. Another indication of their identity lies in the fact that Ogden made no attempt to name them, yet records two days after his arrival at the village "thirty Klamaths visited the camp."

Along with the arrival of the Klamaths one of Ogden's express men—near death—was found some four miles from camp so weak he was unable to walk or even crawl. He and his partner, who was still missing, had never reached the Columbia with Ogden's dispatches to company headquarters. They had been attacked by the Snakes on the Deschutes River, losing horses, weapons and all supplies. When rescued the messenger had been without food for fourteen days and nine days without water. On this unhappy note Ogden headed for the Mexican border.

Christmas found the expedition reduced to one meal a day and New Year's Day, 1827, was observed with the men receiving tobacco and a dram of spirits each. One mountain goat brought in by the hunters provided a token of food. The local Indian merchants becoming increasingly aware of the expedition's dependency on dogs for food had inflated the price. The going rate was now four buttons or a like number of brass rings for one dog or two dogs for a scalper (knife). By February the expedition was trapping in northeastern California on what may have been a branch of the Klamath River. On the thirteenth, buffeted by a gale force wind and in sight of a great unnamed Cascade peak Ogden wrote, "There is a mountain equal in height to Mount Hood or Vancouver. I have named it Mt. Sastice." Today it is called Mt. Shasta.

With starvation nearer than usual, the main expedition slowly trapped through the Siskiyou Mountains battling grizzly bear and working toward the Klamath Lake region to reunite with McKay's detachment which had been left to trap the upper Deschutes. In late April McKay overtook Ogden with good news. In defiance of the Snakes, he had taken 735 beaver and otter without loss of men or equipment. Encouraged by this change of events, Ogden proposed that McKay search for the source of the Willamette River which at this time had never been seen by any white man in the Pacific Northwest, including the far-ranging McDonald. McKay who had been flirting with death for the past three months was not in any mood to become seriously engaged and he refused. Wise enough not to incite the explosive half-breed,

Ogden changed plans, striking northeast from Klamath Lake across an unexplored region bound for the southern Blues.

In a twelve day march across the northwest rim of the Great Basin two horses died from drinking poisonous water, three more were killed for food and another fifty-six were stolen by the Snakes. Adding to this misery, several men, complaining of the heat, bathed in the alkali charged waters of a small lake. Shortly thereafter, their bodies resembled brine-soaked cucumbers. As Ogden put it, "they became as red as if they had been in pickle and the pain was severe."[201]

By June third with the glistening peak of Snow Mountain in sight, one-fourth of the party were disabled from drinking stagnant water. Five days later they reached Malheur Lake intending to set up camp but the stench of the water was so bad it sickened the men. Ogden then decided to head into the Ochoco but weakened from the heat and contaminated water he became bed-ridden for ten days. Reflecting on the past months of hardship, Ogden would sadly note, "I have done my duty examining this barren country but our loss has been greater than our profit." And so it was.

Once again able to straddle a horse Ogden steered a course toward Snake River. This final passage across the Ochoco was without incident other than the loss of a horse to Snake thieves when crossing Sylvaille's river. At the head of the Malheur River his trappers took another 81 beaver in prime condition in spite of the fact that it was summer. On July 16 in "terrible heat and short of food" he reached the Snake River and on July 18, 1827, made the final entry in his journal... "5 a.m. Not wishing to lose any time at Ft. Nez Perce, I take my departure with 4 men to make necessary preparations, leaving Mr. McKay in charge of the party."

He then took off with the season's catch reaching Fort Vancouver on August 5. Eight days later he loaded his furs on board the British trade vessel *William and Ann* bound for the Orient and so ended Ogden's third Snake Expedition and the Company's fourth probe into the Ochoco.

---

[201] All direct quotations are taken from Ogden's third *Snake Country Journals*, entries dated from September 11, 1826 to July 16, 1827.

Although Ogden hadn't done too well and had missed the 1827 rendezvous held at Bear Lake on the border between Shoshoni and Ute hunting grounds, the Americans faired well. They had taken a half-million dollars in furs out of Shoshoni country. Then, when Jedediah Smith turned up at Fort Vancouver in 1827 to report the massacre of his men on the Umpqua River, Hudson's Bay Company really became alarmed. The Americans were getting too close. It seemed that the British policy of killing off all the game animals south of the Columbia had only incited them to hunt deeper into Oregon. And when it came to cleaning out beaver from a given area nobody could compare with the American mountain man. He was not interested in conservation; he wanted to make a killing and quit.

CHAPTER 36

AMERICAN RAIDERS

It is laughable, so many attempts on both sides and no success. Was it not I feared a strong American party here I should undertake the journey myself and would succeed.

Peter Skene Ogden
February 10, 1828

By 1827 Hudson's Bay was running into plenty of trouble with American trappers and the main offenders were the young upstarts working for Rocky Mountain Fur, soon to be known as the SJ&S Company. In 1826 Gen. William Ashley—for 120,000 dollars—sold his interest in the company to three soldiers-of-fortune who held no fear of the Bay Company, the Indians or the territory. It was a strange partnership which found William Sublette—ex-gambler, knife fighter and saloon keeper from St. Charles, Missouri—teamed up with quiet first-class brigade leader David Jackson and Jedediah Smith, a novelty in mountain men. Smith was unique simply because he was a highly educated man who read the Bible daily, never smoked, drank or slipped off to the nearest friendly village in search of a willing Indian girl.

Despite their contrasting personalities—or perhaps because of it—Smith, Jackson and Sublette had what it took to get furs out of the west at a thousand percent profit and with these men calling the shots the Americans were getting increasingly more brazen in poaching on Hudson's Bay territory. Because of this the Snake country expedition of 1827-28 was to be more brutal than any of the previous.

With the exception of John McLeod, who had all the country west of the Cascades to himself, McLoughlin in a rush against time sent every available man in the Pacific Northwest into Shoshoni country. Leading the advance, Jess La Forte and Louis Andre were to scout the entire region for fur-bearing animals. By mid-August 1827 brigades under the guidance of John Work and Joe La Pierre were working the lower

Deschutes, John Day and Umatilla rivers on a course to intercept Ogden's main column moving south out of Fort Nez Perce. At the same time McKay, La Bonte and Sylvaille—stripping the Ochoco, Crooked, Silvies and Blitzen rivers—were also bound for a reunion with Ogden. Francois Payette and Mickele La Framboise leading brigades along the Burnt, Powder, Grande Ronde, Clearwater, Imnaha and Salmon rivers would meet Ogden on the eastern boundary of the Ochoco. Simon McGillivray was making a trans-Canadian push from York Factory on the southwest shore of Hudson's Bay to reinforce Ogden on the lower Snake. McGillivray—a good friend of Ogden's and an old Nor'wester—had departed York Factory at about the same time Ogden left Fort Nez Perce and was expected to rendezvous with Ogden in late December. At the point of expected American intrusion, Ogden—in command of the total operation—would personally supervise all trapping on the Malheur, Payette, Weiser, Owyhee and middle Snake rivers. These men in a ruthless thrust were taking every fur-bearing animal they encountered, leaving desolation in their wake for the winter of 1827-28 saw the beginning of the end of the beaver trade in the far west.

Preceded by the advance parties, Ogden launched the main expedition on September 5, 1827. Traveling with him was Billy Smith, an eager youngster fresh out of England who within forty years would lead the first white homestead party into the upper Ochoco valley. In a drenching rain with the passage made more difficult by fallen pines the main party crossed the northern Blues, reaching the Grande Ronde River on September 14. At this point Ogden intended to enter the Ochoco and trap the headwaters of the main stem and south fork of the John Day River. This plan was soon to be aborted when a Cayuse Indian reported American trappers on their way to Fort Nez Perce. He also carried grim news from the interior.

McKay, who had camped at the 1825 campsite on Crooked River, sent five men to trap the Ochoco River and its tributaries. They were never seen again. La Bonte who was working the upper Deschutes received word that a party of Snakes were camped nearby loaded with furs. In a haggle over prices one of his men accidentally killed a Snake warrior and La Bonte's brigade was chased back to Crooked River where they joined forces with Sylvaille.

Sylvaille who was to rendezvous with McKay in the big prairie on the headwaters of the north fork of Crooked River was having troubles of his own. Snake raiders had stolen most of his pack horses loaded with traps. Later at the rendezvous the Snakes slyly tried to trade them back to Hudson's Bay for hatchets and gun powder. One of the Snake merchants was shot and the McKay-La Bonte-Sylvaille enterprise was chased out of the Ochoco. Joining Work's brigade in the middle Blues, they caught up with the main party on Burnt River four days after Ogden had conferred with the Cayuse messenger.[202]

Reinforced by his second-in-command and with rumors of American trappers in the area, Ogden laid plans to stall their progress. McKay would proceed to the south, trapping the Malheur, lower Snake and Owyhee rivers, while Ogden with the added strength of the main expedition would reenter the hostile Ochoco to clean out the Powder, Burnt, John Day and Crooked rivers including all feeder streams. In the process—if the Americans were in fact around—he would serve as a cover for McKay's activities. This plan for distraction was well founded. It was an accepted fact that Ogden was one of the toughest brigade leaders in the Pacific Northwest and though the Americans hated the British-controlled Hudson's Bay Company, they respected and perhaps even feared Ogden. Now, he was going to earn their respect.

On September 21 McKay with eleven veteran trappers slipped out of the Burnt River camp to devastate the Owyhee River from mouth to source. They had barely gotten out of sight when Payette charged into camp to report the "traps of strangers" along the Weiser River. Shortly, an American named Johnson appeared, informing Ogden that he and five others were trapping the Weiser and that they belonged to a party of forty who with some Nez Perce were working toward the Malheur and McKay's brigade. Forty Americans and a band of Nez Perce was bad news. Ogden himself—after detaching Sylvaille to Payette's river—was left with only sixteen men. This was a strange position for a partisan of Hudson's Bay Company, being caught with the smallest brigade in the mountains. He immediately decided to turn around and head back up Burnt River to the headwaters of the John Day. This proved to be a poor decision.

---

[202] Details of McKay and Sylvaille's push through central Oregon as remembered by William (Uncle Billy) Smith and descendants of Joseph Delore. Both Smith and Delore were members of Ogden's Fourth Snake Country Expedition.

Far from feeling unwelcome Johnson and his fellow Americans tagged along and that evening camped with Ogden, announcing their intention of keeping him company and returning with him to the Columbia. In an attempt to discourage this turn of events Ogden told them he would give no better terms for the pelts they caught than what his own men had agreed to. (By company policy Ogden was bound to pay his trappers no more than 50¢ a pound as opposed to the American's three dollars a pound.) No problem. Johnson was not turning back. This called for some quick action as Ogden had no desire to acquaint Rocky Mountain Fur with the beaver paradise of the Ochoco.

That night a courier slipped out of Ogden's camp with a message alerting McKay to a change of plan. From the headwaters of the Owyhee McKay was to work toward Godin's River (today Big Lost River in southeastern Idaho), mowing a swath of destruction between the American outpost at Great Salt Lake and the middle Snake River to the north. Meanwhile, Ogden would run interference for this new move and rendezvous with McKay in Day's Defile sometime during the coming winter.

In a surprise move to Johnson, Ogden abruptly reversed course and headed into the Eldahow. This served the purpose of getting him out of camp but only far enough to where he could still shadow every move the Canadians made. This was fine by Ogden. However, doing as much bartering as he was trapping, Ogden was running short on his hottest item. . . trade rifles. By year's end, the rate of exchange had dropped drastically from eighteen pelts for one gun to one gun for five pelts. The Snakes were increasing their arsenal.

Mid-October found Ogden on the northern portion of the two Malheur rivers with a Rocky Mountain Fur detachment in bad need of supplies. Ogden, well-outfitted and with long experience in the Snake country, had the upper hand. In exchange for provisions he accepted the American's furs at twenty five percent less than what he gave the Shoshoni. In the party—besides five men belonging to Johnson's outfit—was Thierry Godin who had defected to the Americans three years before and was the only deserter who hadn't settled his debt with Ogden over the humiliating defeat at the hands of Johnson Gardner. Now in Ogden's sight, Godin, being an honest man, delivered thirty-five large beaver skins in payment of his debt to Hudson's Bay.

Inviting Rocky Mountain Fur to join him, Ogden moved on to Big Lost (Godin's) River. Here on November 2nd, Ogden would reveal the strategy behind his uncommon friendliness with the Americans. "It is my interest to amuse the American party now with us so that McKay's men may have time to trap the beaver where the Americans propose going. As they are not aware of this, it is so much the more in our favor. Should McKay not appear at the appointed place, Day's Defile, there will be grass for our horses and buffalo for our support."

The following day Ogden reached Day's River (Little Lost River) where he intended to wait for McKay only to discover that upwards of 1,500 Snakes trailing 3,000 horses had obliterated the valley. Without buffalo or even a blade of grass Ogden had to return to Snake River in search of food. Before leaving he left a note for McKay, telling him what route to follow.

Two weeks later in a forced march the main party arrived at the western edge of the barren Snake plain. They had barely reached the Portneuf River when Ogden was paid the honor of a visit by one of the aristocrats of the Shoshoni nation. Duly impressed, Ogden was quite extravagant with his gifts. On November 25 he wrote:

> The chief of the lower Snakes with 300 followers paid me a visit, by name The Horse. He carries an American flag. I made him the following presents—1 calico shirt, 2 scalpers, 1-1/2 lb. ball, 1/2 lb. powder, 1 looking glass, 1/4 lb. glass beads, 1 half axe, 2 awls, 3 flints. They departed but not without some petty theft.

Ogden had little room for complaint. He was trading The Horse North West Fuzils [$24 each]—hardly the best choice in weapons—for 50 beaver skins each. Nevertheless, these mis-firing antiques were providing the Shoshoni with fire-power.

On the last day of November the Americans who had attached themselves to the expedition on the Malheur River—getting more nervous as they headed deeper into Shoshoni country—left for their headquarters at Great Salt Lake. Ogden smugly notes, "the beaver we have traded from them exceed 100. During the time they have been with us they have trapped only 26, so they lost more by the meeting with us than we have."

They weren't the only one to lose in Ogden's ruthless competition for furs. In other meetings with the Americans, there was much gambling. Although Simpson tried to keep cards away from his trappers they were seldom in short supply as Ogden would later gleefully note: "By the arrival of the Americans we had a new stock of cards in camp, eight packs. Some of the American trappers have already lost upwards of $400, or to the Americans, 800 beavers. . . . " He would also note in this same entry that ". . . Old Goddin is in a fair way on going to St. Louis, having sold his 8 horses and 10 traps for $1,500." Godin [*Godin* is the correct spelling] would never make it. Within two months after leaving Ogden, Johnson and Godin would become casualties of war.

With the departure of the Americans, Ogden was reduced to a dozen men and December arrived "with a wild storm of wind and snow," promising the winter was going to be a bad one. His trappers—working in freezing water up to their chests—were coming in covered with ice and nearly frozen. Adding to the uncertainty of survival, five Shoshoni lodges joined their camp causing Ogden plenty of concern. "I had rather they kept at a distance as they answer as a screen for horse thieves. Our numbers are but 12 men; the Snakes exceed 1,500. We are completely at their mercy." Ogden's only hope for peaceful co-existence based on his earlier bribery of The Horse was: "I am on good terms with the chiefs and will try to remain so." However, he was plenty worried about McKay's party and the other detachments strung out through the territory.

A few days later the Shoshoni moved out and Ogden followed the barren lava plains to the Snake where he intended to ride out the winter storm on an island in mid-river. By late December there was still no word from McKay or Simon McGillivray who had started from Canada some four months before. Certain that McGillivray had been stopped by bad weather, Ogden was more concerned about McKay. Finally, on December 20 some Americans wandered into camp with both good and bad news. Sam Tullock, leader of this six man party, told Ogden that McKay now had five hundred beaver but he was blocked off in Day's Defile because of snow with his horses so weak they couldn't cross the lava fields. Tullock's own party in their effort to reach Ogden's camp had been forced to buy forty nine horses from the Nez Perce "at the extravagant rate of fifty dollars a head." Crossing the lava plain west of Day's Defile, the Americans lost nineteen horses; were forced to kill six for food; and had ten stolen by the Shoshoni. They did not fare well on that transaction.

Tullock also revealed that at least one large body of Rocky Mountain Fur trappers had moved west from Bear River and had reached the Owyhee River in eastern Oregon before McKay arrived. From that point the two groups moved together for the sake of mutual protection to the scheduled rendezvous in Day's Defile. With this unexpected intelligence, Ogden was again in motion heading up river with Tullock and party in tow.

Tullock—"a decent fellow," according to Ogden—"was most amiable" when he came for a visit on Christmas Eve—perhaps more amiable than truthful. He told Ogden that his company (the SJ&S) would readily enter into an agreement regarding deserters and promised to bring in one of the partners to arrange such an agreement. This would have been a little difficult as Smith had just been released from jail in California, Jackson was either in St. Louis or snowed in at Bear Lake and Sublette was up in Blackfoot country.

On New Year's Day, 1828, the Americans, paying their respects to Ogden and receiving his best wishes and a dram of spirits, left for their Salt Lake headquarters. At Fort Vancouver company officials were celebrating in grand style. In the last three months of 1827, Hudson's Bay had increased their normal take of pelts by one thousand and jumped their earning from 90,000 dollars to 103,000, but in doing so the Canadian company was paying dearly in lives. Following McKay's September loss of five men in the Ochoco, Alexander McKenzie and four trappers were killed on the Salmon River in January, 1828. As usual, Concomly's daughter, the Princess of Wales, was McKenzie's travelling companion. As earlier noted, the Princess was making a lucrative living in the traffic of female slaves for "illicit purposes." Some of these unwilling call-girls had Shoshoni blood flowing in their veins. Unfortunately for the Princess, she was taken captive by the Snake war-party and thus ended her career.

Most trappers had Chinook wives. It was the practice of these women to gather as many female slaves as possible during the summer months and then accompany their husbands into the interior during the trapping season to trade for furs, horses or whatever else struck their fancy. "A Chinook matron," wrote Alexander Ross, "is constantly attended by two, three or more slaves." And this traffic was not limited to young women. The Lewis and Clark expedition had hardly arrived on the Pacific Coast when an Indian approached Clark and offered to sell him a ten year old boy. In 1824, Governor Simpson would comment on the slave trade: "I conceive a Columbia ṣlave to be the most unfortunate wretch in existence; the proprietors exercise the most absolute authority over them, even to life and death, and on the most trifling fault maim them shockingly." In view of such reports it can be assured that the Princess of Wales did not fare favorably in a Shoshoni war camp.

Shortly after McKenzie's demise, Alex Carson, grizzled old veteran of the 1814 Grande Brigade, was packed out of "the Valley of Troubles" with an arrowhead embedded in his chest. Carson survived only to be killed by his Indian guide on Alec's Butte in north Yamhill County in 1836. His remains were left to the wolves but later such portions as were found were buried by settlers in the 1860s. His supposed jawbone was picked up and became a relic of the Oregon Historical Society.[203]

With increasing hostilities, Ogden was more than ever worried about the safety of his far flung detachments; especially for Payette, stringing traps in the stronghold of the Sheep Killer Snakes and McKay still blocked off in the Lost River country. In his attempt to make contact with Payette, Ogden would glumly observe. . . "only 3 men have seen Salmon River. One is next to blind, the other 2 lame." One of the cripples, well-supplied with ammunition, was given the thankless task. At the same time Portneuf, armed with a map of the different streams McKay might be trapping and a letter to the Columbia headquarters, set out in search of his lieutenant.

Well supplied with blankets and ammunition, Portneuf insisted on traveling alone so as not to attract the attention of a Shoshoni-Blackfoot war party. In that he was successful, but his search for McKay was fruitless. A week after leaving camp he stumbled into Ogden's tent at midnight partly snow blind and packing a rifle with a broken hammer. Apparently the disabled messenger sent into the Salmon River country made contact with Payette's brigade for on February 12, sixteen days

---

[203] *Oregon Historical Quarterly*, Vol. XXXIX, pp. 16-21.

after Portneuf's failure, Payette with two men again set out to locate McKay.

During this period, the Shoshoni alliance backed by severe weather was taking its toll on the Americans. While serving as messengers, John Johnson and Thierry Godin in an attempt to pass from Tullock's camp to Bear River were killed by the Indians. Tullock, unable to get through the snow to the American depot on Bear Lake, returned to Ogden's camp where he offered eight beaver and fifty dollars for a pair of snowshoes. Failing in this, he then offered a prime horse to anyone who would carry a letter to the American camp. There were still no takers. Then a report came in that the Snakes had stampeded all the buffalo out of that area and the Americans, reduced to eating horses and dogs, were starving. It was during these futile attempts by both Ogden and Tullock to get messages to their respective detachments that Ogden made the remark that "it was laughable" that all efforts undertaken to cross the mountains were without success.

Adding to the gloom which now prevailed over the Rocky Mountain Fur brigade, an Earth Eater arrived in Ogden's camp with word that an American cache with goods valued at six hundred dollars had been robbed by the Snakes. Although it was neither a time nor a place for nice ethical standards, here and there examples of a smoother, more pleasant side did occur. Ogden, who had been bending over backwards to deal with the Shoshoni, could sympathize with Tullock:

> The Americans are most willing to declare war against them and requested, if they did in the spring, would I assist them. To this I replied if I found myself in company with them, I would not stand idle. I am most willing to begin but not knowing the opinion of the Company it is a delicate point to decide. Acting for myself, I will not hesitate to say I would willingly sacrifice a year or two to exterminate the whole Snake tribe, women and children excepted.

During a ten-month period the Snakes were reported to have killed thirteen Americans besides stealing a large number of traps and horses.

United on the subject of war against the Shoshoni, the British and Americans were still trade rivals with Ogden seeing to it that no snowshoes reached their feet. But since the Americans couldn't hunt without them, Ogden supplied them with meat which presented no problem. One hunter ran twenty-two antelope into a snowdrift where he proceeded to kill them with a butcher knife. . . "not allowing one to escape." Ogden would further complain that. . . "200 of antelope have been killed wantonly in the last week" and so it went from feast to famine.

Ogden was also aware that the American camp at Bear Lake was having liquor shipped in from Mexico which would serve to get all the beaver pelts away from the Indians and out of Hudson's Bay hands. However, he was philosophical as he mused, " . . . had I the same chance they have, long since I would have had a good stock of liquor here and every beaver in the camp would be mine. . . . "

In this chaotic atmosphere, Julia Ogden went into labor. On February 1, 1828, she presented Pete with a son they named David. Conceived in the desert south of Hampton Butte and carried over countless miles of prairies and mountains, he seemed already tired of the Snake country and a month later in a freezing snow storm his little body was buried in a willow grove on the Snake River.

The morning Payette had set out in quest of the missing McKay word came in that a Blackfoot war party was headed for Bear Lake and the Americans giving further proof that the Snakes and Blackfeet had ceased internal hostilities. The next few days were spent in nervous waiting for a like visit to the British camp. Shortly after noon on February 16, the suspense was intensified by the yelping of strange dogs, the shouted commands of unfamiliar voices and the novel sight of loaded dog sleds pulling into camp. The party was under the command of an American, Robert Campbell, who in himself was a novelty on the Oregon frontier. Twenty-four years old, brother to Hugh Campbell, the wealthy Philadelphia business backer of Sublette's enterprise, scion of a prominent Irish family, Robert Campbell—a St. Louis fur buyer and partner in Rocky Mountain Fur—was a new force to be reckoned with. He was also bursting with news.

The Americans at Bear Lake had tangled with the Blackfoot war party. During the course of battle, they lost sixty horses and Old Pierre, the Iroquois trapper who had deserted to Gardiner's Americans four years earlier, was killed and his body cut to ribbons. Whatever his faults, Ogden was not overly sentimental. On receiving word of the old Iroquois' death—a man he had known since the days of his youth—Ogden's only comment was; "Pierre owes a debt to the Company, but as we have a mortgage on his property in Canada we shall recover." In short Ogden would not condone a breach of trust to the company no matter who it was or how it was done.

Campbell also brought word of the death of Lord Selkirk and joyfully reminded Ogden that the Bay Company's stranglehold on the Columbia would soon be broken. Taking this in stride, the British trader calmly replied that Hudson's Bay had until November, when the treaty of joint occupation expired, to lay waste to the Columbia fur harvest which he fully intended to do. Unknown to either man, while Ogden had been outfitting for this latest push into Snake country in the summer of 1827, the United States and Great Britain had mutually agreed to extend joint occupation for an indefinite period.

After the Americans lost 800 beaver pelts to the Hudson's Bay trappers in a high-stakes poker game both groups parted peacefully. Campbell pushed south toward Bear Lake and Ogden's main party headed north toward the Columbia. Ogden himself remained behind awaiting word of McKay whom he now believed to be dead.

At daybreak March 1—in time for little David Ogden's burial—Payette stumbled into camp with four snow-blind men, his two express-men and two members of McKay's party. Payette had found McKay camped on the forks of the Salmon River in good condition. Three times he had sent parties in search of Ogden and each time they failed. The messenger Ogden had started from Burnt River in the fall with the letter notifying McKay of the change of plan never arrived. This led to the conclusion he had been killed by the Snakes. The good news: McKay had 350 beaver with him and another 500 enroute to Fort Nez Perce.

Twenty-five days would pass while Ogden waited impatiently for McKay to join him. Finally on March 27 two of McKay's men arrived with a letter for Ogden. Because of the great depth of snow, McKay was unable to reach Ogden's camp and unaware that the main party was already enroute to the Columbia; he suggested Ogden come to him. With his skeleton force this was impossible. Ogden quickly dispatched a message back stating "our numbers are too weak to face the war tribes" and ordered McKay to try to join him. After waiting a few more days, Ogden nervously broke camp and headed in the general direction of McKay's last known position, posting double guards day and night.

By the twenty-fourth of April, Ogden had completed his second thousand of beaver independent of McKay's catch but his trappers were having "hair-raising escapes" from the Indians. And he would lament: "I wish to God McKay's party would make their appearance and relieve my anxiety. Should an accident happen to us, all is lost." Having the bulk of the winter's harvest in his possession, Ogden had ample reason to be worried. Sixteen days before—expecting to make contact with McKay at any moment—he had divided his already weakened force by sending Sylvaille with six men to trap through to the mouth of the Walla Walla. Now, with no sign of snow in the area, Ogden was at a loss to account for McKay's delay.

After eleven more days of waiting with no sign of his missing lieutenant, Ogden began the treacherous journey back to Fort Vancouver on May 6, 1828. Presently he heard shots fired in quick succession across the river and sent a party to reconnoiter. The scouts returned with five of McKay's men who reported McKay only a few miles behind. McKay arrived the next morning with 440 beaver having added another 90 pelts since his last contact with Ogden.

Two days after McKay's arrival, the Canadians were intercepted by an armed party of Snake dog soldiers. It was a tense moment but the warriors were in a jovial mood claiming to have just raided a Blackfoot camp. Ogden was quick to observe that in their loot "were clothes, hunter's hats, shoes, etc., horses belonging to the Americans who had wintered with us." The Snake war chief—most likely Red Wolf's able lieutenant, Iron Wristband—told Ogden he had left the furs they had stolen on the Snake plain which to Ogden was "convincing proof the Americans have been murdered and pillaged. . . the sight of this caused deep gloom in camp. We may be doomed to the same fate. God preserve us."

It soon became obvious what the dog soldiers had in mind. Having little use for such junk as clothing, the war chief told Ogden they were on their way to Salt Lake to find the Americans and obtain a reward for restoration of the property. It was his hope that the reward would be in the form of arms and ammunition.

Even with this forewarning Ogden was quick to blame any and all bloodshed on the Blackfeet; and this, after his own admission that given their war-like nature, he was willing to exterminate the whole Shoshoni male population. Two weeks after meeting with the dog soldiers—in the heart of Robber Snake hunting grounds—the Shoshoni drew blood. Following a stormy night of rain, two of Ogden's men dashed in with news that Louis La Valle had been killed by "Blackfeet" within half a mile of camp and four other trappers were unaccounted for. Ogden immediately gave orders to secure the beaver-laden pack horses and sent McKay with twelve men to rescue the missing trappers.

McKay returned at noon with the four men who had hidden from the Indians and the naked but unscalped body of La Valle found lying where he had been killed. Ogden recorded, "I had the body interred— valuable smart loss. He leaves a wife and 3 children destitute."

It was becoming painfully obvious that, although he had experienced narrow escapes during three previous expeditions into Snake country, Ogden had never run greater risks of being cut off from his whole brigade than this year. A few days after LaValle's death, Louis Andre was attacked by a Snake war party. After shooting one brave, Andre managed to reach camp in time for Ogden to set up a line of defense. It was an extremely touchy situation as only twelve trappers had guns that would fire; the tumblers of the rest were broken. Surrounded by 200 dog soldiers, the Canadians prepared to die. St. Anne, patron saint of the trappers, would show mercy toward her wayward children this day. The Snakes, not realizing Ogden's weakened position, gave up the attack and rode off.

The month of June was spent dodging Snake raiding parties as the Bay men recrossed the southwestern mountains of the Eldahow. In early July, within striking distance of the Owyhee River and reentry into the Ochoco, Ogden sent McKay on ahead to intercept Sylvaille and his trappers. They were found the same day with gains and losses to report. On May 20, within the tribal holdings of the White Knife Snakes, they had been attacked by "150 Blackfeet" who killed a trapper's wife and ran off all the horses. One warrior had been killed in the skirmish but Sylvaille had saved 650 beaver skins cached on the Malheur River.

By mid-July Ogden was on Burnt River and on the seventeenth he was met by twenty men on Powder River. They had been sent out by his old friend Samuel Black to escort the trappers to Fort Nez Perce. The hazards of the expedition were over. Leaving Payette in charge, Ogden went on ahead, reaching Fort Nez Perce on the nineteenth. On July 22, 1828, Ogden arrived at Fort Vancouver and made the final entry in his journal:

Brigade arrived safe. Mr. McKay's party will join us at Fort Vancouver. So ends my 4th trip to the Snake country and I have to regret the loss of lives. The returns far exceeded my expectations.[204]

After the comedy of misadventures in the winter wilderness of Shoshoni Land, Ogden no longer worried about the American fur raiders.

---

[204] All quotations for this chapter are taken from Ogden's *Fourth Snake Country Journal*, entries dated from September 1, 1827 to July 22, 1828.

CHAPTER 37

AND THEN THERE WAS ONE

Sent 6 men to Burnt River. . . also sent off
5 men across country to rejoin us on the
forks of the Malheur. It is only by
dividing that returns can be made.

Peter Skene Ogden
Powder River,
September 30, 1828

There would be no rest for the lucrative Snake brigade. Two months after returning from his fourth expedition Ogden again hit the trail. On a pleasant Monday morning, September 22, 1828, he gathered up Julia and the children and with horses already worn out from the spring hunt headed into the Blues. On the second day nine of the "indifferent" horses, as he called them, gave out. Even so within eight days from his departure of Fort Nez Perce, the main party had crossed Grande Ronde Valley and in an autumn heat wave camped on Powder River. At this point Payette with ten trappers (three of whom were Iroquois) was dispatched into the Ochoco to trap the headwaters of the Burnt, John Day, Ochoco and Crooked rivers on a course that would reunite him with the main party at the forks of the Malheur River. To play it safe Payette was given a "small trading assortment" in the event he ran into any competition from the Americans.

Ogden continued up the Snake River where a Shoshoni guide was supposed to meet him at the mouth of the Malheur. He did not appear. Instead men from the advance party arrived with word that eight of their horses had been stolen while Snake raiders had hampered any success at trapping. It should be noted that the loss of horses was equivalent to destruction. Besides making the trappers easy prey for mounted warriors, they were dependent upon horses for transportation of trade goods, traps, pelts and an alternative source of food. Any serious loss could doom the expedition to failure.

On this unwelcome note, Ogden proceeded warily up river and in mid-October arrived at the forks of the Malheur some forty miles east of the present site of Burns, Oregon. It was still unseasonably hot. Ogden struck out across unexplored country toward the Owyhee River, leaving interior Oregon to be trapped by Payette and McKay who had entered the area from the west. The main party was now trespassing on hunting grounds claimed by the White Knife Snakes.

Having no idea where they were, the brigade wandered north of the Steens Mountains, skirting the bleak Diamond Craters. As Ogden put it, "travelling to little purpose." They discovered a salt lake seven miles long by four wide with no outlet. This may have been Turnbull Lake (now dry) north of the Sheepshead Mountains. Turning west, they passed a boiling spring with a strong smell of sulphur, empty huts and the tracks of fleeing Indians. Ogden was about to renew acquaintance with the Washoes. On November first—dodging rattlesnakes which were still active due to the warm weather—the trappers seized two Indians who had possibly never seen white men before. Dragged into camp, they were questioned about the country in every language known to the expedition. . . to no avail. "More stupid brutes I never saw nor could we make them understand our meaning. Gave them a looking glass and their liberty. In less than 10 minutes they were far from us."[205]

Two days after this uneventful encounter, the expedition came to three large lakes (perhaps Warner Lakes) covered with wild fowl and the waters tasting like "Globular salts." (Glauber's salt, found in mineral waters, is used as a cathartic). They also ran into a large encampment of Washoes who took off in all directions. Ogden suspected that "they think we have come with no good intentions," which was probably a correct assumption on the part of the Washoes.

Cruising east along the Oregon-Nevada border, Ogden apparently reached Trout Creek in the southeast corner of Oregon which he described as a very long, narrow stream emptying into a lake (Alvord)

---

[205] Quotations for this chapter, unless otherwise noted, are taken from Ogden's *Fifth Snake Country Journal*, entries dated from September 22, 1828, to July 5, 1829.

with no outlet. Still continuing eastward across the headwaters of the Owyhee with his traps producing from forty to sixty beaver a day (the catch was now approaching the one thousand mark) he was overrun with Washoes. "There are Indians everywhere, almost naked and most of them without bows or arrows but fat and in good condition." Ogden was quite upset to find them wearing beaver moccasins which he thought was a misuse of good skins, but he was relieved that with 300 Indians milling about camp, scaring off the beaver, at least they were "very peaceable."

November 21 arrived in the teeth of a gale-force wind bringing with it rain and three White Knife braves. These wanderers casually mentioned that six Americans had been killed in the Snake camp at Twin Falls. This intelligence would cause Ogden much anxiety. Cuthbert Grant—his backup from York Factory on Hudson's Bay—working the middle Snake River was in the hostile zone and Payette with his handful of men in the Ochoco was in extreme danger of being cut off by the Bear Killers if the Shoshoni continued to remain in a surly mood. As if to confirm Ogden's uneasiness, a few hours after the White Knives departed, the temperature plunged turning the wind-driven rain into snow.

Near midnight, a sleepless Ogden was jarred from his blankets when a snow-plastered trapper stumbled into his tent and with a wrenching groan collapsed. It was Joseph Paul described by Ogden as. . . "a steady young man and one of the expedition's best trappers." One look was enough to tell Julia Ogden that Paul was mortally ill. The cause of the sudden seizure was unknown but the local tribesmen seriously believed it was the curse of Twisted Hand. Whatever, the stricken trapper—not yet thirty—was old in the history of Shoshoni Country. In 1819 at age twenty, he had been a member of the North West Company's first Snake expedition. Now, nine years later, he was one of the two survivors of that party.

Next morning Paul was no better but with the weather turning more ugly and worried about his detached parties, Ogden decided to move on. However, when Paul told him he couldn't walk or even mount a horse and requested "as an act of charity to end his sufferings by throwing him into the river," the normally calloused trader changed plans. He stalled operations for twelve days doing whatever he could to make the dying trapper comfortable but nothing seemed to alleviate the pain. Finally, on December fourth with their provisions running danger-ously low and starvation looming on the horizon, Ogden gave the order to move out. With much misgiving he noted in his journal " . . .we have no alternative left. God forbid it should hasten his (Paul's) death." On that melancholy note, Ogden had the bed-ridden trapper strapped on a horse and following a Paiute guide—who assured him there was buffalo nearby—struck out to cross the Ruby Mountains and make contact with the American camp on Great Salt Lake.

Some two hundred miles southeast of the Ochoco, Ogden was more or less following the "Unknown River." Later he named it Paul's River. His trappers called it Mary's River for Julia Mary Ogden who had shared their daily hardships on that desolate stream. Later trappers either conferred sainthood on Julia or took the river from her by calling it St. Mary's River. Still later—in 1845—Captain John Charles Fremont took the river from everyone, giving it the name of Humboldt for the respected German geographer, Alexander Humboldt. That name stuck, although one of the tributaries is still called Mary's River.

Six days after breaking camp Ogden was forced to make a decision between the quick and the dead. It was rendered less painful when two trappers volunteered to remain with their sick comrade who had been begging Ogden for days to go on and let him die. Fully aware that if the whole party went into winter quarters in this bleak area they would starve within the month Ogden agreed. All he could offer in the way of survival was a bag of dried peas and a colt. He also warned the Paiutes in the area that if they harmed those left behind not only would he retaliate against them but also kill the guide who accompanied the main party.

On that bleak note, the Canadians crossed the snow drifted Ruby range into Ute country, passing through a "barren gloomy country covered with wormwood, where there were no tracks of any animals but wolves and the streams were salt." On December 22 they found evidence of a large Shoshoni migration heading north. In the early fall a Snake raiding party had ridden into Mexican territory in search of horses. Now returning to the Ochoco, trailing hundreds of Spanish horses, it was their track that Ogden had crossed believing it to be a "large migration of Snake Indians." Following the Indian track, Ogden passed through country hidden under a heavy fog and by Christmas Eve was thoroughly confused. To make matters worse, that evening in a quarrel over a horse, their Paiute guide deserted.

By the twenty-eighth, Ogden had reached and explored the north end of Great Salt Lake where he wrote in his journal " . . .can safely accept as the Americans have on the south side that it is a barren country destitute of everything." Trapping was now temporarily halted as every available man in the starving camp was dispatched in search of game.

New Year's Day, 1829, brought with it one of the trappers who had stayed behind with Joseph Paul. The trapper reported that Paul—after surviving for 25 days of agony—had died eight days after the main party left and was buried beside the Unknown River in northern Nevada.[206] Mourning the death of the twenty-nine-year-old veteran who had been with the Snake Expedition since the beginning, Ogden cancelled plans for observing New Year's Day. He sadly noted that of the 300 man brigade which had followed him into Oregon in 1819 only one man, Joseph Delore, was yet alive. "All have been killed with the exception of 2 who died a natural death and are scattered over the Snake country. It is incredible the number that have fallen in this country."

These memories brought worry about the fate of Payette and Grant. Any chance of making contact with Payette in the Ochoco was out of the question; but Grant, believed to be only sixty or seventy miles to the north on the middle Snake, was worth the effort. Taking a gamble, Ogden hired a Ute chief with nine warriors to take a message to Grant, notifying him that because of exhausted horses, Ogden could not form a union with the York Factory brigade at this time. A few days later the Utes returned with word they could find no white traders on the Snake.

During this interval a trapper reported that his wife, two children and six horses loaded with furs and traps had been missing for three days. Fearing the worst, a search was begun. Meantime, the missing woman rode into camp with all the missing property and a most pleasant surprise. According to her, she had become lost and was rescued by two Shoshoni hunters who "behaved most kindly toward me, defended my

---

[206] Today, Joseph Paul's unmarked grave is somewhere between Golconda and Winnemucca, Nevada.

property from marauding Utes who attempted to molest me and guided me back to camp."

For the next two months Ogden—with no hint as to the fate of Grant or Payette—strung traps in Ute country following what was to become Ogden River into Ogden's Hole where the city of Ogden now stands. During this push, marked by a noticeable lack of journal entries, the Canadians encountered trouble with the Utes resulting in one man being killed. By March, with detachments now working northwest toward the Ochoco, Ogden with fourteen men made a dash to the Owyhee River in hope of joining Payette. Unsuccessful in this attempt, Ogden swung south to the Humboldt where again he found Paiutes dressed in beaver skins and the trapping good. It was in fact so good that by the end of April he had 1,700 beaver pelts strapped on his pack animals.

By mid-May, in an effort to escape the unbearable heat, Ogden was well on his way to a cooler climate crossing through the desolate Black Rock Desert where his horses sank knee deep in sand at each step as they passed such landmarks as Disaster Peak, Blizzard Gap and Guano Lake. He was searching for the illusive Pit River which he believed—as all explorers of that period—had its source in south central Oregon near present day Summer Lake. He was also on a collision course with the Pit River (Mono) Snakes. Already, signal fires dotted Hart Mountain with answering smokes from the distant Steens. On May 17, the trappers saw two mounted warriors in the distance who refused to come near. Four days later while visiting traps an Iroquois had his horse stolen. Another trapper returning from Guano Creek was ambushed by four Indians who fired arrows at him, seized his gun and would have taken his life had he not outridden them.

These games of chance alerted Ogden to the fact that maybe he had penetrated a little too far into hostile country. Beyond doubt, he had run afoul of a strong and very daring group who were "probably the same branch as in Pitts River." Up to this point, Ogden believed there were no Shoshoni in this quarter. From the apparent lack of effort to wipe out Ogden's brigade it appears they were after more interesting game—and they were. The Snakes were staging one of their periodic raids on the Modoc clan.

On May 27—again thanks to a fast horse—a trapper narrowly escaped death when twenty mounted warriors "gave the war cry" and chased him back to camp where he reported the hills covered with

Indians. Oddly, it was not the Snakes who would place their souls in jeopardy. As Ogden prepared a meager defense, his scouts reported upwards of 200 footmen marching on camp. Ogden quickly determined from "their dress and drums and the fact only one elderly man was with them" that this was not a social gathering.

Out beyond the end of the explored world Ogden—tough as he was—must have felt fear facing two hundred unrestrained Modoc warriors with only twelve guns and fourteen men. Obviously he showed no fear for when the army was still half a mile away, he walked out alone and met the Modocs some 500 yards from camp. Through his Paiute interpreter he bid the warriors who had come to exterminate him to sit down for a parley. Taken completely by surprise at this show of bravado, they meekly complied. From them Ogden gained much knowledge about the country but when the Modocs wished to enter camp, the trader—still running a bluff—refused the offer.

The night that followed, rent by thunder and lightning and with Indian fires all around was not pleasant. At daylight Ogden calmly gave orders to break camp and move out. As if he needed any excuse, he dutifully recorded in the company log that by going farther west he. . . . "would infringe on McLeod's territory." As further justification for retreat he noted that he only had fifty traps left and was too weak to advance. Covering for his men as they rode north toward the southern Blues, Ogden told the Modoc chief he would see him again in three months.

Five days later, south of Wagontire Mountain, his journal entry for June 2, 1829, would reveal: "We are directing our course to Sylvaille's (Silvies) River, Day's Defile (John Day Valley) and Snake River." Fortunately for this ragged Hudson's Bay Company detachment, the White Knives were occupied in helping the Pit River Snakes deal misery to the Modocs while the Bear Killers were keeping a wary eye on the Americans who were converging on the Popo Agie River on the eastern boundary of Shoshoni territory for their annual drunken brawl.

As Ogden slipped over Dixie Pass in the middle Blues, being careful not to arouse the suspicions of local natives, the U. S. Congress was vigorously plotting more mischief for its non-voting public. In 1829 this august body devised the first of nearly 100 separate treaties to divide and reapportion Indian lands. Under this arrangement, the Indians would be allowed a small parcel of their tribal holdings while the remainder would be opened to white settlement. By 1831, the first permanent Indian reservation called Indian Territory was established on public lands west of the Mississippi River.[207]

While Congress ironed out the details of this legislation, Ogden was on the final leg of his march through Shoshoni country where he had left so many fallen comrades behind. He, too, was leaving something of himself in the Snake country where for five years his iron constitution had been tested by heat and cold, winds that eroded the desert rock, starvation, contaminated water, dead horse flesh and poison hemlock. In the country of which he once said that six months could turn a youth into a man of sixty, he was leaving much older than the passage of time would indicate.

On July 5, 1829, as the Americans some 500 miles to the east on the Popo Agie continued their celebration of independence from British rule, Ogden completed his journey and headed down the Columbia for Fort Vancouver. His sole comment was "we have no cause to complain of our returns." Nor did McLoughlin. He was so impressed with the season's catch that in a generous mood he took it upon himself to give the trappers one schilling extra (5 cents) in wages because of such good pelts.

Enroute to company headquarters Ogden was surprised to find a new company post—named Bache Fort—which had been established that summer by James Bernie at the dalles on the Columbia. The winds of progress were blowing ever closer to the smoldering Ochoco fanning the flames of mutual distrust to brighter intensity.

---

[207] *Historical Highlights of Public Land Management*, USDI-BLM, 1962, pp. 19-20.

CHAPTER 38

TAPS FOR A SNAKE TRADER

*Chief Trader Ogden. . . I am sorry. . . but
the injury his constitution has sustained. . .
will render it necessary to relieve him of duty. . . . .*

Governor George Simpson
Fifth Snake Country Expedition

Governor Simpson had viewed with alarm the deterioration of Ogden in his fifth year of harsh survival in Shoshoni country and sensed that he was near the breaking point. In early March, 1829, while Ogden was being harassed by the Utes in his dash back to the Owyhee country, Simpson wrote to the Hudson's Bay Company in London expressing his concern. He sorrowfully noted that although Chief Trader Ogden was still one of the Company's best men, "by the privations and discomfort to which he has been so long exposed, will render it necessary to relieve him as soon as we can find a gentleman qualified to fill his place to advantage."[208] At the moment that man was not forthcoming and Ogden was destined to continue on.

In the short interval between the fifth and sixth Snake country expeditions it became obvious that Ogden believed he was living on borrowed time when he threw all responsibilities overboard to save himself. It began with the breakup of his family. Uppermost in his mind was that his oldest son, Peter, must have a chance at the education he had thrown away; and the most convenient place to begin the boy's academic career was the now enlightened Red River settlement where

---

[208] Letter from Sir George Simpson, Fort Vancouver, Columbia District, Oregon Territory to the Governor and Committee of the Hudson's Bay Company, London, England, dated March, 1829.

years before young hotheads like Ogden had bathed in fire and blood. Red River had a highly respected schoolmaster, the ex-brigade leader, Alexander Ross. A man baptized in the carnage of Snake country, Ross had seen both sides of the coin and could be trusted to educate a half-breed boy in the "bombast and marvelous nonsense" that Simpson so despised but which young Peter would need to keep from sinking to a freeman's level. The phrase was a sarcastic reference to Simpson's evaluation of Ross' management of the Snake operations in which he claimed among other things: ". . . this important duty should not in my opinion be left to a self-sufficient, empty-headed man like Ross. . . whose reports are so full of bombast and marvelous nonsense that it is impossible to get at any information that can be depended upon from him." Thus the judgment of the man of action on the man of letters.

And so in the summer of 1829, Peter Jr. was put on board a pack train and shipped off to the Red River settlement in southern Manitoba with instructions to find Mr. Ross. It is doubtful that ten-year-old Peter who had trudged the high mountain meadows of the Ochoco and smelled the aromatic sage after a desert rainstorm would find the Red River settlement to his liking.

Next on the agenda was what to do with Julia and the rest of the children. He soon decided to leave Julia with her mother at Fort Nez Perce under the watchful eye of his old friend Sam Black, chief trader at the fort. Black's days were also numbered. In 1841 he would be murdered by Indians while trading on the Okanogan River. During these final arrangements it appears that Ogden was secretly planning to go out with a bang, dealing misery to beaver and Americans alike. Now, near the breaking point, he began his sixth and final campaign in charge of the Snake brigade. The expedition was to be the most far-flung and hazardous of all. Ironically, there would be no surviving record of this epic journey which covered the full width of Shoshoni country from the John Day Valley to the mouth of the Colorado River—a distance of nearly 1,200 miles through the harshest country in the far west.

At the head of a sixty man force—not counting women and children—Ogden left Fort Nez Perce in the late summer of 1829 and true to his promise to the Modocs laid a path of destruction across the Ochoco toward the Klamath basin.[209] As he knifed through Central Oregon, a new development was taking shape.

In the early fall of 1829, Bill Sublette and Jim Bridger—in a move to outmaneuver the Hudson's Bay Company—led sixty men and 180 pack animals deep into Snake country where they hoped to meet with Jed Smith at the mouth of the Malheur River. Working their way down the Payette River, they arrived at the Snake on October 29, about the same time Ogden entered Modoc country. According to Sublette, across the Snake lay the Malheur and strung up its northern bank were "the lodges of the whole Shoshoni nation." At least that is the way it looked to Sublette. He and Bridger went into council and decided that Bridger would cross the river to find out if the Indians were friendly and if they had seen anything of Smith.

After about two hours, Bridger reported back having seen close to 400 lodges on the Malheur and was told by the chiefs there were that many more camped some sixty miles to the north on the Powder and an equal number downstream on the middle Snake. As near as the trappers could tell that meant there were close to 8,000 Shoshoni holed up around them. Red Wolf also claimed that 150 lodges of Bear Killers were moving out of the Ochoco to join them and trade with the Hudson's Bay Company. Some Paiutes who had drifted up from the Humboldt had seen a party of white men on the south fork of the Owyhee. Sublette believed this to be Smith, Fitzpatrick and the Meek brothers.

The Americans traded for 1,500 dollars worth of prime beaver and would have taken more but the price was too steep for Sublette who was working on a thousand dollar markup in prices delivered at St. Louis. The Shoshoni were very arrogant so Sublette headed back for the Rockies.

---

[209] The known men in Ogden's brigade included Francois Payette (35 year old ex-Astorian and highest ranking engage); Alexis Aubichan, Alex Carson, Antoine Sylvaille; Pierre L'Etang; Michael Otoetomie; Joseph Grenier and the Iroquois trappers Antoine Hoale, Antoine Plante, Charles Ponte and Louis Kanota. Many of these men would drown in the Columbia at The Dalles July 6, 1830. It is probable that Tom McKay was attached to the brigade as second in command.

Meantime, Smith, having spotted the Shoshoni encampment on the Malheur, swung wide and struck the river some ten miles upstream. From this point Smith's detachment worked up the middle fork of the Malheur and over the divide into the Crooked River drainage along a route that was to bring Steve Meek no end of trouble some fourteen years later in 1845. Encouraged and somewhat amazed at the lack of Ogden's presence, the Americans were stringing traps on the Beaver fork of Crooked River when they blundered into a Snake hunting party. The hunters took a fancy to the trapper's pack animals and in a running battle which carried them onto the edge of the Great Basin, Rocky Mountain Fur lost one pack horse with an estimated 800 dollars worth of fur and close to 100 steel traps left along Beaver creek. In the course of this skirmish, Fitzpatrick's musket blew up and tore two fingers off his left hand. From that day forward he was known to Indian and trapper alike as "Broken Hand."

At the narrows between Harney and Malheur lakes, Smith struck a retaliatory blow. Slipping up on a White Knife camp, Joe Meek, under the protection of his buddies who hid out on a low ridge overlooking the encampment, sneaked down and stole four horses. Then in a spirit of bravado, the Americans stampeded the remainder of the herd through camp and then lit out for the Rockies.

Striking up the Boise River, they ran into John Work—who was being groomed to fill Ogden's moccasins—and a severe tongue lashing. Work was not only miffed about their stringing traps in Hudson's Bay Company's back yard but his temper hit the boiling point when he found out they had swiped ponies from the Snakes. Work knew this horseplay would bring trouble to the Baymen for the remainder of the season.

On this sour note, he apparently dispatched Charles Plante and Jean Favel, (Iroquois hunters), across the Ochoco to intercept Ogden in Modoc country.[210] It seems they were successful for eight months later

---

[210] Plante's brother, Antoine, was attached to Ogden's command and it appears that both men had been in Warner Valley a couple of years before John Work first explored the region between October 12 and 15, 1832. (California Historical Society Quarterly, Sept., 1943, p. 203). Also, Arrowsmith's map of North America, corrected to 1832-33 shows a string of lakes connected by Plante River in the locality of what is now called Warner Valley. It seems obvious that

Ogden had a chat with the guilty culprits on his return leg to Oregon territory. The outcome of this meeting was that Smith and Meek gave their solemn word that Rocky Mountain Fur would stay out of Snake country. Sublette took a dim view of this arrangement but with Astor's American Fur Company trying to hamstring his little enterprise at every opportunity he finally agreed to Ogden's terms thinking it best to fight one battle at a time.

Now aware of Rocky Mountain Fur Company's latest move, Ogden in a daring raid into Mexican territory was stripping beaver streams on the eastern slope of the high Sierra Nevadas in a vicious plunge that would take him to the Gulf of California—searching for furs in a region more productive of scorpions than beaver. Meanwhile, speculation was running high among the Americans in Snake country as to the whereabouts of the tough British trader. They were soon to find out.

By spring 1830, Ogden had done such a thorough job of trapping southern California that he left poor pickings for Ewing Young's American brigade which came through after him. During this excursion across Ogden's newly created beaver desert Young gained the everlasting hatred of Kit Carson when he remarked, "You're too small for gettin' up to beaver, bub. Them fellers would laugh in your face." Later, Kit caught Young scalping an Indian he had killed and threatened to kill him. After that they became grudging friends.

Young—suspicious that Hudson's Bay was working the area—managed to catch up with Ogden who apparently hadn't lost a man as Young numbered the brigade at "sixty men strong."[211] This force was stronger than Young cared to argue with and besides he had not fared so well in his crossing of Mohave hunting grounds. Based on American documents, it is evident that Ogden had succeeded in his secret plan to trap the San Joaquin River "from its sources to its discharge in the Gulf of California." Although beaver streams were few and far between in eastern California, when Young caught him Ogden already had a thousand hides stashed in his packs. The rival companies traveled together for ten days during which Ogden became acquainted with Kit

---

Plante River bears either Antoine or Charles Plante's name.

[211] Quaife, Milo Milton, *Kit Carson's Autobiography*, pp. 14-15.

Carson, the veteran trapper with Young's outfit. They parted on friendly terms with Ogden moving north to Oregon and Young heading west to the Sacramento River.

While these two outfits spent the winter in balmy weather, it was a different story in the Ochoco. Winter had struck with a vengeance. With the absence of Ogden to hold them at bay, Bridger with a Rocky Mountain Fur detachment was trapping the Ochoco and if one can believe Joe Meek, the going was rough. Following is Meek's account of Bridger's foray into the Blues. It may be taken for what it is worth:

> Winter o' 1830 was the wust this child ever seen. Seventy days and seventy nights the snow come down. Seventy foot deep it set on the ground. Old Gabe and his boys was holed up north o'the Great Basin in the Blues that year. Half the buffler in the west yarded up just below 'em and froze solid. Come spring Old Gabe had his boys skin 'em out, roll 'em down and pickle 'em in the Great Salt Lake. Kept hisself and the whole Ute Nation fed for more'n ten years, I knowed it for a fact.[212]

Somewhere in that yarn is a grain of truth, for it is documented that the winter of 1829-30 was extremely severe, followed by a heavy spring runoff which would play havoc with Ogden's return to Fort Vancouver.

By early summer of 1830 things were getting critical in the Blues. The Indian trail through South Pass had become the white man's ever-widening thoroughfare and with the added nuisance of Americans underfoot, the Shoshoni's lukewarm tolerance of the British in an effort to obtain arms and ammunition was dropping to absolute zero. The impending loss of Ogden's tight control over the war chiefs was being felt. British traders were reacting with panic. Contrary to strict company policy, "Wild Bill" Kittson was offering anyone two horses for every Shoshoni they killed. At the same time McLoughlin went so far as to suggest to Donald Manson—clerk at Fort Vancouver—that he give out false information as to how low the company would go in the price of trade guns. Anything to drive the American traders out of Shoshoni

---

[212] As told to Mrs. Frances Fuller Victor and recorded in her *The River of the West*. Also see Vestal, *The Merry Mountain Man, Joe Meek*.

country was considered fair game. The moment the opposition was over, the price for weapons would be doubled or tripled. Then, company officials sent orders from Hudson's Bay headquarters to: "Give as much as two years credit to a wild, pagan Indian; but as soon as he cuts his hair and pretends he is civilized, don't trust him, even overnight." Adding to this malaise, at the 1830 Wind River rendezvous, Bridger and Fitzpatrick formed a partnership with three other trappers and were attempting to buy out Rocky Mountain Fur.

This is what greeted Ogden as he entered the Ochoco. As he topped the summit of the Blues, the U.S. population topped 12 million. As far as the Shoshoni were concerned, this uninhibited populace was all crammed between the crest of the Cascades and the summit of the Rockies.

By mid-summer, Ogden was riding the crest of the swollen Columbia to Fort Vancouver when disaster struck. At The Dalles his boats were caught in a whirlpool. Nine men drowned, including Joe Grenier and the old, experienced steersman, Pierre L'Etang. Packs containing 500 beaver pelts sank to the bottom and Ogden's journal was swept to sea. All that remains in the record of the 1829-30 expedition are a few lines in a letter which Ogden wrote to John McLeod on March 10, 1831. Accustomed to bringing in upwards of three thousand pelts, Ogden would comment in his usual laconic way, "I was not so successful in my last year's trapping. . . although I extended my trails by far greater distance to the Gulf of California but found beaver very scarce. . . ."

Ogden did receive some good news. Governor Simpson had found the "gentleman qualified" to ramrod the Snake brigades and that gentleman was John Work who had accompanied Ogden west with the Columbia Express. As for Ogden his new assignment was no less challenging—breach the Russian stronghold in Alaska. To accomplish this, he was to sail for the Nass River, build a fort within shouting distance of the Russian outpost of Ketchikan and ". . . regardless of profit or loss secure all furs that have been going to the Americans." Furthermore, this was to be done without upsetting the Russian-American Fur Company. As an after-thought, Dr. McLoughlin warned: "The Indians of the Nass are numerous and particularly hostile to whites." After six years of dodging hostile Indians in Shoshoni country, Ogden was unimpressed by the warning. He was, however, dubious about the outcome of the project. Writing to John McLeod, he confided, "I am not of the opinion our wealth will be increased."

At Sitka, Baron Wrangell—governor of Alaska—had other ideas. From afar he had watched Ogden exterminate the beaver in Shoshoni country and had also noted his vigorous warfare against American traders. What he had seen from a distance, he did not wish to experience at closer range. Chief Trader Ogden had stepped from the frying pan into the fire.

CHAPTER 39

SNAKE COUNTRY IN TURMOIL

First, they trapped almost all the beaver,
then killed all the buffalo. Then they
practiced a little genocide on the native
population. . . .

James Crumley
Roping Some Western Questions

Some three months before Ogden's return from Mexican territory other events were unfolding in Oregon that would temporarily alter company plans to ship him off to Alaska. Arriving with the spring thaw, malaria rode rough-shod over the Columbia basin, leaving death and destruction in its wake. In a letter to Governor Simpson dated March 20, 1830, McLoughlin reported the loss of "three fourths of the Indian population in our vicinity." Whole Indian villages were wiped out and the trees were blackened by buzzards "gorged on human flesh." The Chinooks were now taking the brunt of this awesome plague which would exact a horrible toll on the lower Columbia tribes for another thirty years.

When Ogden arrived at Fort Vancouver, he found it turned into a hospital and the supply ship from London—Ogden's intended passage to the Nass River—converted to a floating hospital ship. Leaving so many decomposing bodies would cause further problems so McLoughlin placed Ogden in charge of the burial detail where he too came down with the dread disease. It was a tribute to McLoughlin's skill—having studied medicine in Canada, Scotland and France, where he obtained his M.D.—that there were so few fatalities among the Hudson's Bay employees.

Then, to encumber an already serious situation, word drifted down the Columbia that Work was cut off by the war tribes somewhere in the interior. Two trappers had been killed and Alex Carson, who had

335

survived the raid through California, had been severely wounded. Racked with alternate chills and fever, Ogden was dispatched to the rescue.

During the interlude between malaria and the rescue mission, Ogden was beginning to enjoy single bliss. Apparently on his sojourn through California, Ogden found the Spanish girls quite tempting. However, it is doubtful that between malaria and rescue mission he had the energy for dangerous liaisons at Fort Vancouver. By virtue of being left behind on the sixth Snake country expedition, Ogden's family escaped the boating disaster at The Dalles and the plague at Fort Vancouver. Even so, Ogden's shielding of them did nothing for family unity. While Julia waited patiently on the other side of the mountains, Ogden at Fort Vancouver lapsed into the patterns of his bachelor days. Just how much was revealed in the spring of 1831 when Ogden, in a letter to John McLeod, admitted that since he had last seen him (which wasn't all that long ago) "I have increased my children by ten." He then boasted: "the Bachelor Flag I have hoisted and if ever I leave it, it will not be in the H.B. Company's territories."[213]

So much for wishful thinking. On his return from the Alaska assignment, Peter and Julia—whom he now referred to as "my Old Lady"—reunited but though McLoughlin urged him to formalize the marriage, he refused. According to Ogden, Christian marriage was alright for the new generation but Indian wedlock was good enough for his generation and he was not going to change.

Inland, other domestic quarrels were in the making. By mid-winter of 1830-31 Astor's American Fur, specifically the Northern Department of American Fur, soon to be bought by Ramsay Crooks "and associates," was hampering the operations of Rocky Mountain Fur more than Hudson's Bay and the Shoshoni combined. In an effort to build up their capital Smith, Jackson and Sublette took in Fitzpatrick and Bridger as full partners. Then, to strengthen their supply lines, Bill Sublette took charge of the pack trains to and from St. Louis while his brother, Milton

---

[213] Ogden, *Correspondence and Miscellaneous Family Papers*, Oregon State Archives.

took over the trapping end. None of these ardent suitors of beaver were expressing any love toward the Shoshoni.

Meanwhile, under the field leadership of Kenneth McKenzie, the shrewdest and most unprincipled trader in the entire fur empire, American Fur, driven by the Ochoco hardened veteran, Ramsay Crooks, was slowly crushing Rocky Mountain Fur. McKenzie, only twenty-nine years old, had already acquired the reputation that gave him the title "King of the Missouri." In his headquarters at Fort Union he lived like a feudal lord, wearing an ornate uniform of his own design while maintaining military discipline among his trappers at all times. His rooms were lavishly furnished and his Assiniboine call girls were dressed in the latest St. Louis fashions.

Having learned well from Crook's near fatal plunge into the Ochoco, McKenzie was not about to gamble by exploring new fur frontiers. Instead, he preferred to overrun the territory small companies had already proved to be profitable. And so by 1831, it was Astor's money, Crooks' mastermind and McKenzie's ruthlessness pitted against the skill, experience and daring of the Sublettes, the Meek brothers, Bridger, Smith and Fitzpatrick. Lurking in the background, the gigantic, immeasurably powerful Hudson's Bay Company was waiting for the right moment to crush both parties.

William Sublette, immersed in profit and politics, had his sights set on Hudson's Bay. At the inception of the Rocky Mountain Fur Company it is interesting to note that all of Smith, Jackson and Sublette's information on the Oregon country was addressed to Gen. William Clark, Superintendent of Indian Affairs. Then, when it became obvious that Hudson's Bay Company was in control of the area all communications would be directed to the Honorable John H. Eaton, Secretary of War, stressing the inequities of the 1818 convention with Great Britain and hinting that the treaty of joint occupancy should be terminated in favor of the United States.[214]

In contrast to Sublette's belligerent attitude towards Hudson's Bay, Jed Smith in his correspondence at least had the grace to acknowledge the Company's good side, noting: "as an act of justice the treatment I

---

[214] Documents in *The Missouri Historical Society*, Sublette Papers.

received at Fort Vancouver was kind and hospitable. I wish to extend my personal thanks to Governor Simpson and the gentlemen of the Hudson's Bay Company for the efficient and successful aid received in the recovery of furs and horses stolen from me by the Umpqua Indians in 1828."[215]

The first blood drawn in this struggle for supremacy came from an unexpected quarter. Apparently Red Wolf had opened lines of communication with the Comanches alerting them to the instability of trade with the Americans. Whatever, the spring of 1831 found Jed Smith, in an effort to corner the southern Rocky mountain fur market, leading a supply train from St. Louis to Santa Fe. While Snake country was inundated with a record spring run-off that was destroying beaver traps by the hundreds, Comanche hunting grounds were suffering an extreme draught. On May 27, while riding ahead of the supply train in search of water, Smith's luck ran out. The quiet mountain man who had challenged Ogden in his own backyard and survived three major Indian attacks in Shoshoni country fell under the thrust of a dozen Comanche war lances. Jedidiah Smith died as he had lived, alone with only his God for comfort in the lonely Cimarron Desert.

In his search for water, Smith had made a disheartening discovery. Following the dusty stream bed of the Cimarron River, he came upon Fitzpatrick who was leading the main supply train into Cache valley for the summer rendezvous. Fitzpatrick was lost. As a consequence, Rocky Mountain Fur was dangerously low on traps, knives and ammunition to carry on a full campaign. Worse yet, there was no liquor and rendezvous 1831 would not be remembered with pleasure. In a state of confusion search parties were sent out to locate the missing partner who was finally found coming—not west out of St. Louis but north from Santa Fe. Fitzpatrick, who had blundered into Smith's caravan, had wandered several hundred miles off course.

Meanwhile, Bridger and Milton Sublette, giving up hope of seeing the lost supply train, headed for the Powder River country for some winter poaching in Hudson's Bay Company territory, thinking to out-maneuver McKenzie's blood hounds. Other than a brush with Hudson's

---

[215] See Morgan, Dale L., *Jedidiah Smith and the Opening of the West*.

Bay Company the winter of 1831-32 went fairly smoothly. Although the British partisan John Work mentions contact with the Americans, he gives no details as to what happened other than the Rocky Mountain Fur trappers had a superior quantity of whiskey in their packs which says much for the continued destruction of the Shoshoni fur supply. By Now the Snakes referred to the Americans as tibos—barbarians— who had suddenly come into their midst taking possession of tribal streams as if they belonged to them. Sadly, there was no Sacajawea to pave the way toward an understanding between the Snakes and the trappers; nor would her once-accommodating brother, Black Gun, serve as a friendly host. It was now a matter of dog eat dog and the devil take the hindmost. By 1831 the Indian trail through South Pass into Green River—known to the Shoshoni as the Sisk-ke-doc—had become the Americans link to the Ochoco. And Green River became the scene of approximately half of the annual rendezvous, all of which took place on lands claimed by the Shoshoni.

On this sour note and with Fitzpatrick's blunder still fresh in mind, spring found Bill Sublette once again in command of the Rocky Mountain Fur supply train. Working feverishly to get trade goods into Oregon territory in time for the summer's rendezvous at Pierre's Hole, he was making fifteen to twenty-five miles a day pulling twelve heavily loaded freight wagons. It is quite unlikely that Sublette wasn't aware that he was shaping history on this nine hundred mile route worked out by trial and error on his annual trips from Independence, Missouri to South Pass; a trail pioneered some five years earlier by Ashley when he pulled a cannon-mounted artillery wagon over South Pass in 1827. Within a decade of Sublette's 1832 passage, this dim trapper's trail would become a three hundred foot right of way so heavily travelled buffalo would refuse to cross it and on which not a single blade of grass would grow. Bill Sublette was blazing the Oregon Trail and he would make certain of its impact on the settlement of the Oregon controversy between Great Britain and the United States.

A political animal at heart, Sublette must have reasoned that U.S. colonization of Oregon territory was an expedient way to hamper Hudson's Bay Company operations. All that was holding back the flood of immigration was easy access to the region. Now that he was focusing on merchandising rather than trapping, he would also envision a profitable market in the export of goods to settlers. In view of this there is little doubt that Sublette would lose any time in contacting the Hon. Lewis Cass (Eaton's successor as Secretary of War), informing him of his success in bringing wagons across the Continental Divide into Oregon territory. Trader Bill was also adding more competition to the hide war.

Following in the dust of Sublette's freight wagons came Nathaniel Wyeth, a New England merchant who wanted to break into the fur trade. It was said of Wyeth that he was the "kind of Yankee trader who'd tunnel his way to hell if there was a loose dollar there." And so Rendezvous 1832 got off to a roaring start with the customary Indian trouble.

To get things rolling, Sublette unpacked his raw alcohol kegs; watered the stuff down; threw in a pound of tobacco for color; added a handful of red peppers for flavor; and then settled back for some serious trading. The attending Shoshoni—potential clients who were accustomed to Hudson's Bay Company's very fine rum—were consoled by the addition of a quart of black molasses to their devil's brew. Camp kettles, serving as mountain goblets, were passed around, emptied and refilled with amazing regularity as the dog soldiers bartered away furs, daughters and anything else that took the trapper's fancy. During this debauch, the Americans were every bit as uninhibited as their red brethren. Francis Bacon, British philosopher and statesman, once mused. . . "a Christian gentleman, well born and bred. . . will of his own free-will quit his high station and luxurious world to dwell with savages and live their lives, taking part in all their savagery. But never yet hath it been seen that a savage will of his own free will give up his savagery and live the life of a civilized man." The Snake country rendezvous' were fast proving Bacon correct.

After demonstrating their skills on beast, bottle and brown-skinned beauty, Fitzpatrick, Bridger and Milton Sublette headed for the mountains trying their best to outmaneuver McKenzie's blood hounds. Luck was not to be their lot. Crossing the Sawtooth range, they picked up a shadow led by Major Henry Vanderburgh—a West Point graduate and ex-Missouri Fur Company partner—who found McKenzie's pay was about triple that of the army. He and his partners, Andrew Dripps and Lucien Fontenelle, latched onto Bridger's brigade like leeches and the chase was on. With all their skill and tricks learned from the Indians, Rocky Mountain Fur couldn't ditch Vanderburgh who anticipated their every move like a stalking cat. In desperation, Bridger and Sublette came up with a brilliant idea. Remembering the promise given Ogden the previous summer to stay clear of his hunting grounds or suffer the consequences, they headed west into the Ochoco. If the Shoshoni or the British didn't get Vanderburgh, the land would. As it turned out, the Shoshoni were trying their best to accommodate when it surfaced at the next summer's rendezvous that they were searching for Vanderburgh.

When Sublette and Bridger arrived at the mouth of Powder River, instead of settling down for a quiet winter of trapping, they split forces. Bridger headed north toward the Columbia with Steve Meek and Robert "Doc" Newell where they hid out most of the winter with the Nez Perces. Sublette, Joe Meek, Moses "Black" Harris and Ewing Young with an Iroquois deserter from one of Ogden's expeditions acting as a guide, headed for the gaunt desert south of the Blues initially hoping to cover Bridger's retreat and making no attempt to hide their trail. In so doing, Sublette embarked on a four hundred mile journey in an unsuccessful effort to elude his rivals.

From the headwaters of the Malheur, Sublette's brigade veered into the Great Basin area of southeast Oregon toward the Owyhee uplands. Crossing over the Snow (Steens) Mountains at the 9,000 foot summit in an effort to obliterate their trail and again on a westerly course, Sublette plowed through a treeless region into Catlow Valley. Now let American Fur see how well they liked the high desert for trapping!

Sublette had this to say about the tortured land south of the Ochoco. "It is a country dry and parched with little vegetation. Found only some stunted sage and scattered bunch grass that is so short the horses have trouble finding enough forage to sustain them. . . largest game animal found is beaver and precious few of them. . . facing starvation."[216]

Near the head of a north-flowing stream (probably the Blitzen River) the Rocky Mountain Fur brigade encountered a Snake hunting camp where friendly inhabitants offered to share a meal, an invitation most gratefully accepted. Climaxing a day of trade and celebration, steaming kettles made from the paunch of an elk were placed in the middle of the tipi. First on the menu was a delicious concoction of powdered pinenuts, a highly-prized flour made into tasty dishes only on very special

---

[216] Rutherford, *Mountain Man*, p. 131.

occasions. Thick soup, gravy and pan bread were cooked from the richly-flavored pine-nut meal. Then the pan bread, fried on a flat stone, was passed from hand to hand. Chunks were broken from this tough dish, dunked into the gravy soup and relished by all who tasted it. Next came cutlets of white-fleshed beaver which the Shoshoni ate with impunity. The Americans didn't fare so well. Try as they might, they couldn't keep the meat down.

Deathly sick, Sublette made a discovery which he carefully noted in his journal. . . "these beaver are different. . . smaller as they have no willows, cottonwoods or aspen, so they subsist on wild parsnip which is poisonous to horses and mules." Ogden could vouch that these beaver also dined on the equally deadly water hemlock. This tainted the beaver meat so that it was poisonous but for some unknown reason not to the Shoshoni. Apparently, they had stomachs like cast-iron kegs.

Suspecting treachery on behalf of their Snake hosts, the nauseated trappers moved ever deeper into the Great Basin eventually drifting into Nevada's Black Rock desert where they ran into the Washoe Indians, identified by the Iroquois guide as "Shoshoni." Smaller than the mountain warriors, the Washoes were stoop-shouldered, shy, but in perfect physical condition. When walking, they bent forward, eyes to the ground, occasionally stooping to snatch up an insect. It was not as funny as the mountain men first believed. Before they reached the "Unknown" (Humboldt) River such stalwarts of Rocky Mountain Fur as Ewing Young lived on crickets and mice while Joe Meek went so far as to try a handful of ants to stave off starvation.

Daily, they bled the mules and drank the blood to maintain strength. It was a rather parasitic existence for the trappers didn't dare drain off too much blood or the animals would give out and their very lives depended on keeping the pack animals alive. Finally, Sublette ordered one mule killed. Following two more weeks of famine, they reached Raft River teeming with trout. From here Sublette swerved south for a reunion with Bridger at Great Salt Lake. All in all it would have been worth the suffering if Sublette had lost Vanderburgh but he had not. Vanderburgh, after tracking Sublette to the rim of the Great Basin, had figured out the ploy and instead of following him he took to Bridger's trail.

Reunited at Ogden's Hole east of Great Salt Lake, Rocky Mountain Fur tried another tactic. Bridger hired John Gray, an Iroquois deserter from Ogden's Snake expedition—described by Ross as a turbulent blackguard and a damned rascal—with seven of his tribesmen to again guide them into the wilderness to shake off Vanderburgh. In the process, Bridger was trying to talk Gray into running traps for Rocky Mountain Fur on the Burnt and Powder rivers in eastern Oregon in an effort to get furs away from Hudson's Bay Company. While Gray was trying to make a deal with Bridger, a graceful young girl who would have taken the eye of any man red or white, ran into camp screaming her lungs out. Unfortunately it was Gray's daughter and a trapper had tried, without success, to rape her. Gray took an unsportsmanlike attitude concerning the episode and immediately went looking for the "chief" of the fur trappers, Milton Sublette. Sublette made a run for it but Gray, being accustomed to the chase, soon caught his man and split him from belly to chest with a Hudson's Bay knife. In the ruckus that followed, Gray and the girl slipped off. Sublette remained in critical condition for forty days while Joe Meek faithfully stayed with him. Expecting him to die any moment, Bridger had left Meek on burial detail while he and the other trappers—still attempting to elude Vanderburgh—headed for upper Green River and the 1832 rendezvous at Pierre's Hole with Vanderburgh still in pursuit.

There, they learned that the Blackfeet, beating the Snakes to the punch, had taken care of that piece of business for them. Vanderburgh inadvertently ran into a Blackfoot war party where, after his horse was shot out from under him, his men abandoned him. Freeing himself from the dead horse, Vanderburgh killed one warrior with his rifle and was raising his pistol for a second shot when he was cut down. The Indians chopped off his arms, then hacked the flesh from his bones and threw it in the river. The savages were still carrying both arms as war trophies when they showed up at Fort Union in the spring of '33 to buy more powder and lead.

Nevertheless, Vanderburgh's partners, Fontenelle, Dripps, and Robidaux would carry on the fight. If Rocky Mountain Fur thought they were having problems, Hudson's Bay wasn't faring much better. Floods in the interior ranging from Warner Valley across the southern Blues into the Seven Devils were destroying traps and the beaver catch was pitifully small. In desperation Work gathered his far flung brigades and headed for Idaho. Besides chaperoning 29 women and 45 children his brigade consisted of 38 trappers, a Paiute slave and "two youths able to bear arms." One of these youngsters was eleven-year-old Peter Delore who became a prominent figure in the settlement of the Ochoco.[217]

Pirating furs in American Fur territory, the British got caught in the backlash of Vanderburgh's skirmish. While camped on the headwaters of the Missouri with twelve lodges of Flatheads, Hudson's Bay Company was attacked by Blackfeet. One of the first to go down was Joe Delore, shot through the chest with the bullet coming out through his shoulder blades. Four French trappers were killed and two Flathead braves before they downed the Blackfoot war chief, thus ending the battle. Joe was carried to a Flathead lodge where his son Peter nursed him back to health. Joe, having survived another Snake expedition, lived to the ripe old age of 97. Another survivor of this attack, although severely wounded, was the seemingly indestructible Alex Carson. However, less than four years into the future Carson's allotted time on earth would terminate on a lonely western Oregon hillside compliments of his Indian guide.

Work would believe to his dying day that this attack was ordered by King McKenzie and he would show no mercy in his dealings with American Fur. In a bitter message to company officials at Fort Vancouver Work would report ". . . the people wandering through this country in quest of beaver are continually in danger. . . and certain of losing their

---

[217] Work, John, *Fur Brigade to the Bonaventura; John Work's California Expedition, 1832-1833, for the Hudson's Bay Company.* The son of Joseph Delore and a Spokane maiden, Peter was born January 1, 1821, on an earlier Snake Country expedition where the town of La Grande now stands. He learned from his mother every Indian language spoken in the Pacific Northwest. Peter Delore married Lizzett Depree and helped erect the first Catholic mission in the Willamette Valley. The priest paid him in gold coin and Pete thought them to be buttons. Joe told him always to bring home "such buttons." Peter and his family lived solely on meat with the exception of some flour on Christmas. The first peas he saw he thought were beads and was afraid to eat them. His tableware consisted of quaking aspen dishes and spoons of buffalo and elk horn. During the Shoshonean wars, Pete served as a scout from 1864-1869, the last three years under the command of General Crook. In 1878 he and his sons, Joseph, Baptiste and Peter Jr., scouted for General Howard. The Delore family settled in what became Crook County in 1880. (*History of Central Oregon*, pp. 751-804).

lives in the most barbarous manner. . . . " On this matter Sublette, McKenzie and Work could all agree.

CHAPTER 40

TRAPPER'S LADIES

*Maybe you're thinkin' of some sickly gal
from the settlements. . . or some wench
from Santy Fee. Do you here now? Leave the
Spanish slut to her greasers and the pale-faced gal
to them as knows no better. . . . What a
mountain man wants is an Injun woman.*

"Blackfoot" Smith
Advice to Kit Carson

Back on Bear River time was weighing heavily on Meek's hands. Sublette refused to die. Forty days after the Iroquois John Gray had carved him like a Christmas ham, Sublette was able to mount a horse and they moved out to catch up with Bridger's party or, failing that, to meet them at Pierre's Hole for rendezvous 1832. Unknowingly, Bridger's trail was leading them into danger. During Sublette's struggle for survival the Snake war chief, Red Wolf, had left the Ochoco and was now encamped on upper Green River. Without warning Meek and Sublette rode into the midst of some Bear Killer braves grazing their horses. Realizing they couldn't escape, the mountain men galloped through the startled warriors and charged into the main encampment. Wise in Indian protocol, Sublette headed directly for the chief's lodge identifiable by its gaudy trappings. Once inside they were officially under the hospitality of Red Wolf—at least until discharged from the neutral ground.

Inside, the hapless Americans stood panting as the angry Shoshoni began to converge on them. Within a half hour, the lodge was full of scowling braves who refused to speak to the trappers. Instead, they went into conference discussing whether to kill the Tibos or let them live. Operating on a perfectly democratic principle, anyone who had anything to say was given a chance to express his view whether it pertained to the situation at hand or not. Actually, the decision had been made before the arguments ever started. For some reason—perhaps seeing an opportunity for improved trade relations concerning armament—Red Wolf acted as counsel for the defense. This went on for the rest of the day. The verdict was unfavorable.

Everyone else having gone to prepare for the ceremony, Red Wolf was the last to leave. Not that they had a great deal of choice, Red Wolf motioned for Meek and Sublette to be quiet and remain in his lodge. Then he winked. What it meant, neither man knew but at dusk there was a loud noise and much confusion as dust boiled up from the far end of camp. Something was wrong with the horse herd. All villagers ran to see what was going on. Red Wolf appeared at the lodge and motioned the prisoners to follow him. At the outer edge of camp in a pine thicket a tall, fine-featured Indian girl held their horses ready to mount. Joe and Milt were stunned by her beauty. Always the gentleman, Sublette bowed to the smiling girl, thanked her in Shoshoni and rode off.[218]

This frontier beauty was Umentucken Tukutsey Undenwatsy, the Mountain Lamb, daughter of Red Wolf.[219] Within a year, Mountain Lamb would become Milton Sublette's wife. Besides powder and ball, it cost him four of his best horses, a bolt of cloth, five strings of beads, a red ribbon and two silk scarfs. Two years later, he would bequeath her to Joe Meek, beginning one of the great romances of the Oregon fur trade.

It gives pause for thought that in 1827 when Jedediah Smith was outfitting for his second California expedition, he recruited eighteen men and two women. Without doubt, the women were following their men to the field but there is no record as to which men may have been their husbands. Perhaps some explanation is in order as to why the fur men were so eager to acquire Indian helpmates.

When alien people meet, the saying goes, first they fight and then they fornicate. The trappers and Indians did both as mood and circumstances might dictate. This trend began in 1787 when the young Hud-

---

[218] Joe Meek's narrative (Victor, *River of the West*), pp. 104-105.

[219] In the Shoshoni language, Umentucken Tukutsey Undenwatsy—the Lamb of the Mountain—is translated in this manner: Umentucken (of the mountain); Tukutsey (bighorn ram or male mountain sheep); Undenwatsy (his child).

son's Bay employee David Thompson—an acknowledged womanizer—courted the granddaughter of a Blackfoot medicine man as a means to launch the first modern warfare on the unsuspecting Shoshoni.

It soon followed that men spending a winter in the mountains had two basic needs and liquor was only one of them. There were three ways of getting the other—bargaining with Indian fathers and husbands who brought their women to rendezvous for the same reason they brought their furs and horses; bargaining with the Indian wives of the Hudson's Bay Company trappers who dealt in slaves; or using the direct approach with beads or pretty cloth from Bill Sublette's packs.

The British Company wives also provided a means of economic support for other entrepreneurs, specifically the Modocs. During the peak of the fur trade, the Modocs—unable to snare beaver and lacking horses for barter—resorted to their ancient commerce. Prior to 1835 when they made their first trip to Celilo after being cut off by the Snakes in the late 1700s, these slavers worked through the Klamath and Wascos who served as middlemen in the trade. Their main source of supply was Shastas with an occasional Paiute tossed in for good measure. Neither were these gentlemen averse to selling their own wives, sisters or daughters. The going price to the Chinook madams was two ponies for young girls and five ponies for mature women depending upon attractiveness. What the madam charged is anyone's guess.[220]

By 1830, the Americans were using the word "netop" as a form of greeting when they encountered the inland tribes. In the Shoshoni language this could mean friend or comrade, but more literally it translated into "be my woman."[221] This invitation caused much confusion when addressing the dog soldiers.

Kit Carson who played only a minor role in Shoshoni history, was affiliated with them through his marriage to a Paiute girl. As the story goes, he and Isaac Rose were hunting one day along the Oregon-Nevada border when they startled a young girl from a clump of sagebrush.

---

[220] For more on this practice see Nash, "Intercultural Community on Klamath Reservation" in *Social Anthropology of North American Tribes*, p. 381; Gatschet, *Klamath Indians*.

[221] Stoutenburgh, *American Indian*, p. 283.

According to Rose, she "ran like a deer, her long black hair streaming behind her in the wind." She appeared to be about fifteen years old, small and graceful. Carson vowed that she was the prettiest Indian he had ever seen. "I'm goin' to make a dicker for that gal," he told Rose. "I'll have her if it takes the best horse I've got." He would give much more than that for Waa-nibe, the girl called Grass Singing. Shortly before Carson's encounter with Grass Singing, Shenwa—an Iroquois trapper attached to Work's brigade working southeast Oregon—had attempted to have her. It cost him two horses and his life when he was killed by Short Man, Grass Singing's brother. Carson eventually paid a horse, five North West blankets and a new Hawkins rifle for the privilege of her hand in marriage.[222] This marriage was terminated when Carson's Paiute wife was killed by the Arapaho.

Awhile after this tragic incident, Carson was sent to Washington D.C. where in 1847, he was invited to a gala affair at Senator Benton's home. It soon became apparent that he was very ill at ease. After questioning, Kit revealed that he was afraid that it was wrong for him "to be among such ladies" when they might not like to associate with him if they knew he had an Indian wife. Although embarrassed, Carson was staunchly loyal to his dead mate, saying: "She was a good wife to me. I never came in from hunting that she did not have the warm water ready for my feet."[223]

Others were equally proud of their Indian companions but none more so than Joe Meek. One of the most passionate attachments was that between Milton Sublette's former wife and the "Merry Mountain Man." Sublette's marriage to Mountain Lamb, whom he called Isabel, gave him the distinction of being one of the first Americans to marry a Shoshoni girl. This was of great importance for it linked Sublette with Red Wolf, thus giving Rocky Mountain Fur a distinct edge in trade relations with the Snake war tribes. However, this advantage would be shortlived. In the winter of 1833-34 Sublette made the mistake of riding

---

[222] Marsh, James B., *Four Years in the Rockies*, pp. 92-94. Carson later married fifteen year old Josepha Jaramillo, sister to Maria Jaramillo, wife of Charles Bent, a trader who established Bent's Fort on the Arkansas River in Comanche territory and the most important fur trade center in the Rockies.

[223] Fremont, John Charles, *Memoirs of My Life*, p. 74.

with a Crow war party into a Snake ambush. He took a musket ball through his right leg which was so badly shattered that he had to be sent to St. Louis for surgery. Word came back in the spring of 1834 that his leg had been amputated. Sublette would never again return to the mountains.

Before leaving, Milt got Meek's word to take care of Isabel and their "little lambkin" until he returned. This placed Meek—who had never taken an Indian wife—in a dilemma. The trouble was that the woman Meek found so attractive was the wife of his close friend and brigade leader. Now that Mountain Lamb was put under his protection it posed a serious problem. Shortly after Sublette's departure, Meek found Mountain Lamb and her baby freezing in a snow storm. Stripping off his heavy blanket coat, which left him naked to the waist, Meek wrapped this around Mountain Lamb and her baby to keep them warm, placed her on his horse and sent her to Red Wolf's camp. Mountain Lamb would be forever grateful for this act of kindness but her baby would die of exposure on the ride to her father's village. It is recorded that the winter of 1834 was the worst the American fur companies had ever witnessed in the west.

Everyone in the mountains expected daily to receive word from Sublette sending for Mountain Lamb. It did not arrive. Then one day she walked into Meek's camp carrying all her worldly possessions. Her sole remark was "he has found a white woman" and handed Meek a letter from Sublette. Actually, he hadn't. He wrote that he was invalided with cancer and would be dead within a year. The letter concluded by giving Mountain Lamb to Joe with Milton's blessing.

Meek was jubilant. Sublette, while kind to the girl still treated her like a squaw. Meek would treat her like the princess she was and this would get him into much trouble. Mountain Lamb usually wore a short skirt of beautiful blue broadcloth and a bodice and leggings of scarlet cloth. Like all Indian women she also rode a horse astride like a man. Needless to say this caused considerable comment and much speculation on the gentlemen who viewed her.

One day an Irishman named Ben O'Fallon rode into camp. From his temperament this may have been Major Benjamin O'Fallon, ex-Indian agent for Louisiana Territory and a known trouble maker. As early as 1822 he was stirring up anti-British feeling among the Americans at a very high level. In a letter to John C. Calhoun, Secretary of War, he

351

Courtesy of the Oregon Historical Society, OrHi 3474.

Joe Meek, c. 1853.

would liken Hudson's Bay traders to "greedy wolves, not satisfied with the flesh, they quarrel over the bones." He would further claim that Hudson's Bay Company was inciting the Indians against Americans and furnishing them with "the instruments of death and a passport to our bosoms." It was his belief that American scalps "are now bleeding on their way to the British trading establishments." Through William Clark, Secretary Calhoun assured Major O'Fallon that he would check into the matter. A congressional committee would determine that O'Fallon had been exaggerating the threat of Hudson's Bay Company.

Whatever, O'Fallon rode into Meek's camp with two Ute prisoners he had bought—so he claimed—announcing they were his personal slaves. When the Utes escaped in less than two days after he arrived, O'Fallon accused Mountain Lamb of freeing them and announced publicly he was going to "horse-whip Meek's squaw." The whole camp turned out as he strode toward Meek's lodge carrying a shot-loaded whip.

Mountain Lamb saw him coming and slipped out of the lodge and came around to the front. "Coward!" she said with a toss of her braids, "You whip? Would you dare whip the wife of Meek if Meek were here? Meek is not here to kill you but I will!" At this she pulled a pistol from the folds of her skirt. O'Fallon, not completely ignorant, realized she meant business. Sweating and begging for his life, he let the Indian girl run him out of camp which won her the approval of every man in the brigade.

When nearly sixty, Joe Meek would remember Mountain Lamb:

> She was the most beautiful Indian woman I ever saw, and when she was mounted on her dapple gray horse, which cost me three hundred dollars, she made a fine show. Her hair was braided and fell over her shoulder, a scarlet silk handkerchief tied on hood fashion, covered her head; and the finest embroidered moccasins her feet. She rode like the Indians, astride, and carried on one side of the saddle a tomahawk for war and on the other the pipe of peace.

The name of her horse was "All Fours." His accoutrements were as fine as his rider's. The saddle, crupper and bust girths cost one hundred and fifty dollars; the bridle fifty dollars and the muck-a-moots fifty dollars more.[224] All of these articles were ornamented with fine cut glass beads, porcupine quills and hawk's bells that tinkled at every step. Her blankets were of scarlet and blue and of the finest quality. Such was the outfit of the trapper's wife, Umentucken.[225]

According to Meek's daughter, Olive, Mountain Lamb's bridle was covered with Mexican silver dollars.[226]

Prior to the run-in with O'Fallon, Mountain Lamb had a narrow escape from the Blackfeet. While picking berries with other trapper's wives on the Yellowstone River, a Piegon war party rushed the women and caught several. Mountain Lamb ran for the river and jumped in with bullets slapping the water around her head. A strong swimmer, she reached the opposite bank and took cover, thus eluding capture. Meek was mighty proud of his "handsome Lamb for she had plenty of spunk."

Another time on Powder River, a party of trappers were running buffalo. The women followed with travois and pack mules to bring in the meat. Mountain Lamb and her helpers had butchered out several cows and were on their way back to camp. Enroute, Mountain Lamb's pack mule balked because of a slipped pack saddle. As always when in Indian country, the men rode ahead on the lookout for danger with the women bringing up the rear. Meek in his usual gabby manner was engrossed in a tall tale with the advance party and unaware his wife had lagged behind. Before she could catch up twelve Crow warriors appeared out of nowhere and surrounded her.

---

[224] Muck-a-moots is probably a misspelling of the Shoshoni word maishoo-moe-goots, meaning a saddlebag they used for putting crickets and grasshoppers into after gathering them. Mountain Lamb used hers to store trinkets and knick-knacks which couldn't be crowded on the decoration of her horse or herself.

[225] For more on Sublette, Meek and Mountain Lamb see Victor, *The River of the West*, p. 175; Vestal, *Joe Meek*, pp. 160-166; Berry, *A Majority of Scoundrels*, pp. 249, 282, 290, 317-18.

[226] Statement of Joe Meek's daughter, Olive Branch Riley, quoted in Fred Lockley, *Oregon Folks*, Chapter II.

By that time Meek had missed her and with six other trappers rode back to see what the trouble was. Topping a ridge, Meek saw Mountain Lamb encircled by her enemies who had stripped her and were dividing her clothes among them. In blind rage Joe laid spurs to his horse and galloped into the middle of the Crows. This charge startled the warriors giving Meek a momentary advantage. Losing no time, Meek killed the first brave he saw. As Mountain Lamb dashed for safety, two more braves went down before the rest escaped. Once again Mountain Lamb had cheated death.

Then in 1836, a tragic series of events would shatter the Meek's love affair forever. A few days after Kit Carson had married Grass Singing, Jim Bridger could see the old gang breaking up so he married a Flathead girl. This union didn't last long. To the embarrassment of her father, she returned to his lodge. In an effort to make amends, the Flathead father gave Bridger some horses—as it turned out, horses stolen from the Robber Snakes—he had gotten from the Nez Perce. Unfortunately, a Banattee war party spotted the stolen horses in Bridger's camp. No explanation asked; none given. In the fight which followed, Mountain Lamb took a kinsman's arrow through the chest killing her instantly and leaving Joe with an infant daughter.

This baby whom Joe had christened Helen Mar after a heroine in the Jane Porter novel *Scottish Chiefs*, a romance much admired among literate mountain men—would play her part in the shaping of Oregon history. Repercussions from this raid were quick in coming. Being the granddaughter of Red Wolf, her mother's death brought a temporary split in the powerful Snake war tribes. Red Wolf severed all relations with Sweet Root—Pash-e-co—the powerful prophet-head chief of the Robber Snakes and specifically he was out to wreak vengeance on Walking Rock, the Robber war chief.[227] This family feud lasted for nearly a decade.

With an infant daughter to take care of Meek, in desperation, married a Nez Perce woman. Soon after, Doc Newell married her sister thus

---

[227] Walking Rock (Oderie or sometimes called Omr-shee, war chief of the Banattee (Robber) Snakes is often confused with Rock Way (Ora'ibi), the equally powerful head chief of the Sheep Killer (Took-a-rika Snakes) who was killed in 1845.

making him and Joe Meek brothers-in-law. Helen Mar's new step-mother soon tired of trapper's life and in 1839 she walked out on Joe. In the process she also kidnapped his baby girl. When Meek got Helen Mar back, he took her to the Whitman mission (established the same year Mountain Lamb was killed) for a proper upbringing. Narcissa Whitman would describe Helen Mar as "Meek's sullen little creature. Twice as savage as any full blood, she was as venomous as a wounded rattler, as verminous as a Cayuse dog."

Meanwhile, Bridger was having his share of matrimonial woes. After his Flathead wife left him, Bridger was looking for a more stable companion when he spotted "a pert little Eutaw (Ute) girl" and he, too, entered the Shoshoni clan in 1836. A loving and faithful companion, it appears that the rigors of time took their toll on Jim's "pretty little Ute girl." Thirteen years later, a traveler stopping at Bridger's fort on Black's fork of Green River would say of Mrs. Bridger: "She is a stolid, fleshy, round-headed woman, not oppressed with lines of beauty."[228]

Shortly after this unflattering description, Mrs. Bridger died in childbirth leaving Jim—besides three older children—an infant daughter Virginia whom he kept alive by feeding her buffalo milk. Now in the same predicament as Meek, Bridger again went wife hunting. He found his third wife, Rutta, a Shoshoni girl, in the lodges of Gourd Rattler's tribe. Jim would call her Mary Washakie.[229]

Jack Robertson, a Snake country trader who persuaded Jim to build Fort Bridger, also married a Shoshoni girl. Known to all the trappers as "Madame Jack," she was the niece of the powerful Banattee prophet, Sweet Root. Because of his intimate association with the Snake war tribes, Robertson—better known as "Uncle Jack Robinson" served as interpreter and scout for the First Oregon Cavalry during the Shoshoni war. During this campaign, Robertson was instrumental in preventing Sweet Root from burning Fort Bridger. Robertson was the only early day trapper who spent his complete life in the country that would become Wasco County, Oregon Territory.[230]

---

[228] Vestal, *Jim Bridger, Mountain Man*, pp. 164-65.

[229] Alter, J. Cecil, *James Bridger*, pp. 101, 518-20; Vestal, *Jim Bridger, Mountain Man*, p. 112.

[230] Trenholm and Carley, *The Shoshoni*, pp. 95-96, 191, 203.

Tom "Broken Hand" Fitzpatrick, the celebrated Rocky Mountain Fur partner, at age fifty married Margaret Poisal, the daughter of Snake Woman and a Hudson's Bay Company trapper. At the time, Margaret was serving as an interpreter for the U.S. Army. Because of their difference in age, Fitzpatrick—suspecting she would outlive him—provided in his will for any child born within nine months after his death.[231]

Jim Baker, another prominent Snake trader, was married to a Big Lodge girl. At age twenty one, Baker accompanied Bridger into Green River in 1839 beginning his education as a Snake country trapper. In the spring of 1841, Baker was sent into the northern Rockies to warn Bridger of a Sioux uprising and found him west of the Laramie mountains just inside the border of Shoshoni territory.[232] Here, he also found and married Little Traveler—Me-at-eet-se. Baker, yearning for the good life, moved his wife and family into the Colorado boom town of Denver City. Before her 10th child was born, Little Traveler, depressed with city life, returned to the Shoshoni where she remained until her death.[233]

The fur trappers adopted everything about Indian life; dress, morals, attitudes, skills, language frequently and religion fairly often. And along with the benefits of the Indians' good life they also took over some of the disadvantages. Mainly, they were thoroughly exploited as economic resources and looked down upon by the "civilized" whites and an Indian wife was not considered an asset.

No one who actually saw the Indian maidens of the fur trade era failed to comment on their beauty. Most native women dressed more neatly and washed more often than the average white woman of the time. Back in civilization, only the daughters of the wealthy knew what perfume was. Every Indian girl made her own. Among most mountain and plains tribes with the exception of the Shoshoni—and this would change with the arrival of the white men—the girls began experimenting with sex at an early age. Furthermore, they enjoyed it. Such enjoyment was forbidden by both morals and religion to the women back on the

---

[231] Hofen, Le Roy R. and W. J. Ghent, *Broken Hand, the Life Story of Thomas Fitzpatrick*, pp.220, 261-62.
[232] Chittenden, *American Fur Trade*, Vol. I, p. 400.
[233] Mumey, Nolie, *The Life of Jim Baker 1818-1898*, pp. 206-33.

other side of the Mississippi. No, never pity the mountain man because he lacked the genteel and uplifting companionship of white women.

CHAPTER 41

ABSENT WITHOUT LEAVE

*In looking to the interests which the United
States have on the Pacific Ocean. . . the
propriety of establishing a military post at
the mouth of the Columbia river. . . is
submitted to the consideration of Congress.*

The Hon. Caleb Cushing
Committee on Foreign Affairs

Now back to Pierre's Hole and the rendezvous of 1832. The New England ice merchant wasn't the only newcomer to Snake country. Sometime after Wyeth's arrival on the Columbia, Benjamin Bonneville—captain of the 7th U.S. Infantry Regiment—marched into Fort Nez Perce with 110 men, as motley and savage a crew as the Snakes through whose hunting grounds he had just crossed. When Bonneville made known his desire to enter the fur trade, Pierre Pambrum, chief clerk at this outpost, soon spread the word and Bonneville received no help from the Hudson's Bay Company. For that matter, the Rocky Mountain Fur Company already pushed to the wall by the American Fur Company, refused any cooperation also. It was soon deemed that Bonneville's venture was another American failure. Perhaps not. There is convincing evidence that Captain Bonneville was on a mission of espionage for the U.S. government.

A fugitive from the Napoleonic wars, Benjamin Louis Euloilie de Bonneville—known to the Shoshoni as Bald Head—was a graduate of the West Point class of 1815. For some unexplained reason, the War Department granted a 26-month leave of absence running from August, 1831, to October, 1833, during which time Bonneville was to explore Oregon territory. This was to include the natural history of the region, climate, soil, geography, topography, mineral production, geology of the various parts of the country as well as the character of the local Indian tribes. What wasn't mentioned was ferreting out secrets of British activity in the Columbia Basin. It appears the army was unaware of his actual instructions as later confirmed by his court martial.

On the surface, Bonneville was to engage in the fur trade. Over a two year period his trapping, if it could be called such, amounted to nothing. The army gave him no money yet expenses were contributed by private individuals. Bonneville's main backing came from Alfred Seton, one of the original Astorians and a group of anonymous gentlemen with a strong presumption that one of these was John Jacob Astor himself.

When Bonneville arrived at Green River in the fall of 1832, pulling twenty loaded wagons, it was believed that his mission was to prove that wagons could be taken across the divide at South Pass. This seems unlikely since Bill Sublette had preceded him by several days and word of this accomplishment had already been dispatched to the Secretary of War. However, Bonneville got credit for piloting the first wagons over South Pass but he was still 800 miles short of reaching the Willamette Valley. In his push from Fort Osage on the Missouri River, Bonneville had hired as field lieutenants Michael Cerre and Joe Walker. Tough, experienced brigade leaders, both men had been involved in the Santa Fe fur trade and Cerre had worked the upper Missouri for Astor's American Fur.

First on the agenda was construction of a fur-trading post that would never see use. History books call it Fort Bonneville; the mountain men called it Fort Nonsense. From this outpost Joe Walker was dispatched to the Pacific coast while Bonneville with the main party drifted into the head of the Salmon River and eventually into Fort Nez Perce on the Walla Walla River dutifully mapping the location of the various forts and other points of importance. Apparently Bonneville was not overly concerned about the accuracy of his maps. At Fort Bonneville, he got the longitude wrong by about 125 miles; but he only missed his position in the Salmon river country by 50 miles. On these wanderings, he picked up the 10-year-old Enos—nephew to Gourd Rattler—as a guide.[234]

---

[234] *The Wind River Rendezvous*, Vol. XIV, No. 2, June 1984.

Meantime, Walker recruited forty free trappers, including Joe Meek, and headed into the desolate country northwest of Great Salt Lake.

In this crossing of the Great Basin, Walker was not out to make friends. He even skirmished with the totally unaggressive Earth Eaters. Meek, reporting on this incident, quotes Walker as saying, "we must kill a lot of them boys" and that they did. Firing point-blank into a mass of curious Indians, Walker's party "massacred about twenty-five of the miserable creatures." Later, Bonneville would express "horror" at Walker's action.[235] After this show of arms, Walker at least had the good sense to rely on Meek's advice to alter his course which was taking him into the hostile Ochoco and follow a starving course into California. After much wandering, Walker's party became the first whites to see the awesome valley of Yosemite.

Somewhere in this probe, Walker had to have crossed the trail of the Hudson's Bay Company partisan John Work. At about the same time Walker left Green River, Work led one hundred men, women and children through Central Oregon into northern California via Warner Valley. Because of an earlier incident, Work had no desire to trap the Ochoco. On January 10, 1832, Sasty—a Snake warrior who had served as Ogden's guide into Shoshoni country—was fatally shot at Fort Nez Perce by a Cayuse brave. The word was soon out that The Horse—Red Wolf's capable war chief—would annihilate foreigners, white or red, foolish enough to enter Shoshoni hunting grounds; and Horse was in an exceptionally bad frame of mind. Burning Ember—his mother—had died in the summer of 1832 from the white men's dreaded mountain fever.

On his return from California in the spring of 1833, Work gambled and dropped off Amity McTavish to work the southern Blues. It was a high-stakes bet that paid off. McTavish was not bothered by Shoshoni or Americans for he was accompanied by three grizzly bears named Old Blue, Little Blue and Pepper.

---

[235] For more on Bonneville's thrust into Oregon see DeVoto, *Across the Wide Missouri*; Irving, *Adventures of Captain Bonneville*; *Dictionary of American Biography*, Vol. II, p. 438; Carey, *A General History of Oregon*, Vol. I, pp. 269-72; Bancroft, *History of Oregon*, Vol. I.

By now, Bonneville was also making a name for himself. Whether deserved or not, the historian Bancroft would vilify his reputation with the printed word. Among other barbs he would claim Bonneville "was in his coarse way a bon vivant and voluptuary" (Bancroft's high class way of saying Bald Head was fond of wine, women and song). To make certain everyone got the point, he would explain that "every fortnight a new unmarried wife flaunting her brave finery would enter his tent." Bonneville himself would admit that during his wanderings he acquired among other mementoes of the mountains a Nez Perce wife. . . "not a young giddy girl that will think of nothing but flaunting and finery but a sober, discreet, hard-working squaw." Finally, Bancroft would question, "what were the far-off natives. . . doing that this reckless, blood-thirsty and cruel Frenchman should. . . kill them?"

It will never be known what Bonneville's real purpose was in coming to Oregon. But it is interesting to note that when he returned from this excursion he did not report to Washington as might be expected but went directly to Astor's mansion in upstate New York. It appears the military wasn't fully advised as to what Bonneville was to accomplish. Whatever, he overstayed his leave and was dismissed from the army but was quickly reinstated by the Commander-in-Chief, President Andrew Jackson. Even an admiration for maps (especially of Bonneville's calibre) would hardly have justified a full pardon for a grave military offense.

Within five years the Committee on Foreign Affairs would recommend the establishment of military posts in Oregon Territory;[236] and in 1852 the old Hudson's Bay post of Fort Vancouver underwent intensive development as a U.S. military base under the command of—Colonel Benjamin Bonneville.

---

[236] Cushing's *Report on the Territory of Oregon*, dated January 4, 1839. House Document No. 101, 25th Congress, third session.

CHAPTER 42

HAS NO HORSE

A lone lodge tops the windy hill;
A tawny maiden mute and still,
Stands waiting at the river's brink,
As fond as you can think;
A mighty chief is at her feet.

Joaquin Miller
Bard of the Ochoco

In the fall of 1832 as Milton Sublette guided Nathaniel Wyeth to the Malheur River; Jim Bridger attempted to elude King McKenzie's bloodhounds; and Joe Walker was staging a massacre on the Earth Eaters, Captain Bonneville blundered into a Snake hunting camp on the Salmon River. With his usual luck, he arrived at a critical time.

A mixed band of Bear Killer, White Knife and Big Lodge families were engaged in a final buffalo hunt before their return to the Ochoco. A few hours before Bonneville's arrival they had been attacked by a 150-man Blackfoot war party, accompanied by several women to make the Snakes think they were peaceful. The northern raiders were repulsed and driven into a grove of willows. Led by The Horse, the defenders fired the prairie and almost roasted the enemy alive. When the Blackfeet tried to escape, the Shoshoni chased them three miles across the valley toward the timber at the base of the Sawtooth Mountains. In this running battle the Blackfeet lost forty warriors and five women, the Shoshoni only nine. Among the nine was The Horse.[237]

---

[237] Phillips, Paul C., *Life in the Rocky Mountains; a Diary of Wanderings on the Sources of the Rivers Missouri, Columbia and Colorado from February 1830 to November 1835*, pp. 185-90.

Bonneville found them mourning their loss. The Horse—according to the Shoshoni—was believed to have possessed a charmed life making him invulnerable. In past battles he had managed to deflect bullets of the "surest marksmen." His being killed did not cause the Shoshoni to lose faith for they maintained that the bullet was not lead but a piece of horn. Despite the death of Horse and eight comrades, the Shoshoni continued their daily routine inviting Bald Head to join them in the final buffalo hunt of the season. To give an idea of the power of a bow, Bonneville would record that he saw an Indian shoot his arrow completely through the body of a buffalo cow where it struck the ground beyond.

After the hunt, the Shoshoni let loose with the all important victory dance over the fallen Blackfeet followed by an evening of feasting and bragging. They told the captain of their unstable alliance with the Pahkee horse thieves and how the treacherous Blackfeet had "drenched their villages in tears and blood!" Bonneville and his nervous crew were relieved when "the braves gradually calmed down, lowered their crests, smoothed down their ruffled feathers, and betook themselves to sleep without placing a single guard over their camp."[238]

News of Horse's death spread on the autumn wind, alerting all inhabitants between the Cascades and the Rocky mountains that bad times lay ahead. Now, with the exception of Red Wolf and Hiding Bear—both of whom were content to let passion take its course—there was no one with sufficient influence over the dog soldiers "to restrain the wild and predatory propensities of the young men." To the dismay of the fur traders, they became troublesome and dangerous neighbors "openly friendly for the sake of traffic (in arms) but disposed to commit secret depredations and to molest any small party that might fall within their reach."[239]

Meantime, deep in the heart of the Blues, the weak and the infirm kept a nervous vigil for the return of their tribesmen. Everything depended upon the outcome of the hunt for the abundance of wild game or the lack thereof could spell the difference between life and death. To

---

[238] Irving, *Bonneville*, pp. 206-209.
[239] Irving, *Bonneville*, pp. 126-27.

ensure that this arrival would be fruitful, the Ancient Ones—medicine men now too advanced in years to straddle a horse—were praying to the gods of the hunt. For days the council ground had echoed to the monotonous roll of the medicine drums and the sing-song cadence of the aged chanters each dressed in a skin and headdress of an animal of the hunt. Soon their prayers would be answered.

In a blinding December snowstorm, the hunters arrived at the main Snake encampment in the Ochoco Valley. For many this became a moment of frenzied joy for at last their loved ones had returned home. For others it began an eternity of grief. As the shouting crowd gathered around the victorious warriors and their meat laden horses, a Tussawehee woman clutching her infant daughter to her breast, vainly searched the passing line of warriors for some sign of her husband.

Many women had traveled with the party for they did all the skinning and preparation of the meat along with other camp chores. Because Nana'wu—Little Striped Squirrel—had been expecting her second child when the hunt was organized, she had been forced to remain behind. This was in observance of a time honored Shoshoni custom which forbid a woman to touch cooking utensils or in any way help with the preparation of food during her period of confinement. Therefore, she would have been just so much excess baggage on a trip of this nature.

By now the dog soldiers were parading around camp so that the home bodies upon seeing proof of their valor might scream and faint over the trophies of war. . . the torn scalps of Sioux, Pawnee, Arapaho, Crow and Blackfoot dangling like limpid guidons from their bloody coup-sticks. Frantically, the young mother watched the familiar faces file by. . . saw several women adorned in mourning. . . a young warrior with a white stripe painted across his upper cheekbones and over the bridge of his nose. . . something had happened to his father. Then came the awful realization. . . her husband would not return. The tragic news was soon circulating camp that Old Deer Running had lost a son and Red Wolf a war chief believed to have been impervious to gun-fire. This was a bad omen.

The Horse—prime target for a Blackfoot musket ball—had joined his ancestors in the grassy valley of the Salmon River and there on a platform high above the reach of Ishaui, the wild dog, he awaited his summons to the spirit land. Horse, little more than thirty years old, had been a rich man by Shoshoni standards, owning hundreds of fine ponies. According to tribal custom his property went to his male next-of-kin. Having no son, the great horse herd now belonged to his brother, Deer Fly.[240] By tribal law he left nothing to Little Striped Squirrel but the memory of his love and the clothes on her back. In practice it did not work that way. Little Striped Squirrel now became a member of her brother-in-law's family provided for and protected as one of his own. There she could remain for the rest of her days or until she decided to remarry.

To help dull the shock of losing her husband, Little Striped Squirrel began preparing for her next ordeal. As the time of birth drew near, she retired to a secluded spot on the headwaters of the Ochoco River. . . there to bring forth her child unassisted. And there she would remain alone for another three weeks to a month providing her subsistence as best she could. When the appointed time had elapsed, Little Striped Squirrel would then consider herself purified and be allowed to join her friends again.[241]

During the time when the British and American fur traders would celebrate the beginning of a New Year—the Shoshoni called it the Moon of Small Tracks—Little Striped Squirrel gave birth to a son in a lonely lodge overlooking the ice-choked Ochoco River.[242] A son who in

---

[240] This man was known to the Canadian trappers as Mauche de daim which literally meant "fly of the deer."

[241] For more on this custom see Bancroft, *Native Races*, pp. 436-37. Meriwether Lewis comments on the ease of delivery with reference to childbirth among the Shoshoni. He mentions one Shoshoni woman who had been helping the Corps of Discovery transport its baggage and had halted at a little stream. He inquired of the chief as to the reason. The latter informed him that the woman had stopped to deliver her fourth child and would soon overtake the party. In about one hour she appeared with her newborn babe apparently as well as ever. See O. Farrell, "Medical Aspects of the Lewis and Clark Expedition," *Oregon Historical Quarterly*, Vol. VI, No. 3, p. 219).

[242] Chochoco's descendants would testify that Has No Horse was born in the Ochoco Valley by the stream which name the settlers would bestow upon him. In 1878 Has No Horse in conversation with Capt. Henry Wagner at Fort Bidwell would state that he was born on a creek three days ride to the north, meaning some 200 miles. Wagner interpreted this to mean a creek east of the

manhood would blaze across frontier history as the leader of the Paviotso Confederacy. Looking at the glistening mountains surrounding her, the white-cloaked valley in which she stood and the frozen torrent from which this land had taken its name, it is easy to believe that Little Striped Squirrel would have been tempted to name him for this beautiful spot.

When a Shoshoni child is born, whether a boy or a girl, it is called "baby" . . .afterwards by any childish name until, if a boy, he goes to war. Then, if he counts coup, he is named for something that has happened on the journey or for some accident, some animal killed or some bird that helped him succeed. Normally, over his lifetime, a Shoshoni warrior would take three names. But mothers no matter what the color of their skin have and give special names to their children and always remember them by such.

Little Striped Squirrel would have smiled at the tiny one cradled in her arms thinking how proud his father would have been. Then a painful thought would occur. The Horse would be very saddened this day as he looked down from the spirit world for he who had owned more ponies than any man in the White Knife tribe had left his son destitute for his vast herds now belonged to Deer Fly. Her next thought must have been "poor little man without a horse." Whatever the circumstances, she would call her son cho'cho'co—Has No Horse.[243]

Unlike so many, baby Chochoco would keep this name (although altered into Ochoco by the first Central Oregon settlers) for the remainder of his stormy life whether by choice or by chance will remain a

---

garrison and so it was recorded. (Captain Henry Wagner, 1st Cavalry to Assistant Adjutant General, March 11, 1878, Letters Received, Office of Indian Affairs, Oregon Superintendency.) At the time, Has No Horse was hiding out from the army to keep from being placed on the Malheur Reservation and it is doubtful that he would have made an effort to correct Wagner's mistake.

[243] Notice the similarity in pronunciation between chochoco (show-show-ho) which means "a walking person or a person who has no horse" and Ochoco (ooo-she-hoo) meaning "red willow." Unable to distinguish, the whites quite naturally called Has No Horse "Ochoco" or as his name was most often spelled in military records, "Ochiho" and thus was entered on the reservation rosters and how his descendants now spell their name.

. mystery. It would be nice to think that the savage war chief held on to this name in memory of the Indian mother who so proudly bestowed it upon him.

And so, while John Work's 1832-33 Snake Expedition forged north toward the southern Blues from their California raid, cursing the wind, the snow and the lack of game, an uncomplaining Indian woman gave birth to her son in a frost covered lodge on the Ochoco River; a boy who would take the scalp of an American soldier before his seventeenth birthday.

CHAPTER 43

THE BOSTON WHIRLWIND

He says he came. . . to make a business of
curing salmon. . . and it is impossible for
us to say. . . if these are his views or not.

Dr. John McLaughlin
Letter to Gov. Simpson,
October 29, 1832

The autumn of 1832 found Shoshoni Country in a state of confusion. While a pregnant Shoshoni girl waited expectantly for a husband who would never return, thus throwing a road-block into the inland fur trade, Rocky Mountain brigades were probing the Ochoco to steal pelts from the British. Ignoring this intrusion, Hudson's Bay was sending trappers into California to wrench furs from the Mexicans. American Fur was negotiating a peace treaty with the Blackfeet in an effort to pilfer hides from both companies. The suspected U.S. military spy was cavorting around the Sawtooth Mountains aiding the Snakes in a buffalo hunt and making no attempt to snare beaver. And the New England merchant was eagerly homing in on the Columbia to toss a wrench into the British fur monopoly.

Near five o'clock on the evening of October 14, 1832—some two months before Little Striped Squirrel went into labor—a thirty-year-old Boston speculator trudged into the Hudson's Bay Company post on the Walla Walla River. As one historian put it, "now he was amongst the dragons that guarded Oregon's gates." Following in his footsteps were eight bedraggled men; all that remained of the glorious cavalcade which entered Shoshoni land in early summer. After the struggle across the Blues where his men—suffering from exposure, dying of starvation, withstanding Indian attacks—deserted in great numbers including his brother Jacob who had come along as company surgeon, Nat Wyeth held little fear of the British "dragons."

Somewhat to his surprise, Wyeth was "received in the most hospitable and gentlemanly manner" by Pierre Pambrum, chief clerk at Fort Nez Perce. Pambrum, a lifelong company man described by Simpson (who had an opinion on all of his employees) as "an active, steady dapper little fellow" may have been friendly but he was also wary. During Wyeth's five-day stay at the outpost, Pambrum dispatched a fast oarsman downriver to alert McLoughlin of this new development. Meanwhile, Wyeth drank to his friends "from the waters of the Columbia mixed with alcohol and eat of a buffalo cow." Wyeth was well on his way to being a mountain man.

By month's end, Wyeth arrived at Fort Vancouver where he expected to find his supply ship anchored in the Columbia. It wasn't. Wyeth was shocked to find the British not only civilized but the outpost stocked with books and men who could and did read them. They also read newspapers. McLoughlin was fully aware that Wyeth had strong ties to Hall Jackson Kelley.

Kelley, a Boston teacher, had been enamored with Oregon for fifteen years before Wyeth's arrival on the scene and was one of the higher-pitched voices of Manifest Destiny. In 1818, he conceived the idea of founding a new republic of civil and religious freedom on the Pacific coast. Ten years later he presented a memorial to Congress on the subject including a plat for a city at the mouth of the Willamette River where Portland now stands. By 1829, Kelley had organized the American Society for the Settlement of Oregon Territory and had signed up 400 emigrants for that purpose—among them Nathaniel Jarvis Wyeth. Lacking financial backing, Kelley had to momentarily give up the idea but by 1832, Wyeth—abandoning the American Society for Settlement—struck out on his own.[244] McLoughlin was aware of Kelley's fervent dream. As early as March, 1831, McLoughlin had seen an article in a Boston paper of Kelley's plan to colonize the Willamette Valley. McLoughlin had more knowledge of his New England visitor than the visitor knew.

---

[244] For more on Hall J. Kelley, see *Dictionary of American Biography*, Vol. X, p. 297; Carey, *A General History of Oregon*, Vol. 1, pp. 259-62; Scott, *History of Oregon*, Vol. 1, pp. 199-201; *Oregon Historical Quarterly*, Vol. II, pp. 381-99.

Though given a warm welcome, McLoughlin was not taken in by Wyeth's "salmon pickling" story. Wyeth arrived at Fort Vancouver around noon on October 29, 1832. Before nightfall McLoughlin had a letter on its way to Governor Simpson in Canada stating that he believed Wyeth was up to more than what met the eye. He was right. Beside salmon, Wyeth—knowing tobacco was an important part of the fur trade—was contemplating cultivating it in Oregon. Like it or not, Wyeth was going to be hard to get rid of. Word arrived that his depended-upon supply ship, the *Sultana,* had broken up on a reef and sinking took with her the last of Wyeth's hopes for a foothold in Oregon. Now he was completely destitute, without men, without supplies and without prospects having lost most of his capital.

Undaunted, he immediately began devising plans for a second expedition to Oregon country. Wyeth was also determined to start a Columbia River fishing and trading company in competition to Hudson's Bay Company which would include the export of pickled salmon to the Hawaiian Islands. Against his better judgment, McLoughlin agreed to let Wyeth stay at Fort Vancouver until he could get passage back to the states. Wyeth then went so far as to write to Governor Simpson to receive financing. Although Simpson didn't want to alienate American-British relations, he was not about to accept this offer. On February 3, 1833, McLoughlin placed Wyeth with a Hudson's Bay Company brigade bound for Flathead House. From this outpost, Wyeth began to heckle Rocky Mountain Fur and lay plans for a second Oregon expedition.

During this period, Kelley—the Boston Moses—was enroute to Oregon by way of New Orleans and Mexico. He, too, was having bad luck. All his supplies were confiscated by the Mexican government for non-payment of import duties.

In a whirlwind of wheeling and dealing, Wyeth reentered Snake country in the late spring of 1833. Attaching himself to a thousand Flatheads driving nearly two thousand horses before them, Wyeth headed for the Green River rendezvous. On this southward push, he found some of Bonneville's men who told him that Bonneville was still in the Salmon River country. Wyeth's always flexible plans took another turn. He dispatched an express inviting Bonneville into a partnership to trap the country south of the Columbia—in short, the Ochoco. In fact, Wyeth planned to work as far south as San Francisco, never once considering that Hudson's Bay and the Mexican government might have different plans.

When he finally contacted Bonneville on July 4, the latter apparently agreed to the proposition. However, something happened to change his mind. For unknown reasons, Bonneville backed out of the deal. Perhaps he could foresee diplomatic constraints placed on British-Mexican-American relations or maybe Wyeth's plan didn't correspond with his government mission. At any rate when Wyeth and his Indian escort arrived at Bonneville's camp, a Hudson's Bay Company brigade under Francis Ermatinger was already there and undoubtedly Ermatinger would notify McLoughlin of this latest proposed infringement on Company hunting grounds.

From Bonneville's Salmon River camp, the two groups travelled together to Green River already overflowing with American trappers and Snake gun-buyers. For the next few days Wyeth was busy negotiating a contract with Rocky Mountain Fur Company whereby all trade articles would flow through him by way of the Columbia River. According to Wyeth, he could deliver $3,000 worth of trade goods from a supply depot on the Columbia River for less than $5,000; just half of what Sublette was charging for delivery out of St. Louis. This sounded good to Rocky Mountain Fur and they accepted. With that finalized the various fur companies fanned out for the fall hunt.

Wyeth was now travelling momentarily with Fitzpatrick and Robert Campbell's brigade. Near the mouth of the Malhuer River, they ran into four men from Bridger's brigade who had recently ran afoul of a Snake war party. One of the party named Thompson had taken a musket ball through the head just below his eye where it passed downward and lodged behind his ear in the neck. While knocked out, an arrow was shot into the top of his shoulder which penetrated almost six inches into his chest. Thompson was not in good shape. According to Wyeth another member of the party, "Charboneau" chased the Snakes on foot. This man may have been one of the most famous half-breeds in American history: Baptiste Charbouneau, the child born to Sacajawea who appears in the Lewis and Clark journals as the baby Pomp who spent the winter of 1805 at Fort Clatsop, the first American settlement on the Pacific Coast.

However, the most excitement of the year would happen in mid-autumn. To start the ball rolling, a man named Guthrie in Henry Fraeb's

Rocky Mountain Fur brigade was struck by lightning. As reported by Joe Meek, Fraeb rushed out of his tent shouting, "Py gott, who did shoot Guttery?" Meek's answer was "Gawd a'Mighty, I expect: He's firing into camp." That was just the first salvo.

Three hundred miles to the west in the heart of the Ochoco a gentle wind rippled the short tufts of bunch grass dotting the level top of Twelve Mile Table. On the western rim overlooking Crooked River, forty lodges stood stark and white against the deep blue of the chill evening sky. All was quiet for the inhabitants were watching the scene below. A Hudson's Bay Company fur brigade was setting up camp in the bottom land. Some six hours later the forces of heaven were unleashed.

On November 13, 1833, from midnight to dawn Ermatinger on Crooked River, Wyeth on the Missouri, Bonneville in the Big Horns and everyone else who happened to be awake were scared half to death by what astronomers called the most brilliant meteoric shower in history. Named the Renoids, it consisted of some 200,000 shooting stars bombarding western America from outer space, possibly from the constellation Leo. This one-night event so disturbed the Sioux that on their calendar the year 1833 became known as Wicarpioki-camna—When the Stars Were Falling.

Back on Twelve Mile Table a baby's cry shattered the dawn stillness. The Hudson's Bay Company brigade would hear the first sound made by a man whose cry would chill the blood of every white man, woman and child between the Cascades and the Rockies in the years to come. During the Renoids a Shoshoni woman had given birth, perhaps induced by this event. It seems prophetic that blazing meteors introduced an Indian child who would become a personality almost as unusual as this visitation from outer space. To the Shoshoni he would become revered as Paluna—the War Spirit. To the Americans he would become feared as Paulina—the Brutal Devastator.

Ironically, another child was born that night. As one of an elite group of women prophets, she would take the name Falling Star. She would also become the wife of War Spirit.

By the time spring of 1834 arrived, Wyeth, who had returned to the States, found new financing and the brig, *May Darce*—stocked with trade goods and supplies—was sailing toward the Columbia River. Loaded with additional trade goods, Wyeth was back on the scene.

Milton Sublette, his principal ally in this venture, had been forced to return to St. Louis because of his infected leg when only ten days out on the plains. In his absence Wyeth would be torpedoed by Milton's big brother, Bill. He arrived in Idaho in July in time for the rendezvous only to find the fur companies in turmoil. The Yankee trader was doomed to see another of his grand notions explode into nothing.

Rocky Mountain Fur Company was in dissolution and unable (or unwilling) to fulfill the guarantee to purchase his supplies. When Wyeth produced the 1833 contract, Fitzpatrick blandly told him that Rocky Mountain Fur had decided to give its business to Bill Sublette. On this, Wyeth threatened to return to St. Louis and to file suit against the company. Bridger then told Wyeth he had an agreement alright with Rocky Mountain Fur but "there ain't no more such company. . . this outfits Bridger, Fitzpatrick and Sublette, all licensed and legal." At this point according to Meek, Wyeth snapped back, "Gentlemen, I will roll a stone into your garden that you will never be able to get out!" And he did.

In cold anger, he rebuilt Hunt's old supply cache on the middle Snake River into a permanent fur trading post. On August 6, he christened it with "a bole of liquor" and named it Fort Hall after Henry Hall, his principal backer. Leaving some of his men and all trade goods there, he headed directly to Fort Vancouver where he sold the post at a loss to the Hudson's Bay Company bringing the British monopoly into the heart of the territory Rocky Mountain Fur had been fighting for. From that ideal position, John Work began stripping the country of all fur-bearing animals. Before 1834 drew to a close, Hudson's Bay Company took in more than 98,000 pelts worth some 320,000 dollars in hard cash. In the following three years it reaped a total of 307,180 pelts. Unfortunately for all, the hide war was lowering profits. It was also playing havoc with company receipts. A blanket which customarily produced ten or twelve beaver pelts was only getting five; and the hot item, trade guns, were only bringing in at best, six hides. Wyeth's trade war was producing fruit.

In retaliation, Fitzpatrick staged an invasion of his own and moved into eastern Oregon, acknowledged Hudson's Bay territory and learned firsthand just how well organized and controlled his rivals were. Confused in the unfamiliar valleys of the Ochoco, Fitzpatrick made his first mistake when he refused an offer from McLoughlin of a company guide to escort him back to the Snake River. Soon he discovered that no Shoshoni or free trappers would sell furs to him. Fort Nez Perce refused to sell him supplies. As a consequence his men were reduced to eating their horses and, as winter set it, he lost men and animals in crossing the snow-choked Blues. It was not a profitable venture.

Back at Fort Vancouver, McLoughlin was having his share of internal problems. To start things off Meredith Gairdner, post physician, risked his neck—not to mention the company's peaceful existence with the Chinook nation—to steal the skull of Chief Concomly. He then sent it to England where it was lodged in a London museum for the next 117 years. Burnby Bell, secretary of the Clatsop County Historical Society, managed to get the skull returned from England in 1953. Then in 1956, under $1,000 insurance, it was mailed to the Smithsonian Institution for study.[245] Today it is the most popular object in Astoria's Flavel House museum.

Concomly's skull was a minor concern compared with what was happening to the north. While Wyeth was busy constructing Fort Hall, Chief Trader Ogden—assigned to Alaska duty—was ordered to abandon Fort Simpson on the Nass River and set up a trade with the Indians on the Stikine River. Ogden who had gotten along fairly well for three years with the Nass Indians was now walking a political tightrope. Competition from the Americans, who were plying the local natives with liquor added another danger to the situation. On the last day at Fort Simpson, Ogden decided to fight fire with fire. He authorized his medical officer, John Kennedy, to sell the Indians all the rum they could

---

[245] Suzan Shown Horjo—executive director of the National Congress of American Indians, based in Washington, D.C.—has this to say about state-sanctioned grave robbery: "Some of my own Cheyenne relatives' skulls are in the Smithsonian Institution today, along with those of at least 4,500 other Indian people who were violated in the 1800s by the U.S. Army in an 'Indian Crania Study'. . . . At the infamous Sand Creek massacre many Indian bodies were decapitated and their heads shipped to Washington by freight. Some had been exhumed only hours after being buried. Imagine their grieving families' reaction on finding their loved ones disinterred and headless." The ordinary American would say there ought to be a law—and there is, for ordinary Americans. But then, they are not archaeological property of the United States.

pay for. That was on the morning of August 30, 1834. Dr. Tolmie (Ogden's Russian interpreter) would record in his journal that this was a big mistake: "... some of them getting intoxicated were very turbulent from noon until sunset, when we embarked, we were all under arms in momentary expectation of having to fight our way on board or being butchered on the spot."[246]

Ogden and crew finally made it on board the company brig *Dryad* by leaving behind a cask containing 25 gallons of Indian rum. But their troubles were not over. Attempting to enter the Stikine River they found the passage blocked by a Russian gunboat. An international problem was now brewing. After nearly being killed by drunken Nass Indians and threatened by the Russian navy, Ogden set sail in early October for Fort Vancouver.

Three weeks before Ogden's departure from hostile waters, Nat Wyeth stomped into Fort Vancouver on September 14. He brought with him Jason and Daniel Lee, the Methodist missionaries; the scientists Thomas Nuttall and John Kirk Townsend; and John Bull who became Oregon's first schoolmaster. If this disturbed McLoughlin, he did not let on. Besides, he had some cheerful news for his American competitors. Wyeth's supply ship, the *May Darce,* had been struck by lightning off the coast of Chile and had to put into Valparaiso for repairs. His first ship, the *Sultana,* had been lost in a storm off the Oregon coast; now, the second had been struck by lightning. The Chinook sea-gods were trying to tell Wyeth something but he wouldn't listen.

Ogden wasn't faring much better. A trip that normally took eight days would stretch into an eternity. After eight weeks of struggle against head winds and laboring in wild Pacific storms, the little brig was still at sea. It would be December 14 before she dropped anchor in the Columbia at Fort Vancouver.

By the end of October, McLoughlin was anxiously awaiting Ogden's arrival when another sick and penniless group of Americans hailed the Fort. Not particularly wanted, this group was led by Ewing Young, the Santa Fe trader and Ogden's old opponent. Seeing the handwriting

---

[246] From Dr. Tolmie's Journal, reprinted in Binns, *Peter Skene Ogden: Fur Trader*, pp. 266-67.

on the wall, Young was the first to quit the mountains. In May, while touring California, Young ran into the Oregon evangelist—and Wyeth's original backer—Hall J. Kelley, now on the dodge from the Mexican government. Kelley soon persuaded Young to try his hand at farming in the Willamette Valley. And so, Young and Kelley with twelve others plus a pack string of horses and mules arrived at Fort Vancouver on October 27, 1834, adding to McLoughlin's problems. Welcomed as horse thieves, Young remained under a cloud of suspicion for years after he took up a homestead at the foot of Chehalem Mountain.

Neither did McLoughlin trust Kelley. Aware of his connection to Wyeth, he stuck him on the first outbound ship for Hawaii. But by 1836, Kelley was again agitating Congress for settlement of Oregon so the Chief Factor didn't gain much breathing space. Young wasn't contributing much to his peace of mind either.

Within three years, Young had organized the Willamette Cattle Company. Then, with fourteen buckaroos (three of whom were Snake Indians), he started the west's first cattle drive into the Oregon country. In 1837, Young arrived in the Willamette Valley with 800 head of Mexican longhorns which he sold to the farmers at $7.75 a head. Not only did this make him a leader in the Oregon community but also the wealthiest man in the territory.[247]

While waiting for the *May Darce* to arrive, Wyeth began construction of Fort William on Sauvies Island under the eagle eye of John McLoughlin. Here, he established the Columbia River Fishing and Trading Company. As promised, his sell-out of Fort Hall to Hudson's Bay Company was causing drastic changes in the U.S. fur companies. In an effort to present a united front against the British company, Rocky Mountain Fur and American Fur buried the hatchet and divided the trapping grounds east of the Rockies agreeing to respect the territory of the other. In short they had to join forces to survive.

Even so, Wyeth wasn't through with stirring up trouble. Shortly after Ogden arrived back on the Columbia on December 14, 1835, Wyeth

---

[247] Some accounts claim that Young only brought in 600 head of cattle. For more on Ewing Young see, *Dictionary of American Biography*, Vol. XX, p. 627; *Oregon Historical Quarterly*, Vol. XXI, pp. 171-315, Vol. XIII, p. 182; Cleland R G. *This Reckless Breed of Men*, pp. 209-45.

took to the Ochoco. A real character, on his march up the Deschutes River, he issued bayonets for repelling Shoshoni attacks and bugles for signalling back and forth among the peaks of the Blues. No one had told him that trappers of the same company often worked hundreds of miles apart. Anyway, his bugles had the desired effect. The Shoshoni were convinced that the white barbarian was mentally unbalanced and his motley crew arrived at the present site of Bend, Oregon, on January 5, 1835, without mishap. Backtracking to the Metolius River, he traded for supplies with a Snake encampment and by January 29 was back at Warm Springs where he began his plunge into the interior.

Red Wolf kept a respectful distance as Wyeth's grand brigade tooted its way across eastern Oregon. There wasn't a brave in the whole Shoshoni nation foolish enough to risk his personal medicine against a group of deranged white men who packed their scalp knives on the end of gun barrels. And thus Wyeth arrived at the 1835 rendezvous without suffering a Snake attack. Neither did he have much to offer in the way of furs which is probably just as well.[248]

The old West was changing rapidly. In the midst of the 1835 rendezvous' drinking, brawling and gambling, missionaries showed up to convert the Indians to Christianity. No missionary ever made even a half-hearted attempt to convert the trappers. But one of them, a skilled surgeon named Dr. Marcus Whitman who was on his way to die in Oregon territory, did remove the Blackfoot arrowhead Bridger had been carrying in his back for years.

During this, Nat Wyeth's salmon pickling kettle—under head brew-master Lawrence Carmichael—was turning out whiskey in defiance to Hudson's Bay. To ensure that he received no competition from the American quarter Wyeth had, in the spring of 1834, tipped off a federal agent that King McKenzie was operating a distillery at Fort Union. This was the straw that broke Astor's hold on the fur market.

For years American Fur had been paying off a number of government officials to keep McKenzie in business. Less than a year before Wyeth squealed on him an uproar had been raised when McKenzie

---

[248] Background on Wyeth can be found in *Dictionary of American Biography*, Vol. XX, pp. 576-77; Clarke, Samuel A., *Pioneer Days in Oregon Country*, Vol. I, pp. 277-85; Fuller, George W., *A History of the Pacific Northwest*, p. 181.

kidnapped and imprisoned a rival trader named Le Clerc. Then a letter from Tom Fitzpatrick to General Ashley telling of his robbery by the Blackfeet had been leaked to the press, exposing the fact that one of McKenzie's men led the Blackfoot attack. The distillery was the death blow. Acting on this information, the federal watchdogs belatedly came to the conclusion that the King of the Missouri was carrying the theories of free enterprise a little too far.

American Fur managed to save its license but only after a desperate fight by Daniel Webster and Thomas Hart Benton, the company's hired men in Congress. Even so, McKenzie had to be rushed out of Indian country and packed off on a long vacation to Europe. The formidable John Jacob Astor was also wounded. This unwanted publicity left such a bad taste in Astor's mouth that he dissociated himself from the fur trade entirely, selling out to Ramsay Crooks in the fall of 1834.[249] The gigantic monopoly now shattered, Crooks began splitting up the American Fur Company into small individual firms in 1835. Beyond doubt, Nathaniel Wyeth had "rolled a stone" into the western fur trade that would see its final demise.

It was believed if the American trapper could be discouraged from drifting west of the Rockies then so would be the settler. To the surprise of everyone, it was a religious movement which brought the downfall of the all-powerful Hudson's Bay Company.

With his typical flair for stirring up trouble, Wyeth had introduced the first evangelists to Oregon territory the previous summer. The Green River rendezvous of 1835 had seen a major crack in the flood-gates. That same year, a young showman named Phineas Taylor Barnum was taking the east by storm. He came into the world on July 5, 1810, in Bethel, Connecticut, a straight-laced community where the price of a

---

[249] Ramsay Crooks was born in Scotland in 1787 and died in New York City on June 6, 1859. One time owner of the American Fur Company, Crooks occupies a high place in Central Oregon history which he does not rightfully deserve. Crook County was not named for this man nor was it named in honor of his son, Colonel William Crooks, an official of the Union Pacific Railroad who died at Portland, Oregon on December 17, 1907. Through no fault of the Crooks family, this has become a common belief among the inhabitants of Crook County.

cuss word—if overheard by a church official—was forty lashes. Indians and Hudson's Bay Company traders alike had best beware.

CHAPTER 44

GOD IN HIS WISDOM CREATED THEM ALL

> *. . . there are a great many*
> *Indians in Oregon territory that*
> *will have to be civilized; and*
> *though I am no missionary, I*
> *have no objection to helping in that.*
>
> **Wilson Morrison**
> *Emigration of 1845*

"Let there be light among the heathen," intoned the preacher, "and let us pacify them while we're at it. White people may be wanting to go to Oregon." One Methodist Bishop put it more bluntly, "We will not cease until we have planted the standard of Christianity high on the summit of the Stony Mountains."[250]

What caused all this religious fervor? Unfortunately, the Indians themselves though certainly not intentionally. In late summer of 1832, a delegation of Nez Perce and Flathead Indians appeared in St. Louis—bewildered and totally unfit for their mission—looking for General William Clark simply because he was the only white man they knew in the so-called civilized world. By sign language which was poorly interpreted, they communicated to Clark that they had come to secure "religious instruction." What the Indians wanted was not salvation. They were desperately seeking knowledge and the Nez Perce-Flathead delegation had hoped to get the jump on the Shoshoni-Blackfoot alliance by courting the white medicine chiefs.

---

[250] De Voto, *Across the Wide Missouri*, p. 9.

All Indians on the North American continent had been impressed with European trade goods. Rifles, pistols, knives, saddles, liquor, cloth, mirrors, tools. . . were a mystery to them. Pacific Northwest natives soon deduced through contact with Hudson's Bay Company's half-civilized French and Iroquois trappers that white power was centered in the white man's religion the same as Indian power was centered in Indian religion. Therefore, the white man must have superior medicine and superior gods who accounted for the white man's power. Following this line of thought, Ignace La Mausse, an Iroquois trapper, became an apostle to the Nez Perce. It was Big Ignace's glowing words which sparked this 2,000 mile trek to obtain knowledge not of prayers, psalms and worship but of arms, steel and industry.

The tragedy of this great pilgrimage and its unexpected outcome lay in the eastern press. Supposedly quoting the Indian spokesmen, headlines screamed: "Savages search for Book of Heaven." Apparently no one saw fit to entrust heathens with the Bible for the attached copy to the headlines in which various reporters outdid themselves in interpretation read: "You make my feet heavy with gifts. . . yet the book is not among them; when I tell my poor blind people. . . that I did not bring the book, no word will be spoken; my people will die in darkness. . . no white man's book to make their way plain. . . ."[251]

There was probably good reason for not supplying Indians with the printed record. If put to the test, missionaries sent out to convert the heathen could hardly point to the blood-spattered pages of religious history as proof of the superiority of their divine beliefs. Yet, how could anyone refuse to send the light of salvation to these poor, supplicating Indians? Not the Methodists nor any other red-blooded young missionary in the United States.

However, since such things take time, it wasn't until the summer of 1834 that Jason Lee—pious, determined and Calvinist—arrived in Oregon territory tagging along behind Nat Wyeth's pack train. He was fully prepared to wage a hard war on heathenism for it was rumored that a "sect of fanatics called Mormons" were already taking over Inde-

---

[251] Ibid.

pendence, Missouri in their rush to get west of the Rockies in search of the lost tribe of Israel.[252]

Jason and Daniel Lee founded the first Protestant mission west of the Rocky mountains on the Willamette River some ten miles north of Salem under the protective arm of Hudson's Bay Company. McLoughlin, which he would later regret, offered them every possible assistance that he could. It soon became apparent that Lee's main purpose—more important than saving the souls of a few miserable savages—was the settlement and building of a state.

At the time of the U.S. missionaries arrival, there were only two churches in Oregon country. The Roman Catholic which had no priest and the Royal Hawaiian both located at Fort Vancouver. At this time McLoughlin—baptized in the Roman Catholic faith but who, for the next half century, would live and practice the faith of the Established Church of England—read the service of the Church of England to his officers at the fort.

So, while the servants of God understood the Nez Perce to be yearning for the heritage of Moses, Christ and the apostle Paul, what they really wanted was the knowledge of Jake Hawken, Eleuthere DuPont and Sam Colt. On that piece of misunderstanding, the missionaries within the next ten years convinced the red brother of two things—not only were they out to steal his land but they were also establishing squatter's rights on his immortal soul. This bit of claim-jumping was to stir up bloodshed. While not as spectacular as the Skull Hollow massacre of 1845, it would gain a thousandfold more publicity.

Deeply religious in their own way, the Indians were not taking to this interference kindly. It took a special breed of men to perpetrate this infringement and few were forthcoming. Those who qualified were Joab Powell, an untutored Baptist missionary; the Reverend Samuel Parker, a Congregationalist doctor of divinity; and a handful of Jesuit priests.

Joab Powell, less than six feet tall but weighing over three hundred pounds, was of that rare school of ministers known as circuit riders. Strong as a bull, he soon convinced the unbelieving that he could be gentle and kind for all his power and bulk. Powell couldn't read (he

---

[252] Berry, *Majority of Scoundrels*, p. 359.

memorized the Bible) or write, but he rode throughout Oregon territory telling of the wonders of God.[253] He commenced all sermons by saying, "I am Alpha and Omegay" —the beginning and the end. Once when acting as chaplain of the Oregon Legislature he gave the invocation thus: "Lord, forgive them for they know not what they do."[254] But it was not so much the words he used but his voice which brought both white and red to the faith. When Brother Powell sang a hymn everyone listened. Even the rowdy mountain men became reverent in his presence. Soon his voice became known as "the harp with a thousand strings," for it could be heard for a distance of two miles on a quiet day. With the aid of this natural gift he wooed and won the Indians.

Rev. Samuel Parker at 54 was an old man by western standards when he applied for Oregon missionary work in the summer of 1834. Fired with missionary zeal after reading accounts of the Indian's search for "the white man's Book of Heaven," he offered himself as a volunteer to take the word of God west. Parker arrived at Green River rendezvous in the summer of 1835 with the Whitman-Spalding group. Parker alone—the others being interested only in the forty lodges of Nez Perce and Flatheads present—moved cautiously among 2,000 Snakes (by Whitman's count), winning them over with sincerity and kindness. This would be his approach throughout his career and the Snakes came to trust him and ultimately some would share his religious beliefs.

Realizing the futility of trying to make white men out of red men, the Jesuits long schooled in the missionary field were sticking solely to religion while keeping their noses out of Indian internal affairs. However, their rigid doctrine of what constituted mortal sin was hardly compatible with Indian lifestyle. Even so, the priests were making gains having converted some six thousand natives to the faith during the first six years of work in Oregon territory. The paganistic rituals and colorful ceremonies of the Roman Catholic church appealed to the Indian's sense of the dramatic. In short, the natives came to regard the priests as religious men and the Protestant ministers as the vanguard of the white

---

[253] Information on Powell from an interview with his granddaughter, Effa Powell Calbreath.
[254] Blankenship, *And These Were Men*, pp. 121-37.

plague. Because of this, the priests were soon placed in the same class as the Indians themselves—not to be trusted.

The Jesuits were accused of nurturing the desire to keep the Indians ignorant, the more easily to exercise their "priest craft" on the benighted savages.[255] This accusation gained great popularity during the 1840s. The explanation was simple. All the priests wanted to accomplish was to make the savages better people—but still remain Indians. The failure to grasp this rather fundamental point was the reason for the many and tragic failures made by others in the field of Indian education.

In 1883 Senator George Vest of Missouri visited many Indian schools. He reported back to Congress in 1884: "In all my wanderings last summer I saw but one ray of light on the subject of Indian education. I am a Protestant—born one. . . educated one. . . and expect to die one—but I saw that the system adopted by the Jesuits is the only practical system for the education of the Indians and the only one that has resulted in anything at all."

On the minus side of the ledger there was Jedediah Strong Smith, Jason Lee and the Rev. Henry Harmon Spalding to name but a few.

Smith, "the praying mountain man," tried to make the Indians believe that he carried the key to heaven in one hand and a one-way ticket to hell in the other. He proved the latter on several occasions but at least he offered a choice.

The Rev. Jason Lee could give a damn less about the heathens plight. Lee had been detailed west to set up a mission for the Flatheads. When several Flatheads and Nez Perce visited him at the 1834 Rendezvous anxious to have the missionary or some of his party stay, Lee politely shook hands with them, said he might be back in two or three years and promptly set out for the Willamette Valley with Wyeth. At the time, it was something of a mystery as to why the missionary to the Flatheads moved so quickly on. That was soon solved. All his efforts in Oregon were not for soul saving but for empire building. He was not overly tolerant of his white congregation either.

Emigrants who had to depend on The Dalles mission under the capable leadership of Lee's nephew, the Rev. Daniel Lee, had little good

---

[255] For more on Catholics see O'Hara, *Pioneer Catholic History of Oregon.*

to say about the hospitality received. Usually arriving in a sick, starved and destitute condition, they would be refused help of any kind. Elisha Packwood—a member of the 1845 emigration—had this to say about the Mission: "When it came to sheer heartlessness, avarice and a desire to take advantage of the necessities of the immigrants to the utmost, the Mission at The Dalles exceeds any other institution in the Northwest."[256] This is a strong charge but a check of the records from 1838 to 1850 will satisfy anyone that what Packwood said was true.

Then there was the Rev. Spalding who saw little but eternal damnation for his red brothers. Perhaps he had reason. Spalding was an unhappy and bitterly disappointed man. Not only in the missionary field was he overshadowed by Dr. Marcus Whitman but it was Spalding's fiancee, Narcissa Prentiss, a physical beauty, who became Whitman's vibrant bride at the advanced age of 28. Narcissa was not cut out to be a missionary to the Indians of Oregon or any other heathen for that matter. While the Whitmans honeymooned in the next tent on Green River in 1836, Spalding's second choice wife, Eliza Hart, a plain, quiet girl prone to sickness was too ill to get out of bed and see the assembled Indians.

On the other hand, Whitman saw nothing but good in the Indians. A deeply religious man, Whitman was not a doctor of divinity but a doctor of medicine and in this field the Indians considered him slightly ignorant especially when a Cayuse medicine man apparently beat him at his own game. Each of these men in his own way told the Indian that his way of worship and appeal to the Great Spirit, the way he lived, his outlook on life—everything he did—was sinful.

The missionaries zeal did not stop at bringing the word of God to the heathen. They were determined to make them one of the upper five hundred or die trying—which some almost did. In an attempt to civilize them, the missionaries misjudged how far they could push the Indians when it came to cramming white culture down their throats and the red men in a final showdown turned on such men as Spalding and his associates blaming them for all of their troubles from running sores to unanswered pleas to the Great Spirit.

---

[256] Excerpt from Morse, *Washington Territory 1868.*

Adding to this strained situation, wagon trains began plodding across Indian hunting grounds, leaving death in their disease-ridden wake. It is said without exaggeration that fatalities along the Oregon Trail were so numerous the emigrants averaged one grave every 200 feet between the Missouri River and the Willamette Valley.

In 1846 when Whitman met with the Shoshoni in the John Day Valley, he should have gained some insight into their religious beliefs. During the effort to gain converts, he talked to Weasel Lungs, their equivalent to a medical doctor. The old man explained that to the Shoshoni the only great sin was desecration of their hunting grounds. In their minds plowing the land was the same as wounding the earth which provided all of their material needs. He also noted confusion in Whitman's message for it appeared to him that the white man's creed was "the fear of dying" while the Shoshoni believed "in the joy of living." With deep-rooted faith such as this—at least from the missionaries viewpoint—Indian salvation was beyond redemption.

CHAPTER 45

THE LAST BRIGADE

I can state with undiminished confidence,
that the Snake country towards the Rocky
Mountains is and will be rich in furs for
generations to come.

Alexander Ross
Winter of 1813

.

With religious turmoil hovering over the territory, 1836 arrived in a state of convulsion. Cholera swept the land from the Pacific Coast to the crest of the Rockies hitting Christian and pagan alike. Originating in India, it was the third trip around the world for the Asiatic plague—a highly malignant intestinal disease often terminating in death. Striking hard in the ranks of the Snakes, one of the first to succumb was Old Deer Running—grandfather of the infant Has No Horse—whose wife had been taken by the epidemic in 1832.

Neither was it confined to the lodges of the Snakes. By early autumn cholera had swept across the United States and on October 3, 1836, claimed the great war chief of the Fox tribe, Black Hawk. Four years before his death, this man with 40 warriors of the Sauk and Fox nations had handed Major Stillman, with his 270 crack Kentucky riflemen, the most humiliating defeat of the Blackhawk War.

During the epidemic while trappers died in the mountains, easterners were extolling the virtues of a new patent medicine which sold under the name of "Dr. Miles Compound Extract of Tomato." Regrettably, it did little to relieve the symptoms of cholera. Today we call it ketchup.

Down in Comanche country a handful of Texans escaped the plague by getting massacred at the Alamo; in the process Texas gained independence from Mexico, promising more bulk to U.S. possessions. Nine years later the promise would be fulfilled.

Back in Oregon territory, as if it needed more upheaval, Red Wolf's daughter, the Mountain Lamb, was killed by a Banattee horse rustler causing a diplomatic split in the Snake war tribes. As Mountain Lamb lay dying, the apostle Whitman was establishing a mission on the Walla Walla River within spitting distance of Fort Nez Perce. Whitman would be allotted eleven years to complete his salvation of the Indians—hardly enough time for such a strenuous task.

Rendezvous 1836 is hardly worth mentioning except for the arrival of Narcissa Whitman and Eliza Spalding. With the Snakes in a surly mood and beaver scarce the grand carousal had lost its luster. The ceaseless slaughter of fur-bearing animals had taken its toll. Coupled with the new fashion of silk hats, the margin of profit in beaver hides was dwindling fast. Prime beaver had dropped to four dollars or less a pelt though goods from the settlement still sold at the same outrageous prices. A pint of coffee, sugar, cocoa or flour sold at an average of two dollars and this at a time when the most expensive dinner in the States could be had for fifty cents. More essential commodities such as guns, powder and ball, flints, bear traps, beaver traps, blankets and handker-chiefs sold at enormous profits to the suppliers. And the real necessities such as a jug of diluted alcohol brought four dollars a pint, while chewing tobacco sold for two dollars a plug.

In the old days at rendezvous trappers had lived like lords. It was nothing for a single trapper to blow a thousand dollars in a couple of days of riotous living. But the days of glory were past. Only the coarse-haired animals such as wolves, bear, elk and buffalo were bringing in any money at all. Although a few independent trappers like Bridger, Meek and Carson still clung on, the two big outfits, Hudson's Bay and American Fur, had complete control of the fur industry. By now with Nat Wyeth's Columbia distillery pumping it out by the barrel, the whiskey trade was going full bore.

The traders operated on the theory that the coming of the settlers meant the ruination of the fur country and the end of the fat profits they made from the natives. Although the fur supply was already on the decrease, it was still big business. To protect it, the whiskey runner not only supplied the Indian with liquor but incited him to attack white settlements and wagon trains. In this manner he hoped to keep Oregon country free of whites, full of Indians and to add more money to his growing bankroll. And grow it did. Ogden once made the statement,

"We Indian traders cannot afford to give supplies to the Indian for free. Before this happens a wonderful change must happen." Yet it goes on record that one trader secured six thousand dollars in furs for a single iron file. This they could afford to do!

At the 1837 Wind River rendezvous there were few beaver to trade. Among those present was Sir William Drummond Stuart, captain in the British army and a veteran of Waterloo.[257] According to him, "1833 was the last good year in the mountains for in 1834 came the spoilers, the idlers, the missionaries and the seekers after money." Sir William would be further disappointed this year.

Wandering into rendezvous was the 27-year-old Dr. William Gray—physician and lay missionary—accompanied by four white women who heeded the call of God.[258] These fair-skinned ladies caused considerable uproar among the Indian lads but not as much as the arrival of Wooton's brigade. Dick Wooton, veteran trapper, had been severely wounded in a skirmish with the Snakes. At that he fared better than his partner, LaBonte. In trying to escape the Snakes, Wooton's brigade ran into their allies, the Utes and LaBonte was killed. According to the survivors, the Utes cut the flesh off LaBonte's bones, roasted it over a fire and ate it.[259] It can be guessed that the lady missionaries seriously questioned just what they had volunteered for.

While the Utes were dining on LaBonte, the old trapper Ewing Young was scouring the mesquite thickets of California rounding up long horns for the west's first cattle drive into Oregon. One of his partners in this venture was none other than Chief Factor John McLoughlin which tells something about the condition of the fur market.

---

[257] Victor, *The River of the West*, p. 238.

[258] Dobbs, *Men of Champoeg*, pp. 93-97. Gray, the son of a Presbyterian minister, first came to Oregon in 1836 with Whitman and Spalding. He helped form the Provisional Government in 1843 and was a member of the Provisional Legislature. He entered the sawmill business and wrote a *History of Oregon*. Buried at Astoria in 1889, his remains were later removed and placed beside those of Dr. and Mrs. Whitman at Waiilatpu (the Whitman Mission).

[259] Coutant, Charles G., *The History of Wyoming*, Vol. I, p. 698.

By spring 1838 more changes were in the offing. Jason Lee, having wooed and won Anna Pittman, celebrated his honeymoon by establishing a Methodist mission at The Dalles—western gateway to the Ochoco, Red Wolf's undisputed domain.[260] Those God-fearing souls at the mission included Ben Wright whose experiments with strychnine would bring on the Modoc War.

Hand in glove with mission building, typhoid fever took up residence in the mountains. Among those dying were Swooping Eagle (Tobe), Shoshoni guide for the Lewis and Clark expedition and Blue Bird (Chosro), the maternal grandmother of Has No Horse. Twisted Hair, head chief of the Banattees, was shot—whether by Red Wolf or Joe Meek is unknown—but the Shoshoni oath of "blood for blood" had been satisfied repairing the rift in the Snake war tribes precipitated by the murder of Mountain Lamb at the hands of a Banattee brave.

Further disruption was forthcoming when the U.S. government dispatched Co. J.J. Abert (Chief, Bureau of U.S. Army Topographical Engineers) to complete the job Captain Bonneville should have accomplished. Abert spent the summer of 1838 mapping eastern Oregon from the summit of the Blues to the California-Nevada border. Dodging Snake war parties, the survey was not entirely accurate and within six years, M. Mofras (attache of the French legation to Mexico) would map the same area in the summer of 1844.

By spring of 1839, the fur trade was in a state of collapse. The last rendezvous ever held in the far west took place at Green River but it was only a mockery of the past. In October 1839, staging a last-ditch effort, a detachment of Hudson's Bay Company trappers under the leadership of a grizzled veteran, Tom McKay, bored straight into the Ochoco. At the northeastern base of a glowering butte eight miles from the present city of Prineville, they pitched camp on the edge of the dark, quiet waters of Crooked River. "Tomorrow," McKay solemnly

---

[260] The Dalles was officially named Dalles, Nov. 5, 1851. The name was changed to Wascopam on September 3, 1853. This was the name of the Chinook tribe living there at that time and means "Makers-of-small-bowls-made-of-horn." On March 22, 1860, Wascopam was renamed "The Dalles City" which has now been shortened to The Dalles. (McArthur, *Oregon Geographic Names*, pp. 721-22.)

vowed, "the beaver will catch hell." Hardly had this promise been given when the chill evening air was rent by the hunting call of the Shoshoni pack.

McKay's brigade had been sighted as it moved up Willow Creek, crossed the head of Newell (now called Newhill) Creek and worked down McKay Creek toward the lower Ochoco Valley. Messengers well in advance of his trappers had carried the word into Wolf Dog's camp on the upper reaches of the Ochoco River. With missionaries constructing log churches on two sides of their territory and the white man's sickness entering their lodges, the Bear Killer and White Knife Snakes were in no mood to be tampered with.

McKay had barely started up Crooked River when the battle-scarred Wolf Dog led a pack of hot-blooded young braves across the mountains towards McKay's line of march. On that late September evening Wolf Dog taught his young students the artistic execution of a pre-dusk attack. Throughout the night their soul-tearing shrieks were punctuated by the throb of the victory drums which the welcoming committee used to guide them home. Morning had dawned cold and clear before the raiding party joined the celebrants in the Ochoco Valley. Another party some twenty miles to the southwest was not so lucky. Only McKay and the indestructible Joe Delore had escaped.[261]

Yes, times were hard in the Blues. A month before McKay's ill-fated push into Crooked River, Steve Meek—Joe's older brother—turned scalp hunter when he joined up with James Kirker's company of some 200 men, made up of American trappers, hunters, Indians and half-breeds headed for Mexico.

Born in Ireland, Kirker—called Don Santiago by the Mexicans—came to the U.S. when he was seventeen. During the 1820s, he engaged in the fur trade on the upper Missouri where he trapped and fought Indians. By the 1840s, Kirker was serving as scout and interpreter for wagon trains headed west. Between times, Kirker hunted Apache scalps for bounty in the pay of the governor of the northern Mexican states of Chihuahua and Sonora—the going rate being set by the

---

[261] As remembered by early settlers of Crook County and members of the Delore family, this event took place in the vicinity of Hat Rock on Powell Buttes. The buttes were named for descendants of the circuit rider, Joab Powell.

authorities at one hundred dollars for a man's, fifty dollars for a woman's and twenty-five dollars for a child's scalp.

The Apaches became a nuisance when Comanche invaders shoved them off their ancestral hunting grounds. These outcasts had to survive and survive they did. By the late 1830s, Apache raids on Mexican villages and farms had become so widespread and devastating that they wiped out whole villages. And so contemptuous were the Apaches of the Mexicans they dared to attack Mexican herdsmen and farmers on the very outskirts of the capital city of Chihuahua itself. They drove off herds of sheep, cattle and horses, slaughtered the Mexican men and took captive the women and children.

Unable to stop the raids with the military forces at their command, the Mexican authorities engaged the enterprising Kirker to organize his company and hit the Apache trail. The demand for beaver skins and the price paid for them had diminished to such an extent that hunting Apache hair was a far more lucrative business.

Kirker's band was large and more than able to cope with the Apaches. Acquainted with every water-hole in the arid southwest, Kirker knew just where to find his Apache and the bloody business prospered. In fact at times the scalp hunters brought back so many bales of scalps that the Mexican authorities could not—or would not—pay the promised bounty. But as soon as the barbarous business ceased, Apache raids increased and the scalp hunters would be recalled.

Other trappers were also changing occupation. Their numbers dwindled with the trade itself and most of them who survived settled down at last on frontier farms—although few were satisfied with such a drab existence. A few months after Steve Meek's change of profession, Doc Newell turned to guiding wagon trains west along with his brothers-in-law Joe Meek and Caleb Wilkins—all of whom had married Nez Perce sisters.

This is what the fur trade had degenerated into. Hudson's Bay was now concentrating on Alaska fur and American Fur, pulling back onto the plains, was collecting buffalo hides. For both company's managers it was a bad choice. McLoughlin would suffer great personal sorrow while Ramsay Crooks would be forced to break up his company to avoid bankruptcy.

Hudson's Bay shipped McLoughlin's son to Russian territory to establish trade on the Stikine River, which Ogden had failed to do in 1834. In April, 1842, John McLoughlin Jr. was murdered by his own men at Fort Stikine.

The Russian-American Fur Company was also feeling the heat. Fort Ross, the only Russian settlement in California and the colony founded to extend Russia's fur trade into Oregon territory, had become unprofitable. When opportunity knocked in 1841, the company sold Fort Ross for 30,000 dollars to John Sutter, who the year before had become a Mexican citizen. This transfer of title came with the full blessings of Governor Juan Alvorado who was getting tired of British, American and Russian trappers trespassing on Mexican soil.

Less than two generations had passed since Ross made his observation in 1813; and in that period the fur trade had flourished and died. The day of the trader was over but that of the emigrant had just begun.

Appendix A
LIST OF SHOSHONI NAMES

LIST OF SHOSHONI NAMES

The following is a list of the known Shoshoni who fought to protect the Ochoco from American invasion

TRANSLATION	NAME	OTHER INFORMATION
Always Ready		Signed Bruneau Treaty 1866.
Annette Tallman	Odukeoi	Daughter of Tall Man, resident of Prineville, born 1859; mother killed by Warm Springs scouts along the John Day River in 1859.
Arrow	Ouray	Head chief Northern Utes 1859. Part Apache.
Bad Face	Wobitsawahkah; Winnemucca the Younger; Mubetawaka, Poito	Son-in-law to old Winnemucca (One Moccasin), The Giver of Spiritual Gifts; wife Tuboitonie; surrendered June 1868; poisoned 1882.
Beads		War chief Bannock War; shot 1878.
Bear Claw	Honaunamp	Hung at The Dalles 1855.
Bear Hunter	Honauka	Chief; shot 1863.
Bear Skin		Medicine chief killed by the Arapaho in 1824. Father of Little Bearskin Dick.
Big Man	Oapiche; Oulux; Oualuck; Youluk; Howlock; Howlark; Nampa; Bigfoot; Chickocclox; Starr Wilkerson	Married Running Deer 1864; married Rainbow Woman 1867; shot 16 times in 1868 and survived; disappeared in 1869.
Big Porcupine	Muinyan	Red Wolf's war chief.
Big Rumbling Belly	Kwohitsauq	Medicine chief; father of White Man; grandfather of Wovoka (The Cutter).
Big Water	Pahwuko; Yahuskin (Water Belly)	Head chief; died in 1816.
Biting Bear	Haune Shastook; Annoyed Bear; Irritated Bear	Signed 1865 treaty; shot 1868; Always Ready's war chief.
Black Beard	Toomontso	Man Lost's war chief.
Black Buffalo	Chocktote; Chewhatney; Chatchatchuck; Chewhatne; Chokkosi; Sahtootoowe; Chocktoot; Tchaktot; Chowwatnanee; Chacchackchuck; Tchatchaktchaksn	War chief during the Sheepeater War of 1879; father of Dave Chocktote.
Black Coal	Tovuveh	Twisted Hand's war chief.
Black Eagle	Wahweveh; Weahshau; Kwahu (Eagle Eye)	Often confused with Weahwewa (Wolf Dog) his half brother; brother to Paulina, Bright Eyes and Cactus Fruit. Head war chief in Sheepeater War of 1879.
Black Gun	Cameahwait; Tooitecoon	Brother to Sacajawea; died of smallpox 1847.

399

TRANSLATION	NAME	OTHER INFORMATION
Black Spirit	Tamanmo; War Jack	Spiritual leader in Sheepeater War of 1879; killed by firing squad 1879.
Bloody Antler	Alatuvu	Married Mourning Dove; son-in-law to Has No Horse; daughter Rose married Dave Chocktote; shot in 1898.
Blue Bird	Chosro	Wife of Weasel Lungs; mother of Little Striped Squirrel; died of typhoid in 1838.
Boy	Natchez	Son of Bad Face; brother to Sarah Winnemucca.
Bright Eyes		Sister to Paulina and Black Eagle; married Lake Hunter; died in 1867.
Broken Knife	Shenkah; Shezhe; Shaka	Brother to Tall Man and Running Deer (sister). Brother-in-law to Has No Horse and Pony Blanket. Married to Half Moon. Shot in 1866. Signed treaties of 1855 and 1865.
Buffalo Horn	Kotsotiala	War chief; shot in 1878.
Buffalo Meat	Ahtootoowe; Amaroko; Buffalo Meat Under the Shoulder	Signed 1865 treaty; shot in 1867.
Buffalo Tail	Peter Pahnina	Paulina's son; taken captive by Oregon Volunteers 1865; served as Warm Springs scout during Modoc War in 1873.
Burning Ember	Kooyahtovu	Wife of Old Deer Running; grandmother of Has No Horse; died of cholera 1832.
Burning Wagon	Enkaltoik; Enkaltoak; Tovucoona	Brother-in-law to Paulina, Black Eagle and Wolf Dog; shot in 1864.
Butterfly	Buli	Wife of Lost His Arrow; mother of Dawn Mist and Evening Star.
Buzzard Man	Urie-wishi	Has No Horse's medicine man. Picture in *Handbook of American Indians*, p. 556.
Cactus Fruit	Puna	Sister to Paulina, Black Eagle, and Bright Eyes; married Burning Wagon.
Cold Wind	Kinauni; Kinauney	Ochoco's son; married Snow Bunting; killed in 1868; 17 years old at the time of death.
Cougar Tail	Tahretoonah; Tonouh	War chief; shot 1867.
Cow Lick	Nowweepacowick; Nowhoopacowick	Warrior; signed 1865 treaty; shot in 1868.
Coyote Hair	Ishauya	Warrior; signed treaty of 1855 (No. 88).
Crooked Leg	Paseego	Married Lost Woman; Washakie's father; killed by Blackfeet in 1824.
Cut Hair	Wiskin	Medicine chief; succeeded by White Cloud (a white man named James Kimball).
Dancer	Genega Taniwah; Tauwadah; Tanwahda; Tanwah	Spiritual leader; shot in 1878.

TRANSLATION	NAME	OTHER INFORMATION
Dawn Mist		Daughter of Lost Arrow; wife of Has No Horse; mother of Mourning Dove, Mountain Breeze, Red Willow, Cold Wind and Spotted Fawn; shot in 1866.
Dead Deer	Masiduedeeheah; Mike Daggett; Shoshoni Mike	Shot by the Nevada State Police in 1911.
Death Rattle	Tamowins	Paulina's medicine man; shot in 1864.
Deer Fly	Mohwoomkah; Mouche De Daim (Fly of the Deer)	Son of Old Deer Running; brother to The Horse and Iron Wristbands; shot in 1856.
Elk Calf	Chaizralelio	War chief; married to Summer Hair; shot in 1865.
Elk Tongue		War chief; shot in 1787.
Evening Star	Ashohu	Sister to Dawn Mist; married to Pony Blanket; shot in 1878.
Falling Star	Shohu	Wife of Paulina; spiritual leader; sometimes called Wild Wind.
Fish Man	Numaga	Minor Paiute head man who signed the 1863 Ruby Valley Treaty.
Four Crows	Watsequeorda	Clan chief; face branded in 1845 by members of Lost Wagon Train; shot as a prisoner of war in Oct. 1867.
Fox	Wahi	Surger, son-in-law to Left Hand; married Willow Girl; shot in 1878.
Funny Bug	Leliotu	Sister of Lame Dog; wife of Black Eagle; sister-in-law to Paulina.
Good Man	Teyuwit, Tasowitz	Clan chief.
Gourd Rattler	Washakie; Washaki; Washano; Washekeek; The Rattler; Pinaquanah (Smells of Sugar); Rawhide Rattle; Shoots Straight; Sure Shot; Shoots-On-The-Fly; Shoots Buffalo Running; Gambler's Gourd; Buffalo Killer	Son of Crooked Leg and Lost Woman; head chief eastern Shoshoni nation; died February 23, 1900 of old age.
Grass Woman	Boinaiv; Porivo; Sacajawea	Sister to Black Gun; died December 20, 1812 at Fort Manuel.
Gray Head	Tosarke	Spiritual leader; shot in 1866.
Great Rogue	Tasokwainberakt; Le Grand Coquin	Weighed 275 pounds; head chief.
Ground Owl	Tecolote	War chief; shot in 1866.
Hairy Man	Poemacheoh	Clan chief; shot in 1864.
Half Horse	Peeyeam	War chief; shot in 1879.
Half Moon		Sister to Has No Horse; wife of Broken Knife; mother of Mattie Shenkah; prophet; murdered in April 1864.

TRANSLATION	NAME	OTHER INFORMATION
Has No Horse	Cho-cho-co; Chocho-co-i; Shosho-ko; Chok-ko-si; Ochoco; Ocheko; Ocheo; Otsehoe; Ochoho; Ochiko; The Man Who Has No Horse; Albert Ochiho	Son of The Horse and Little Striped Squirrel; grandson of Old Deer Running; married Dawn Mist; children—Red Willow, Cold Wind, Mourning Dove, Mountain Breeze and Spotted Fawn; granddaughter Agnes Banning Philips; grandsons Tom, Dick, and Harry Ochiho; great grandson Burdette Ochiho. Signed 1869 treaty; shot in 1898 but survived. He was serving a two year prison sentence in Reno, Nevada when he died in 1914.
Hawk	Walkara (Hawk of the Mountains)	Head chief of the southern Utes.
High Head	Kalama; Kalim.	Clan chief; signed treaty of 1855.
Honey Bear	Penointi	Sister to Pony Blanket; married Pipe; shot, 1878.
Horn	Ala;. Mopeah	Sometimes called Horned Chief or Horn of Hair on Forehead; war chief in Bannock War; shot in 1878.
Horse Trap	Hadsapoke	War chief; shot in 1867.
Iron Crow		Gourd Rattler's war chief.
Iron Wristbands	Pahdasherwahundah. Hiding Bear	Brother to The Horse and Deer Fly; Has No Horse's uncle; succeeded Yellow Hand in 1842; died in 1842 of natural causes.
Jerk Meat		Married Grass Woman's (Sacajawea) imposter; had five children; warrior with Gourd Rattler's eastern Shoshoni.
Lake Hunter	Pagorits; Lapakugit	Warrior; imprisoned at Fort Klamath in 1866; killed in 1867.
Lame Dog	Shirriitze; Sheapchis; Shezhe	Brother to Funny Bug; brother-in-law to Black Eagle; executed in 1867.
Laughing Hawk	Tambiago; Laughing Jack	War chief; hung in 1878.
Lean Man	Torepe	Warrior; married Sorrowful Woman; shot in 1864.
Left Hand	Otiz; Owitze; Oete; Oits; Awiteitse; Owits; Oytes; Oitis; Oites; Puhiawatse	Prophet; grandson of Twisted Hand; father of Willow Girl; father-in-law to Fox.
Leggins	Cheegibah	Son of Natchez; grandson of Bad Face; associated with Yellow Jacket.
Little Bearskin Dick	Honalelo.	Medicine chief; shot under a flag of truce in 1878. Son of Bear Skin.
Little Cloud	Okuwa	Married Red Willow.
Little Foot	Walsac	Associated with Big Man.
Little Lizard	Nana; Nawi; Nuni; Nooey	Signed 1865 treaty at Fort Klamath.
Little Rattlesnake	Sieta; Chihiki	Pit River war chief; surrendered in 1868; shot in 1878.
Little Shadow	Siwiin.	Wife of Tall Man and mother of Annette Tallman; shot in 1866.

TRANSLATION	NAME	OTHER INFORMATION
Little Striped Squirel	Nanawu	Daughter of Weasel Lungs; wife of The Horse; mother of Has No Horse (Ochoco).
Lost Arrow	Paiakoni	Father of Dawn Mist and Evening Star; married Butterfly; father-in-law to Has No Horse; clan chief.
Lost Woman		Daughter of Weasel Lungs and Blue Bird; wife of Crooked Leg; Gourd Rattler's mother.
Magpie Man	Uriposiwu	Sheep Killer chief; shot in 1864.
Man Lost	Pocatello; Pikatello; Pocatellah; Bokatellah; Paughatello; Man-Who-Strayed-From-The-Trail	Head chief; sons were Tom and John Pocatello.
Mattie Shenkah		Daughter of Broken Knife and Half Moon; died on death march to Fort Simcoe, Washington Territory, in 1879.
Moses Brown	Motcunkasket; Moshunkoskkit; Moshenkosket; Moskosket; Moskosket; Moghenkaskit; (Modoc name: Pomoaks)	Head chief; listed in historical records as a Yahooskin Snake, but there was no such tribe.
Mountain Breeze		Has No Horse's daughter; married Wolf Jaws; shot in 1868.
Mountain Fog	Pogonip	Deer Fly's son; cousin to Has No Horse; shot in 1868.
Mountain Lamb	Umentucken	Red Wolf's daughter; married Joe Meek; killed by a Banattee arrow in 1836.
Mourning Dove	Huwitubic	Has No Horse's daughter; married Bloody Antler.
No Ribs	Kewatsana; Kepoweetka	Sub-chief; signed 1865 treaty; shot in 1867.
Old Bull	Teverewera	Warrior in Bannock War; escaped to Canada in 1878.
Old Deer Running		Father of The Horse, Iron Wristbands, and Deer Fly; married Burning Ember; died of cholera in 1836.
Old Woman	Lamneya	Taken prisoner on Lookout Mountain, June 1864.
One Eye	Giltewa	Warrior blind in one eye; prisoner at Fort Klamath in 1866.
One Moccasin	Wunamuca; Winnemucca; Onennemucca; Captain Truckee; The Giver of Spiritual Gifts	Medicine chief; prophet; father-in-law of Bad Face; died in 1859 of natural causes.
Otter Bear	Pansookamotse; Pahagiveto; Otter Beard	Clan chief; killed in May 1864 during a raid on Fort Maury.
Pigeon Hawk	Kela; Kele	War chief; first Shoshoni to sign 1855 treaty; beheaded in 1860.
Pipe	Chongyo (Charlie)	Medicine man; war chief; brother-in-law to Pony Blanket; shot in 1878.

403

TRANSLATION	NAME	OTHER INFORMATION
Pit Viper	Chukai; Chumi; Chua (Mud Lizzard)	Warrior in the Bannock War.
Pony Blanket	Egan; Eegan; Ehe-gant; Ezichquegah; E.E. Gantt; Weegant; Enkaltoik	Son-in-law to Lost Arrow; married Evening Star; Has No Horse's brother-in-law; succeeded Buffalo Horn as war chief in Bannock War; beheaded in 1878.
Prairie Flower	Olsombunwas	Sister to Turkey Buzzard; threatened to kill Kit Carson; married Snake Hawk.
Race Horse	Pohave; Parvekee; Pahvissign	War chief in 1878.
Rainbow Woman	Tahaka	Second wife of Big Man; taken captive in 1868.
Red Sand	Tuwa; Tabby; Taiwe; Tabbi; also known as White Eye	War chief; ally to Has No Horse; signed treaty March 2, 1868.
Red Willow	Ochiho	Son of Has No Horse and Dawn Mist; married Little Cloud; natural death.
Red Wolf	Gotia; Roux Loup; Rougeatre Loup	Head chief Shoshoni nation; often confused with Twisted Hand; father of Mountain Lamb; father-in-law to Milton Sublette and Joe Meek; died of cholera in 1852.
Rippling Voice		Daughter of Sits-Under-The-Pine; married Wolf Tail.
Rock Way	Oraibi	Sub-chief; shot in 1845.
Running Deer		Sister to Broken Knife; called "Little Dear Legs" by soldiers; married Big Man; killed in 1866.
Runs Behind		Warrior in Bannock War; friend of Laughing Hawk.
Setting Sun	Tawasi; Tawash	Wolf Dog's son; Paulina's nephew; signed treaty of 1855 at age 17.
Shell Flower	Tocmetone; Sarah Winnemucca; Sally	Daughter of Bad Face; Paiute activist; U.S. Army scout and interpreter.
Six Feathers		Warrior; leader of Snake scouts; killed by Gourd Rattler in 1867.
Snake Hawk	Wakachau	War chief; married Prairie Flower; signed 1865 treaty; shot in 1865.
Snow Bunting	Chisro	Daughter-in-law to Has No Horse; married Cold Wind; killed in April 1868.
Snow Spider	Kokyou	War chief; shot in 1868.
Sorrowful Woman		Wasco slave found in 1859; married Lean Man.
Speaking Spring	Chakpahu	Medicine chief; died in 1854.
Spotted Elk	Chaizra; Boss; Medicine John	Spiritual leader; shot in 1878.
Spotted Fawn	Sowinwalelio	Has No Horse's daughter; married Woman Helper; shot in 1868.

TRANSLATION	NAME	OTHER INFORMATION
Spotted Rabbit	Sowiette	Sometime friend of Gourd Rattler; peaceful chief 1840-1860; Snakes wanted his scalp for being a traitor.
Starving Dog	Goship	Clan chief; bullet removed all of his teeth.
Stiff Finger	Taghee	War chief; died in 1871; signed the Treaty of Peace and Friendship in 1863.
Storm Cloud	Gshaneepatki; Shaw-nee	War chief; shot in 1878.
Summer Hair		Sister to Turkey Buzzard; married Elk Calf; their daughter, Rosa Summer Hair, was placed on the Umatilla Reservation where her picture was taken by Major Lee Moorehouse.
Sun Hunter	Tebechya; Tebachne	Warrior; member of treaty council of 1868.
Swamp Man	Pahragodsohd	Warrior; shot in 1866 on Dry Creek.
Sweet Root	Tashego; Jageon; Pasego; Passequah; Pashego; Petego; Pasheco	Snake prophet who caused much religious unrest among the Pacific Northwest tribes in the 1860s and 70s.
Swooping Eagle	Tobe	Guide for Lewis and Clark; died of typhoid in 1838.
Tall Man	Odukeo; Tokio; Injun Charley	Father of Annette Tallman; warrior; brother to Broken Knife; shot in 1866.
The Climber	Tendoy	Chief of the Lemhi Snakes; defector.
The Cutter	Wovoka; Jack Wilson	Son of White Man; founder of the Ghost Dance religion; died September 20, 1932.
The Horse		Father of Has No Horse; son of Old Deer Running; brother of Iron Wristbands (Hiding Bear) and Deer Fly; shot by the Blackfeet in 1833.
Three Coyotes	Ponce; Shoshoni Jack; Bannock Jack; Snake John; Big John; Paiute John; Ishaui; Big Bill; Bannock Bill	With the Mormon John D. Lee in the Mt. Meadow massacre in southwest Utah September 11, 1857. Mother was Apache; tracked down Cochise for the army.
Tiny Ant	Leliotu	Married Sun Hunter; captured and imprisoned at Fort Vancouver in 1864.
Tobacco Root	Kooyah; Chemma; Cheonma	Warrior; signed 1865 treaty.
Turkey Buzzard	Wishoko; Wiskaka	Brother to Prairie Flower and Summer Hair; brother-in-law to Snake Hawk and Elk Calf; doctor who treated Lt. Fremont; signed treaty of 1855; shot in 1868.
Twisted Hair		Clan chief; shot in 1838.
Twisted Hand	Owitze; Bad Left Hand; Mauvais Gauche	Took control of Shoshoni nation in 1785; grandfather of Left Hand; shot in 1837.

TRANSLATION	NAME	OTHER INFORMATION
Walking Rock	Oderie; Omrshee	Chief of Nevada Snakes; ally to Has No Horse.
War Hoop	Weerahoop	Warrior.
War Spirit	Paulina; Paluna; Pushican; Paninee; Panaina; Poloni; Paulini; Paunina; Pichkan; Pelinis; Pannina; Purchican; The Brutal Devastator;	Has No Horse's number one war chief; had a scar on his forehead from Gourd Rattler's war axe; signed treaty of 1855; married Falling Star; brother to Black Eagle, Bright Eyes, and Cactus Fruit; half-brother to Wolf Dog; father of Buffalo Tail shot in May 1867.
Water Lizard	Momobic; Monoa	Medicine man; at Council Ruby Valley, Nevada, October 1, 1863.
White Cloud	James P. Kimball	Succeeded Cut Hair as Wolf Dog's medicine chief; a native American born in New York state in 1829; taken captive by Bear Killer Snakes in 1848; escaped in 1859.
White Man	Tavibo; Taviwunshear; Taysoba	Married into Walking Rock's band; father of Wovoka (The Cutter); spiritual leader; died 1870.
Willow Girl	Ohoctume	Daughter of Left Hand; married to Fox; shot in 1867.
Winter Frost	Oyike	Prophet.
Wolf Dog	Weahwewa; Weahweah; Kwewa; Wasenwas; Wewawewa; Weyouwewa; Yewhowewa	Succeeded Red Wolf as head chief of the western Shoshoni nation; half-brother to Paulina, Black Eagle, Bright Eyes and Cactus Fruit; signed treaty of 1855; shot in 1878.
Wolf Jaws	Kwewu	Son-in-law to Has No Horse; married Mountain Breeze; in 1880s was Has No Horse's medicine man. Shot by IZ sheep shooters, 1898.
Wolf Tail	Kwewatia	War chief.
Woman Helper	Tonnat; Tonoyiet	Head game driver, son-in-law to Has No Horse; married Spotted Fawn; shot in 1868.
Yellow Badger	Sikamonani; Skytiattitk	War chief; shot in 1865.
Yellow Hand	Ohamagwaya; Amaquiem; Yellow Wrist	Commanche prophet; often confused with Twisted Hand; associated with Shoshoni by 1820; succeeded by Iron Wristbands (Hiding Bear) in 1842; died natural death, 1841.
Yellow Jacket	Potoptuah; Paddy Cap; Paddy; Whitka; Padé Kape	Head chief; army scout; served as a double agent; signed treaty of 1855; placed on the Duck Valley reservation on the Oregon-Nevada border in 1878; listed as a "mounted Paiute."

Note:
All historical documents and newspaper articles refer to Big Man as Oulux,
which in Chinook Jargon means The Snake.

Symbol of the Western Shoshone National Council

Seal of the Western Shoshone Nation

Flag of the Western Shoshone Nation

It was decided by the Western Shoshone National Council that it is necessary to have a flag separate from our traditional sacred flag that would be recognized by the international community. The Western Shoshone People were invited to create designs for their new flag. For three years designs were collected from our citizens which included children and elders from numerous communities. The selected design was chosen by the Newe People at the 1995 Fall Gathering held at Stoneburger Creek. The creator of the design is Johnnie Bobb from Yomba.

Symbolic meaning: Red (power of the people), Green (new born), Blue (life line), White (purity), Eagle Feather (honor), Circle (circle of life), Baby basket symbols of diamond (female) and diagonal lines (male).

Appendix B
BIBLIOGRAPHY

Adams, James Truslow. *The Epic of America.* Washington, D.C.: 1931.

Alter, J. Cecil. *James Bridger, Trapper, Frontiersman, Scout and Guide.* Salt Lake City: 1925.

Bailey, Vernon. *Mammals and Life Zones of Oregon.* Portland, Oregon: 1950.

Baldwin, Ewart M. "By A Fur Trader." *Traits of American Indian Life and Character.* Boston: 1853.

Baldwin, Ewart M. *Geography of Oregon.* University of Oregon Press, N.D.

Ballantyne, Robert Michael. *Hudson's Bay: Or Every Day Life in the Wilds of North America.* Boston: 1859.

Bancroft, H.H. *History of Oregon,* 2 vols. San Francisco: 1886-1888.

Bancroft, H.H. *History of the Northwest Coast 1800-1842.* San Francisco: 1876.

Bancroft, H.H. *Native Races of the Pacific States of North America,* 2 vols. Library of Congress: 1874.

Barker, Burt Brown (ed.). *The Letters of Dr. John McLoughlin.* Portland, Oregon, 1948.

Barrington, _____. "Mourrelle's Journal." *Miscellanies.*

Berreman, Joel. *Tribal Distribution in Oregon.* American Anthropological Association Memoir 47: 1937.

Berry, Don. *A Majority of Scoundrels: An Informal History of the Rocky Mountain Fur Company.* New York: 1961.

Binns, Archie. *Peter Skene Ogden: Fur Trader.* Portland, Oregon: 1967.

Blankenship, Russell. *And There Were Men.* New York: 1942.

Bonner, T.D. (ed.). *The Life and Adventures of James P. Beckwourth.* New York: 1853.

Bradbury, John. *Travels in North America.* Boston: 1834.

Brebner, John B. *The Explorers of North America.* New York: 1933.

Bryant, Edwin. *Rocky Mountain Adventure.* New York: 1885.

Bryce, G. *The Remarkable History of the Hudson's Bay Company.* New York: 1900.

Burton, Richard. *City of the Saints and Across the Rocky Mountains to California.* London: 1861.

Canfield, Gae Whitney. *Sara Winnemucca of the Northern Paiutes.* University of Oklahoma Press, 1931.

Cannon, Miles. "Snake River History." *Oregon Historical Quarterly, Vol. XX, No. 1.* March, 1919.

Capps, Benjamin. *The Great Chiefs.* New York: 1975.

Carey, Charles Henry. *A General History of Oregon Vol. 1* (6 vols.). Portland, Oregon: 1922.

Catlin, George. *Manners, Customs and Conditions of the North American Indians*, 2 vols. London: 1841.

Celand, R.G. *This Reckless Breed of Man*. N.D.

Chaney, R.W. *Geology and Paleontology of the Crooked River Basin*. Carnegie Institute Publication 346. Washington, D.C.: 1927.

Chittenden, Hiram M. *The History of the American Fur Trade of the Far West Vol. 1* (2 vols.). New York: 1935.

Clark, Robert. "Who Was Oregon's Mystery Pioneer?" *The Sunday Oregonian*. Portland, Oregon: December 26, 1965.

Clark, William. *Cash Book*. Unpublished.

Clarke, Samuel A. *Pioneer Days in Oregon Country Vol. 1* (2 vols.). Portland, Oregon: 1924.

Collins, John W. "The Opening and Development of the Region." *Atlas of the Pacific Northwest*. Portland, Oregon: 1958.

Condon, Thomas. *Oregon Geology*. Portland, Oregon: 1910.

Cones, Elliott (ed.). *History of the Expedition Under the Command of Lewis and Clark* (2 vols.). New York: 1893.

Cook, Warren L. *Flood Tide of Empire: Spain and the Pacific Northwest 1543-1819*. New Haven: 1973.

Coutant, Charles G. *The History of Wyoming Vol. 1*. Laramie: 1899.

Cox, Ross. *The Columbia River*. University of Oklahoma Press, 1957.

Cressman, L.S. *Archeological Research of the John Day Region of North Central Oregon*. American Philosophical Society Proceedings 94. Philadelphia: 1950.

Cressman, L.S. *The Sandal and the Cave: The Indians of Oregon*. Portland, Oregon: 1964.

Cushing, C. *Report on the Territory of Oregon*. House Executive Document No. 101, 25th Congress, 3rd session, January 4, 1839.

Dale, Harrison, C. *The Ashley-Smith Explorations and Discovery of a Central Route to the Pacific*. Cleveland: 1918.

Davidson, Gordon. *The North West Company*. Berkeley. 1918.

De Calves, Don Alonso. *Travels to the Westward or Unknown Part of America (Confirmed by Three Other Persons)*. Boston: 1793.

De Voto, Bernard. *Across the Wide Missouri*. Boston: 1947.

De Voto, Bernard. *Journals of Lewis and Clark*. Boston: 1951.

Dobbs, Carolene C. *Men of Champoeg*. Portland, Oregon: 1932.

Dunn, John. *The Oregon Territory and the British North American Fur Trade*. London: 1844.

Dunne, Peter Masten. *Pioneer Black Robes on the West Coast*. Los Angeles: 1940.

Eastman, Dr. Charles A. *The Soul of the Indian*. Portland, Oregon: N.D.

El Hult, Ruby. *Lost Mines and Treasures of the Pacific Northwest*. Portland, Oregon: 1957.

Elliott, T.C. "Coming of the White Women." *Diary of Narcissa Whitman*. *Oregon Historical Quarterly*.

Evans, Jim. "Klamath, Blues Hold Most Oregon Gold." *The Bulletin*, Bend, Oregon, January 31, 1979.

Farely, _____. *San Francisco Medical Journal Vol. III*. N.D.

Farnham, Thomas J. *Life, Adventures and Travels in California*. New York: 1846.

Farnham, Thomas J. *Travels in the Great Western Prairies*. New York: 1843.

Fell, Berry. *America B.C.: Ancient Settlers of the New World*. New York: 1976

Fenton-Fenton. *The Rock Book*. New York: 1946.

Flandreau, Grace. "The Verendrye Expedition in Quest of the Pacific." *Oregon Historical Quarterly Vol. XXVI, No. 2*. June 1925.

Franchere, Gabriel. *Adventures at Astoria 1810-1814*. University of Oklahoma Press, 1967.

Franchere, Gabriel. *Voyage to the North West Coast of America in the Year 1811-1814*. Montreal, Canada: 1819.

Fremont, John Charles. *Memoirs of My Life*. Chicago: 1887.

Frost, Robert. *The Complete Poems of Robert Frost*. Henry Holt & Co., Inc., 1928.

Fuller, George W. *A History of the Pacific Northwest*. New York: 1931.

Gatschet, Albert Samuel. *The Klamath Indians of Southwest Oregon*. Washington, D.C.: 1890.

Gebou, Joseph A. *A Vocabulary of the Snake or Sho-Sho-Nay Dialect, 2nd Edition*. Green River City, Wyoming: 1868.

Ghent, W.J. *The Road to Oregon*. New York: 1929.

Glassley, Ray Hoard. *Pacific Northwest Indian Wars*. Portland, Oregon: 1953.

Gluckman, Arcadi. *United States Muskets, Rifles and Carbines*. New York: 1948.

Gould, Jane. "Journal 1862." *Oregon Historical Quarterly*.

Greenhow, Robert. *The History of Oregon and California and Other Territories on the Northwest Coast of America*. New York: 1845.

Grinnell, George Bird. *Beyond the Old Frontier*. New York: 1913.

Grinnell, George Bird. *Blackfoot Lodge Tales*. New York: 1892.

Haines, Aubrey L. (ed.) *Historic Sites Along the Oregon Trail*. Denver: 1973.

Hebard, Grace R. *Sacajawea*. Cleveland: 1933.

Hebard, Grace R. *Washakie: An Account of Indian Resistance of the Covered Wagon and Union Pacific Railroad Invasions of Their Territory*. Cleveland: 1930.

Hendricks, R.J. *Innnnng Haaaaa! (A Trilogy in the Anabases of the West)*. Salem, Oregon: N.D.

Highsmith, Richard M. Jr. (ed.) *Atlas of the Pacific Northwest*. Corvallis: 1973.

Hodge, E.T. *Geology of North Central Oregon*. Corvallis: 1946.

Hodge, Frederick Webb (ed.). *Handbook of North American Indians North of Mexico*. Bureau of American Ethnology, Smithsonian Institution Bulletin 30, 2 vols. Washington, D.C.: 1907.

Hofen, LeRoy and W.J. Ghent. *Broken Hand, The Life Story of Thomas Fitzpatrick*. Berkeley: 1949.

Holman, Frederick V. *Dr. John McLaughlin, the Father of Oregon*. Cleveland, Oregon: 1907.

Hosmer, James K. *History of the Expedition of Captains Lewis and Clark 1804-5-6 (2 vols.)*. Chicago: 1902.

Howard, Gen. O.O. *Famous Indian Chiefs I Have Known*. Hartford: 1908.

Hunt, John Clark. "Wild Horses Fade From Scene." *Sunday Oregon Journal*. Portland: June 22, 1958.

Irving, Washington. *Astoria*. New York: 1832.

Irving, Washington. *Captain Bonneville: A Tale of a Traveler*. New York: 1868.

Jacobs, James Ripely. *Tarnished Warrior: Major General James Wilkinson*. New York: 1938.

James, John. *My Experience With the Indians*. New York: 1925.

Johnson, Connie. *The John Day Country: A Living Memorial*. Published by the Blue Mt. Eagle. John Day, Oregon: N.D.

Johnson, J.J. *Index of the Shoshoni Language*. N.D.

Joseph, Alven M. (ed.) *The American Heritage Book of Indians*. New York: 1961.

Judge, _____. *Half Alligator, Half Horse*. University of Oklahoma Press, 1953.

Judson, Katherine R. *Early Days in Old Oregon*. N.D.

Keane, A.H. *Ethnography and Philology of America*. London, 1878.

Kelsey, Henry. *Papers*. Ottawa, Archives of Canada, 1929.

Lavender, David. *The Great West*. New York: 1965.

Lewis and Clark. *Travels to the Source of the Missouri*. London: 1814.

Lewis, William S., and P.C. Phillips. *The Journals of John Work*. Cleveland: 1923.

Liljeblad, Dr. Sven. *The Idaho Indians in Transition 1805-1960*. Pocatello, Idaho: 1972.

Lockley, Fred. *Oregon Folks*. Portland: N.D.

Longstreet, Stephen. *War Cries on Horseback*. Garden City, New York: 1970.

Luttig, John C. *Journal of a Fur-Trading Expedition on the Upper Missouri 1812-1813*. Boston: 1820.

Mack, Joanne. *Cultural Resources Inventory of the Potential Glass Buttes Geothermal Lease Areas, Lake, Harney and Deschutes Counties*. University of Oregon Department of Anthropology, December 1, 1975.

MacKenzie, Alexander. *Voyage From Montreal Through the Continent of North America to The Frozen Pacific Ocean in 1789 and 1793*. London: 1801.

Marsh, James B. *Four Years in the Rockies*. Newcastle, Pennsylvania: 1884.

McArthur, Lewis A. *Oregon Geographic Names*. Portland, Oregon: 1974.

McLaughlin, Major James. *My Friend the Indians*. Chicago: 1868.

Meacham, Walter E. *The Old Oregon Trail: The World's Most Historic Highway*. Baker, Oregon: 1922.

Meek, Stephen Hall. *Autobiography of a Mountain Man 1805-1889*. Glen Dawson (ed.). Pasadena, California: 1948.

Merk, Frederick. *Fur Trade and Empire*. Cambridge: 1931.

Miles, Jim. "Cahokia: First American Metropolis." *Fate, Vol. 35, No. 10*. October: 1982

Miller, Joaquin. *Poetical Works*. New York: 1923.

Moberly, Henry John. *When Fur Was King*. New York: 1929.

Monagham, Jay (ed.). *The Book of the American West*. New York: 1963.

Morgan, Dale L. *Jedidiah Smith and the Opening of the West*. University of Oklahoma Press, 1964.

Morse, Eldridge. *Notes of the History and Resources of Washington Territory MS., 24 vols*. N.D.

Mosion, L.R. *Les Bourgeois de la Compagnie du Nord-quest, Vol. II (2 vols.)*. Quebec: 1890.

Mumey, Nolie. *The Life of Jim Baker 1818-1898*. Denver: 1931.

Nash, _____. "Intercultural Community on Klamath Reservation." *Social Anthropology of North American Tribes*.

Newsom, David. *The Western Observer 1805-1882, MS*.

Norall, Frank. *Bourgmont; Explorer of the Missouri 1698-1725*. University of Nebraska, 1988.

O'Hara, Edwin V. *Pioneer Catholic History of Oregon*. Paterson, New Jersey: 1939.

Ogden, Peter Skene. *Correspondence and Miscellaneous Family Papers*. Oregon State Archives.

Ogden, Peter Skene. *Snake Country Journals 1824-1829*. Hudson's Bay Record Society. London, England: 1950.

Packard, E.L. *Preliminary Report of the Cretaceous of Central Oregon.* Geological Society of America, Vol. 40. 1929.

Phillips, Paul C. *Life in the Rocky Mountains: A Diary of Wanderings on the Sources of the Rivers Missouri, Columbia and Colorado from February 1830 to November 1835.* University of Oklahoma Press, 1961.

Pollard, Lancaster. *Oregon and the Pacific Northwest.* Portland, Oregon: 1938.

Porter, Kenneth. *John Jacob Astor, 2 vols.* Cambridge, Massachusetts: 1931.

Priestly, Herbert (ed.). "The Log of the Princess by Estevan Martinez." *Oregon Historical Quarterly, Vol. XXI, No. I. March, 1920.*

Prince, _____. "Shoshoni Lifestyles." *California Farmer.* October 18, 1861.

Quaife, Milo M. (ed.) *Kit Carson's Autobiography.* Madison, Wisconsin. 1919.

Quaife, Milo M. (ed.) *The Journals of Captain Meriwether Lewis, Sergeant John Ordway, Kept on the Expedition of Western Exploration 1803-1806.* Madison, Wisconsin: 1916.

Rees, John. "Oregon—Its Meaning, Origin and Application." *Oregon Historical Quarterly, Vol. XXI, No. 4.* December 1920.

Rick, E.E. (ed.) *McLaughlin's Fort Vancouver Letters, Third Series 1844-46.* Hudson's Bay Company Publication VII. London: 1944.

Roe, Frank Gilbert. *The Indian and the Horse.* University of Oklahoma Press, 1955.

Rollins, Philip. *The Discovery of the Oregon Trail, Robert Stuart's Narrative.* New York: 1935.

Ross, Alexander. *Adventures of the First Settlers on the Oregon or Columbia River 1810-1813.* New York: 1969.

Ross, Alexander. *Fur Hunters of the Far West, 2 vols.* London: 1825.

Rusell, Osborne. *Journals of a Trapper: Or Nine Years in the Rocky Mountains 1834-1843.* The Syms-York Company, Inc. Boise, Idaho: 1921.

Rutherford, G. Montgomery. *Mountain Man.* New York: 1957.

Schoolcraft, Henry R. *Personal Memoirs of a Resident of Thirty Years Among the Indian Tribes on the American Frontier: With Brief Notices of Polling Events, Facts and Opinions, A.D. 1812 to A.D. 1842.* Philadelphia, 1851.

Schuette, C.N. *Quicksilver in Oregon.* State Department of Geology and Mineral Industries Bulletin No. 4. 1938.

Scott, H.W. *History of the Oregon Country, Vol. I (6 vols.).* Cambridge, Massachusetts: 1924.

Scott, Hamilton. *Trip Across the Plains in 1862* (personal diary).

Seton, Ernest Thompson. *The Gospel of the Red Man.* Los Angeles: 1948.

Shaver, Fred (ed.). *The History of Baker, Grant, Malheur and Harney Counties.* Spokane: 1902.

Shaver, Fred (ed.). *The Illustrated History of Central Oregon.* Spokane: 1905

Simpson, George. *The Oregon Territory*. London: 1846.

Sprague, Marshall. *Massacre: The Tragedy at White River*. Boston: 1957.

Stewart, Wallace (ed.). *Documents Relating to the North West Company*. Toronto, Canada: 1934.

Stoutenburgh, John L. *Dictionary of the American Indian*. New York: 1960.

Strong, Emery. *Stone Age on the Columbia*. Portland, Oregon: 1969.

Strong, Schenck, Stevord. *Archeology of The Dalles-Deschutes Region*. University of California Publication in American Archeology and Ethnology 29. Berkeley: 1930.

Taylor, James. "Shoshoni." *California Farmer*. April 27, 1860.

Teit, James. *The Middle Columbia Salish*. University of Washington, 1928.

Thompson, David. *Narrative of Expedition of 1807*. London: 1925.

Thwaites, Reueben Gold (ed.). *Original Journals of the Lewis and Clark Expedition 1804-1806*. London: N.D.

Timmens, A. *Who Was John Day?* N.D.

Toepel, Kathryn Anne and Stephen Beckham. *Cultural Resources Overview of the Brothers EIS Area, Prineville District, Oregon*. Department of Anthropology, University of Oregon, June 1978.

Trenholm, Virginia Cole and Maurine Carley. *The Shoshonis: Sentinels of the Mountains*, University of Oklahoma Press, 1964.

Tyrrell, John (ed.). *David Thompson's Narrative of Exploration in Western America*. Toronto, Canada: 1916.

Vestal, Stanely. *Jim Bridger, Mountain Man*. Caxton Printers, 1959.

Vestal, Stanely. *The Merry Mountain Man: Joe Meek*. Caxton Printers, 1952.

Victor, Frances Fuller. *The River of the West*. Hartford: 1870.

White, Catherine M. (ed.) *David Thompson's Journals*. Missoula, Montana: 1950.

Whiting, Beatrice Blythe. *Paiute Sorcery, Anthropology Publication No. 15*. New York: 1950.

Winnemucca, Sarah. *Life Among the Paiutes: Their Wrongs and Claims*. San Francisco: 1883.

Winther, Oscar Osburn. *The Great Northwest*. New York: 1947.

Work, John. *Fur Brigade to the Bonaventura: John Work's California Expedition 1832-1833 for the Hudson's Bay Company, MS*. Provincial Archives. Victoria, B.C.

Work, John. *Journal August 22, 1830-April 20, 1831, MS*. Provincial Archives. Victoria, B.C.

Young, F.G. (ed.) *Correspondence and Journals of Captain Nathaniel J. Wyeth 1831-36; Sources of the History of Oregon, Vol. I*. Oregon Historical Society, 1899.

GOVERNMENT DOCUMENTS
AND MISCELLANEOUS PUBLICATIONS

The American Educator, Vol. II, (26 vols).

California Historical Society Quarterly. September, 1943.

Central Oregonian. Old Timers Edition, August 4, 1939 from the files of 1880.

Dictionary of American Biography, Vols. II, X, XII and XX. American Council of Learned Societies.

Explorations into Cahokia, Illinois. Archeological Survey Bulletin No. 7.

"Hall J. Kelly." *Oregon Historical Quarterly, Vol. II.*

Historical Highlights of Public Land Management. USDI-BLM. 1962.

House and Senate Executive Documents 1803-1839.

Hudson's Bay Record Section. Publication VI. 1821.

Humboldt Register. Unionville, Nevada. December 5, 1863.

Idaho Yesteryears, Vol. II, No. 2. 1958.

"Indian Distribution in Oregon." Atlas of Oregon.

"Medical Aspects of the Lewis and Clark Expedition." *Oregon Historical Quarterly, Vol. VI, No. 3.*

The Montana Historical Quarterly, Vol. VI, No. 2.

The National Geographic Magazine, Vol. LVI, No. 6. December, 1929.

The North American Review. January, 1839.

The Oregon Historical Quarterly, Vols. X, XI, XXXIII, XXXIX and LXXVIII.

The Oregon Statesman. December 9, 1851.

"Probing the Riddle of the Bird Woman." Montana: The Magazine of Western History, Vol. 23. 1973.

The Public Records Office, Colonials Office Case 323, Vol. 18. London, 1792.

The San Francisco Alta. December, 1851.

"Sublette Papers," *The Missouri Historical Society.*

Surgery, Genealogy and Obstetrics, No. 85. November, 1947.

"Thomas Condon, Pioneer Geologist of Oregon." *Oregon Historical Quarterly, Vol. VI.*

The Washington Historical Quarterly, Vol. XXIV. October, 1933.

The Wind River Rendezvous, Vol. XIV, No. 2. June, 1984.

Appendix C
INDEX

THUNDER
OVER THE OCHOCO

VOLUME I: *The Gathering Storm*

Covering hundreds of years from pre-Columbian times to the collapse of the world fur trade in 1840, Volume I meets the Shoshoni Indians before the arrival of the Europeans and tracks their rise from peaceful eastern Oregon agriculturists to the aggressive Snake war tribes, rulers of the Pacific Northwest. By 1812, they had clashed with every major world power in their jealous guardianship of a land they called Oyerungun. Their undisputed hunting grounds beyond the setting sun would soon become coveted by white foreigners searching first for precious metals and later for valuable fur-bearing animals. The gathering storms of hatred would hover ominously on the distant horizons. Volume I chronicles the events which inevitably would lead to war.

VOLUME II: *Distant Thunder*

The twenty-year period between 1840 and 1860 would see overland migration across the land known to the Shoshoni as the Ochoco—Land of the Red Willow. The Americans would call it eastern Oregon. Never on friendly terms with the white invaders, the Shoshoni tolerated passage across their ancestral hunting grounds only so long as the American homesteaders stayed strictly on the dusty thoroughfare called the Oregon Trail. When they transgressed, the distant thunder of gunfire reverberated across interior Oregon like the tolling of a death knell. Volume II narrates the suffering, heartache and death of those unfortunate souls who dared to venture into the Ochoco; and it covers the first brutal Indian wars fought west of the Mississippi River.

VOLUME III: *Lightning Strikes!*

Between 1860 and 1869 rich deposits of gold were discovered in eastern Oregon, and the citizens of the Willamette Valley were out to claim their share at any cost. Shoshoni dog soldiers were equally determined that they keep to their side of the Cascade barrier. War was officially declared. The opposing forces went for each other's throats locked in a death struggle that seemed endless. The crashing crescendo of thunder was accompanied by lightning strikes of destruction which ricocheted into four western states—and the military campaign they thought would last but a few weeks stretched into years. In flashing raids, Shoshoni dog soldiers humiliated the Oregon Cavalry, taking a deadly toll on mining settlements, homesteads, stagecoaches and wagon trains. It would take a battle-hardened army baptized in the carnage of the Civil War four years to bring the Shoshoni to their knees: an aggressor with unlimited resources pitted against a foe that was undermanned, undernourished and outgunned—but desperately fighting for survival. Volume III is the story of the first violent Shoshoni outbreak, which would again erupt in the 1870s.

VOLUME IV: *Rain of Tears*

The thirteen year interval between 1866 and 1879 would witness monumental changes in the Ochoco. With the surrender of Has No Horse's battered army, western Oregon had free rein to exploit the Ochoco as it saw fit. In a blind daze, the Shoshoni would witness frontier towns springing up where their lodges had once stood. As thousands upon thousands of bawling cattle and sheep trampled their ancestral hunting grounds to dust, the proud warriors of a by-gone year again rebelled. And, for a fleeting moment, shook the state of Oregon to its very foundations. Then it was over. Stripped even of reservation rights, the few survivors drifted between the four winds on their final journey into the bitter rain of tears.

VOLUME V: *And the Juniper Trees Bore Fruit*

Between 1880 and 1916, the birth of industry would give vent to new bloodshed in the Ochoco. Six-shooters roared in the night, ranchers disappeared never to be seen again ... and the Juniper trees bore fruit: the dangling bullet-ridden bodies of men whose only crime was to oppose the land barons who ruled old Crook County with a Winchester rifle and a rawhide rope. As the 19th century staggered to a close, a Shoshoni visionary born in the Ochoco foretold the rebirth of Indian supremacy. His wondrous dream was buried in a common grave at Wounded Knee, South Dakota. By the time the 20th century blundered onto the scene, saddle-blanket blazes hacked into the Ochoco pines marked the deadlines between sheep and cattle range and woe unto him who crossed these barriers. Rifle shots echoed the length and breadth of the Deschutes canyon as the Hill-Harriman railroad giants battled to link central Oregon to the outside world. Ironically, the last Indian war fought in the United States would explode on the Oregon-Nevada border in 1911 when a Shoshoni chief led his followers, armed only with bows and arrows, in a suicidal charge against a group of stockmen. Thus ended the *Thunder Over the Ochoco*. Would the new owners do a better job of managing the land they had wrenched from the Shoshoni? I leave that to other writers to decide.